ELEMENTARY CLASSROOMS

Teaching Students with  *Needs*

Edited by

JAC ANDREWS

University of Calgary

Nelson Canada

I(T)P An International Thomson Publishing Company

Toronto • Albany • Bonn • Boston • Cincinnati • Detroit • London • Madrid • Melbourne
Mexico City • New York • Pacific Grove • Paris • San Francisco • Singapore • Tokyo • Washington

I(T)P ™

International Thomson Publishing
The ITP logo is a trademark under licence

© Nelson Canada
A division of Thomson Canada Limited, 1996

Published in 1996 by
Nelson Canada
A division of Thomson Canada Limited
1120 Birchmount Road
Scarborough, Ontario M1K 5G4

Canadian Cataloguing in Publication Data

Main entry under title: '
Teaching students with diverse needs: elementary classrooms

Includes bibliographical references.
ISBN 0–17–604856-1

1. Special education.   I. Andrews, Jac, 1952–
LC3965.T4   1995   371.9   C95–931780–5

Team Leader	Michael Young
Acquisitions Editor	Charlotte Forbes
Developmental Editor	Heather Martin
Production Editor	Jill Young
Senior Production Coordinator	Carol Tong
Art Director	Liz Harasymczuk
Cover Design/Interior	Sharon Foster
Cover Illustration	Daphne McCormack
Senior Composition Analyst	Alicja Jamorski
Input Operator	Elaine Andrews

Printed and bound in Canada
1 2 3 4   BBM   98 97 96 95

▨ Table of Contents

◈ Preface

Teachers are well aware of the student diversity in their classrooms. They are also aware of the challenges arising from teaching students who have exceptional learning conditions (i.e., learning disabilities, developmental delays, advanced cognitive abilities, behavioural disturbances, and physical and health impairments) as well as different racial, ethnic, and religious backgrounds. No longer is exceptionality equated with separate classrooms and programs, rather, a dramatic increase of students with special learning needs are being taught in regular classrooms. Hence, many teachers are being tremendously impacted by the changes in their roles and responsibilities as they are facing the reality of contemporary education in Canada.

This book is about teaching students with a wide range of needs in Canadian schools and classrooms. The major aim of this book is to provide practical information that teachers can apply in their schools and classrooms to meet the increasing student diversity. However, it is *not* a recipe book because teaching students with varied backgrounds, identities, frames of reference, abilities, interests, and belief systems is too complex for simple solutions. It is a book that presents theoretically grounded and empirically based procedures for addressing the operational issues related to teaching and managing a heterogeneous population of students in the educational mainstream. Beyond the provision of practical techniques, this book attempts to provide an accountable foundation for the recommended educational practices and promote a deeper understanding with respect to their usage.

The idea for this book grew out of my numerous conversations with colleagues within the field of education and teachers at conferences and workshops, as well as my students in pre-service and in-service courses. All of these people expressed the need for additional educational resources to assist them in addressing the challenges of accommodating the growing crowd of diverse students within Canadian schools and classrooms. To this end, Canadian educators were asked to contribute chapters in relation to the central focus and critical components of the book and in accordance with their areas of expertise.

Central Focus and Critical Components of the Book

The underlying position throughout this book is that schools throughout Canada are including more students who have special needs within regular classrooms and segregating fewer students into special classrooms. Moreover, an increasing number of schools across the country are adopting a philosophy of *inclusive* education that reflects the view that schools are communities in which everyone should feel that they belong, are accepted, and are respected and valued for their individuality. Accordingly, the emerging mission for these schools is on how to operate classrooms so that student diversity is valued, potentials of all students are maximized, and teachers have the necessary support and assistance to provide appropriate educational experiences for all of the students in their classrooms. Hence, the central focus of this book is on ways schools can deliver educational services in accordance with their philosophy of inclusive education; classrooms can accommodate student variance; students can achieve appropriate educational goals; and teachers can be empowered to deal with the changes in their roles and responsibilities. This is accomplished by presenting and discussing what are considered to be critical components of teaching students with diverse needs:

1. Understanding the nature of student diversity and inclusive education,

2. Knowing how to prepare oneself for educational reform and student diversity,

3. Knowing how teachers, administrators, parents, and other professionals can collaborate with one another and collectively meet the diverse needs of students,

4. Knowing how to identify the learning needs of students,

5. Knowing how to plan for accommodating the wide range of students' needs,

6. Knowing some instructional strategies that can meet the learning needs of all students in the classroom,

7. Knowing how to manage students within inclusive classrooms,

8. Knowing how to enhance social competence and acceptance among students in the classroom,

9. Knowing how to promote sociocultural development and awareness,

10. Knowing how to build mutually beneficial family-school partnerships,

11. Knowing how to use computer technologies to better serve the needs of all students, and

12. Understanding the major factors and enabling conditions conducive to inclusive education.

Audience

Teaching Students with Diverse Needs: Elementary Classrooms is written primarily for all pre-service teachers in colleges and universities across Canada who will be faced with the reality of student diversity in their future classrooms as well as for in-service teachers who are presently facing this reality. However, this book is also considered to be useful for parents and professionals (i.e., teachers' aides, psychologists, social workers, physical and occupational therapists, and counsellors) who work with special-needs children and collaborate with teachers in preparing and delivering educational services.

This book can stand on its own as a primary text for any course that is aimed at preparing teachers to manage diversity or as a supplementary text for course work related to collaboration and consultation, assessment, instructional methods, individualized program planning, classroom management, social skill development, second language and second culture learning, family-school partnerships, and computer instruction.

Features of the Book

This book provides interesting and useful information relative to inclusive education in Canadian schools. At the beginning of the book, a conceptual overview is provided to highlight some of the important ideas covered in each of the chapters. Throughout the text case studies and realistic vignettes that are drawn from the authors' experiences in teaching students with diverse needs are presented. In addition, tables and figures are included which expand the text discussion and illustrate how some of the information can be used by teachers and their students. Moreover, a resource section concludes each chapter so readers can pursue further information and materials for assistance and support.

Acknowledgements

Many people contributed to the preparation and completion of this book. I would like to thank all of the authors of this book who demonstrated a great deal of commitment to this project and who submitted very readable and creditable chapters. I would also like to thank all of the people who are cited in this book for providing us with a body of work that positively impacts the lives of many.

Thanks also to all the editors at Nelson Canada. Thank you Charlotte Forbes for accepting the proposal of this book and for providing continual support, guidance, and encouragement. Most importantly, thank you for having faith in me and in this project. Thank you Heather Martin for always being there and for always being positive, helpful, and responsive to the issues and challenges that emerged throughout the process of finishing this book. Thank you Jill Young for all your efforts in transforming the manuscript into a polished product in a timely fashion.

I would like to thank Rick Freeze, University of Manitoba; Nancy Hutchinson, Queen's University; Gladene Robertson, University of Saskatchewan; Liz Stenson, Toronto Board of Education; John Walsh, University of Victoria; and Jack Wendt, Acadia University, for their reviews of the original manuscript and for their constructive feedback and support for the project. I also owe a large debt of gratitude to Anne Waddell who helped prepare my work so it was presentable for further reviewing and editing. As well, I would like to thank all of my students over the years who have taught me how to be a better teacher.

Finally, at the top of the list of all the people who made this book possible are my wife Debbie and my children Jenna and Chad who make all things possible for me.

◈ An Introductory Overview

Teaching students who have a wide range of needs within regular classrooms is one of the biggest challenges of Canadian educators in the 1990s. This book addresses the issues related to student diversity in today's schools and classrooms. The authors in this book recognize that contemporary efforts to educate students with diverse needs differ from earlier attempts in at least two significant ways. First, current approaches are characterized by a more collaborative system of educational service delivery because teaching has become an increasingly complex task. Teachers need to network with each other and develop partnerships within the community to address the unique learning needs of all students and deal with the issues created by sociocultural, political, and economic changes. Second, while the education of students with diverse needs has been the responsibility of schools for many years, they have tended to provide segregated educational programming and instruction rather than inclusionary educational practices. The current trend in Canadian education is the inclusion of students with diverse needs within regular education settings. This book provides a description and discussion of some practical approaches that can be used by elementary teachers to provide high-quality education for the diverse population of students in their schools and classrooms.

The first two chapters of this book provide some introductory thoughts about teaching students with diverse needs and some ideas about how to cope with student diversity and educational reform. In **Chapter 1**, Jac Andrews draws upon his academic and applied experience to discuss the past and current trends with respect to the education of students with diverse needs. He maintains that all students have needs that require various levels of support to maximize their potential, and that all teachers have to assume a shared responsibility to ensure quality instruction for all students. He acknowledges that the nature of teaching in today's schools has become very complicated due to increasing student diversity and highlights collaborative, dynamic, proactive, and empathic approaches as ways of teaching and managing students with different needs.

In **Chapter 2**, Donna Patterson reminds us that many teachers might find educational reform and student diversity to be overwhelming. She asserts that schools exist as much for teachers as for students and that they need to become effective change managers and agents to cope with their new roles, responsibilities, and functions. She believes that teachers need to take care of themselves in times of change and recommends that they build a network of support to help each other adapt to the changes. She argues that teachers should prepare for transitions in education by creating personal goals and determining the processes for achieving these goals. Having goals and steps for reaching them strengthens one's resolve and mobilizes energies for change. Patterson points out that many teachers might experience occasions of discouragement with the change process and recommends that they take one step at a time, have patience and confidence in their efforts, and consider how the innovations can make things better for themselves as well as their students.

Growing diversity within our schools and classrooms coupled with increased fiscal constraint has resulted in more attention to educational alternatives that make more efficient use of limited resources. One innovative response to this situation has been the utilization of collaborative approaches to educational service delivery. Many benefits can come from a collaborative work environment. Benefits will accrue from the varied perspectives, skills, and knowledge available from the different disciplines represented in the collaborative team. Benefits will also come from the group interaction that can broaden as well as focus upon ideas relative to serving children with a wide range of needs. Collaborative approaches provide opportunities for teachers to access information from one another, share materials and instructional techniques, and to have more responsibility in school-based problem solving and decision making.

In **Chapter 3**, Rick Freeze discusses collaboration and consultation in elementary schools. In the first section of his paper, Freeze identifies and describes what he considers to be essential characteristics of a school climate that allow for effective collaboration and consultation (i.e., parity among participants, voluntary participation, mutual goals, common resources, cooperative values, and shared accountability and resources) and introduces some ways that teachers can share their professional experience and knowledge at their school (e.g., literature circles, roundtables, methods presentations at staff meetings, and team teaching). In the following section, he discusses the professional skills (e.g., one's professional knowledge and experience), interpersonal skills (e.g., listening skills, communication ability, and conflict-resolving strategies), and process skills related to effective problem solving (i.e., problem identification, assessment, program development, program implementation, program evaluation, and follow-up) that are needed to collaborate and consult with others. In addition, Freeze presents some solutions to the most common forms of resistance with respect to collaboration and consultation.

An underlying message throughout his paper is that student diversity has created the need for teachers to work together and be involved in shared problem solving. However, according to Freeze, a team process is only as effective as the knowledge, skills, values, and attitudes the team members possess relative to collaboration and consultation. Accordingly, he stresses the importance of everyone having a commitment and responsibility to the collaborative and consultative process and a mutual understanding and respect for each other.

Effective teaching of students with diverse needs requires an evolving process of student assessment, program planning, instruction, and classroom management. The next four chapters in this book focus on ways to identify students' learning needs, plan and make accommodations for student diversity, provide learning experiences that help students reach appropriate educational goals, and arrange classroom environments that promote successful learning. Assessment, program planning, instruction, and classroom management are ongoing and interactive aspects of teaching. Although each of these components is presented separately in this book, all of the authors of these four chapters point to their interconnections.

Over the past two decades, sociocultural, developmental, and cognitive orientations to learning have been emphasized over behavioural theory and practice. This theoretical shift in educational psychology has resulted in assessment practices that are sensitive to the situational contexts, developmental levels, and cognitive processes of students. Although the product of cognitive activity is still important, the way students acquire, store, retrieve, and apply knowledge is a major focus of current assessment practice. Concomitantly, a current trend in education has been to view assessment and intervention as interactive practices that influence the direction of student learning. Hence, finding out how students process information and approach their learning helps teachers plan for instruction. Concern for both the process and product of learning along with a growing realization of the importance of differing stages in child development as well as the interactive social basis of learning has resulted in emerging changes in assessment practices.

In **Chapter 4**, Marion Porath describes and discusses a variety of classroom-based assessment strategies that teachers can use to gain greater insight about their students' learning and to help them plan for teaching. Porath begins her chapter by overviewing four general types of assessment (norm-referenced, criterion-referenced, curriculum-based, and performance-based) and points out that there is an important relationship between the form of assessment and the purpose of assessment. Throughout this section of her chapter, she notes some salient issues with respect to the different types of assessment and provides some practical steps teachers can follow to evaluate their students' levels of understanding and performance potential. Moreover, she focuses on ways teachers can talk with, listen to, and observe their students to find out more information about their knowledge base and incorporate it into learning activities. According to Porath, classroom assessment should be an ongoing activity that helps teachers plan more effectively to improve their students' cognitive processing and learning competence. She stresses the importance of evaluating student ability in relation to contextual factors (i.e., the nature of the task) and knowing where students are on the developmental continuum. She recognizes that teachers will need a multiplicity of assessment approaches due to the large range of areas and tasks for assessment and encourages teachers to include the involvment of other teachers, parents, and students in the process.

Classroom assessment of students and the identification of their learning needs is the foundation from which teachers can prepare lessons, specify learning goals and objectives, gather materials, monitor their lessons, and evaluate their interventions. Holistic and comprehensive program planning is essential for effectively responding to student diversity. In **Chapter 5**, Rick Freeze provides a program planning framework that teachers can use to adapt curriculum and instruction for students in elementary classrooms. He begins by delineating important variables in learning that form the basis of program planning (i.e., students' prior knowledge and their repertoire of cognitive strategies; behavioural interventions that shape classroom climate; social dynamics and cultural dimensions of the classroom; physical characteristics of the classroom environment; students' emotional needs; and developmental factors in curriculum design and instruction) and elements of instruction (i.e., an inclusive philosophy that values student diversity; student learning that is facilitated by the in-class participation of parents, tutors, volunteers, mentors, and other support personnel; active instructional milieu in which students are encouraged to be autonomous learners; a commitment to child-centred approaches to teaching; multifaceted methodology that captures students' individuality and differentiated learning needs; and cooperative tasks that link the product of learning with the process of learning). Freeze maintains that elementary teachers can weave these diverse learning variables and instructional elements into a coherent program plan to address the learning needs of all students in their classrooms. After presenting the holistic program framework, Freeze exemplifies two classroom situations that illustrate the use of this framework for adapting the curriculum and accommodating the diverse needs of students.

Teaching with respect to individual differences among students is the "bottom line" expectation for today's teachers. Instructional approaches must be flexible to accommodate variations in students' abilities and learning progress. Moreover, instructional programs should enable students to experience success in learning, reach their desired academic and social goals, enhance their ability to self-regulate learning, and adapt to changes in their lives.

Students who are able to engage in self-regulation can better react to the academic tasks in their classroom and adapt to changes inside and outside the school. However, in today's classrooms there are many students who do not possess the required skills to guide their own learning. Hence, it is important that instruction of self-regulation become an integral part of the teaching regime. In **Chapter 6**, John Walsh and Dawn Howard-Rose overview the psychology (theoretical and empirical evidence) of self-regulated learning and provide some examples of how instruction can promote this skill.

Walsh and Howard-Rose maintain that self-regulation is not a fixed characteristic of students, rather, it is an approach to learning that is teachable, learnable, and improvable. According to these authors, teaching students to be more self-regulated involves getting students to be much more aware of the nature of their classroom work and resourceful in the ways they approach academic tasks. They argue that to teach students to be more autonomous in their learning requires a knowledge of the content of instruction in self-regulation. They point out that classroom tasks pose conditions and goals that require students to be purposeful in the way they direct their efforts. Self-regulated learners employ effective strategies to accommodate the task conditions and complete the task goals. Moreover, the authors note that self-regulated learners are highly motivated because they have a repertoire of efficient strategies that help them sustain and control their efforts.

Walsh and Howard-Rose outline some approaches teachers can undertake to promote self-regulation in the classroom. According to these authors, the presentation of classroom and homework assignments offers a good time for teachers to show students how they can be more self-regulated. They indicate that task directions offer an opportunity for teachers to model the cognitive plans and strategies students might employ to complete the assigned tasks. Moreover, they suggest that teachers can talk aloud while working through this approach to help students become more aware of the important cognitive skills and attitudes to be developed. Their suggestions for teaching self-regulation in the classroom emphasize ways for teachers to promote self-management and self-responsibility within their students. They discuss the importance of establishing a classroom climate that provides opportunities for students to set their own learning and behavioural goals, promotes the view that mistakes are part of learning, develops mastery goal orientations, and reflects a multidimensional value system. An underlying theme throughout their chapter is that students can be taught to be more active, independent, and motivated in their learning by teachers who encourage self-regulation.

In **Chapter 7**, Don Dworet, Clint Davis, and Janice Martin discuss classroom management within the context of teaching in elementary classrooms. From their perspective, teachers should follow a proactive and preventative approach to classroom management. This approach involves the use of effective instructional procedures to promote and sustain successful learning and appropriate behaviour and prevent misbehaviour from occurring. In the first part of their chapter, the authors discuss the three stages of the proactive and preventative model of classroom management. Planning, the first stage, involves the consideration of classroom space, the modifications required to manage student diversity, classroom rules, procedures, routines, and the use of support personnel and special materials to maximize students' learning potential. The second stage of the model deals with the implementation of the management plan. Dworet, Davis, and Martin stress the importance of communicating the plan with all members of the school as well as with the students and their parents. The third stage of the model involves the maintenance of the management system by monitoring students' behaviour, reinforcing student compliance with the classroom procedures and routines, reacting appropriately to student misbehaviour, and continually evaluating and modifying the system.

Dworet, Davis, and Martin also present and discuss strategies for specific behavioural concerns. These authors note that sometimes misbehaviour will occur in the classroom even though the teacher has created a comfortable classroom environment, established appropriate classroom rules and routines, employed effective instructional procedures, and involved students in meaningful and enjoyable learning experiences. When this happens, they recommend that teachers explore the need the student is indicating from his or her misbehaviour, deal with the student calmly and directly, demonstrate concern for the student, refocus his or her attention, choose an intervention in accordance with the student's need, make adjustments to short and long-term goals if necessary, and consult and collaborate with others regarding the student's misbehaviour as required.

Success in school is a function of both academic achievement and social development. This is not a new phenomenon in education. Traditionally, teachers have been aware of the important and reciprocal relationship between academic and social competence. Teachers have always wanted their students to be cooperative and respectful to one another and have generally guided their students toward appropriate social behaviour. However, it should be recognized that for a variety of reasons contemporary efforts to interface academic and social development are distinguishable from earlier attempts in a few important ways. First, many more children who have marked difficulty developing social networks, gaining acceptance from their peers, and making friends are entering regular classrooms. In essence, many students within contemporary regular classrooms do not have the prerequisite social skills that are required for them to work, share, and learn together.

In response to this situation, teachers are currently finding it necessary to provide systematic instructional procedures that effectively promote personally satisfying and beneficial interpersonal experiences for their students and concurrently enhance their academic mastery. Second, while social skill development has always been considered educationally relevant, social skill programs have been traditionally directed at special education students outside the regular classroom. Current approaches to social skill development are designed to benefit all students within the context of the regular classroom. Third, today's educational approaches tend to emphasize proactive methods for promoting appropriate social behaviour rather than reactive methods that respond to social problems. Hence, teachers plan for social skill development as a part of the daily routine rather than reinforce social skills only when needed.

The next chapter in this book presents some ways for promoting social development within the elementary classroom. In **Chapter 8**, Kimberly Schonert-Reichl and Shelley Hymel maintain that the growth of positive peer relationships can play an important role in determining students' academic and social success. Moreover, they advise us that the facilitation of social ability requires an understanding of the nature of social development. In the first half of their chapter, they review critical aspects and stages of social-emotional growth related to such areas as social participation, empathy, perspective taking, pro-social reasoning, person perception, friendship conceptions, biases, prejudices, and moral reasoning. In addition, they provide recommendations and strategies for teachers to foster the social development of students with respect to these domains. They continue with a discussion on approaches teachers can undertake to facilitate social awareness and acceptance among students and help them resolve social problems and interpersonal difficulties by themselves. The authors acknowledge that the process of social development is gradual and that it takes a lot of time and energy. However, they believe that the promotion of social development should be an important part of the teachers' daily classroom practices to ensure both the academic success and social competence of their students.

One of the most compelling concerns of Canadian educators is the dramatic increase of second culture and second language students in their schools and classrooms. Teachers must recognize that many cultures exist in Canada and that our society expects multicultural education and demands that schools value and respect cultural and ethnic diversity. Students in today's classrooms are members of different racial, ethnic, and religious groups who have different identities, frames of reference, and belief systems. These students should be provided with learning environments that promote acceptance and respect for individual differences and that fosters understanding and appreciation of others.

In **Chapter 9**, Jacquelyn Baker-Sennett and Gina Harrison present their views on how a sociocultural perspective can be applied to the teaching and learning transaction in elementary classrooms. They begin their chapter by reviewing the theoretical foundation of a sociocultural framework for educational practice. In contrast to educational theories that focus on specific learning tasks, environmental conditions, conceptions of intelligence, learning strategies, and stages of development, sociocultural theory emphasizes the importance of culture, language, and the interactive social basis of learning in students' cognitive development. According to Baker-Sennett and Harrison, this perspective on teaching and learning has important consequences for classroom instruction and assessment. They believe that teaching and learning should be a process of collaboration between the teacher and the student who both contribute to and share a responsibility for learning. Baker-Sennett and Harrison see assessment as a key to effective instruction because it is aimed at finding out the amount and type of assistance that is necessary for students to reach mastery performance. Hence, both instruction and assessment are interactively linked in the sociocultural practice of fostering learning processes and potential for change. Moreover, teachers and students are linked in the sociocultural practice of accomplishing things together that are often a struggle to do alone.

Over the last decade, a widespread trend toward inclusive education and growing support for collaborative exchanges within the field of education has resulted in a greater movement towards school-family partnerships. During this time, teachers have increasingly recognized the value of parents as active contributors to student program planning and intervention. Much of the basis for this increased focus on school-family partnerships is that teachers have come to realize that greater understanding of student behaviour can emerge from greater awareness of the family's influence on an individual's behaviour. In **Chapter 10**, Gerry Kysela and his colleagues L. McDonald, S. Brenton-Hadan, J. Alexander, and J. Cunningham provide details of an approach designed to help teachers identify important dimensions of family functioning and assist them in forming working partnerships with parents to provide the best educational experiences for students. The authors argue that family adaptation is an important factor affecting child development and that a family adaptation framework would be useful for working with families that have children who have serious learning difficulties. Accordingly, they delineate what they consider to be five critical and interactive dimensions that help educators understand families who experience a build-up of demands or stress because of their endeavours to deal with their child's special needs. They suggest that if educators learn more about stressors affecting families, the family's strengths, capabilities and resources available to them, appraisals and perspectives influencing their judgments, and coping patterns assisting adaptation, they would be able to better collaborate with families in ways conducive to the academic and social development of children with learning and developmental difficulties.

Teachers must also be aware of the dramatic changes in the business world that have placed greater demands on the educational system to prepare student to effectively learn and adapt to the post-industrial information age. Over the last decade, microcomputers have been increasingly used by teachers as a tool in the classroom. They have been used to stimulate students' interest, help them understand and review concepts, improve their academic skills, store and organize information, develop problem-solving skills, complete classroom assignments, and accommodate individual learning needs. In addition, they have also been used as tools to help teachers prepare individualized lesson plans, assess students' performance, record their grades, and monitor their progress. In **Chapter 11**, Leonard Haines and Gladene Robertson draw upon their considerable experience with the application of computer technology in schools to discuss how computers and related technology can help teachers address student diversity within elementary classrooms. They assert that computers can be used as a tool to direct and promote collaborative educational activities in support of students who have diverse needs. Coincidentally, they maintain that there should be greater use of computers as a tool to support the work of teachers than has been currently realized. In light of these views, Haines and Robertson first discuss the connection between computer support and collaborative instructional delivery with particular regard to educational planning, communication, teaching, record keeping, and reporting. From this discussion, they describe and present information relative to the use of a software program called the "Instruction CoPlanner," which they believe can be used to support teamwork and thereby support students with diverse needs in elementary classrooms.

The authors report that the "Instruction CoPlanner" consists of several elements that are designed to facilitate and support collaborative teamwork. First, team members (e.g., classroom and resource teachers, psychologists, social workers, parents, and students) share their views regarding an educational plan for a student. Next, this information can be stored, organized, and modified by the computer. Another feature of the software program is that each member can insert information independently and communicate with each other electronically. In addition, the program allows for storage and use of various assessment and instructional forms and methods and provides a system for planning and preparing progress reports for students.

In **Chapter 12**, Jac Andrews provides a thematic review of the entire book, which emphasizes group effort, proactive and adaptive teaching, and classroom climate. He presents a few more ideas relative to future educational efforts for improving the teaching of students with diverse needs. In the first part of the chapter, specific dimensions related to these themes are presented and expanded. In the second part of the chapter he discusses three conditions that can enable teachers to better accommodate student diversity in their classrooms (i.e., administrative leadership and support, professional training and development, and educational research). Andrews concludes his chapter with the view that our current challenge is to prepare ourselves with the knowledge and skills that can empower us to deal with the changes in our schools and the changes in our students.

Some Thoughts about Teaching Students with Diverse Needs

Jac J.W. Andrews

University of Calgary

All students are different from one another. They vary with respect to their academic abilities, social competence, interests, motivation, behavioural tendencies, cultural backgrounds and approaches to learning. Moreover, they differ in terms of their family and general life experiences. Although some students have greater challenges in responding and adjusting to their environmental conditions compared to their peers, all students have needs that require various levels of support in order to maximize their potential.

The dramatic changes in the nature of families in our country (e.g., immigrant families, single-parent and two-wage-earner families), along with the rapid technological developments in many fields and inflated requirements for students to meet their potential as adults (e.g., higher educational attainment), have significantly increased the demand for schools to provide expanded educational services for students. According to Murray (1993, p. 173), "there are simply too many students with too many needs. Fewer and fewer students fit neatly into the traditional teacher-centred classrooms of the past. Teachers who overemphasize large-group activities and teach to the middle are reaching fewer and fewer students."

The social and economic developments occurring contemporaneously over the past number of years, along with the growing discontent about educational service delivery and student outcomes, have culminated in an intensification of reform movements within the field of education. Although there are disagreements about how the educational system should change to accommodate greater diversity within our schools, many agreements can be found among parents and educators. Most reformers want our schools to change in ways that minimize the possibility of children falling between the cracks of the system and maximize the availability of higher quality education for all students. Most reformers want more effective schools without segregation. Most reformers want educational environments in which people are tolerant and respectful of student diversity. Most reformers want students to receive fair, equitable, and excellent instruction in ways that meet their needs without social stigma. Most reformers want to encourage increased parent participation in student programming and instruction. Most reformers want greater collaboration among all educational stakeholders and service providers. Finally, most reformers want changes to be made through a bottom-up rather than top-down process where educators and parents can team together in open-ended ways in order to develop and practise innovative educational service delivery approaches.

Educators have debated for decades about how to best meet the diverse needs of students. Typically, the focus of the debate has been on *where* students with special learning needs should be taught. During the 1950s and early 1960s, special class placements were favoured by educators for children who were unsuccessful with the age-appropriate curriculum. In the mid- and late 1960s, children typically qualified for special education services on the basis of intellectual functioning. For example, by the late 1960s, special education programs for students with educable mental retardation had the greatest number of children receiving special education services (Reschly, 1988). During this time, reformists opposed the narrowness of this criterion, and various parental and professional groups lobbied governments to broaden the qualifications for special education services. This activity, along with increasing discontent over the placement policies, led to a burgeoning of operational definitions of students by category of special need and became the basis of educational funding support. This resulted in the establishment and proliferation of special education classes and schools. It also dramatically increased the number and type of students serviced in special education programs (e.g., students with gifts and talents, behavioural disturbances, and learning disabilities). At the same time, it also increased labelling practices for placement determinations and the segregation of students with special learning needs from their peers in the mainstream.

In the early 1970s, many teachers and parents in the general public were becoming concerned with the viability of special education classes, particularly for mildly handicapped children (Dunn, 1968; Deno, 1970). A philosophical and attitudinal move away from categorical approaches in special education and toward the integration of children with particularly mild disabilities emerged. Along with a growing social consciousness of desegregation and legislative initiatives such as the

U.S. federal legislation of Public Law 94-142 and similar provincial and territorial policies within Canada (see Csapo & Goguen, 1989) to facilitate integrated placements and ensure the least restrictive educational environment for exceptional children, school boards during the 1970s and 1980s were being pressured to mainstream students with special learning needs into the regular classroom. Today, the concept of mainstreaming has been replaced by the concept of inclusive education whereby school boards are attempting to more fully integrate handicapped students within their schools and classrooms by restructuring their schools (Reynolds, Wang & Walberg, 1987; Villa, Thousand, Stainback & Stainback, 1992), melding special education and regular education services (Stainback, Stainback & Bunch, 1989; Mesinger, 1985), and instituting innovative instructional strategies and professional teaming approaches (Glomb & Morgan, 1991; Nevin, Thousand, Paolucci-Whitcomb & Villa, 1990; Porter, 1991).

These trends represent a paradigm shift for meeting the diverse educational needs of students. The traditional paradigm that has been widely adopted and practised in schools throughout the country is represented by a dual system of educational service delivery (regular education and special education) for meeting the diverse educational needs of students. This dual system has been characterized by static and standardized assessment, student labelling, classification and categorization, segregated learning environments, fragmented programming and instruction, and top-down decision making. The "new" paradigm represents the merging of the regular and special education systems into one unified system of service delivery to address the individual needs of all students. This "inclusive" model has been adopted and implemented in an increasing number of schools and school systems across Canada *because it is becoming increasingly evident that student diversity is no longer just a special education issue.* This paradigm is characterized by the application of cognitive, developmental, and sociocultural perspectives of teaching and learning, dynamic-, ecological-, and instructionally based assessment procedures, integrated learning environments, holistic programming and instruction, home-school partnerships, collaborative-based decision making, and greater partnership between regular and special educators.

We can no longer depend on special education to be responsible for students who do not fit the middle of regular education classrooms. Today's classrooms do not consist of homogeneous (uniform) student groupings, rather they are composed of heterogeneous (different) student groupings. As our classrooms take on a new look, our teachers' approaches to teaching must change to accommodate student diversity. Teachers should be provided opportunities to work together in teams to make the task of teaching manageable and to ensure quality instruction for everyone. Teaching students with diverse learning needs requires the adoption of more flexible and creative instructional approaches. Traditional teacher-centred approaches where teachers stand in front of the classroom and only provide large-group instruction and direction will not be effective within today's multidimensional classrooms. Instead, multifaceted instructional plans need to be orchestrated in ways that incorporate large-group instruction less often and utilize individualized and small-group instructional formats more often. Successful teaching techniques in today's classrooms include the utilization of team-teaching procedures, cooperative learning groups, peer and cross-age tutoring, formative assessment strategies, self-regulatory management approaches, cognitive strategy instruction, differentiated lesson plans, student assignments and outcome expectations, and other procedures that maximize students' involvement with one another and in their own learning.

The current trend toward greater inclusion of special-needs students in today's regular classrooms has significantly complicated the nature of teaching. The greatest challenge for teachers is to create educational environments that provide structure as well as flexibility for students and that enhance the learning of all students.

Inclusive education means that everyone is welcomed and valued in their neighbourhood school. To be included in your community school means that you have the same opportunities as every other child in the school, you have a variety of choices available, and you can be in the same classes as your peers. All children should have the right for fair and equal access to their community school and for participation in normal school experiences. As with communities, schools are places where diversity should be expected and appreciated. In some cases, this philosophy might result in multi-age and/or multi-grade classrooms where peer uniqueness, student assistance, and child-centred perspectives can be fostered. In any case, student diversity within classrooms can promote learning communities that expose students to differences within and across their peers, sensitize them to the needs of others, and offer opportunities for them to learn how to help one another construct knowledge, solve problems, complete projects, and live and work together collaboratively inside and outside their school. *Essentially, all students benefit from an atmosphere created by student diversity.*

Whereas some people have suggested that inclusion means getting rid of special educators, special education, and its continuum of services (e.g., individualized instruction and tutoring) (see Stainback & Stainback, 1992), others have suggested that inclusion means that special personnel, instructional methods, and a continuum of services get brought into the regular classroom. *Inclusion reflects an important societal value* (Lusthaus & Lusthaus, 1992) *and emerges from a sociology of acceptance, in contrast to a sociology of exclusion* (Flynn & Kowalczyk, 1989). As noted by Little (1992, p. 12),

> …it may help to think of inclusive education as that educational response in which each individual student is included in the thinking and planning process, is included in instruction, included in activities, included as a fully participating *bona fide* member of the class or group. Inclusion

precludes being segregated, or isolated in the ordinary class. Of paramount importance is its opportunity for helping children who have been separated from one another to begin to see each other as real people. It is simply not assigning children with special problems to the ordinary classroom. It is the conscious decision to create a sense of community out of accepted differences.

Inclusion requires variable and flexible educational processes to provide opportunities for children to have meaningful and enjoyable school experiences and then to reach their maximum potential.

Inclusive education embraces the concepts of normalization, integration, and mainstreaming. The concept of **normalization** reflects the idea that all individuals, regardless of their abilities, have a right to the opportunities of everyone else in everyday life (Wolfensberger, 1972). **Integration** refers to the education of handicapped children with their nonhandicapped peers. **Mainstreaming** is a process of integrating students that includes a continuum of services (e.g., professional teaming approaches, resource rooms, teacher aides) that aim to provide students with educational experiences that are the least restrictive and the most ordinary. Inclusion is not a cohesive plan to eliminate special services and place every student, regardless of condition, within the regular classroom. As noted by York, Doyle, and Kronberg (1992, p. 2) *"Inclusion does not mean that students must spend every minute of the school day in general education classes (no student should), that students never receive small-group or individualized instruction, or that students are in general education classes to learn the core curriculum only"* [italics added].

Inclusion should mean that there is more than one acceptable way to organize and structure education; more than one way to provide a differentiated curriculum to children; more than one way for teachers as well as students to share and work together in the teaching and learning transaction; more than one way for teachers to achieve desired educational outcomes for their students; more than one way for teachers to assess and evaluate student progress; and more than one way for teachers to prepare our children for the future. Essentially, inclusion means that everyone has a contribution to make and that the educational career of a child should be one that is maximized and *not* restricted. Lusthaus and Lusthaus (1992, p. 104) note that inclusion means that: "a) the child with the disability is educated for all or most of the day in an ordinary classroom with his or her age peers, b) the educational program is adapted to meet his or her social and academic needs, and c) the child and teacher receive the support they need to succeed. Full inclusion never means simply placing a child with challenging needs in an ordinary classroom without adaptations or supports."

We know that over the past few years there has been a growing institutionalization of successful collaboration-based and consultation-based service delivery systems in schools to help address student diversity. For example, a consultative-collaborative model for serving students with diverse needs in regular classrooms has been developed and practised in the province of Manitoba for many years (Freeze, Bravi & Rampaul, 1989). This model incorporates the use of different support service teams that comprise various personnel (e.g., classroom teachers, resource teachers, clinical specialists, program specialists) to assist classroom teachers in assessing their students, developing and implementing instructional programs, and evaluating the effectiveness of instructional strategies. Conditions for the successful implementation and maintenance of consultative-collaborative models of service delivery include time to implement them, parity among participants, shared participation, accountability, resources (Friend & Cook, 1990), and knowledge of and experience with the necessary problem-solving and management skills.

We know some ways to assess and evaluate students to better understand their diverse needs. Assessment techniques include norm-referenced assessment procedures (to ascertain students' academic achievements and cognitive abilities), criterion-referenced assessment techniques (to determine students' depth and breadth of knowledge and skills relevant to the curriculum), performance-based assessment measures (to determine students' reasoning and problem-solving skills and evaluate how students approach their learning), curriculum-based assessment methods (to continually probe and estimate students' knowledge and performance in order to better design instructional objectives), and informal techniques such as student observations, questionnaires, and interviews.

One way to get students actively involved in their own learning and development is to collaborate with them in the collection and evaluation of material. This can result in a portfolio of information that is chosen by the students under the guidance of the teacher and that reflects the day-to-day performance of the students in the classroom. This type of collection allows students to be participants in the assessment process and provides a way for teachers to monitor their students' performance in relation to a variety of learning tasks. Moreover, it is one example of how assessment practices can be part of the daily instructional routine.

We know that once we gather information about our students we can better address their needs. Planning should incorporate long-term goals, short-term objectives, and instructional strategies to accommodate the diverse needs of the students. We also know that good planning should involve the consideration of key concepts to be understood by the students, and the provision of activities that connect students with their real-world experiences. For example, reading activities might get students to familiarize themselves with world events reported in newspapers, and writing activities might involve students in the completion of job applications that are commensurate with their interests and skills. Moreover, different learning formats need to be considered such as peer tutoring, individual study, and small-group endeavours.

We know some effective ways for managing and instructing children with diverse needs. For example, all students will learn and behave better in classrooms that are well organized and where behavioural expectations and routines are well established as well as monitored and maintained by the teacher (Englert, 1984). Student achievement is also influenced by the degree of positive climate in the classroom. Positive social/emotional behaviour can be created by teachers who demonstrate to students that they care about them and who help them meet classroom expectations.

Social climate as well as academic development can be facilitated by using peer-tutoring arrangements (Jenkins & Jenkins, 1985; Lloyd, Crowley, Kohler & Strain, 1988) where students can instruct and guide one another with respect to various skills. However, materials need to be carefully arranged and structured and sessions should be continually monitored by the teacher. Cooperative learning experiences provide opportunities for students to undertake roles such as leader, encourager, recorder, facilitator, and be significantly involved in group work (Johnson & Johnson, 1986). According to Murray (1993, p. 181) "teachers report that as a result of working in cooperative groups, special students become less hesitant to offer ideas in larger group discussions. They develop more confidence in their ability to think and contribute."

Successful teachers of students with diverse needs prevent problems from occurring. Students need to understand the behavioural rules and routines of the classroom and be helped in making good behavioural choices. Appropriate behaviour is promoted by teachers who make adjustments in the curriculum and in their teaching methods to accommodate student differences. Teachers can maintain and facilitate successful learning and appropriate behaviour by using effective instructional procedures.

We know that many children with learning problems also have social problems that need to be addressed by the teacher in the classroom. Teaching students to become socially skilled and effective social problem-solvers is a challenging task that requires attention to cognitive, affective, and behavioural dimensions. This is another area in which regular and special educators can work together in identifying the social needs of students and providing social skills training for the students. Many programs and strategies are available that have proven to be effective in regular classrooms (see McIntosh & Vaughn, 1993; Vernon & Schumaker, 1993).

Many students do not have the social skills they need to be able to successfully work and interact with their peers. Hence, many teachers are finding it necessary to provide direct social skills instruction. Research has shown that positive peer interactions can be increased and that students can feel better about themselves when cooperative group and peer-tutoring structures have been implemented (Putman, Rynders, Johnson & Johnson, 1989; Delquadri, Greenwood, Whorton, Carta & Hall, 1986). It has also been shown that instructing students in social skills, giving them opportunities to practise these skills, providing feedback with respect to their performance, and providing appropriate behavioural modelling augments sociometric acceptance and status of children (Gottman, Gonso & Schuler, 1976) and helps reduce inappropriate behaviour (Zahvi & Asher, 1978) while increasing conversational behaviours (Bondy & Erickson, 1976). Overall, the literature points out that teachers can effectively teach social skills to their students. According to McIntosh and Vaughn (1993), the best practices involve the incorporation of social skills interventions within the classroom, the delivery of social skills instruction over extended periods of time, the use of individual and small-group instructional formats, and the integration of cognitive-behavioural approaches.

Many children in today's classrooms have second-culture and second-language backgrounds that should be respected and acknowledged in the day-to-day learning activities. The more we are aware of our own cultural values and beliefs, the more likely we can appreciate the variant beliefs and values held by our students and create a community of learners in which there is equality of opportunity and expression. Among other things, students should be encouraged to discuss the issues related to various cultural group membership and be able to share with one another their cultural experiences.

We know that there are many benefits from the establishment of school-home partnerships (Shea & Bauer, 1991). Along with providing useful information regarding student interests, motivations, behavioural tendencies, and learning styles, parents can be trained to work with their children at home in accordance with classroom directives as well as undertake volunteer roles within the school (Shea & Bauer, 1991; Nystul, 1987).

It is also important to note that students with diverse needs come from families that are unique and diverse. Families differ in terms of culture, religion, belief systems, stress levels, educational background, political affiliations, social status, and other dimensions. Just as classrooms consist of heterogeneous groups of students, communities consist of heterogeneous groups of families. To better know the nature of students is to better know the nature of their families.

We know that the use of technology can play an important role in promoting the academic development of students within the classroom. Advances in computer hardware and software make individualized instruction more feasible within the classroom. Moreover, computing technology can be used in ways that support collaborative planning and decision making. Computers can also be used by teachers to more efficiently record student progress and prepare learning profiles of students. At the functional level, computer technology can, for example, help students get more actively involved in their writing through the use of word-processing software programs and help them become more proficient in mathematical computations and problem solving. Technologies are also available to assist students with hearing and visual impairments as well as students with physical disabilities to better communicate with others. At the developmental level, computer technology can be used to prepare students for their future in a workforce that will likely require them to be users of advancing computer technology.

Teaching students with diverse learning needs is not easy. It requires hard work, deep commitment, and perseverance. It is going to take more than occasional professional development workshops and pre-service teacher preparation programs to prepare teachers to deal with the complexity of student diversity within their classrooms. Many teachers are not supportive of the integration of exceptional students into their classrooms (Winzer, 1985) and some are angry and frustrated, particularly if appropriate supports are not provided (Hardman, Drew, Egan & Wolf, 1990). Many teachers worry that their classroom might be disrupted if children with diverse learning needs are placed in regular classrooms (Vacc & Kirst, 1977) and that their programs will be diluted (Bradfield, Brown, Kaplan, Rickert & Stannard, 1973). We know that teachers' attitudes and dispositions regarding teaching children with diverse learning needs are important determinants of inclusive education. In order to facilitate positive attitudes, teachers cannot feel burdened with diversity (Duquette, 1992) and must experience support from the administration within their school, help from their colleagues related to the frustrations and stresses involved in the teaching process, and have positive and successful encounters with their students and their families.

Students with diverse learning needs are unlikely to be taught well by someone who has no desire to develop their teaching skills and who has little interest in learning how to teach students with diverse needs. Teachers should be (among other things) bright, fair-minded, patient, caring, thoughtful, cooperative, inquisitive, resourceful, and willing to learn, grow, and change for the betterment of themselves and their students.

Although we know some things about teaching students with diverse needs there is a lot for us to learn. It seems reasonable to expect that we will always be trying to improve our instructional ability and our students' learning abilities. As we develop over time we will become more knowledgeable about how to teach and manage diverse populations. Hopefully, we can move beyond discussion and debate about where students with diverse learning needs should be taught and focus on how to best achieve excellence while accepting individual differences within the school and community (Gallagher, 1994; Morse, 1994; Pugach, 1990). Integration has not been shown to be flawed (Goetz & Sailor, 1990) and does not preclude the continued investigation of children's learning problems and the resolution of their difficulties. We have moved away from the assumption that children with special needs are the owners of their problems and have come to realize that the school system and the community at large have ownership of children with diverse educational needs (Csapo, 1992). However, we need to continue to research and develop more effective interventions that can expand the continuum of services for children with special needs within community schools and regular classrooms. As noted by Kauffman (1993), we do not want inclusion to exclude remedial assistance for those students who are struggling in their learning. Rather, we want all students to be a part of the educational mainstream that has teachers who are willing and able to accept diversity and who can assess students' needs, accommodate these needs in their programming and instruction, facilitate lifelong learning and self-fulfilment, academic and social skills, school-home partnerships, educational quality and equity, and collaboration among all service providers. *Although perfection in these areas is not reasonable, it is reasonable to improve upon the necessary enabling conditions* (i.e., funding, professional development, empirical studies, and administrative leadership and support) *that can promote these worthwhile targets. Moreover, it is reasonable to increase our understanding of what can be done to improve the teaching of students with diverse needs within the classrooms of our schools.*

SUGGESTED RESOURCES

Andrews, J., & Lupart, J. (1993). *The inclusive classroom: Educating exceptional children.* Scarborough, ON: Nelson Canada.

Bowd, A., McDougall, D., & Yewchuck, C. (1994). *Educational psychology for Canadian teachers.* Toronto: Harcourt Brace & Co.

Bos, C.S., & Vaughn, S. (1994). *Strategies for teaching students with learning and behavior problems* (3rd edition). Toronto: Allyn and Bacon.

Crealock, C., & Bachor, D. (1995). *Instructional strategies for students with special needs* (2nd edition). Scarborough, ON: Allyn and Bacon.

Goodlad, J.I., & Lovitt, T.C. (1993). *Integrating general and special education.* Toronto: Maxwell Macmillan Canada.

Mulcahy, R.F., Short, R.H., & Andrews, J. (1991). *Enhancing learning and thinking.* New York: Praeger.

Smith, T.E.C., Polloway, E.A., Potten, J.R., & Dowdy, C.A. (1995). *Teaching children with special needs in inclusive settings.* Toronto: Allyn and Bacon.

REFERENCES

Bondy, A.S., & Erickson, M.T. (1976). Comparison of modelling and reinforcement procedures in increasing question-asking of mentally retarded children. *Journal of Applied Behavior Analysis, 9*(1), 108.

Bradfield, H.R., Brown, J., Kaplan, P., Rickert, E., & Stannard, R. (1973). The special child in the regular classroom. *Exceptional Children, 39*, 384–90.

Csapo, M. (1992). Special education in crisis. *B.C. Journal of Special Education, 16*(3), 249–58.

Csapo, M., & Goguen, L. (1989). *Special education across Canada: Issues and concerns for the '90s.* Vancouver: Centre for Human Development and Research.

Delquadri, J., Greenwood, C.R., Whorton, D., Carta, J.J., & Hall, V. (1986). Classwide peer tutoring. *Exceptional Children, 52*, 535–42.

Deno, E. (1970). Special education as developmental capital. *Exceptional Children, 37*, 229–37.

Dunn, L. (1968). Special education for the mildly retarded—Is much of it justifiable? *Exceptional Children, 35*, 5–22.

Duquette, C. (1992). Integrating mildly and moderately handicapped children: What goes on in a successful school? *Exceptionality Education Canada, 2*(1&2), 139–53.

Englert, C.S. (1984). Measuring teacher effectiveness from the teacher's point of view. *Focus on Exceptional Children, 17*, 1–14.

Evans, W.H., & Evans, S.S. (1983). Using parents in behavior management. *Academic Therapy, 19*, 37–41.

Flynn, G., & Kowalczyk-McPhee, B. (1989). A school system in transition. In S. Stainback, W. Stainback & M. Forest (Eds.), *Educating all students in the mainstream of regular education* (pp. 29–41). Baltimore: Paul H. Brookes.

Freeze, D.R., Bravi, G., & Rampaul, W.E. (1989). Special education in Manitoba: A consultative-collaborative services delivery model. In M. Csapo & L. Goguen (Eds.), *Special education across Canada* (pp. 47–80). Vancouver: Centre for Human Development and Research.

Friend, M., & Cook, L. (1990). Collaboration as a predictor for success in school reform. *Journal of Educational and Psychological Consultation, 1*, 69–86.

Gallagher, J.J. (1994). The pull of societal forces on special education. *The Journal of Special Education, 27*(4), 521–30.

Glomb, N.K., & Morgan, D.P. (1991). Resource room teachers' use of strategies that promote the success of handicapped students in regular classrooms. *The Journal of Special Education, 25*(2), 221–35.

Goetz, L., & Sailor, W. (1990). Much to do about babies, musky bathwater, and trickle-down politics: A reply to Kauffman. *The Journal of Special Education, 24*(3), 334–39.

Gottman, J., Gonso, J., & Schuler, P. (1976). Teaching social skills to isolated children. *Journal of Abnormal Child Psychology, 4*, 179–97.

Hardman, M.L., Drew, C.J., Egan, M.W., & Wolf, B. (1990). *Human exceptionality: Society, school, and family.* Boston: Allyn and Bacon.

Jenkins, J., & Jenkins, L. (1985). Peer tutoring in elementary and secondary programmes. *Focus on Exceptional Children, 17*(6), 1–12.

Johnson, D.W., & Johnson, R.T. (1986). Mainstreaming and cooperative learning strategies. *Exceptional Children, 52,* 553–61.

Kauffman, J.M. (1993). How we might achieve the radical reform of special education. *Exceptional Children, 60*(1), 6–16.

Little, D.M. (1992). The muddle of mainstreaming: Cross-Canada currents—policy and practice of inclusive education. *Exceptionality Education Canada, 2*(1&2), 9–48.

Lloyd, J., Crowley, E.P., Kohler, F.W., & Strain, P.S. (1988). Redefining the applied research agenda? Cooperative learnings, prereferral, teacher consultant, and peer-mediated interventions. *Journal of Learning Disabilities, 21,* 43–52.

Lusthaus, E., & Lusthaus, C. (1992). From segregation to full inclusion: An evolution. *Exceptionality Education Canada, 2*(1&2), 95–115.

McIntosh, R., & Vaughn, S. (1993). So you want to teach social skills to your students: Some pointers from research. *Exceptionality Education Canada, 3*(1&2), 39–59.

Mesinger, J.F. (1985). Commentary on Rationale for the merger of special and regular education or Is it now time for the lamb to lie down with the lion? *Exceptionality Children, 51*(6), 510–12.

Morse, W.C. (1994). Comments from a biased viewpoint. *The Journal of Special Education, 27*(4), 531–42.

Murray, L.B. (1993). Putting it all together at the school level: A principal's perspective. In J.I. Goodlad & T.C. Lovitt (Eds.), *Integrating general and special education.* Toronto: Maxwell Macmillan Canada.

Nevin, A., Thousand, J., Paolucci-Whitcomb, P., & Villa, R. (1990). Collaborative consultation: Empowering public school personnel to provide heterogeneous schooling for all—or Who rang that bell? *Journal of Educational and Psychological Consultation, 1*(1), 41–67.

Nystul, M. (1987). Strategies for parent-centred counselling of the young. *The Creative Child and Adult Quarterly, 12,* 103–10.

Porter, G.L. (1991). The methods and resource teacher: A collaborative consultant model. In G.L. Porter & D. Richler (Eds.), *Changing Canadian schools* (pp. 107–154). North York, ON: Roeher Institute.

Pugach, M.C. (1990). The moral cost of retrenchment in special education. *The Journal of Special Education, 24*(3), 326–33.

Putman, J.W., Rynders, J.E., Johnson, R.T., & Johnson, D.W. (1989). Collaborative skill instruction for promoting positive interactions between mentally handicapped and nonhandicapped children. *Exceptional Children, 55*(6), 550–57.

Reschly, D.J. (1988). Introduction. In M.C. Wang, M.C. Reynolds & H.J. Walberg (Eds.), *Handbook of special education: Research and practice* (Vol. 2, pp. 3–5). Oxford, UK: Pergamon Press.

Reynolds, M.C., Wang, M.C., & Walberg, H.J. (1987). The necessary restructuring of special and regular education. *Exceptional Children, 53*(5), 391–98.

Sharan, S., & Sharan, Y. (1976). *Small group teaching.* Englewood Cliffs, NJ: Educational Testing Publications.

Shea, T.M., & Bauer, A.M. (1991). *Parents and teachers of small children with exceptionalities: A handbook for collaboration* (2nd edition). Boston: Allyn and Bacon.

Stainback, S., & Stainback, W. (1992). *Curriculum considerations in inclusive classrooms: Facilitating learning for all students.* Baltimore: Paul H. Brookes.

Stainback, S., Stainback, W., & Bunch, G. (1989). A rationale for the merger of regular and special education. In S. Stainback, W. Stainback & M. Forest (Eds.), *Educating all students in the mainstream of regular education* (pp. 15–26). Baltimore: Paul H. Brookes.

Vacc, N.A., & Kirst, N. (1977). Emotionally disturbed children and regular classroom teachers. *Elementary School Journal, 77*, 309–17.

Vernon, D.S., & Schumaker, J.B. (1993). Who benefits from social skills instruction in the mainstream classroom? *Exceptionality Education Canada, 3*(1&2), 9–38.

Villa, R.A., Thousand, J.S., Stainback, W., & Stainback, S. (Eds.). (1992). *Restructuring for caring and effective education: An administrative guide to creating heterogeneous schools.* Baltimore: Paul H. Brookes.

Winzer, M. (1985). Teacher attitudes towards mainstreaming: An appraisal of the research. *B.C. Journal of Special Education, 9*, 149–61.

Wolfensberger, W. (1972). *Normalization in human services.* Toronto: National Institute on Mental Retardation.

York, J., Doyle, M.B., & Kronberg, R. (1992). A curriculum development process for inclusive classrooms. *Focus on Exceptional Children, 25*(4), 1–16.

Zahvi, S., & Asher, S. (1978). The effect of verbal instructions on preschool children's aggressive behavior. *Journal of School Psychology, 16*, 146–53.

Becoming a Change Agent in Your Elementary Classroom

Donna Patterson

University of Regina

Introduction

This chapter begins with an example of how a teacher, Rachel Scott, acts as change agent for herself and her students. The remainder of the chapter focuses on what each of us might do to become such agents in our own classrooms amid the now-occurring merger of special and regular education. Self-care, political astuteness, planning, effective conflict resolution, and a sense of humour are explored as ways to manage the merger successfully.

CASE STUDY

Rachel Scott was taking on a grade-8 class after Christmas. The previous teacher, the vice-principal in the school, Mrs. Tymchuk, was on a maternity leave and would not return until the fall. Mrs. Tymchuk was well thought of by other staff members and her students. This was Rachel's first full-time teaching assignment and she was nervous, as most of us would be.

During the first week, she noticed that there seemed to be a great deal of "to-ing and fro-ing," lots of walking around to sharpen pencils, and lots of conversation. The students didn't seem to be adjusting easily to having a new teacher. Often when she would ask the students a question or to do something, she would hear mutterings of this not being how they did things with Mrs. Tymchuk. She knew some of this was to be expected, but after two weeks it was disconcerting. The class seemed tense, as if everyone had things to say but did not feel comfortable saying them out loud.

Rachel thought about holding a class meeting. She knew it might be risky but she also thought pretending the tension would disappear or waiting for the air to clear by itself was leaving everyone feeling frazzled. She approached another more experienced teacher, Matthew Carver, who seemed to have a good rapport with the students, and who had been friendly to Rachel. She talked with him about how he started his class at the first of the year. He said that he liked to start things off with a class meeting—just to make sure that things got off to a good start and to set the tone for the year. Rachel decided to follow her own inclination and hold a class meeting.

She told her students that she knew that they had really liked Mrs. Tymchuk, that she suspected having a change of teacher mid-year wasn't easy, and that she would like to have a class meeting the following afternoon to talk about how she and the students might structure the class.

After all, they were going to be working together for the rest of the year. A few class members said that it was a good idea, others nodded in agreement, and the rest of the group said nothing. Sensing from this response that the class was unsure about holding the meeting, Rachel suggested they think it over and vote on it the following morning.

The next day there were still some students who were noncommittal but most (20 out of the 27) decided that a meeting was a good idea. The meeting went reasonably well. The class and Rachel made some rules together. The students had an opportunity to talk about what they liked about Mrs. Tymchuk's class, as well as share some of their own ideas about how the class should run. Rachel agreed to try some of their ideas, and she said that though she knew it wasn't easy for them, no matter what she did, she couldn't be Mrs. Tymchuk. Things had changed and it meant everyone had to adjust. Rachel also suggested that the class set up a bulletin board on the computer so that both Rachel and the students could exchange notes about concerns on a daily basis. Some of the tension began to disappear, and there was more on-task behaviour. Classroom life seemed to be getting better.

Then Mrs. Tymchuk dropped in for a visit. She had been asked by the principal to come in and talk to the students about their move to high school the following year. The students were excited when they heard the news, but. Rachel worried about the possible disruption. It had just started to feel like her classroom and the students were just starting to settle down. While the students seemed to enjoy the presentation, after Mrs. Tymchuk left, everyone was tense. Rachel remembered that when she was tense it helped to breathe. She had the class stand up and together they focused on taking deep breaths and slowly exhaling to the count of 10. The class and Rachel repeated this seven or eight times and then sat down. Larry, this week's funster, told the class a joke. Everyone laughed and settled down to talk about what had just happened and to get on with the scheduled mathematics lesson.

This example demonstrates the difference between being overwhelmed by change, being a change manager, and becoming a change agent. No matter what the situation, or what we would wish:

Change must be accomplished by people.
(Evans, 1993)

Change is ubiquitous. It is a constant in our lives, affecting families and schools and most certainly students. Fullan (1985) suggests that change is a process whereby we alter our ways of thinking and doing. It is a process of developing new skills and, above all, of finding satisfaction in new ways of doing things. Cantor (1953) goes as far as to suggest that to learn is to change.

Currently, the classroom is changing. Among many other changes, regular and special education are merging. This merging is often framed in a renewed commitment to meeting the diverse needs of students. Frequently, discussion focuses on what educators can and/or should do for students. This is as it should be, for it is this commitment that brings most of us to and keeps us in the teaching profession (Gold & Roth, 1993). Still, for many of us, this merging of special and regular education can be, and is, overwhelming. Sarason (1990), in his reflections on school reform, suggests that attempts to reform education (and by extension to merge regular and special education) will make little difference until those initiating change understand that the school must exist as much for teachers as for students. Schools will be successful in nurturing students only to the extent that they nurture teachers. The contention in this chapter is that teachers involved in the merger of special and regular education are at the centre of this change (Postman & Weingartner, 1987).

This chapter reflects the belief that change is a process, not an event, that is made by individuals first and then by institutions, and that in the final analysis it's a very personal experience. It focuses on how we can avoid being overwhelmed and how we can navigate this merger to become effective change managers and agents. Managing this type of change must start with ourselves. It requires self-care if we are to persist, political astuteness if we are to find support and/or renegotiate roles, a systematic planful approach if we are not to be overwhelmed, an ability to deal with conflict if we are not to get sidetracked, and a sense of humour to get us over the humps.

> *If you want to know how something works, try changing it.*
> (Lewin, 1935, 1948)

Lewin's statement can be adapted to the personal level: if you want to learn about yourself, try changing yourself.

We are more likely to change if we see the change as desirable or feasible (Beckhard & Harris, 1987); when it is espoused by someone we trust; when it is linked to things we hold as important; and when its target is focused and practical. As an individual teacher in a school or school system, you may become involved in the merging of special and regular education in a number of ways. For some, school or provincial policy will dictate their involvement; for others, the merger speaks to their own commitment to equity. For still others, the merger becomes real only when a student with special needs turns up in their class for the first time or when the number of students with special needs increases beyond two or three.

There are a range of responses to the merging of regular and special education. Some teachers carry on as if nothing were happening (Sikes, 1984; Troyna, 1985). Sometimes teachers suggest that changes have taken place, but the gap between what they say and what they do is wide. Going through the motions of presenting an appearance of change prevents real change from occurring.

Some teachers are already "neck deep" in change. They are the ones most encouraged by the merger. They are already committed, initiating changes for their students in their classrooms. It might be said these teachers are "front runners," showing the rest of us what is possible. Sometimes they are so far ahead of the rest of us that we feel left behind, even resentful, and certainly frustrated.

A novice teacher wanting to include parents in decision making about students' educational programs found the most important thing was to communicate with the rest of the school staff about what she was trying to do. She then communicated with the parents of the students in her class, and, in this way, began to build a circle of support. But she had to try not to do everything on her own, all at once. This chapter will discuss these and other strategies for those finding themselves in a similar position.

Most of the rest of us are beginning to grapple or are in the midst of grappling with the merger. We're starting to develop effective ways to work with and meet the needs of all our students. We are willing to foster the merger, but may not yet be totally committed and/or understand all its implications for us or our practice. Our greatest struggle is not to become discouraged. We need to approach this merger with care.

Of course, there are some things that shouldn't be changed and there are some that can't be changed—at least, not right now, not quickly, and not by ourselves. It is important to identify these and try to accept them gracefully. Remind yourself that you cannot solve every problem or fix everything. However, you can solve *some* problems and begin to change *some* things. At the very least, it is possible to do something, to make a start, to take a step. Some of us are ready to take that step and others have taken it; in both cases the question is what to do next.

Finally, there are those who are actively resisting the merger of regular and special education. Some try to change and fail, but think they are succeeding; other refuse to try. At the very least, many teachers are ambivalent about change (Bolman & Deal, 1991). As Marris (1986) has shown, for many of us the primary metaphor for change is loss. The discrediting of the assumptions by which we live and make sense of our world and our work is often filled with pain and sadness. There are usually good reasons for our resistance to any change. Fear of loss, of incompetence, and of disorganization all fuel our resistance to change. We may not be able to find an "adequate" plan or strategy. How we go about the change becomes a critical question both for the school system and the individual teacher. Our expectations may be high and we may expend a lot of energy looking for a "right" or "best" strategy or plan. In the merger of special and regular education, it would be easy to look for one way to achieve this goal instead of trying a number of strategies to see which works best for us and for our students. We may also resist the merger because of an apparent lack of resources or because we perceive that there has been an underestimation of the issues surrounding resources and feasibility. In this case, it's necessary to go back to the drawing board and rethink what is reasonable given existing resources. High expectations and slight resources often lead to frustration.

Continued resistance requires effort and is often exhausting even if we join a "grumbling clique" (Sikes, 1992, p. 46). Participating in the merger ensures that our needs and those of our students are addressed and that we can live more easily with the form the merger takes in our school or school system. Being involved can give us a sense of continuity, predictability, and control. See Appendix 2A for another way to frame or understand our response to change.

▩ Building in Self-Care

If we don't take good care of ourselves,
we will not be able to give anything to anyone else.
(Coloroso, 1994)

Finding a Buddy

For many of us, the joy of teaching lies in being in the classroom, working with our students. While these days there are many people in and out of the classroom (parents, teacher aides, volunteers, other professionals, even students from other classes), no one else really knows fully what we're doing. Even with conferencing, team, and/or staff meetings we are mostly on our own.

A popular teaching strategy is to set up a buddy system—to pair one student with another to work together on reading, to pair an older student with a student new to a school to help them learn the ropes. This strategy works well for students and, often, for parents. It is one teachers might use for themselves.

In developing such support we would be assisting ourselves in our own professional development. When this kind of support is set up by a school system, Joyce and Showers (1982) and Hord and Huling-Austin (1988) refer to it as "consulting" or "coaching." Their work indicates that change happens most easily when there are at least two people working to effect the change—when we have a buddy.

There is much to be gained from developing support. It provides a safer environment in which to recognize and explore classroom issues and concerns. It can help you think through changes you are attempting in your classroom with your students. It can encourage us throughout the change process by helping us to focus on our successes. Support can help us sustain our efforts, clarify our goals, develop strategies, and generate new ones when the ones we are using aren't working as well as we would like.

Finding someone with whom you feel comfortable, who you can talk to, is a first step. It would be easy to turn to a close friend, someone you know and trust. While these people can be helpful in many respects, they may not always be a good choice; perhaps better is someone whom you respect and with whom you share common experiences in teaching. You may want to choose someone who is a little further along the road, but not so far ahead you can't see them (Odell, 1990; Opuni, 1989; Vann, 1989). Probably you will consider someone teaching at your school or at a school close to you since proximity will make meeting and talking more probable. Usually a support emerges over time, as you develop a working relationship with the other person. The relationship grows with thought, attention, and good communication skills. Of course, it is a two-way street and for most of us must include an understanding that what is discussed is held in confidence. This kind of "being with" helps us feel listened to, understood, and accepted, and makes the risks of change a little less ominous.

Usually we need more support than any one individual can provide. Some teachers find support in professional organizations or in a small group of colleagues. It is important to have a variety of sources of support in your professional life to act just as your family and circle of friends do in your personal life. This need for support, for a circle of caring, in both professional and personal life is so strong that the rate for virtually every major cause of death is significantly higher for the lonely (Hartog, Audry & Cohen, 1980).

This need for support is one we often deal with intuitively without much thought. When support occurs easily, that is wonderful. But sometimes, particularly in new situations, it doesn't hurt to consciously try to establish it by finding a buddy.

Learning to Encourage

As teachers and teachers in training, we tend to see ourselves as problem-solvers. We try to define what is wrong or what is making learning difficult for our students. The more we do this, of course, the better we get at it. We become quick at identifying errors and become critics. We turn this skill on our students, on our colleagues, and on ourselves. What would happen if we concentrated on the positive, on strengths? I often open my classes by asking students to share one positive thing that has happened to them in the past 24 hours. At the beginning of the semester, students often are hesitant and uneasy. Some remain so, others begin to look forward to the activity, and actually find it easy to do by the end of the semester.

Many have written extensively on how we can turn our classrooms into inviting, safe, supportive places for our students (Canfield, 1990; Kearns et al., 1990; Purkey, 1991; Purkey & Schmidt, 1990; Purkey & Novak, 1984, to name only a few). Teachers need to use these same techniques for themselves.

We need to look carefully at how we speak to and about ourselves. Perceiving ourselves positively means applying the labels: valuable, able, and responsible to our lives. Try this: make a list of your strengths as a teacher and beside each strength write an example in which you used that strength. For some, finding one—for others, finding more than five or six—will be difficult. Often we are afraid we will be seen as overconfident, as bragging.

One way to try to increase the number of positive things we say to ourselves is to acknowledge what we do, what we say, and what we try. Often we just don't take the time to notice. We tell ourselves that what we say and what we do doesn't matter, doesn't or didn't make any difference anyway. Simply acknowledging what we have tried, what we have done, and what we have said is a first step in encouraging ourselves. Accepting what we have done means understanding what has taken place and our part in it. We can also agree that what we have done, said, and tried is OK. This kind of self-talk will not take place by itself. We'll need to practise encouraging ourselves until it becomes automatic.

Many of us get too busy to keep a list or to acknowledge our successes. Still we need to talk about and, focus on what succeeds. Often we have five objectives, succeed in four, but because we are rushed and stressed, we focus all our attention on the one objective we haven't reached. It's easy to get frustrated if we ignore our successes. Perhaps we need to build 5 or 10 minutes at the end of the day just to jot down a few notes on what worked that day. Sometimes a tape recorder can be more helpful; often we're tired of paper and writing at the end of the day.

Deboer (1986) deals at some length with what she calls cognitive distortions—illogical and hurtful self-talk. Her advice seems to be not only to avoid being angry, sarcastic, or aggressive with our students but also with ourselves.

Try to treat yourself kindly and with consideration. Think of it as practice for acting positively with your students. Most of us don't need critics, we need friends—we need encouragement. Recognizing and building in supportive self-talk is one way to provide that encouragement.

Sometimes you can catch yourself speaking harshly to yourself, saying things like,

"I must be losing it."
"No one else makes these kind of mistakes."
"I'll never get it right. I must be stupid."
"This would have gone better if I'd been more prepared."

These messages are clearly ones that imply, "I'm not valuable," "I'm not able," and "I'm irresponsible." When you catch yourself making these statements say to yourself, "Stop," or "Interrupt," and then replace the rest of what you were going to say with a reminder that "you are valuable," "you are able," "you are responsible." Think of something that has worked, think of a time when you felt able, and acknowledge that while this time things did not work, they have in the past and they will again. Acknowledge that you tried and pick out what worked. Think about what you did and talk yourself through how you will do it better next time, *later.*

There are other ways to be encouraging. When you made your list of strengths, did you have difficulty? If so, think back to something in your work in the classroom you felt proud of, something that made you want to celebrate. Did you celebrate? How? Most of us overlook our successes; we are so good at identifying and solving problems, we forget to celebrate when things work. In many elementary classrooms, students are rewarded with stars, stickers, praise, and, in some classrooms, cookies. Celebrating our successes is important, and the more ways we put in place to celebrate, the better.

A final tip on learning to encourage: learn to build in successes. Most teachers know to do this for their students, but forget or don't think to do it for themselves. The feeling of competence gained through doing something that works cannot be overstated. If you have not experienced any success for a while, perhaps you need to go back to the drawing board and look at how you are trying to bring about change in your classroom with your students. Lack of success is often a sure sign that our steps or strategies are too big, too ambitious, and that we are trying to do too much, too quickly.

Encouragement—engaging in positive self-talk, celebrating our efforts, and building in successes—maintains our willingness to work toward merging special and regular education. These strategies can help us to take pride in our teaching, to do our work with care, to finish what we start, and to know our efforts will work if we persist.

▨ Developing Political Astuteness

Finding Support and Reading the Political Current

Most of us think of teaching as something we do with and for students. We see our involvement with parents and other professionals as working on our students' behalf. This is true, but there is another part of the job and many of us overlook it. Letting others know what we are doing, finding out about district initiatives, and building a circle of collegial support are important if we are to manage change and not have it manage us.

I like to tell my students about a first-year teacher. She worked in a special education resource room and many evenings she sat up late organizing materials and designing learning experiences. There were many Saturdays she spent gathering resources, arranging field trips, and contacting speakers for her classroom. At the end of the year, when the principal was asked to make decisions on staffing, he voted to let her go. His explanation was that he wasn't aware she had done anything special for her students. This story highlights the issue that if the other members of the school community don't know what we are trying to do, they can't help us. They may even unknowingly make life more difficult for us.

If you are either new or viewed as an outsider to a school system, you need to be cautious about the amount or degree of change you undertake initially. Using familiar systems, procedures, forms, and/or language can help you seem more a part of the school system. Check out school system policies and try to get a sense of system priorities and/or initiatives. District administrators are on the front line, often coordinating change efforts so that those changes are coherent and well managed.

It is in your best interest to work closely with your principal. This can be done by keeping your principal informed about what's going on in your class. You can use video or audio tapes, short memos, student-created newsletters, and/or short, regularly scheduled meetings to do this. In most situations, principals have little idea what it is you need from them in terms of support. Most would like to be supportive, so it is your responsibility to provide the necessary information so that they can be so.

Parents also like to know what's happening in your class. Parents appreciate being acknowledged as caring individuals and as having their child's best interests at heart.

How we get information to parents is a challenge. Parent-teacher conferences are one way. With both parents working, such meetings can be difficult to arrange. Some other ideas that have worked are postcards—notes to parents about something wonderful their child did that day. Writing one of these a day allows 20 of your parents a month to actually get good news from the school. Another idea a teacher used was to videotape occasional classes (one or two a month) and put them on reserve in the public library. The library made a viewing room and videocassette recorder (VCR) available to parents . Whatever we do we mustn't isolate ourselves. Sometimes it helps in all our efforts for our students to remember that the other people involved with our students do the best they can with what they have.

You can find allies if you see others striving toward excellence just as you are. Our resources often determine what and how well we do. You may also find it helpful to remember that your schedule is yours and everyone else has their own. If you want to work well with others you need to accept that you can't always set the pace. Finding ways to communicate and keeping the door open helps everyone. Remember you're on the same side.

Negotiating Roles

With the merging of regular and special education, the classroom is becoming an ever-expanding community. Many people are in and out throughout the day. There are parents and paraprofessionals or teacher associates. There are other students—younger ones and older ones—some acting as tutors and some coming in to be tutored. There are other teachers and other professionals. Coordinating all of these resources so that students' needs are met and the classroom is not disrupted is challenging.

The key to making this kind of situation work for all those involved lies in our working together, in clearly setting out who will do what, and when and where an intervention will take place. Let's look at an example: Johnny is a grade-6 student having some persistent reading difficulties. A reading consultant is requested to work with him. At the same time, the teacher decides to involve the student in a reading buddies program linking grade-6 students with reading difficulties and more accomplished junior high readers. Unfortunately, because there is no discussion about when, where, and how these programs will take place, both the consultant and the buddy turn up to work with Johnny at the same time. This is easily fixed but as time goes by Johnny's reading does not improve. It seems that the consultant and the buddy are working at cross-purposes. Everyone is frustrated, particularly Johnny, when after two months he has made no progress. It is vital in situations like this that the teacher, the consultant, and the buddy sit down and talk through what exactly they think should be going on, where Johnny is in his efforts to learn to read, what steps need to be taken to get him reading, and who will be responsible to see that those steps are taken. If we are really honest, we will involve Johnny in this process, since learning to read, in some ways, is largely in Johnny's hands. Involving the student is not always appropriate but when it is, it can add a helpful dimension to discussions.

Negotiation skills play a large part in these kinds of discussions. Negotiation is simply a means of getting what you want, a kind of back-and-forth communication designed to reach an agreement when you and the other person or people have some common or shared interests and some interests that are not. Fisher and Ury (1981) advise that negotiations be undertaken in a way that allows you to get what you are entitled to and still be decent, to be fair and still protect yourself from being taken advantage of by others. (See Appendix 2B for further exploration of their ideas on how this might be accomplished.)

Good negotiation is marked by three things:

1. It meets the legitimate interests of both sides as far as possible.

2. It resolves conflicting interests fairly.

3. The resolution is durable and community interests are taken into account.

Of course, no matter how skilful you are, there are limits to what you can achieve through this process.

A big key in most negotiation is to remember you are dealing with other people—people who have deeply held values, come from different backgrounds, and have emotions, hopes, and dreams just as you do. In negotiation, it is always worthwhile to ask yourself, "Have I paid enough attention to the other person?" If both parties see themselves as partners in a difficult search for a solution beneficial to all concerned, negotiation becomes easier.

Often the ongoing relationship with the other person is more important than the particular outcome, so it is a good idea to deal with people directly, not by making compromises or concessions. Behind opposing positions, behind the apparent conflicting interests are often shared and compatible ones. Kauffman (1993) suggests that significant agreements can often be found. Nearly all those involved with students (whether those with special needs or those without) want for these students effective instruction in academic and social skills, appropriate education in a supportive but least restrictive environment, parental participation in decision making, and collaboration among all those working with, or on behalf of, the student. These are but a few of the many shared interests possible.

In negotiating roles and responsibilities, there are some questions that it's wise to consider before you begin and/or strategies that may prevent you from grinding to a halt. One question it's important to be clear on is, "Of the interests you bring to the negotiation, which are the most important?" Knowing the answer to this question can help you stay focused or "grounded" in the negotiation.

Perhaps just as important as having a sense of what is central to you is having some idea of what a successful solution or agreement might look like. You'll want to reshape your vision of an acceptable or workable agreement as you discuss and gather more information. It's also helpful to think about some realistic objectives. "What can we do given the present situation?" "How will we work together to make these things happen?" and "How will we know if our strategies are working?" become useful questions when we try to decide how to implement our solutions. It can also be helpful to generate a number of solutions. Of course, if we generate alternatives, we also need to think of some criteria for deciding among them or devise some "rule of thumb" to help us select one to try.

It's always a good idea to remain open to revisiting your ideas on roles and responsibilities. Listen closely to the person who carries through on a strategy. His or her suggestions are more likely to happen. An effective guideline is that if the person who will provide direct assistance to the student (the doer) makes a suggestion, try it first, as long as the student will not be placed at a disadvantage.

Negotiating roles and responsibilities is really about clarifying who does what under what conditions. In a time when the number of people involved in the classroom is growing on a daily basis, this kind of clarification helps create a classroom where students' needs can be met.

◈ Planning

If we don't change our direction, we are
likely to end up where we are headed.
(Ancient Chinese proverb)

In any undertaking, planning is the key to successful change (Barker, 1992). The emphasis here is on the process rather than the product. It's important to plan knowing that no matter how good the plan, the future holds surprises.

Planning really has two components: the decision making regarding the steps to be taken to bring about the desired change and the preparation needed to make these steps happen. (It is not unusual in discussions of planning for this last to be overlooked, but if we want the change to succeed it is as instrumental as the first.) To start, we need to define the change we are trying to make. The clearer we can set out what the change is and how things will look when it has taken place, the more likely we are to know if we are making progress. Having a time frame for the change can help us determine how things are going. We also need to decide how long we will or need to be on the road.

Developing a rationale can also be helpful: what are your reasons for choosing this particular change at this point in time? If you honestly believe everything is fine as it is, change will be more difficult. Usually, it's not enough to think things will be better or that the change is for the good. It's important to identify specifically how the change will make things better for you and for the others affected by it.

Often if we try to make too big a change all at once, we get overwhelmed. It's definitely an advantage if the change we undertake is realistic, if it builds on what we are doing already, if it build on our strengths. Setting a destination that is clear and reasonable is an important first step.

In defining or setting out where you are going, you are wise to involve those who might be affected by the attempted change (Eastwood & Louis, 1992). Students, parents, volunteers, other professionals, even your family, need to know what you are trying to do so that they can be supportive. They may even have ideas about how you could go about the change–ideas you may not have thought of and that may work.

Having set a goal, having involved those around you, it is important then to set out how you will reach this goal. A series of small steps will ensure success and keep frustration to a minimum. If your steps are too large, you will experience little success, and it's important to experience some success if we want to persist.

Reconsidering your steps if you are not experiencing any success is advisable. See if you can make the steps smaller and more doable. Again, it's a good idea to involve those affected by the steps, reviewing whether or not each of the steps is working. It is also usually a good idea to tackle each of the steps sequentially. Setting out how long you think each step will take can be useful.

Take time to consider carefully the particular setting in which you find yourself and the people with whom you are working. Strategies or steps that may work in some situations and with some people won't always work. Strategies that have worked in your own dealings with yourself won't work every time. History, tradition, and experience play a large part in determining what will work and how long a change takes.

Having a goal and a set of steps to reach that goal strengthens our resolve and helps each of us mobilize our energies for change. Setting out the particular steps can help us see our underlying beliefs and priorities and can be a wonderful opportunity to get in touch with our wishes and our dreams.

▣ Dealing With Conflicts

There are no quick fixes.
(Common saying)

It is not possible to try to change things in your classroom, in your students or even within yourself without running into conflict. Conflict, in itself, is not a bad thing, but if conflict occurs, it is important to try to negotiate a resolution. You may find it useful to share these skills with your students so that they can learn to better manage their own conflicts without needing to involve adults. (See Appendix 2C for a possible way to go about this.)

Most of us have strategies for dealing with conflict. Unfortunately, those strategies are not always constructive. To deal with conflict constructively means turning it into a "win-win" situation. The following four steps may help achieve this:

1. *Establish respect.* Prior to meeting, consider outside influences that may affect attempts to resolve the conflict. Ask those involved:

   - "Is this a convenient time to talk?"
   - "Is this a place that is quiet and free of interruptions?"
   - "Has enough time been allotted to discuss the problem and reach a resolution?"

   At the meeting itself, take care in setting the tone. Begin by stating your positive intentions about the relationship and/or the current situation. For example:

   - "I want to resolve this problem."
   - "I want to understand how this problem arose."
   - "I want to hear your point of view."

   Hint: These negotiations will go better if they begin with everyone involved in a calm state.

2. *Pinpoint the issue.* Prior to meeting, some reflection on the following questions may prove useful:

   - What is it that specifically concerns me about the situation?
   - What are my real needs in the situation?
   - How do I view the other person? What are my assumptions and suspicions?
   - What exactly would make the situation better for me?

   At the meeting itself, try to separate the person from the problem—it is important to see yourself as working with, as being on the same side, as trying to attack and resolve the same issue.

   Try to focus on shared interests rather than hard-lined positions. If solving the conflict is really important to us, we need to look beyond our initial position to honestly examine our own real interests and needs in the situation. It also helps to think about what the interests of the other person might be.

Hint: We can find out what has given rise to the conflict only by talking and listening to one another.

3. *Explore Alternatives.* Prior to and in the meeting itself, all alternatives for dealing with an issue should be examined.

In both the work of Deboer (1986) and Fisher and Ury (1981), four common obstacles to generating and exploring alternatives have been identified:

- Premature judgment or criticism
- A search for the "one and only," "very best," "perfect" solution
- The belief that resources are limited and so no new alternative is possible
- The belief that the responsibility for resolving the issue lies with someone else

Hint: Brainstorming may help override or prevent this obstacle from occurring (see Appendix 2D).

4. *Participate in shared decision making.* There must be a new agreement, those involved must reach a decision that establishes clear lines of responsibility.

The people in conflict must decide how they will deal with one another from this point on.

The final decision of what to do must have the active involvement and agreement of those most responsible for carrying through on the decision or it will fail.

The first step in carrying out this decision should be very clear because this is where most resolutions fall apart. The person responsible for the first step is often not sure how to get started. Taking some time on this in the resolution process can help things stay resolved.

An anecdote might be helpful here. Late on Friday afternoon toward the end of the school year, a mother turns up in a school hall looking for Mrs. J., her child's grade-3 teacher. She probably has been thinking about what has been on her mind all week and only now has been able to bring herself to the school.

The classroom teacher meets her in the hallway and they quickly get into a confrontation. The mother wants her daughter kept behind. The teacher doesn't understand and is quite mystified. She recognizes that the student is behind and experiencing some difficulties. She tries to explain to the parent that she understands that the parent wants the best for her child, but that retaining the child is not board policy. The parent, seeing the teacher does not understand and will not comply, asks for a meeting with the principal. The teacher agrees that might be best.

A meeting is arranged for the parents, the principal, the teacher, and the teacher associate working with the student. As they talk, it becomes clear that the parents, in particular the mother, see putting the child ahead as setting their child up for failure. As parents, they care enough to be concerned. The principal says, "We know Sarah isn't able to do the work that is expected of a grade-4 student and what we want to do is work with her at her level." The parents noticeably relax. They ask the principal to repeat the commitment made to dealing with Sarah at her level. They do this to reassure themselves and to check that they have understood.

Only when the underlying concerns have been addressed correctly can positions be discarded and only then can the team—the parents, principal, teacher, and teacher associate—begin to work out ways to best meet Sarah's needs.

A final comment on conflict. Raspberry (1992) suggests that it's important to distinguish between enemies and problems. Problems persist after enemies are vanquished, and diverting energy into battles with real or imagined enemies often prevents or delays solutions. So let's focus on the issues or problems to find solutions that work for our students, for our parents, for our colleagues, and for ourselves.

▩ Getting Over the Humps

There is a caution I should bring to your attention. There will be rough times. There will be instances when you forget your resolve, whene you are overwhelmed. The frequency and extent of these times vary with individuals, but they do happen. (When you are having one of these times, it's important not to get discouraged. Discouragement is one of the most damaging forces against managing change.)

You can also get frustrated when change is not happening fast enough for you. If you feel dissatisfied and think that you are not having the effects you want soon enough, have patience and confidence in yourself and your efforts. A better strategy is to develop your own personal approach to dealing with such moments so that you have a plan of what to do when the need arises.

While this is not how any of us would like it, these humps, these occasions of discouragement, are an integral part of the change process. The new strategies that you are trying to put in place aren't as automatic as the old ones that you are trying to give up. An example may help here. A middle-years teacher was trying to use cooperative groups. Initially, she paid a lot of attention to grouping the students and observing how they participated. In focusing on these elements, she found it difficult to also look at their grasp of the concepts she was teaching. She was like her students learning a new way to work. She found it hard to focus on the curriculum, the teaching/learning process, and her students all at once. As she became more comfortable with cooperative groups, more practised in using them, not only did she feel more comfortable, but she was again able to pay attention to the many elements necessary for an effective lesson.

When you begin to hear yourself saying, "In my class…" rather than "In my class, I am trying…," you will know you have survived your anxiety and frustration and overcome your moment of discouragement.

◈ Keeping a Sense of Humour

When the first baby laughed for the first time,
the laugh broke into a thousand pieces and
they all went skipping about and that was the
beginning of fairies.
(James Barrie, *Peter Pan*)

Question: What do you get when you cross a monster
with a drip dry suit?
Answer: A wash and wear wolf.

A surprise! An unexpected, weird, funny change. Sometimes when these things happen and sometimes when we make them happen, we laugh.

Humour, aptly used, has helped to diffuse a potentially stressful situation, has helped to break the mould of conventional thinking in problem solving, has helped both psychological and physiological healing, and has helped the communication process.

Humour, laughter, play, and fun are powerful tools to use in any change effort. They convey caring and warmth, and generate feelings of confidence. They prevent burnout, increase productivity, and create hope for future possibilities. Robinson (1986, p. 132) says of humour that it's "the human being's built in mechanism for equilibrium and haemostats."

In an article called "Pain by the Gain," John Morris (1994), a primary teacher, relates a story in which the day had hardly begun and already there was vomit on the floor, two children in tears, and a birthday party problem brewing in the background. At almost the end of his rope, he was just wondering if he could handle any more and in walks his principal. The principal took one look around, looked at John and they both started to laugh, shook their heads, and started to deal with the vomit, the tears, and the brewing birthday party problem.

Humour is one way to stop us from taking ourselves and our situation too seriously. Yet in all the pressures and stresses of merging special and regular education, of doing our best for each of the students in our classrooms, it makes sense to remember to occasionally laugh and to laugh at ourselves. Without laughter there would be no bounce in our lives and, in some cases, no way to keep going.

▨ Summary

*Grown ups love figures. When you tell them you have
made a new friend, they never ask you any questions
about essential matters. They never say to you, What
does his voice sound like? What games does he love
best? Does he collect butterflies? Instead they demand:
How old is he? How many brothers has he? How much
does he weigh? How much money does his father make?*
(Saint Exupéry, 1971, p. 16)

Like most grown-ups, discussions on how or even whether to merge regular and special education are well intentioned but misplaced. The wrong questions are asked and the focus is in the wrong place.

There is an old truism that cannot change anyone but oneself. It follows, then, that efforts to change schooling, to make it inclusionary, to merge regular and special education, cannot start with the community, with the classroom, or even with the students, but must start with ourselves. The question we must each ask ourselves is, "How must I be so I can help each child feel she or he counts, so that every child feels included?"

Please remember: as teachers we often tell our students that progress typically comes through everyday activities or efforts, through small steps taken each day. These steps often seem mundane, inconsequential, but they are necessary for "long-term gain." These small steps need to include some attention to ensuring self-care, to developing political astuteness, to planning in a systematic way, to dealing with conflict, and to using humour when all else fails. Please understand that these steps are only a beginning, are not exhaustive, and so invite additions and adjustments.

We don't come to the merger of special and regular education without resources. Many of the strategies suggested here are those we use with our students. That's what, as teachers, we should capitalize on—using our best teaching strategies not only for our students but for ourselves.

Some Tips And Reminders

- If what you desire in the way of change is not immediately forthcoming, take your time.

- Do the best you can and don't stop trying or don't be afraid to make mistakes. Mistakes are human.

- Remember to take one step at a time and to build in success.

- Recognize and build on your strengths.

- The initial stages of any significant change involve anxiety and uncertainty and/or involve taking a risk.

- Support is crucial.

- Change involves learning new skills through practice and feedback.

- The most fundamental breakthrough occurs when you understand how the new way will make things better for you.

APPENDIX 2A

Stages of Concern: Typical Expressions of Concern about the Innovation

	Stages of Concern	**Expressions of Concern**
Impact	6 Refocusing	I have some ideas about something that would work even better.
	5 Collaboration	I am concerned about relating what I am doing with what other instructors are doing.
	4 Consequence	How is my use affecting learners?
Task	3 Management	I seem to be spending all my time in getting material ready.
Self	2 Personal	How will using it affect me?
	1 Informational	I would like to know more about it.
	0 Awareness	I am not concerned about it (the innovation).

Notes: These stages of concern are taken from the Concerns Based Adoption Model (C-BAM). This project has been ongoing for 30 years at the Research and Development Centre for Teacher Education at the University of Texas in Austin. Interestingly, according to this research most of us approach a particular change with a concern about, "How will using it affect me?" or "How will I have to adjust my practice?" (stage two). It is a while before we become concerned about, "How is my use affecting students?" (stage four).

Researchers in the project (Hord, 1989; Hord & Huling-Austin, 1988; Hall & Hord, 1987; Hall & Rutherford, 1976) suggest that to fully implement a significant change in our classrooms may take three to five years. So taking our time, moving slowly and steadily, and being patient with ourselves and with others become important skills if the merger of special and regular education is to be successful.

APPENDIX 2B

Change the Game/Negotiating on the Merits

1. Be Principled.

   Participants are problem-solvers.

   The goal is a wise outcome reached efficiently and amicably.

2. Separate the people from the problem.

   Be soft on the people, hard on the problem.

   Proceed independent of trust.

3. Focus on interests not positions.

   Explore interests.

   Avoid having a bottom line.

4. Insist on objective criteria.

   Try to reach a result based on standards independent of will.

   Reason and be open to reason; yield to principle, not pressure.

Source: Taken from Fisher and Ury (1981, p. 13).

APPENDIX 2C

Teaching Your Students to Manage Conflict

Consider teaching your students to negotiate constructive resolutions to their problems. Students who know how to manage their own behaviour have a definite advantage over those who do not. If students are to learn how to resolve their own conflicts, they must have opportunities to practise conflict resolution, to resolve conflicts, and to follow through on these resolutions.

Johnson and Johnson (1987, 1991, 1992) suggest a useful six-step format:

1. State what you want: "I want my book back now."

2. State how you feel: "I'm frustrated. You had the book for two weeks. If I don't get the book back soon, I won't have enough time to study for the test on Friday. It's frustrating to have to wait."

3. Summarize your understanding of what the other person wants, how the other person feels, and the reasons underlying both.

4. Invent three optional plans to resolve the conflict.

5. Choose one plan and the first step in that plan carefully.

6. Shake hands and take that first step.

Students need to learn a conflict resolution procedure such as the one above and become skilful in its use in relatively easy situations before they try to use it to resolve real conflicts. The procedure, along with listening and assertive skills, needs to be overlearned so that they are readily available when emotions run high and feelings of fear and anger are intense.

Students should learn to handle conflict one-on-one before learning to mediate someone else's conflict (Roy, 1993). It's easy for these procedures to sound simplistic, but to teach these strategies to students, we need to practise and master the techniques ourselves (Scherer, 1992).

Resources for teachers:

The Canadian Institute for Conflict Resolution, St. Paul University, 223 Main Street, Ottawa, ON, K1S 1C4, promotes and provides educational services in conflict resolution for communities and schools. This nonprofit organization has a newsletter for educators called *Common Ground.*

"From Peer Conflict Resolution through Creative Negotiation" is a program developed by Sandy Kalmakoff and Jeanne Shaw for Public Education for Peace Society, #208 – 1956 W. Broadway, Vancouver, BC, V6J 1Z2. Phone: 604–736–2918.

APPENDIX 2D

Ground Rules for Brainstorming

1. Rule out all criticism or evaluation of an idea. Ideas are suggested and placed before the group without evaluation or critical analysis.

2. Expect wild ideas when the group suspends judgment. Practical considerations are not important at this point. The session is to be freewheeling.

3. The quantity of ideas counts, not quality. All ideas should be expressed, and not screened out by an individual. A great number of ideas will increase the likelihood of discovering good ones.

4. Build on the ideas of other group members when possible. Pool your creativity. Everyone should be free to build on to ideas and to make interesting combinations from the various suggestions.

5. Focus on a single problem or issue. Don't skip around on problems or try to brainstorm a complex multiple problem.

6. Promote a congenial, relaxed, cooperative atmosphere.

7. Make sure all members, no matter how shy and reluctant, contribute and get their ideas heard.

8. Record all ideas.

SUGGESTED RESOURCES

Becoming a Change Agent

Dedrick, C.V.L., & Raschke, D.B. (1990). *The special educator and job stress.* Washington, DC: National Education Association. This monograph examines stresses encountered by special educators, ways of coping with professional demands, and reasons why some teachers handle job stress better than others. Symptoms of burnout are reviewed. Ten stress management techniques are discussed.

Friend, M., & Cook, L. (1992). *Interactions: Collaborative skills for school professionals.* New York: Longman Publishing Group. This book is about collaboration. It can be used as a tool to learn skills that have immediate use such as interpersonal problem solving, resolving conflict, and program planning.

Idol, L., Nevin, A., & Paolucci-Whitcomb, P. (1994). *Collaborative construction* (2nd edition). Austin, TX: Pro-Ed, Inc. This book is intended to stimulate and encourage collaboration among classroom, special education and remedial education teachers, other support staff, and administrators who are jointly responsible for students with special needs. This text provides a detailed six-step process for working together and is perhaps more useful for the more experienced reader or teacher in the field.

REFERENCES

Barker, J.A. (1992). *Future edge: discovering new paradigms of success.* New York: William Morrow and Co.

Beckhard, R., & Harris, R.T. (1987). *Organizational transitions* (2nd edition). Reading, PA: Addison-Wesley.

Bolman, L.G., & Deal, T.E. (1991). *Reframing organizations: Artistry, choice and leadership.* San Francisco: Jossey-Bass.

Canfield, J. (1990). Improving Students' Self-Esteem. *Educational Leadership, 48*(1), 48–50.

Cantor, N. (1953). *The teaching-learning process.* New York: Holt, Rinehart and Winston.

Coloroso, B. (1994). *Kids are worth it!* Toronto: Somerville House Publishing.

Deboer, A.L. (1986). *The art of consulting.* Chicago: Arturus Books.

Eastwood, K.W., & Louis, K.S. (1992). Restructuring that lasts: Managing the performance dip." *Journal of School Leadership, 2,* 212–24.

Evans, R. (1993). The human face of reform. *Educational Leadership, 51*(1), 19–23.

Fisher, R., & Ury, W. (1981). *Getting to yes: negotiating agreement with giving in.* New York: Penguin Books.

Fullan, M. (1985). Change processes and strategies at the local level. *The Elementary School Journal, 85*(3), 391–421.

Fullan, M. (1991). *The new meaning of educational change.* New York: Teachers College Press.

Gold, Y., & Roth, R.A. (1993). *Teachers managing stress and preventing burnout: The professional health solution.* London: The Falmer Press.

Hall, G.E., & Hord, S. (1987). *Change in schools: Facilitating the process.* (SUNY Series in Educational Leadership). State University of New York-Albany: SUNY Press.

Hall, G.E., & Loucks, S.F. (1978). Concerns of teachers about implementing team teaching. *Educational Leadership, 34*(3), 227–33.

Hall, G.E., & Rutherford, W.L. (1976). Teacher concerns as a basis for facilitating and personalizing staff development. *Teachers College Record, 80*(1), 36–53.

Hartog, J., Audry, J., & Cohen, Y. (Eds.). (1980). *The anatomy of loneliness.* New York: International Universities Press.

Hord, S. (1986). "Recent results of research on school leadership: The principal and beyond." Presentation to the Faculty of Education, University of Calgary (March 14).

Hord, S. (1989). Facilitating change in secondary schools—Myths & management. *NASSP—Bulletin, 73*(516), 68–73.

Hord, S., & Huling-Austin, L. (1988). Curriculum implementation: How to know if it's there (or not there). *Journal of Rural and Small Schools, 1*(3), 23–26.

Johnson, D.W., & Johnson, R. (1987). *Creative controversy: Intellectual challenge in the classroom.* Edina, MN: Interaction Book Co.

Johnson, D.W., & Johnson, R. (1991). *Teaching students to be peacemakers.* Edina, MN: Interaction Book Co.

Johnson, D.W., & Johnson, R. (1992). Effects of mediation training on elementary school students. *Mediation Quarterly, 10*(1), F.

Joyce, B.E., & Showers, B., (1982). The coaching of teaching. *Educational Leadership, 40,* October, 4–10.

Kauffman, J.M. (1993). How we might achieve the radical reform of special education, *Exceptional Children, 60*(4), 6–16.

Kearns, J.R. et al. (1990). "The London project: The implementation of invitational strategies at the secondary school level." Paper presented at the annual meeting of the American Educational Research Association, Boston, MA (April 16–29).

Lewin, K. (1935). *A dynamic theory of personality.* New York: McGraw-Hill.

Lewin, K. (1948). *Resolving social conflicts.* New York: Harper.

Louis, K.S., & Milles, M.B. (1990). *Improving the urban high school: What works and why.* New York: Teachers College Press.

Marris, P. (1986). *Loss and change.* London: Routledge and Kegan Paul.

Morris, J. (1994). Pain by the gain. *Principal, 73*(3), 54.

Odell, S. (1990). "Mentor teacher program. What research says to the teacher." Document Eric ED 323185.

Opuni, A. (1989). "The teacher induction program." Document Eric ED 322104.

Postman, N., & Weingartner, C. (1987). *Teaching as a subversive activity.* New York: Dell Publishing.

Purkey, W.W. (1991). "What is invitational education and how does it work?" Paper presented at the Annual California State Conference on Self-Esteem (Santa Clara, CA, February 22–24).

Purkey, W.W., & Novak, J.M. (1984). *Inviting school success.* Belmont, CA: Wadsworth Publishing Co.

Purkey, W.W., & Schmidt, J.J. (1990). "Invitational learning for counselling and development." Ann Arbor, MI: University of Michigan ERIC Counselling and Personnel Services Clearing House.

Raspberry, W. (1992). Address at the Annual Invitational Team Case Competition. University of Virginia, Charlottesville (May 24).

Robinson, V.M. (1986). Humour is a serious business. *Dimensions of Critical Care Nursing, 5*(3), 132–33.

Rossman, G., Corbett, N.D., & Firestone, W. (1988). *Change and effectiveness in schools.* Albany, NY: State University of New York Press.

Roy, I. (1993). Violence if preventable: How some schools are educating students to be peacemakers. *Brock Education, 3,* 116–18.

Saint Exupéry, A. (1971). *The little prince.* New York: Harcourt, Brace and World, Inc.

Sarason, S.B. (1990). *The predictable failure of educational reform.* San Francisco: Jossey-Bass.

Scherer, M. (1992). Solving conflicts—Not just for children. *Educational Leadership, 50*(14), 15–18.

Sikes, P.J. (1984). Teacher careers in the comprehensive school, in S. Ball, (Ed.), *Comprehensive schooling: A reader.* London: The Falmer Press.

Sikes, P.J. (1992). Impose change and the experienced teacher, in M. Fullan and A. Hargreaves (Eds.), *Teacher development and educational change.* London: The Falmer Press.

Troyna, B. (1985). The great divide: Politics and practices in multi-cultural education. *British Journal of Sociology of Education, 6*(2), 209–24.

Vann, A.S. (1989). A principal's guide to the hiring and induction of new teachers. *Principal, 69*(1), 26–29.

Collaboration and Consultation in Elementary Schools: Strategies to Manage Diversity

Rick Freeze

University of Manitoba

Introduction

Educational change has been, and likely will continue to be, most evident in elementary schools. This climate of change has been brought on by a number of factors working in tandem. Foremost, students with a wide diversity of needs are entering the educational system and the regular classroom. As a result, teachers are faced with classrooms in which students vary widely in their backgrounds, levels of preparation, learning styles, and abilities. In addition, teaching practices are undergoing a reformation in part due to: a) the growing presence of new information technologies in the classroom, b) improved instructional methods focused as much on how students construct understanding and acquire strategies as the learning of subject area content, c) approaches to classroom management in which cooperative learning, problem solving, and the social aspects of learning are stressed, and

d) a renewed commitment to real partnerships with parents. Furthermore, the distinctions separating traditional subject areas have become blurred. For example, in a world where the telephone largely has replaced the letter, and where television and computer screens have become the electronic pages of interactive books, language arts necessarily have expanded from reading and writing to include listening, speaking, viewing, and producing. Finally, instruction that is thematic, process oriented, and cooperative, and that is supported by new technologies in the classroom, requires approaches to assessment that are relevant to an interdisciplinary curriculum, group problem-solving processes, and that measure how, as well as what, students are learning.

All of these factors are contributing to the emergence of a new classroom environment in which parents, paraprofessional teaching assistants, and cross-grade peer tutors may be working collaboratively with teachers in the classroom. In addition, teachers increasingly are being asked to consult with parents, resource (learning assistance) teachers, special education integration teachers, librarians, counsellors, clinicians, and others either as individuals or as members of an early- or middle-years team of teachers. Consequently, collaboration and consultation are interwoven in the day-to-day lives of educators in inclusive elementary schools.

▩ A Positive Climate for Collaboration and Consultation

In general, collaboration involves shared work (Friend and Cook, 1992) and consultation involves shared problem solving (Brown, Wyne, Blackburn & Powell, 1979).

Consultation and collaboration are vehicles for the educational reform and renewal process under way in inclusive schools and school systems. In order to succeed as mediums of change and growth, collaboration and consultation must occur in a professional climate in which several essential characteristics are valued and encouraged. These include: a) parity among the participants, b) voluntary participation, c) mutual goals, d) common resources, e) shared responsibilities, f) shared accountability, g) cooperative values, and h) shared expertise (Brown, Wyne, Blackburn & Powell, 1979; Block, 1981; Friend & Cook, 1992; Morsink, Thomas & Correa, 1991).

Parity

Not all relationships between elementary school educators are reciprocal. Sometimes relationships involve supervision, mentoring, evaluation, or even disciplinary action. When educators meet to collaborate or consult, however, it is best if each person's contribution is equally valued and each has equal power in decision making. Even though administrators, specialists, teachers, paraprofessionals, parents, and students are not on a par as far as power and authority are concerned in many situations; they can have parity when they work together on a particular collaborative activity.

Those with power and authority can enhance the climate for collaboration and consultation by clarifying when parity exists, minimizing the number of situations when it does not, and by playing by the rules. This means, of course, accepting the decisions you disagree with in a spirit of cooperation that prizes the process of team building as much as specific outcomes and more than personal triumphs.

Voluntary Participation

In order to work effectively together, participants must feel they are involved because they need and want each other's assistance and not because they have a duty to attend. All participants must feel they are free to actively contribute without prejudice, choose from a range of options without pressure, and withdraw from the process without penalty.

Mutual Goals

In essence, collaboration means working to achieve a common goal and consultation means joint decision making to solve a common problem. A sound basis for deciding if a collaborative or consultative relationship is needed is to determine if all participants share at least one important goal.

Common Resources

Once collaborative partners are working together, it is important that they combine their resources to better achieve their common goals. If someone is seen to be holding back access to information or resources, the relationship is undermined. Conflict often arises when people attempt to collaborate but do not share a common understanding of the problem they are trying to solve. Shared access to the same database of information dramatically increases the chances of a common vision and usually brings everyone on side.

Shared Responsibilities

Collaboration and consultation are processes that often blur the traditional areas of responsibility and lines of authority in an elementary school. While it is very important for individuals' roles and areas of expertise to be known and understood by everyone in the group, it is also very important for everyone to feel an equal responsibility to participate, solve problems, make decisions, and implement solutions.

Shared Accountability

Once a collaborative or consultative relationship develops, accountability is shared. If accountability cannot be shared for legal or other reasons, then attempts to work in a collaborative manner will sit uncomfortably with all participants unless the domains of what is negotiable and what is not are clearly defined.

Cooperative Values

Collaboration and consultation are enhanced greatly when cooperative values are prized by the group. It is best if relationships are open and trusting. This can be accomplished if each person's role and agenda is transparent to all others. Information and opportunities should be openly shared. Ethical guidelines with respect to confidentiality help to prevent missteps. Interdependence and community are built by taking the time to achieve the high levels of agreement that lead to consensus and not the lower levels of agreement needed to win a majority vote. Consensus and cooperation are easier to achieve when people pay close attention to their own feelings as well as those of others. In collaboration and consultation, the process is always as important as the outcome it is designed to achieve (Block, 1981). A positive climate for collaboration and consultation is built when schools adopt strategies designed to: a) foster the development and sharing of professional expertise, b) initiate systemic interventions, and c) encourage instructional themes and projects that cross the traditional boundaries between classrooms, subject areas, and grade levels.

Sharing Expertise

Several ways that educators can facilitate the sharing of the professional experience and knowledge at their school are briefly reviewed in this section (also see Stainback & Stainback, 1990). A **literature circle** is a good way to begin. At a literature circle, each member provides a reading for everyone else. The readings are then discussed informally at successive meetings of the circle until everyone has taken a turn. Participation in a literature circle is voluntary, exploratory, and informal.

A **roundtable** is similar to a literature circle except there is usually an agreed theme (e.g., a roundtable on inclusive schooling) and a broader range of activities on the theme such as guest presentations, field trips, debates, and joint projects by members. A trusted external facilitator with expertise in the area often is recruited to help stimulate and organize activities.

Methods presentations by teachers at staff or team meetings or at an in-service sharing day are an excellent way to build professional skills and team spirit. All teachers are invited to participate by sharing a single, short (5 to 10 minutes) teaching strategy that works well for them.

The **teachers' pantry** is another extremely useful idea. The pantry is a storehouse of the teaching and learning materials used by all staff. The materials are organized by grade level, subject area, and topic, and are usually stored in the resource room or library. The teachers' pantry greatly reduces teacher preparation time and enhances the availability of quality topical materials that are otherwise difficult to find or develop (e.g., maps, pictures, charts, practice sheets, games, resource kits, assignments, checklists, tests, and adapted materials for students with special needs).

There is probably no better way for two teachers to share their expertise than through **team teaching**. Team teaching is more likely to emerge in a school where it is encouraged by administration and allowed by the timetable. At first, it is best to encourage short-term commitments to defined projects so team members can test the waters and change course if necessary.

The special educator in the inclusive school can play a very active role in encouraging staff to share their expertise (Stainback and Stainback, 1990). The special educator can facilitate this type of sharing by agreeing to take one of the two teachers' classes so they will have time to meet.

Schoolwide interventions designed to prevent the development of learning, behaviour or integration problems often depend on joint planning and team implementation. There are a tremendous number of **systemic interventions** that address the academic, social, and behavioural needs of students throughout an entire school population. Most focus on prevention, practice, consistency, and maintenance (Bos & Vaughn, 1991; Gearheart, Weishahn & Gearheart, 1992). Some examples of commonly used systemic interventions are Uninterrupted Sustained Silent Reading (USSR) (Tearney, Readence & Dishner, 1990), Circle of Friends (O'Brien & Forest, 1989), and schoolwide programs in behaviour management (Jones & Jones, 1986), writing (Tearney, Readence & Dishner, 1990), and spelling (Thomas, 1979).

Programs that bring students together in novel patterns of interaction also increase staff contacts and shared work. Some examples of programs that may cross the boundaries between classrooms and grades are peer tutoring; cooperative learning; reading-writing process conferencing; project learning; whole school festivals, celebrations, and sports days; and in-school science fairs and arts presentations (Slavin 1994; Stainback & Stainback, 1990). Schools that share and honour the expertise and skills of their students and staff are likely to be rewarded with a climate in which collaboration and consultation are promoted easily.

◈ How to Collaborate and Consult

Collaborative and consultative relationships in elementary schools occur in a variety of ways for a variety of reasons.

Common Relationships

Two types of relationships are most common: individual and team. The first typically involves two individuals. There are many possible combinations. For example, two teachers may work together by both covering half of the responsibilities for two classes at the same grade level. This arrangement gives the students two role models and may help prepare them for a secondary school where they will see more teachers per day. The teachers may benefit by having less subjects to prepare and by being able to focus on the subjects they most enjoy or best match their expertise. In the context of inclusive schooling, a cooperative relationship between special educators (including resource and special-needs integration teachers) and classroom teachers is essential. Some of the reasons why this pair of educators might collaborate and consult are listed in Figure 3.1.

FIGURE 3.1

Typical Reasons for Collaboration and Consultation between Classroom and Special Education Teachers

- To implement early identification screening procedures
- To conduct data-based observations of student behaviour
- To collect and analyze samples of student work to identify academic success and error patterns
- To provide support for differentiated instruction
- To help get modified programs of instruction and behaviour management "up and running" in the classroom
- To demonstrate adaptive teaching methods
- To help introduce new curricula, materials, or instructional methods
- To conduct individual or group-student assessments
- To help train a teaching assistant
- To act as a peer coach or mentor to the classroom teacher

A second common type of consultative or collaborative relationship involves teams of several educators and may include students, parents, administrators, clinicians, or community services representatives. For example, the early years and middle-years teams may coordinate the scope and sequence of instruction for grades K to 3 and 4 to 6 or 8 respectively. A team of subject area teachers may meet to strengthen instruction by sharing materials and methods. In all cases, whether it is two individual teachers or a school team, the collaboration and consultation process requires professional, interpersonal, and process skills.

Professional Skills

Each partner brings his or her professional knowledge and experience to the process. Knowledge about educational policy and ethics, curriculum and modified programming, student learning and development, teaching and behaviour management methods, and social, cultural, and economic factors that impact on school life are the substance that is worked with by those who collaborate and consult. It is important that each partner knows what the others are talking about. This can be achieved by:

- Providing written information about each partner's professional role and areas of expertise
- Defining professional terms in lay language
- Sharing the policy or curriculum guidelines under which team members work with others
- Using concrete examples and recent valid assessment data to focus discussions
- Asking for information when it is not provided

Interpersonal Skills

There are many dimensions to the interpersonal skills needed to collaborate and consult with others. Some of the most important are discussed in this section. They include: a) clarifying roles, b) listening, c) communicating, d) understanding nonverbal behaviour, e) dealing with feelings, f) dealing with conflict, and g) supporting others.

Role Clarification

Role clarification is an essential component in successful collaboration and consultation. Resource and special-needs integration teachers, for example, must make it very clear that their role is to provide support to the classroom teacher and not to teach students directly themselves. Classroom teachers, for their part, must make it very clear that interventions in their classrooms must not compromise their effectiveness with the class as a whole. For special educators, the three most common role mistakes are being an "expert," being "Ms. or Mr. Fix-it," and being "an extra pair of hands."

The expert role puts the special educator at a distance and above the classroom teacher and tends to lead to some consultation but very little collaboration. As a result, classroom teachers seek support elsewhere and the "expert" is left with little to do but administer formal assessments (often for no obvious reason or benefit) and write lengthy reports that usually do little more than confirm what the teacher already knows.

The Ms. or Mr. Fix-it role casts the special educator as a surrogate teacher who is supposed to outperform the classroom teacher, fix the child, and return him or her to the regular classroom to live happily ever after. Unfortunately, children sent to resource, learning assistance, and special classes tend to stay there year after year and often fail to transfer the new skills they master back to the regular classroom. Over time, they suffer a tremendous blow to their self-esteem that may undermine their education permanently. This is not to say that children should never be removed from the classroom. There are times when children's integration needs are best met outside the classroom. In an inclusive school, all opportunities to integrate individualized programming into regular classroom activities, shared by the whole class, are pursued aggressively. Often, there are ways to include nondisabled students in the individualized activities of those with disabilities; providing all with valuable learning experiences.

The extra pair of hands role places the special educator in an assistant role with respect to the classroom teacher. This usually results in the special educator doing unimportant tasks around the classroom or school and failing to fulfil his or her professional mission.

Inclusive schooling challenges special educators to stop trying to "fix" kids or "change" teachers, and to start supporting classroom teachers struggling to include the full spectrum of students in the learning adventure of the regular classroom. In general, roles are clarified and strengthened when they are: a) consistent with the school mission statement, b) defined through a consensus-building process involving all staff, c) described in the school handbook, and d) reviewed and clarified at the initial meeting when teachers meet to collaborate or consult with each other.

Listening

Good listening skills are essential to productive relationships. The feeling that your contribution was wanted, was heard, and was understood is a prerequisite to engagement and commitment for most people. Friend and Cook (1992) suggest several strategies designed to help professionals become good listeners (see Figure 3.2).

FIGURE 3.2
Strategies for Good Listening

- Mentally rehearse the information you are being given.
- Confirm what you have heard by sharing your summary with the others at the meeting.

- Categorize the information you are receiving so you have a structure within which to address the issues being raised.
- Make brief notes as you listen.
- Avoid interrupting (jot down the responses you wish to make later so you won't forget).
- Avoid daydreaming, tuning out, doing other work, or mentally rehearsing what you will say next when you are supposed to be listening.
- Avoid projecting your ideas onto what someone else is saying or assuming you already know what they are going to say.
- Try not to stumble on "hot words" that you react to strongly (instead, keep listening).

Source: Adapted from Friend & Cook (1992).

Communicating

Statements and questions can be used to provide or seek information, to reflect on experience or imagine new possibilities, and to confirm or dispute what others have said. Statements and questions are most effective when they: a) affirm, or at least acknowledge, what others have said, b) lead to common ground and build consensus, (c) are concrete, specific, and unambiguous, d) are focused on issues and not people, e) confront issues respectfully rather than sarcastically, and (f) are made in good faith.

Understanding Nonverbal Behaviour

Friend and Cook (1992) note that nonverbal behaviour, like a picture, can be worth a thousand words. Facial expressions, posture, stance, eye contact, gestures, the use of personal space, and voice tone and pace are all valuable clues about how someone may be feeling. Of course, they are also clues for others about how you may be feeling. It is a good idea to practise paying attention to the nonverbal communications of yourself and others until you are conscious of the messages you are sending and receiving.

Dealing with Feelings

Inevitably, you will have to deal with strong feelings when you are collaborating and consulting with others. Block (1981) suggests: a) recording your feelings in a private journal, b) waiting to do something about your feelings until after you have cooled off and thought through all the implications of your actions, c) remembering that resistance, fear, and tension are inevitable when you are dealing with difficult issues and may indicate that you are on target, and d) remembering not to take conflict personally as hostility often has its sources in other areas of the person's life of which you may not be aware.

Dealing with Conflict

While serious conflict is not a common problem in educational collaboration and consultation, it is something educators worry about because it is extremely uncomfortable for most of us. When others are aggressive or angry Turnbull and Turnbull (1990), and Morsink, Thomas, and Correa (1991) suggest the following eight-step procedure:

1. Listen intently.
2. Write down what they say.
3. Exhaust their list of concerns.
4. Ask for specific examples to clarify general complaints.
5. Show them the list and ask if it is complete.
6. Ask for suggestions on how to deal with each problem.
7. Write down their suggestions.
8. Ask to meet at a later time after you have had time to reflect on their concerns and tempers have cooled.

During the eight steps, it is important to speak more softly as they speak more loudly, mirror their body posture, and avoid the "verbal swords" that provoke confrontation (listed in Figure 3.3).

FIGURE 3.3
Verbal Swords to Avoid in Collaboration and Consultation

Do Not	Example
Argue	"You're wrong about that, the truth is ..."
Defend	"There is nothing wrong with anything we do at this school, we never ..."
Shout	"I'VE HAD ENOUGH OF YOUR ..."
Belittle	"Yes, but that's hardly worth worrying about ..."
Moralize	"You should ..."
Lecture	"I told you to ..."
Judge	"One of your problems is ..."

Threaten	"If you do that, I'll ..."
Order	"You must ..."
Console	"Don't worry, they'll probably find a cure tomorrow ..."
Analyze	"You're just going through a stage ..."
Interrupt	"Never mind that, I think ..."
Lie	"Don't worry, he'll catch up three grade levels in a few months ..."
Mock	"So you think you've had it bad, just be thankful ..."
Collude	"You're right, my principal doesn't understand ..."
Project	"That's exactly like the problem I had when ..."
Attack	"That's the stupidest idea I've ever heard ..."

Source: Adapted from Morsink, Thomas & Correa (1991).

In the follow-up meeting, Friend and Cook (1992) elaborate on the following strategies to resolve conflict and develop a common ground for decision making: a) seek underlying common ground, b) brainstorm for new ideas, c) use a formal problem-solving strategy, d) look for compromise, and e) be prepared to negotiate. For particularly thorny problems it may be worthwhile to seek a neutral mediator or facilitator or to try piloting alternative solutions to see which works best.

A particularly effective strategy to build solutions in challenging circumstances is the PATH (Planning Alternative Tomorrows with Hope) process developed by Pearpoint, O'Brien, and Forest (1993). With the guidance of a trained creative facilitator, the **PATH process** can be used to help school teams or an entire staff to plan effectively. In group planning, the PATH process involves successive steps that serve to focus the participants on: a) their common guiding values and positive dreams for the future, b) the goals they need to pursue to achieve their dreams, c) how their dreams relate to and build on what is happening now, d) the people, resources, and strategies they will enrol in their progress toward goal achievement, and e) an action planning process that assigns people to tasks with helpers and the guidance of time lines and an effective monitoring and reporting system.

Supporting Others

Turnbull and Turnbull (1990) note that there are a variety of practices that support your partners in collaboration and consultation. They stress treating others with respect and courtesy, respecting their time constraints, being sensitive to cultural, linguistic, and disability differences, acknowledging and reinforcing the participation and contributions of others, and sharing information equally with all partners.

Process Skills

Process is by far the most important factor in successful elementary school collaboration and consultation. Successful meetings require the timely advanced notification of all potential participants with introductory information (e.g., their names, professional, roles, and work phone numbers). A detailed agenda, preferably with input from all participants, with allotted times set against each agenda item, will help everyone contribute at the appropriate time and budget their contribution. In terms of setting, it is important to ensure a comfortable, quiet, private meeting place where interruptions and distractions can be held to an absolute minimum. Personal materials (paper, pens, tissues, drinking water, etc.) and professional materials for participants (files, work samples, program records, curriculum or policy guidelines, etc.) should be readily available. Finally, the meeting should be chaired by a neutral facilitator using an agreed-upon process.

Following the six stages of the collaboration and consultation process over a series of meetings or shared work sessions is the single most important factor in making the process work. The six stages are:

1. Problem identification

2. Assessment

3. Program development

4. Program implementation

5. Evaluation

6. Follow-up

Stage-by-stage activities for educators involved in individual or team relationships are given in Appendix 3A.

Problem Identification

In the first stage, the central purpose of the partnership is established. To do this, each participant should be given the opportunity to: a) clarify their role and responsibilities in the process, b) share their understanding of the problem to be solved, and c) share their expectations for the outcomes of the process.

The last order of business is to work out the logistics for the assessment stage. Specify who will collect what information, by when, and how it will be communicated to the others.

It is in the best interests of educators working in inclusive schools to work with classroom teachers on perennial problems that many students share rather than limiting their involvement to individual students. Proactive educators will scout for problems and look for systemic changes likely to improve the learning climate for all children.

Assessment

The primary purpose of data collection at the assessment stage is to verify the nature of the problem and to develop a baseline against which the success of any action taken can be measured. It is wise for consulting teachers to share data collection. Some curriculum-based strategies for collecting assessment information include: a) reviewing student work samples, b) completing a behaviour inventory or academic skills checklist, c) reviewing the results of curriculum-based tests, d) conducting an academic interview, or e) attempting a trial teaching session using a new approach and analyzing its effectiveness. The methods, content, and results of the assessment measures should be organized so that they relate to the grade level and subject area instructional concerns of the classroom teachers involved (for examples of how to do this for students of diverse ability levels see Bigge, 1991; Luftig, 1987; Freeze, 1989; Salvia & Hughes, 1990; Zigmond, Vallecorsa & Silverman, 1983). Some additional keys to effective assessment in inclusive schools are listed in Figure 3.4.

FIGURE 3.4
Some Keys to Effective Assessment

- Continuous monitoring of student achievement and behaviour in essential areas in cooperation with all teaching staff
- Early intervention for all students who share the problem
- The integration of problem prevention and remedial strategies into normal teaching
- The coordination of assessment across grade levels and subject areas

---

Program Development

The essence of program development is the exploration of possibilities and the testing of choices based on the assessment information that has been collected. The development of an intervention program by the teachers working to solve a problem is a team-planning process. At this stage, instructional and behavioural objectives should be set, materials and methods should be selected, and a schedule of instruction with target mastery dates for each objective and assigned responsibilities for each teacher should be agreed upon. It is most important to remember that it is the classroom teacher who will have to live with a program in the long run, so it should fit his or her teaching style and build on his or her strengths and preferences.

Program Implementation

The purpose of the educators involved at the program implementation stage is to get improved programs up and running in the regular classroom. This may involve them in demonstration teaching, team teaching, coaching, or joint materials preparation over the short term. If assistance in a classroom is required for an extended period, then supports such as peer tutoring, computer-assisted instruction, a learning prosthesis, or the introduction of a teaching assistant may be needed. It is the responsibility of the collaborative team to get new programs up and running in the classroom and to fade involvement as those programs become routine and prove successful.

Program Evaluation

Continuous direct measurement of program objectives is the best approach to evaluation in inclusive classrooms. Such evaluation may take many forms including ongoing portfolio assessment, regular curriculum-based testing, student-teacher conferences or academic interviews, repeated observations, or the comparison of daily performance measures with the baseline information collected during the assessment phase. At this stage, an ongoing evaluation strategy should be embedded in day-to-day instruction in the classroom.

Follow-Up

A series of pre-arranged probes to ensure that program gains have been maintained or generalized should be scheduled as a follow-up measure to successful programs. If a program has been unsuccessful, then assistance requests to other levels of support services (e.g., clinical services, school psychologist, and community services) should be initiated.

▥ Overcoming Resistance in Collaboration and Consultation

The most troublesome part of any collaboration or consultation is overcoming resistance to the process. Most often, resistance is temporary and merely reflects legitimate concerns that distract participants from full cooperation or commitment.

Solutions to Resistance

Some of the most common forms of resistance (Block, 1981; Morsink, Thomas & Correa, 1991; Friend & Cook, 1992) are described in this section with suggested solutions.

It's hopeless. In this case a partner believes that the problem is unique and too complicated to solve. Your partner may be concerned that others will succeed where he has failed. Alternatively, he may be exasperated with the problem and feel worn out. To solve this form of resistance, it is very important that you first acknowledge the uniqueness and complexity of the problem. Note your shared professional obligation to try to solve the problem and affirm your ability to tackle difficult problems (in general) or to solve this kind of problem (in particular). Also, refer to any additional resources you may be able to bring to the problem-solving process. Finally, emphasize that you depend on your partner's cooperation, experience, and insight to work on the problem and that he will be a main player in the eventual solution.

It's not my job. Sometimes a partner may feel that a problem exceeds her area of responsibility. Your partner may be trying to distance herself from the problem because she feels untrained and unprepared. In other instances, your colleague may have a different understanding of the roles the team members play, the problem under consideration, or the methods that possibly may be used. In either case, clarify how you see her role. To do this, it may be helpful to refer to school guidelines that describe who should be involved in problem solving and the process that should be followed. If necessary, acknowledge that her opportunities for professional preparation, to date, may have been impractical or inadequate.

At this point, it is important to move the discussion away from the person to the problem. To do this, objectify the problem by referring to its curricular or classroom management aspects and review some of the methods you or others have employed in prior similar situations. Affirm your confidence in her ability to contribute to the solution and stress the active and practical support you will provide. To engage her immediately, divide the problem up and begin with the parts she feels most prepared to deal with and reinforce her participation in the process frequently.

Expertise lacking. On occasion, a colleague may feel that the team lacks the expertise to solve the problem. The worst response in this situation is to take it personally and recite your credentials. A better approach is to take this concern seriously and review the skills needed to solve the problem in the estimation of all the team members. After completing an inventory of the team members' skills and areas of expertise, determine what is lacking and expand the team to include new partners who will bring the needed knowledge base and skills. Finally, review how similar cases were dealt with in the past and how the expertise already present on the team contributed to the solution.

Low motivation. There are any number of reasons why some team partners may evidence a low level of motivation. If they merely have cold feet, try reinforcing the importance of their continuing participation and stressing the ongoing support you and others will provide. If your colleagues' motivation levels are low because they feel overwhelmed, respond by developing mutually acceptable priorities so the program can be developed in smaller pieces that seem less daunting. To prioritize, try reducing the scope of the program by: a) focusing on essential, as opposed to desirable, objectives and outcomes, b) sequencing the program so that it stretches out over a longer period, and c) looking for additional supports for your colleague in this and other areas of his or her job.

Time lacking. To some extent, time can be created by following the suggestions listed in Figure 3.5. Another approach is to try to use time more effectively by: a) developing a brochure outlining the steps in the process to share with new team members, b) running short effective meetings with an agenda, time line, and the advanced distribution of relevant materials, c) sharing written information as much as possible (e.g., ask colleagues to prioritize problems before a meeting or confirm a program plan by signing off objectives afterwards), d) locating meetings where they consume the least travel time for the most teachers (especially in larger schools), and e) making meetings enjoyable by meeting for lunch or a recess coffee break. It is important to realize that as schools become more inclusive and teachers get used to working together, they begin to find the time to collaborate and consult through their daily work as they team-teach and share other work. As a part of the process, seek additional supports for your school from the school division, community, university, etc.

FIGURE 3.5
Creating Time for Collaboration and Consultation

- Schedule collaboration and consultation periods into the regular school timetable.

- Use existing grade level or subject area meetings as opportunities to collaborate and consult with special education and other support teachers by inviting them to attend on a regular basis.

- Use some of the special education budget to release teachers from the classroom to collaborate and consult.

- Whenever possible, allow teachers to trade traditional school time for time spent meeting with parents or others outside of school hours.

- Schedule meetings when a teacher's students are out of the classroom at music or physical education, etc.

- Train teaching assistants and volunteers to monitor classes during noninstructional time periods (e.g., test writing and independent reading) while teachers meet.

- Allow support-services educators to volunteer their time in return for the time from others (e.g., "I'd like to teach a lesson for you so you can show Mr. Jones how to do repeated readings," or "I'll take your class for math, while you phone to get the large print and talking books from the provincial resource centre.").

Another strategy is to refocus on providing systemic changes that will create more time and resources for you and your colleagues. A volunteer program, a peer-tutoring program, a teaching assistants' training program, a teacher's pantry, or the development of computer-assisted remedial tutorials or study guides for low-achieving students may have a positive impact on the stresses felt by all teachers.

Solution impractical. Occasionally, a partner may doubt the practicality of a particular approach. If the concern is directed towards you, ask to be invited to observe the situation first hand in the classroom and request to see the text or other classroom materials that will improve your understanding.

Alternative approaches to this obstacle include: a) comparing the present situation to past situations (same age group, grade level, curricular area, behaviour problem, type of disability, etc.) that you have dealt with successfully, or b) suggesting an experiment to test the practicality of an approach with a criterion set for its success or failure (in this approach stress that it is the method, not the people, that will succeed or fail).

Passive resistance. Sometimes a colleague may appear to agree to a collaborative project but avoid active involvement. To encourage involvement and commitment, invite your partner into the decision-making process in small ways by asking him or her to: a) complete an inventory or checklist with you, b) prioritize possible objectives, or c) rate alternative methods being considered for the program. Remember to invite his or her opinion often. If you remain uncertain about the commitment of your partners, ask everyone to initial the contracted program. Since most people won't sign something they don't agree with, this may bring hidden concerns out into the open where they can be explored. Passive resistance during meetings often becomes a "flight into health" later. That is, the situation suddenly and miraculously improves and help is no longer needed by those who originally raised the concern. In such a case, ensure the progress of the "miracle cure" will be monitored over the long term.

Leave me alone. Some teachers greatly value their independence and prefer to be their own problem-solvers. In this situation, it is best to approach the teacher through a team to which he or she belongs (e.g. the early-years team). Pose the problem with all team members and establish a common procedure for dealing with the problem. Invite your resistant colleague to pair up with you or another teacher to evaluate the procedure using students from each of your classes. Encourage your new partner to take a leadership role in reporting the results of the evaluation to the team.

I'm confused. Sometimes someone asks too many questions, gives too many details, or goes off on too many tangents. If this is the case, try to help get the process on track by referring to the time line on the agenda. If the problem persists, try saying "You've given us a lot of details, can you pick out the three most important facts," or "in a nutshell, then, the issues are …" Alternatively, ask the team to set two or three priorities and then move on to the next stage in the process with those as the focus.

We've never done it that way before. When a partner is nostalgic for the past, remind them of some of the objective reasons (changing student population, changing society, new curriculum, new educational policies, fewer resources than before, etc.) why change is necessary. Comfort with a new approach can be increased if you explain how it grew out of, or is related to, the old way of doing things. Finally, stress the supports and assistance available in the change process.

Understanding Resistance

Elementary school educators typically do not resist collaboration or consultation with their colleagues. When they do, it is often because their legitimate concerns about the process have not been taken seriously.

When resistance seems to be blocking progress in spite of all your best efforts you still have at least three strategies that may help break the impasse.

Naming the resistance. To name the resistance (Block, 1981), say what you think the other is doing, say how you feel about it, ask for their help in resolving the problem, and then keep quiet and let them respond. For example, if the resistance is "time lacking" say, "You really don't seem to have time for this process, I feel blocked at every turn no matter how hard I try to be flexible, please try to find some time for us to meet," and then await your colleague's response. If the resistance is "passive resistance" try saying, "You are very quiet and I don't know how to understand your silence, please tell me what you think." Do not use this strategy early in the process. It is an all-or-nothing last resort that is likely to win empathy and cooperation, or result in the end of the partnership on that particular project.

Return to the facts. It may be that a colleague's resistance is rooted in a different understanding of the facts at a fundamental ideological or philosophical level. It may be useful to set aside the project at hand and tackle the underlying issues that are preventing cooperation. While this may be time-consuming, it sometimes results in understanding even if agreement is not reached. Mutual understanding and respect can be a foundation for future progress in collaboration and consultation.

Personal appeal. Finally, it is sometimes possible to break through resistance with a personal appeal or by prefacing further negotiations with an attempt to get to know the other person better as a professional colleague.

When resistance is encountered, it is extremely important to keep the following key points in mind. First, it is methods, and not people, that succeed or fail. Second, if you spend the time needed to build strong partnerships and a good decision-making process, you will save time in the long run. Third, clarify the roles of all your partners early in the process. In particular, special educators, administrators and other support services personnel need to remember they are guests in classrooms—there to support, but not to fix.

⬔ Conclusion

In this chapter, the prerequisites for successful collaboration and consultation have been reviewed. They include: a) the establishment of a positive school climate for shared work and problem solving, b) the professional, interpersonal, and process skills needed to work with individual and team partners, and c) the strategic skills needed to recognize and help overcome resistance in yourself and others.

Several underlying themes emerge from our review. First, the growing importance of collaboration and consultation is linked to changes that are under way in Canadian elementary schools. Second, collaboration and consultation are important skills because they are emerging as the preferred methods of decision making and problem solving in areas as diverse as assessment, curriculum innovation, program modification, support-service delivery, behaviour management, and school reform. Third, a team process is only as effective as the knowledge and skills of the team members. Educators require more pre-service and in-service professional development in how to collaborate and consult efficiently and effectively. The active commitment of teacher educators and school administrators to professional development in collaboration and consultation skills is essential. Finally, the processes of collaboration and consultation require values that place the emphasis on "building" consensus rather than "winning" support, "sharing" responsibilities rather than "protecting" traditional interests, and "overcoming" resistance to change rather than "surrendering" to pessimism and inaction in the face of the changes that challenge us in our professional lives.

APPENDIX 3A

Stages in a Collaborative-Consultative Model

Stage/Duration   Activities

Problem   • Contact significant people involved.

Identification   • Schedule consultation.

(1–5 Days)   • Clarify roles of all participants.

                           • Review process with all participants.

                           • Review technical information needed by participants.

                           • Review existing information about the problem.

                           • Share expectations for the outcomes of the process.

                           • Agree on a common definition of the problem.

                           • Explore possible outcomes objectives.

                           • Explore possible assessment procedures.

                           • Agree on how to get started and assign tasks.

                           • Schedule ecological- and curriculum-based assessment procedures or other data collection activities.

                           • Arrange for record keeping and information dissemination.

Stage/Duration   Activities

Assessment   • Select and conduct assessment procedures:

(5–10 Days)   — in-class observations

                               — work sample analysis

                               — curriculum-based testing

                               — academic interviews

                               — analytic teaching

                               — behavioural recording

                               — curriculum analysis

	— checklists and inventories
	• Organize assessment information.
Program Development (1–10 Days)	• Review assessment information.
	• Agree on broad goals of program.
	• Set instructional and behavioural objectives.
	• Determine measurement methods.
	• Set criteria for success for each objective.
	• Develop teaching methods and materials.
	• Develop behaviour management plan or motivational strategy.
	• Conduct trial teaching.
	• Work out relationship to ongoing classroom instruction.
	• Schedule sequence of instruction.
	• Outline liaison with support services if needed.
	• Agree on time line for program implementation and set target mastery dates for objectives.
	• Record and disseminate program information.
Program Implementation Stage/Duration (1–8 Weeks)	**Activities**
	• Implement program in the classroom:
	— demonstration teaching
	— ongoing materials support for differentiated instruction
	— team teaching
	— guide teaching assistant support
	— manage ongoing systemic support (e.g., peer tutoring and computer-assisted instruction)
	• Implement continuous direct measurement.
	• Monitor sequence of instruction and achievement of criteria for success.

	• Fine tune program and supports.
	• Disseminate information on the progress of the program.

Program Evaluation (Variable)
- Evaluate mastery of program objectives against criteria for success at target dates.
- If program has been successful:
  — agree on measures to monitor maintenance or generalization of program gains
  — disseminate information on the success of the program
- If program has been unsuccessful:
  — re-enter assessment stage with the benefit of experience
  — consider referral to another level of support services
  — disseminate information on the evaluation of the program

Follow-up (Variable)
- Monitor implementation of maintenance and generalization.
- Disseminate information on the outcomes of the process.

Source: Adapted from Freeze, Bravi & Rampaul (1989).

SUGGESTED RESOURCES

Block, P. (1981). *Flawless consulting.* San Diego: University Associates.

Friend, M., & Cook, L. (1992). *Interactions: Collaboration skills for school professionals.* New York: Longman.

Morsink, C., Thomas, C., & Correa, V. (1991). *Interactive teaming: consultation and collaboration in special programs.* New York: Macmillan.

O'Brien, J., & Forest, M. (1989). *Action for inclusion.* Toronto: Inclusion Press.

Pearpoint, J., O'Brien, J., & Forest, M. (1993). *PATH.* Toronto: Inclusion Press.

Stainback, S., & Stainback, W. (1990). *Support networks for inclusive schooling.* Baltimore: Paul H. Brookes.

Turnbull, A., & Turnbull, H. (1990). *Families, professionals and exceptionality: A special partnership.* Columbus: Merrill.

REFERENCES

Andrews, J., & Lupart, J. (1993). *The inclusive classroom.* Scarborough, ON: Nelson Canada.

Bachor, D., & Crealock, C. (1986). *Instructional strategies for students with special needs.* Scarborough, ON: Prentice-Hall.

Bigge, J. (1991). *Teaching individuals with physical and multiple disabilities.* New York: Macmillan.

Block, P. (1981). *Flawless consulting.* San Diego: University Associates.

Bos, C., & Vaughn, S. (1991). *Strategies for teaching students with learning and behavior problems.* Boston: Allyn and Bacon.

Brown, D., Wyne, M., Blackburn, J., & Powell, W. (1979). *Consultation: Strategy for improving education.* Boston: Allyn and Bacon.

Csapo, M. (1989). From minor stream to mainstream: A sociological perspective. In M. Csapo & L. Goguen (Eds.), *Special education across Canada: issues and concerns for the '90s.* Vancouver: Centre for Human Development and Research.

Csapo, M., & Goguen, L. (1989). *Special education across Canada: Issues and concerns for the '90s.* Vancouver: Centre for Human Development and Research.

Freeze, R. (1989). *Achieving.* Winnipeg: Peguis Publishers.

Freeze, R., Bravi, G., & Rampaul, W. (1989). Special education in Manitoba: A consultative-collaborative service delivery model. In M. Csapo & L. Goguen (Eds.), *Special education across Canada: Issues and concerns for the '90s.* Vancouver: Centre for Human Development and Research.

Friend, M., & Cook, L. (1992). *Interactions: Collaboration skills for school professionals.* New York: Longman.

Gearheart, B., Weishahn, M., & Gearheart, C. (1992). *The exceptional student in the regular classroom.* New York: Macmillan.

Jones, V., & Jones, L. (1986). *Comprehensive classroom management.* Boston: Allyn and Bacon.

Luftig, R. (1987). *Teaching the mentally retarded student.* Boston: Allyn and Bacon.

Morsink, C., Thomas, C., & Correa, V. (1991). *Interactive teaming: Consultation and Collaboration in special programs.* New York: Macmillan.

O'Brien, J., & Forest., M. (1989). *Action for inclusion.* Toronto: Inclusion Press.

Pearpoint, J., O'Brien, J., & Forest, M. (1993). *PATH.* Toronto: Inclusion Press.

Salvia, J., & Hughes, C. (1990). *Curriculum based assessment.* New York: Macmillan.

Seifert, K. (1991). *Educational psychology.* Boston: Houghton Mifflin.

Slavin, R. (1994). *Educational psychology.* Boston: Allyn and Bacon.

Stainback, S., & Stainback, W. (1990). *Support networks for inclusive schooling.* Baltimore: Paul H. Brookes.

Stainback, S., & Stainback, W. (1992). *Controversial issues confronting special education.* Baltimore: Paul H. Brookes.

Stainback, S., Stainback, W., & Forest, M. (1989). *Educating all students in the mainstream of regular education.* Baltimore: Paul H. Brookes.

Tierney, R., Readence, J., & Dishner, E. (1990). *Reading strategies and practices.* Boston: Allyn and Bacon.

Thomas, V. (1979). *Teaching spelling.* Toronto: Gage.

Turnbull, A., & Turnbull, H. (1990). *Families, professionals and exceptionality: A special partnership.* Columbus, OH: Merrill.

Ysseldyke, J., & Algozzine, B. (1982). *Critical issues in special and remedial education.* Boston: Houghton Mifflin.

Ysseldyke, J., Algozzine, B., & Thurlow, M. (1992). *Critical issues in special education.* Boston: Houghton Mifflin.

Zigmond, N., Vallecorsa, A., & Silverman, R. (1983). *Assessment for instructional planning in special education.* Englewood Cliffs, NJ: Prentice-Hall.

Classroom-Based Assessment for Instructional Planning at the Elementary Level

Marion Porath

University of British Columbia

Introduction

The focus of this chapter is on classroom-based assessment techniques that can help teachers learn more about children's understandings of their world in order to facilitate a "match" between the learner and the curriculum (Donaldson, 1979). Assessment should be an integral component of classroom activity (Gardner, 1993). Recognizing the range of activities that takes place in classrooms, **classroom-based assessment** is broadly interpreted in this chapter to mean ways of increasing our knowledge of *what* children know and *how* they come to know it. A number of assessment options are presented with emphasis on approaches to help teachers understand children's points of view on the curriculum and how these points of view are constructed. Examples of how teachers then can use their understanding of children's points of view to plan for teaching in an inclusive classroom are provided.

Inclusive classrooms are complex environments in which children's academic abilities, personalities, physical and sensory abilities, and social skills interact with those of the teacher and their peers and are brought to bear on their attempts to master the curriculum. One of the challenges of teaching is to identify children's strengths, weaknesses, and ways of understanding to enable all the children in a classroom to reach their potential. The first part of the chapter focuses on the different forms assessment may take to meet this challenge. Short profiles of children, including those with physical and sensory disabilities, are featured as examples of how assessment can help to optimize a match between the learner and the curriculum. The chapter concludes with two case studies. Children with exceptional learning needs—one with language difficulties and one with advanced cognitive and academic development—are the focus of discussions on how theory can be put into practice.

◨ Types of Assessment

The magnitude of diversity in a classroom is great and instruction that acknowledges diversity is believed to optimize children's progress in school (Biemiller, 1993). Assessment has been defined as "a process of collecting data for the purpose of making decisions about students" (Ysseldyke, Algozzine & Thurlow, 1992, p. 199); these decisions are relevant to understanding diversity and improving instruction.

There are a number of ways of assessing children for the purpose of instructional planning. No one way will provide a teacher with the "the answer"; rather, a **multiple assessment approach** (Sattler, 1992) is advocated to better understand how children learn. A number of options are presented, all of which have relevance to informing decisions about instruction. In deciding on the form the assessment will take, a clear relationship between form, purpose, and educational aims must be evident (Floden, 1994).

Norm-Referenced Assessment

Children's academic achievement and general cognitive skills can be assessed using standardized measures. Measures such as the Canadian Test of Basic Skills (Heironymous, Lindquist, Hoover & King-Shaw, 1990) and the Canadian Cognitive Abilities Test (Wright, Thorndike & Hagen, 1988) sometimes are given on a districtwide basis and results made available to teachers. On these tests, an individual's performance is compared to that of a **norm group**, or others of the child's age who have taken the test. Norm groups should contain children whose background and experience are similar to the population as a whole; that is, norm groups should be *representative* of the children on whom the test will be used (Sattler,

1992; Ysseldyke et al., 1992). Both the Canadian Test of Basic Skills and the Canadian Cognitive Abilities Test were normed on 40 000 students across Canada. Norm-referenced tests have the advantage of being reliable indicators of a child's general cognitive skills, how well a student is learning in comparison to others in his or her age group, or at what grade level a student is achieving (Keating, 1991; Sattler, 1992). Disadvantages include the possible lack of relationship between what the test measures and what a child has been taught in school, the provision of limited information about *how* children learn, and the need for careful interpretation of grade-equivalent scores.

Criterion-Referenced Assessment

Rather than comparing a child's performance to others of his or her age as in norm-referenced testing, criterion-referenced assessment identifies a child's level of mastery of specific skills as determined by an established criterion relevant to the curriculum (Sattler, 1992; Ysseldyke et al., 1992). These tests are developed by teachers to ascertain how well a student has mastered particular curricular objectives. For example, Jill can read curriculum materials at the grade-6 level. She can multiply and divide fractions accurately and knows 90 percent of the words in the current spelling unit. Criterion-referenced assessment is useful in understanding what and how much a child has mastered, which, in turn, can guide subsequent instruction.

Shapiro and Lentz (1988) have cautioned that criterion-referenced tests be examined to determine if the items on the test are fairly representative of the skill being assessed. If not, mastery of skills may be incorrectly judged. Shapiro and Lentz (1988, p. 90) stress that the measure "ask the right questions." This can be optimized by matching the questions to curricular materials.

Curriculum-Based Assessment

Curriculum-based assessment involves *ongoing* analysis of students' performance across the curriculum; that is, it is used to monitor and evaluate students as they deal with curricular demands throughout the year. It includes observing students at work, analyzing the learning environment and the child's approach to tasks, examining students' products (Ysseldyke et al., 1992), and testing understanding of the curriculum. Curriculum-based assessment is naturalistic in that it evaluates student performance in the relevant environment—the classroom. For example, Laurie, who has low visual acuity, is a student in a grade-7 classroom organized with desks in groups of four, learning centres, and several private work spaces. Mr. Ferguson, the itinerant teacher with responsibility for children with visual impairments, has supported Laurie's teacher, Ms. King, by supplying large print materials and advising on appropriate lighting. He has also supplied word-processing software with a large print option so that Laurie can complete assignments more easily. He and Ms. King, incorporating Laurie's feedback, have collaborated to make sure that all areas of the classroom are accessible to Laurie.

Laurie chooses to do her work in reading at a private work space. She needs concrete directions set out in a specific temporal sequence. The open-ended tasks that Ms. King uses to build inferential comprehension abilities are stressful for her. Laurie responds to tasks like, "Think of a different ending for this story and predict what the main character would do," with "I don't know," or "I don't get it." Laurie's assignments, projects, and tests indicate good language skills, vocabulary, and literal comprehension. Ms. King speculates that Laurie's difficulty with inferential comprehension may stem from lack of confidence due to limited experience with making inferences and that Laurie may not wish to have others know about her difficulty with these tasks. Ms. King and Mr. Ferguson believe it is unlikely that Laurie's difficulties are sight-related since she is able to complete other assignments.

Ms. King regularly works with the whole class to have the children reflect on their thinking about various concepts and activities and she models acceptance of individual styles. She also has the students keep learning logs in which they describe and reflect on what they know and how they learn. On an individual basis, she helps Laurie to impose her own order on open-ended tasks by having her map her ideas (Brownlie, Close & Wingren, 1990) and encouraging her to suggest ways to complete the task. At first, Ms. King gives considerable guidance with these strategies, then gradually encourages and reinforces independence. With this approach, Laurie's ability to deal with open-ended tasks increased gradually and she became capable of using her knowledge in innovative ways. As this ability increased, Laurie began to seek out group learning opportunities more often.

Curriculum-based assessment also can be used to break down tasks into their component parts in order to allow teachers to describe what has and has not been mastered (Shapiro & Lentz, 1985). Teacher-made tests of curricular content help teachers to monitor pupils' progress throughout the curriculum (Ysseldyke et al., 1992).

Performance-Based Assessment

It has been argued that performance-based assessment measures the "thinking curriculum" not the "remembering curriculum" (Resnick, 1990, cited in Ysseldyke et al., 1992). Performance-based assessment focuses on problem-solving ability rather than simply knowledge acquisition (Slavin, 1994; Ysseldyke et al., 1992); looks at pupil performance over a period of time (Ysseldyke et al., 1992); and commonly includes the following characteristics:

1. Uses open-ended tasks
2. Focuses on higher order or complex skills

3. Employs context-sensitive strategies

4. Often uses complex problems requiring several types of performance and significant student time

5. Consists of either individual or group performance

6. May involve a significant degree of student choice (Baker, O'Neil & Linn, 1993, p. 1211)

Performance assessments involve "real-life" demonstrations of skills (Slavin, 1994) and can include conducting a science experiment to solve a problem, giving an oral presentation, writing a letter or speech that demonstrates understanding of the issues addressed, dramatizing historical events, or producing a painting.

Gardner (1993, pp. 150–51) provides guidelines for teacher assessment of students' performance in art, music, and writing. A student could be considered to be making excellent progress in writing production, or thinking *in* the domain of writing, if:

1. The student has mastered grammatical and stylistic conventions.

2. The student develops a work through thoughtful revisions.

3. The student generates his or her own topics and writes about them in a creative, expressive fashion.

Similar guidelines are given for reflection, or thinking *about* the domain, perception of the domain (for example, awareness of word patterns and ability to make discriminations about works of writing), and approach to work (for example, ability to work both independently and collaboratively).

Performance-based assessment is believed to be valuable because it incorporates *multidimensional evidence* about students and can involve students in assessments that are of consequence to them (Moss, 1994). Baker et al. (1993), however, caution that surface features of performance can be misconstrued as evidence of higher-order thinking; students' cognitive processes are often not documented. Patricia Arlin, of the University of British Columbia, who worked with bright grade 4 math students, went beyond the students' formulaic responses to probe their understandings of area and perimeter.

> *Arlin:* Okay, you're saying perimeter can measure many shapes; area cannot measure many shapes.
> *Student:* Square or rectangle.
> *Arlin:* Okay, the area can only be a square or rectangle. Why do you think area can only be a square or a rectangle?

Student: You can't have many other shapes to measure in area 'cause it has to be in square feet; you have to measure in square feet (Arlin, in preparation).

Subsequent to discussing their notions of area and perimeter, the students were given the assignment of calculating the number of tiles needed to retile their classroom. Both the discussion and the activity gave the students the opportunity to test their conceptions of area and perimeter. Based on their applications of formulae, a teacher may have believed the students' understanding to be complete. However, with discussion and application, their understandings and misunderstandings were revealed. Without these opportunities, they may not have thought deeply about measurement and Arlin would not have been able to document their thinking processes.

Baker et al. (1993) suggest that performance-based assessments focus on a student's knowledge representation, problem representation, inference, integration of knowledge, procedures, and explanations to optimize the assessment of higher-order thinking. They also suggest that the nature of students' instructional experiences and practice of the task be considered to decide whether a student is demonstrating rote knowledge or genuine understanding. Instruction and practice that have emphasized the learning of facts and application of rules and procedures can sometimes result in student responses that may *appear* to demonstrate understanding but which, in fact, do not utilize higher-order thinking skills.

Gardner advocates the use of **portfolios** as an assessment tool compatible with the goals of performance-based assessment (Brandt, 1987–88). The portfolio contains samples of a student's work gathered throughout the year in collaboration with the teacher. Gardner (1991) suggested that portfolios may, however, emphasize the final product and proposed that a **process-folio** be considered, which would contain, for example, initial ideas, first and interim drafts, critiques, journal entries on moments when ideas changed and/or thoughts came together, and the final product. The process-folio may offer a more representative view of a child's performance. Wolf (1987–88, p. 29) supports this view, stating that "students' abilities to formulate new questions, pursue work over time, and arrive at standards of excellence" cannot be tapped in product-oriented assessment but must, rather, focus additionally on the process students engage in as they think critically about their own work.

Slavin (1994) offers a number of helpful guidelines for planning, organizing, and implementing assessment of process and performance using portfolios:

- Plan enough time that students can prepare and talk about items for their portfolios.

- Start small, perhaps with one subject area or one aspect of learning, and gradually incorporate more topics as you and the students become more familiar with the portfolio process.

- Choose items that show progress toward or mastery of curricular objectives.

- Collect items that show progress toward required or "core indicators"—things that all children are working on—and items that demonstrate individual styles, interests, and strengths. Keep a list of objectives and a record of optional items in the front of the portfolio.

- Help students gain responsibility for selecting, evaluating, and keeping up-to-date the items in their portfolios.

- Record teacher and student comments on the spot and attach them to the relevant portfolio item.

- Be selective about the items included in a portfolio. The selection should be thoughtful and linked to instructional objectives (Based on Slavin, 1994, pp. 555–56).

Performance-based assessment may also help teachers to better understand children who possess relevant skills as measured by norm-referenced or criterion-referenced instruments but have difficulty in performance; that is, the child who has the knowledge but doesn't perform in the classroom. Shapiro (1989, p. 52) has described this as a "won't do" rather than a "can't do" problem. Performance-based assessment can help to describe environmental and individual variables that may be influencing a child's performance in school and is, thus, an important supplement to the assessment of academic skills (Shapiro, 1989). Performance-based assessment can be useful for optimizing *all* children's learning, not just that of the child who seemingly "won't do."

Listening to Children

Lohman (1993, p. 21) pointed out the necessity of seriously considering the learner's perspective and "not simply the common perspective codified in the curriculum." Listening to how children respond to curricular tasks, their peers, and you, the teacher, can be extremely informative (Paley, 1981, 1986). Consider the following excerpt from *Wally's Stories* (Paley, 1981) in which listening to kindergarten children as they grappled with measurement issues helped the teacher to come to grips with five-year-olds' understanding of rulers. Wally has determined that a classroom rug is a "four-person rug" in size. However, on measuring with four different classmates, some of the rug is left uncovered. Discussions ensue about the relative merits of using short people, big people, dolls, and rulers and the advisability of waiting for Warren, who is just the right size, to return to school, after which the teacher asks the children if the rug is 10 rulers and 2 dolls long. There is no response to the question and she suggests using one of the rulers over again to measure the rug. The following conversation takes place:

> *Eddie:* Now you made *another* empty space.
> *Teacher:* Eddie, you mentioned a tape measure before. I have one here. (We stretch the tape along the edge of the rug, and I show the children that the rug is 156 inches long. The lesson is done. The next day Warren is back in school.)
> *Wally:* Here's Warren. Now we can really measure the rug.
> *Teacher:* Didn't we really measure the rug with the ruler?
> *Wally:* Well, rulers aren't really real, are they? (Paley, 1981, pp. 15–16)

The teacher incorporates her knowledge of the children's understanding of measurement into subsequent activities (Paley, 1981). In introducing new curricular content, students' level of understanding must be considered (Wang, Haertel & Walberg, 1993, cited in Peterson, 1993). Patricia Arlin at the University of British Columbia has described this activity as "teaching as conversation with children around the topics we call the curriculum." This sort of teaching emphasizes the inclusion of the child's point of view, the involvement of children in *mental activity* as opposed to activity for activity's sake, and the provision of concrete experiences that emphasize "concepts in action" (Arlin, in preparation). Frameworks for understanding children's points of view can be established by asking them questions such as:

> "What is it that you know about ...?"
> "What is ...?"
> "What are three things you would like to find out about ...?" (Arlin, in preparation)

By asking the question, "What is heat?" *before* beginning a science unit, the experience of fourth-grade children became the concepts to work with in understanding heat (Watson & Konicek, 1990). They tested their notions that sweaters, hats, and rugs were very hot. While it is necessary to keep in mind that conceptual change is slow and influenced by a child's stage of development (Arlin, in preparation; Watson & Konicek, 1990), incorporating children's points of view into our instructional planning can lead to the acquisition of more accurate and complete conceptual understandings.

To the extent that one carries on a conversation with a child, as a way of trying to understand a child's understanding, the child's understanding increases "in the very process." The questions the interlocutor asks, in an attempt to clarify for herself what the child is thinking, oblige the child to think a little further also (Duckworth, 1987, p. 96).

Teachers also can listen to determine how self-directed a learner a child is. Andrew Biemiller at the University of Toronto and Donald Meichenbaum at the University of Waterloo have shown that the most competent learners engage in regulating their own learning, including self-interrogating, self-monitoring, and asking for help (Biemiller & Meichenbaum, 1992). Less competent learners engage in far fewer self-regulatory behaviours. Listening to children's task-related speech can provide indicators of their degree of competence in a subject. Teachers should also be aware that self-regulatory language can vary from subject to subject (Biemiller & Meichenbaum, 1992).

Observing Children

Children's lives in classrooms entail more than just academic work. The classroom is a complex, dynamic social setting and observing children within this setting can contribute to understandings that ultimately benefit their learning. Peterson (1993, p. 322) describes the "case knowledge" that teachers demonstrate in their observations of children—knowledge that "interweaves the academic, affective, personal, and social realms …" and that informs instruction. This knowledge can be recorded in journal form at the end of the day or the week, or jotted down on index cards or in a notebook as relevant observations are made. The following is an excerpt from mid-September journal entries described by Peterson (1993). The children are fifth and sixth graders.

> *Keisha*: sometimes says things which appear to be unrelated to what's going on or with the intention of getting everyone's attention and getting others to laugh at her. *Andrei*: right on the ball, active in discussions, making suggestions (wanted more geography). Reading *Voyage of the Dawn Treader* and says he wants to read the whole Narnia series (Peterson, 1993, p. 321).

This teacher's case knowledge is developed as she converses with students while they work. Her knowledge is "continually developing and being revised" (Peterson, 1993, p. 322).

One way a teacher might utilize case knowledge is to jot down observations in a notebook during the day. Good and Brophy (1987) have several suggestions for how this might be done. The page could be divided in half and observations noted on the left-hand side. Observations *only* should be recorded during the school day and they should be dated and note taken of what was happening at the time of the observation. Time at the end of the day could then be used to make inferences about the observations with the inferences recorded to the right of the observations. If inferences are made at the time of observation, there is the danger of observations being influenced by "perceptual blinders" (Good & Brophy, 1987, p. 59); that is, observations may reflect a biased point of view based on hasty interpretation. Thoughts about academic or social implications could be added at this time. Suppose that Keisha and Andrei are members of an inclusive classroom; Keisha wears a leg brace and walks with difficulty. Within this context, Table 4.1 shows how the teacher's observations might be used to make inferences and to help her think about classroom implications.

TABLE 4.1
Using Observations to Plan Teaching Strategies

Andrei	Right on the ball, active in discussions, making suggestions (wanted more geography)	Skill in geography?
		Go ahead to more complex activities?
		Some independent study?
		Discuss with him.
	Reading *Voyage of the Dawn Treader* and says he wants to read the whole Narnia series.	Same with reading—more challenge.
		See Mark (Gifted Resource Teacher) for ideas.
Keisha	Sometimes says things which appear to be unrelated to what's going on or with the intention of getting everyone's attention and getting others to laugh at her.	Attention seeking? Her attempt to be "normal"? How intentional? Is this my bias? Making different connections to information? Monitor and talk to counsellor.

Source: P.L. Peterson (1993), p. 13, 321.

A plan for observation can be made; for example, the teacher could focus on three or four students per day. However, the plan should be flexible. There will be the occasional day when it is not possible to find time to make notes and days when other children will be added to the planned observations because something noteworthy has happened.

Using Developmental Level to Plan Remedial Instruction

Knowing where children are on a developmental continuum can help teachers plan instruction. This is particularly relevant for the child who is experiencing difficulties in learning. Research done at the Ontario Institute for Studies in Education showed that instruction that takes a child's developmental level into account and helps him or her bridge the gap to the next level is effective for children who experience difficulty learning (Case, 1991; Case, Sandieson & Dennis, 1986). This approach to instruction, when compared to instruction based on adult strategies for solving tasks, results in greater gains in achievement, greater ability to do tasks that are similar conceptually, and longer lasting effects (Case, Sandieson & Dennis, 1986). To plan remedial instruction, teachers need to know what sort of development is typical for the average child. The developmental psychological perspectives of Piaget and neo-Piagetian theorists have been operationalized to guide teachers in recognizing typical development (Arlin, in preparation; Case, 1991; 1992; Donaldson, 1979; Duckworth, 1987; Paley, 1986; Watson & Konicek, 1990). A teacher's observations and knowledge of the children in his or her classroom are also important sources of understanding in planning remedial instruction as are curricular scope and sequence. The following steps provide general guidelines for incorporating children's developmental level into instructional planning:

1. Identify what average children typically do in a subject area at different points in their development.

2. Assess the point of development for children experiencing learning difficulty.

3. Build a series of "conceptual bridges" from the child's current level to the next level of development in a context that simplifies the concepts and makes them concrete for the child (Case, 1991), that is, in a "conceptually meaningful" fashion (McKeough, 1992).

These guidelines are operationalized in the following way:

1. Start with tasks that children can do.

2. Make children aware of how they are solving the task by using some kind of representation or analogy that is meaningful to them.

3. Allow children to practise the task using the representation or analogy until they can do it automatically.

4. Add an element to the representation in a way that captures the next step in conceptual development. The objective is to highlight the new element in a way that helps children to see how it differs from what they are presently doing.

5. Allow children to practise using the new element, first with help and then independently (Case, 1991).

Anne McKeough (1989, cited in Case, 1991) at the University of Calgary taught learning-disabled children to tell stories that were conceptually more well developed. Whereas other children their age could tell stories that consisted of plots involving a problem, the main character's attempt to solve the problem, and finally, a satisfactory resolution, these children told stories involving a series of events that were unintegrated in the sense that no simple plot was apparent. McKeough followed the steps above in planning instruction:

1. The children first told stories until they were comfortable with the activity.

2. The stories were represented by the instructor in a series of drawings in cartoon frames.

3. Step 2 was practised until the children were familiar with it and could produce at least four events including some action and the main character's response.

4. To introduce the notion of a simple plot containing a problem and a resolution, the instructor generated a problem herself and drew it in a cartoon strip format. (McKeough, 1989, cited in Case, 1991, p. 142).

5. Children practised by telling further stories using prepared problem events. Finally, children were asked to tell stories independently.

6. This procedure was then repeated to help children achieve the kind of plots that other children their age were capable of including in stories. An "X" was introduced as a representation for a complicating event that prevented a resolution of the problem—"something that he tried but didn't work" (McKeough, 1989, cited in Case, 1991, p. 143); practice provided; support gradually faded; and independent story telling encouraged (Case, 1991).

As well as demonstrating the importance of considering children's current level of understanding in planning instruction, the approach used by McKeough also demonstrates the importance of practice and support in assessment and instruction, two factors that have been described as **context**.

The Importance of Context in Assessment

The context of the assessment must be recognized as an important contributor to children's performance (Donaldson, 1979; Day & Hall, 1987; Fischer, Bullock, Rotenberg & Raya, 1993; Ysseldyke et al., 1992). Fischer et al., in particular, have addressed the role of practice and support in allowing children to demonstrate their "optimal level" of performance in assessment situations. Questions such as the following need to be considered in determining contextual influences on performance.

- What is being asked of the child in this task?

- How did the child interpret the instructions? Donaldson (1979, p. 159) has emphasized that if we are to improve in helping children, emphasis must be switched from thinking that the child didn't understand the adult to attempting to "make the imaginative leap needed to understand the child."

- What sorts of understandings did the child bring to the task?

- With practice and support, would this child do better? What *kind* of support would be best?

- If another avenue of expression were allowed, would the child demonstrate understanding? Gardner and Hatch (1989) emphasize the need for multiple approaches to the demonstration of knowledge. A child with exceptional spatial skills, for example, may be better able to represent knowledge visually than verbally.

Students may be more likely to reveal understandings when **authentic tasks** (Pea, 1993, p. 273) are used. In science, for example, Pea has emphasized that children be able to "talk" science, that is, predict, experiment, observe, explain, and revise, rather than just "hear" science. This provides the optimal context for students' knowledge to be assessed for the purposes of planning further instruction.

▣ Theory into Practice

It is nearing the end of September and Ms. Green is feeling confident about her emerging understanding of most of the pupils in her multi-aged grouping of 8- to 10-year-olds. She recognizes that the process of understanding how her students learn is a dynamic and ongoing one and will be influenced by the children's development and the variety of things they will attempt during their school year. Two of her pupils pose special challenges, however, and she considers ways of increasing her understanding of their particular learning needs.

Matthew, age 8, is experiencing difficulties with reading and writing. He has received help with language arts since beginning school. Matthew's achievement test results indicate that his reading ability is in the lowest 10 percent for children his age. Ms. Green has organized an individualized reading program and Matthew is reading books at an appropriate level, but she is concerned about his rate of progress. Matthew's written language skills are very weak. He finds spelling difficult and he has been unable to complete the grammatical and dictionary skills assignments that his age group is working on, although Ms. Green realizes that his difficulties with grammar and spelling are influenced by his poor reading skills. Matthew's home background is not one that has offered him reading and rich oral language experience.

Matthew's achievement test results in mathematics showed age-appropriate skills but weakness in reasoning. Ms. Green has given criterion-referenced tests of basic facts and Matthew has demonstrated between 80 and 100 percent mastery on the tests. Her observations in her journal entry of Matthew's interactions during math indicate difficulties with problem-solving and persistent help-seeking behaviours.

September 20. Matthew was very reluctant to read to me at our reading conference today. I sense that his self-esteem is beginning to suffer because of his poor language abilities. His oral language is immature but only in the sense that he doesn't have an extensive vocabulary. His sentence structure is O.K. He seems to have more understanding of concepts than he is able to talk about. Work on enriching his vocabulary! Give him more opportunities to communicate orally. Also—what about tests? He has a tough time reading them. Maybe I'll try doing the social studies test tomorrow orally, one-on-one. And math— his computational skills are fine but problem solving is weak. Is this because of a lack of ability to reason or because he can't read the problems very well? I'll assign someone to read out problems in the math group next week and listen to his responses.

Ms. Green offered Matthew the opportunity to give his responses to a social studies test orally and found that, while his language was simple, he demonstrated excellent understanding of the concepts studied. Later that day, in a class discussion, Matthew offered insightful observations about others' motivations and intentions. Moreover, Matthew appeared more confident in these situations and, in contrast to his behaviour in reading and writing situations, focused on his work.

Ms. Green decides to provide Matthew an opportunity for him to be an "expert" (Biemiller, 1993). She and the first-grade teacher have just planned a buddy system where older children assist younger children and the first-grade teacher has agreed to have Matthew participate in social studies lessons by working with small groups of children on their projects on community life. This arrangement should allow the building of confidence and increased opportunities to strengthen vocabulary.

In math, Matthew did better when problems were read out. Ms. Green suspects that his difficulties stem from lack of practice rather than from fundamental problems in reasoning. She decides to alternate work with peers or herself with independent sessions where Matthew works from a tape recording of math problems and follows along in the textbook. She also will have Matthew review the tasks verbally (Biemiller & Meichenbaum, 1992) when working with others and encourage him to do the same when working independently.

Matthew will continue to receive extra help with reading and writing. Ms. Green keeps in close contact with the resource teacher and she will continue to monitor—through observations and listening, her journal notes, portfolios, and tests—Matthew's academic progress and social-emotional development.

Claudia, age 9, has a very sophisticated vocabulary and her level of understanding of concepts across the curriculum is excellent. She learns quickly and has a good sense of how she learns and what her interests are. She has an inquiring mind and, at times, it seems her thirst for knowledge is insatiable. Claudia has advanced reading abilities, although Ms. Green is not sure just how far advanced she is, nor is she sure what should be done to provide an appropriate curricular match. Claudia's achievement test results indicate that she reads and comprehends better than 99 percent of children her age. However, Ms. Green knows that this test may not have had enough items that challenged Claudia. Daniel Keating, at the Ontario Institute for Studies in Education, has emphasized that, for bright learners, a test's *ceiling* must be high enough (Keating 1975, 1991). That is, unless a test has enough scope for a bright student, it will not reveal just how much the student knows.

Claudia's mathematical ability is clearly advanced for her age. Her achievement test results showed that her mathematical skills and reasoning are in the top 5 percent for children her age. In Ms. Green's multi-age classroom, instructional groupings are flexible and Claudia works on challenging problems with 9- and 10-year-olds who are competent in mathematics. Claudia has achieved 90 to 100 percent mastery on criterion-referenced tests and her performance on open-ended math tasks is excellent.

Claudia has mentioned that she would like more challenge in language arts and Ms. Green recognizes that, without it, the signs of boredom and frustration she has noticed lately will likely increase. Ms. Green wants to keep Claudia's love of learning alive.

October 2. Claudia sure has been vocal lately about being bored in language arts, particularly. I'm really puzzling over how to make sure she's getting enough challenge. In our reading conference, it was clear that she can read extremely well, but her book contained some pretty mature issues. Is she ready for these? Some of her interpretations and answers were sophisticated but others were quite literal. I need to find out more about how she's thinking about the books she chooses. What's making her feel bored? Listen to her explanations to other children in book discussion time for clues. Talk to the librarian and her parents. How does she talk about reading in other contexts? What sorts of books does she read? Her writing isn't very inspired lately. Discuss this with her at portfolio time and get some input on what she'd like to write about.

In discussing Claudia's reading with her parents and the school librarian, Ms. Green realized that a better match between Claudia's abilities and the reading curriculum was possible. Developmental issues are important for academically advanced children too (Porath, 1992) and the librarian suggested that books with sophisticated treatment of issues relevant to bright 9-year-olds would be appropriate (see Halsted, 1988 and Hauser & Nelson, 1988 for excellent suggestions for gifted readers). The librarian agreed to help Claudia select some books and Ms. Green will build assignments around these choices in consultation with Claudia.

Ms. Green also talked to the district resource teacher who works with gifted children and provides support to classroom teachers. This teacher recognized the appropriateness of Ms. Green's strategies and suggested that Claudia also join one of the small groups that she meets with twice weekly. For children who are academically advanced, the opportunity to meet with other children of similar interests and abilities is important for both academic and social-emotional development (Davis & Rimm, 1989). * gifted

Ms. Green recognized that Claudia has significantly advanced abilities in writing and that some provision needs to be made to match instruction to Claudia's level of development. In work with students of high ability, both Dona Matthews at the Ontario Institute for Studies in Education and William McKee at the University of British Columbia have emphasized the importance of an appropriate match of curriculum to students' skill levels (Matthews, 1994; McKee, 1994). Ms. Green plans to investigate the possibility of providing a mentor for Claudia (Matthews, 1994).

In math, Ms. Green decides to try compacting the curriculum (Reis & Renzulli, 1992) for the competent math group. Curriculum compacting involves streamlining the curriculum for those students who are capable of learning quickly. Pretesting allows teachers to identify what a student has already mastered; students can "test out" of certain academic material (Reis, Burns & Renzulli, 1992). Ms. Green decides to give the children in the competent math group end-of-unit tests as pre-tests (Reis & Renzulli, 1992) to see if Claudia and others may be able to do more advanced work than they are currently doing. She decides to use the unit tests in the grade 5 math text for the 9-year-olds and those in the grade 6 text for the 10-year-olds for this purpose. Because all the children in this group scored at the 90th percentile or above on the mathematics achievement test, she believes that starting with a text one grade level above their age may be appropriate. Ms. Green plans to allow the children to skip material they have already mastered and offer some opportunity for them to work ahead, but she also wants to deepen and broaden their curriculum by involving them in math projects. By utilizing the pre-test approach she can also identify any areas of weakness and provide the appropriate instruction. When Ms. Green first heard of curriculum compacting, she thought it would consume an enormous amount of time but a colleague convinced her that it actually saves time that would otherwise be spent marking work that children need not have done (Reis & Renzulli, 1992). (Reis et al. (1992) provide excellent practical guidelines for implementing curriculum compacting. See the list of resources at the end of the chapter for information on where to obtain this publication.) As with Matthew, Ms. Green will monitor how Claudia responds to these provisions, both academically and socially, using classroom-based assessment techniques.

The examples of how theory can be put into practice show how different forms of assessment can be combined to increase knowledge of what children have learned, the ways in which they learned it, and how they appeared to learn best. Assessment should be viewed as an ongoing process in keeping with the dynamic nature of children's development.

◉ Summary and Conclusion

In this chapter, several approaches to classroom-based assessment have been discussed and examples of how these approaches might work in inclusive classrooms presented. It was emphasized that assessment should focus not only on ascertaining *what* it is that students know but also *how* they come to know it. By including both the what and how of children's learning, teachers can use the results of assessment to plan more effectively for instruction.

Several themes emerged in the chapter. First, assessment should be an ongoing process, an integral part of classroom life. Fostering learning and understanding requires ongoing assessment and reassessment—a continual evaluation of where children are on the path to mastery and what instructional and contextual factors are most conducive to helping them reach their goals. A prerequisite for an assessment rationale is a good understanding of curricular scope and sequence throughout the grades. Another feature of the integral nature of assessment is that it is not *just* testing. Tests are a component of assessment but the term "assessment" implies a broad-based approach to monitoring and understanding children's learning.

A second theme implicit in the chapter was the importance of understanding the nature of children's thinking at different stages of cognitive development. In order to validate and incorporate children's points of view, teachers need to understand the qualitative differences between child, adolescent, and adult thought.

Third, assessment should be viewed as a collaborative process that includes consultation with support staff, parents, and the students themselves. Each can contribute valuable insights that, when incorporated with classroom-based assessment information, lead to a more complete picture of the learner.

The goal of this chapter was to provide teachers with information on a number of classroom-based assessment strategies. The importance of including strategies that allow teachers to gain understanding of children's points of view and the ways in which they come to hold those points of view was emphasized. The guidelines for implementing and interpreting classroom-based assessment will help teachers to evaluate children's learning and to consider how subsequent instruction can help children reach their potential.

SUGGESTED RESOURCES

General References

Principles for fair student assessment practices for education in Canada (1993). Edmonton, Alberta: Joint Advisory Committee. This publication covers issues to consider in order to ensure that all students are assessed fairly. A range of assessment methods are covered, including norm-referenced testing and classroom-based methods. Interpretation and reporting guidelines also are given. Available from:

Joint Advisory Committee
Centre for Research in Applied Measurement and Evaluation
3–104 Education Building North
University of Alberta
Edmonton, AB T6G 2G5

Eyde, L.D., Robertson, G.J., Krug, S.E., Moreland, K.L., Robertson, A.G., Shewan, C.M., Harrison, P.L., Porch, B.E., Hammer, A.L., & Primoff, E.S. (1993). *Responsible test use: Case studies for assessing human behavior.* Washington, DC: American Psychological Association. This book presents case studies focused on interpretation of assessment data. Implications for instruction are discussed.

Performance Assessment

Brownlie, F., Close, S., & Wingren, L. (1990). *Tomorrow's classroom today. Strategies for creating active readers, writers, and thinkers.* Markham, ON: Pembroke Publishers. This book presents numerous strategies for instruction that helps to reveal students' thinking processes. Assignments that allow students to demonstrate knowledge in a variety of ways are emphasized. Sample lessons and examples of students' work are included.

Portfolio Assessment

Gardner, H. (1993). *Multiple intelligences: The theory in practice.* New York: Basic Books. This book discusses the philosophy behind portfolio and process-folio assessment and gives examples of how to implement these types of assessment.

Kallick, B. (1993). Portfolio assessment. *The Video Journal of Education, 3* (4). Videotape Program 1: Reflections of learning. Videotape Program 2: Utilizing portfolios. These videotapes provide useful guidelines on implementing and managing portfolio assessment across different subject areas. Student, teacher, and parent comments on using portfolios are included as well as many examples of student work. Available from:

The Video Journal of Education
Salt Lake City, UT
1-800-572-1153

Observation

Braun, C. (1993). *Looking, listening, and learning. Observing and assessing young readers*. Winnipeg: Pegius Publishers. Practical suggestions for assessment and instruction are included as well as guidelines for teacher and student self-reflection.

Good, T.L., & Brophy, J.E. (1987). *Looking in classrooms* (4th edition). New York: Harper and Row. This book includes examples of observation systems and provides guidelines for teacher observation of classroom activities including how to deal with possible bias in observation. Examples of observations are followed by practical, well-informed suggestions for how to use the results to inform instruction and classroom management.

Krechevsky, M. (1994). *Project spectrum: Preschool assessment handbook*. Cambridge, MA: President and Fellows of Harvard College. While this handbook focuses on preschool, the assessment tools would be useful for primary grades and some of the checklists could be adapted for intermediate grades. Assessment across all the curricular areas and the social domain is covered and guidelines for determining children's working styles are included. Available from:

Harvard Project Zero
Graduate School of Education
Cambridge, MA 02138

Curriculum Compacting

Reis, S.M., Burns, D.E., & Renzulli, J.S. (1992). *Curriculum compacting: A guide for teachers*. Available from:

NRC/GT
The University of Connecticut
362 Fairfield Road, U-7
Storrs, CT 06269-2007

REFERENCES

Arlin, P.K. [University of British Columbia] The constructive classroom (1995). Draft book in preparation.

Baker, E.L., O'Neil, H.F., & Linn, R.L. (1993). Policy and validity prospects for performance-based assessment. *American Psychologist, 48,* 1210–18.

Biemiller, A. (1993). Lake Wobegon revisited: On diversity and education. *Educational Researcher, 22*(9), 7–12.

Biemiller, A., & Meichenbaum, D. (1992). The nature and nurture of the self-directed learner. *Educational Leadership, 50*(2), 75–80.

Brandt, R. (1987–88). On assessment in the arts: A conversation with Howard Gardner. *Educational Leadership, 45,* 30–34.

Brownlie, F., Close, S., & Wingren, L. (1990). *Tomorrow's classroom today. Strategies for creating active readers, writers, and thinkers.* Markham, ON: Pembroke Publishers.

Case, R. (1991). A developmental approach to the design of remedial instruction. In A. McKeough & J.L. Lupart (Eds.), *Toward the practice of a theory-based instruction: Current cognitive theories and their educational promise* (pp. 117–47). Hillsdale, NJ: Lawrence Erlbaum.

Case, R. (1992). *The mind's staircase: Exploring the conceptual underpinnings of children's thought and knowledge.* Hillsdale, NJ: Lawrence Erlbaum.

Case, R., Sandieson, R., & Dennis, S. (1986). Two cognitive-developmental approaches to the design of remedial instruction. *Cognitive Development, 1,* 293–333.

Davis, G.A., & Rimm., S.B. (1989). *Education of the gifted and talented.* Englewood Cliffs, NJ: Prentice Hall.

Day, J.D., & Hall, L.K. (1987). Cognitive assessment, intelligence, and instruction. In J.D. Day & J.G. Borkowski (Eds.), *Intelligence and exceptionality: New directions for theory, assessment, and instructional practices* (pp. 57–80). Norwood, NJ: Ablex Publishing Corp.

Donaldson, M. (1979). The mismatch between school and children's minds. *Human Nature,* March, 155–59.

Duckworth, E. (1987). *"The having of wonderful ideas" and other essays on teaching and learning.* New York: Teachers College Press.

Fischer, K.W., Bullock, D.H., Rotenberg, E.J., & Raya, P. (1993). The dynamics of competence: How context contributes directly to skill. In R.H. Wozniak & K.W. Fischer (Eds.), *Development in context: Acting and thinking in specific environments* (pp. 93–117). Hillsdale, NJ: Lawrence Erlbaum.

Floden, R.E. (1994). Reshaping assessment concepts. *Educational Researcher, 23*(2), 4.

Gardner, H. (1991). *The unschooled mind: How children think and how schools should teach.* New York: Basic Books.

Gardner, H. (1993). *Multiple intelligences: The theory in practice.* New York: Basic Books.

Gardner, H., & Hatch, T. (1989). Multiple intelligences go to school: Educational implications of the theory of multiple intelligences. *Educational Researcher, 18*(8), 4–10.

Good, T.L., & Brophy, J.E. (1987). *Looking in classrooms* (4th edition). New York: Harper and Row.

Halsted, J.W. (1988). *Guiding gifted readers from preschool to high school.* Columbus, OH: Ohio Psychology Publishing Co.

Hauser, P., & Nelson, G.A. (1988). *Books for the gifted child.* New York: R.R. Bowker Co.

Hieronymous, A.N., Lindquist, E.F., Hoover, H.D., & King-Shaw, E.M. (1990). *Canadian test of basic skills.* Toronto: Nelson Canada.

Keating, D.P. (1975). Testing those in the top percentiles. *Exceptional Children, 41,* 435–36.

Keating, D.P. (1991). Curriculum options for the developmentally advanced: A developmental alternative to gifted education. *Exceptionality Education Canada, 1,* 53–84.

Lohman, D.F. (1993). Teaching and testing to develop fluid abilities. *Educational Researcher, 22*(7), 12–23.

Matthews, D. (1994, March). *Program planning: Providing a range of options to address individual needs.* Paper presented at the National Association of School Psychologists Conference, Seattle, WA.

Matthews, D. (in press). Beyond identification: Toward assessing developmental advancement by domain. In F.D. Horowitz & R.C. Friedman (Eds.), *The gifted and talented: Theories and reviews. Vol. II.* Washington, DC: American Psychological Association.

McKee, W.T. (1994, March). *Looking for gifts in all the right places: Innovations in identification and assessment practices for school psychologists.* Paper presented at the National Association of School Psychologists Conference, Seattle, WA.

McKeough, A. (1992). Testing for the presence of a central social structure: Use of the transfer paradigm. In R. Case, *The mind's staircase: Exploring the conceptual underpinning of children's thought and knowledge* (pp. 207–25). Hillsdale, NJ: Lawrence Erlbaum.

Moss, P.A. (1994). Can there be validity without reliability? *Educational Researcher, 23*(2), 5–12.

Paley, V.G. (1981). *Wally's stories.* Cambridge, MA: Harvard University Press.

Paley, V.G. (1986). On listening to what the children say. *Harvard Educational Review, 56,* 122–31.

Pea, R.D. (1993). Learning scientific concepts through material and social activities. Conversational analysis meets conceptual change. *Educational Psychologist, 28,* 265–77.

Peterson, P.L. (1993). Toward an understanding of what we know about school learning. *Review of Educational Research, 63,* 319–26.

Porath, M. (1992). Stage and structure in the development of children with various types of "giftedness." In R. Case, *The mind's staircase: Exploring the conceptual underpinnings of children's thought and knowledge* (pp. 303–17). Hillsdale, NJ: Lawrence Erlbaum.

Reis, S.M., & Renzulli, J.S. (1992). Using curriculum compacting to challenge the above-average. *Educational Leadership, 50*(2), 51–57.

Reis, S.M., Burns, D.E., & Renzulli, J.S. (1992). *Curriculum compacting: A guide for teachers.* University of Connecticut: The National Research Center on the Gifted and Talented.

Sattler, J.M. (1992). *Assessment of children* (3rd edition). San Diego: Jerome M. Sattler, Publisher, Inc.

Shapiro, E.S. (1989). *Academic skills problems: Direct assessment and intervention.* New York: The Guilford Press.

Shapiro, E.S., & Lentz, F.E. (1985). Assessing academic behavior: A behavioral approach. *School Psychology Review, 14,* 325–38.

Shapiro, E.S., & Lentz, F.E. (1988). Behavioral assessment of academic skills. In T.R. Kratochwill (Ed.), *Advances in school psychology. Vol. 5* (pp. 87–139). Hillsdale, NJ: Lawrence Erlbaum.

Slavin, R.E. (1994). *Educational psychology: Theory and practice.* Boston: Allyn and Bacon.

Watson, B., & Konicek, R. (1990). Teaching for conceptual change: Confronting children's experience. *Phi Delta Kappan,* May, 680–85.

Wolf, D.P. (1987–88). Opening up assessment. *Educational Leadership, 45,* 24–29.

Wright, E.N., Thorndike, R.L., & Hagen, E.P. (1988). *Canadian cognitive abilities test.* Toronto: Nelson Canada.

Ysseldyke, J.E., Algozzine, B., & Thurlow, M.L. (1992). *Critical issues in special education.* Boston: Houghton Mifflin.

Holistic Program Planning: Adapting Curriculum and Instruction for Elementary Students

Rick Freeze

University of Manitoba

Introduction

The goal of holistic program planning is to provide learning environments where all students can learn safely, comfortably, and successfully. The teacher's role in holistic program planning is to interpret and adapt curriculum requirements so that instructional methods are matched with the cognitive, behavioural, social, cultural, physical, emotional, and developmental needs and abilities of the students they teach. Moreover, holistic program planning involves an orientation to instruction that is inclusive, facilitated, active, child centred, multifaceted, and cooperative.

These two sets of ideas are explored briefly in the following section. Two examples of holistic program planning and instruction are presented in the second section of the chapter. The first exemplar is a grade 5 Language Arts unit on the biography. The second exemplar is a cross-disciplinary approach to teaching numbers at the grade-2 level. Some generalizations and conclusions about holistic program planning and instruction are presented in the final section of this chapter.

◈ Holistic Program Planning

Variables in Learning

In the past, many educators believed that teaching was primarily an act of presentation, and learning was chiefly an act of acquisition. Consequently, teachers were mostly concerned with the selection and organization of what should be presented and the measurement of how much content knowledge the student had acquired. There were many problems with this understanding of teaching and learning. Sensitive educators realized that much of what they were presenting was going over the heads of their low achievers and failing to challenge their most able students. Their conclusion: not enough attention was being paid to students' prior knowledge and the cognitive strategies they used, or failed to use, to process the content being presented (Andrews & Lupart, 1993). In addition, many teachers came to realize that misbehaviour often represented more than wilful misconduct. For some students, it was an expression of their frustrations with academic and conduct expectations for which they were inadequately prepared (Freeze, 1989).

With this understanding, educators began to focus on behavioural interventions that went far beyond the goal of securing classroom control. Their focus shifted to building the classroom climate, routines, and rules that lead to cooperative work and play, to helping students gain an understanding of their misbehaviour, and to teaching self-control and self-management skills. Educators noted that students who were socially isolated, disdained, or teased by their peers tended to become preoccupied with the need to belong at the expense of their learning (Charles, 1992). By contrast, student achievement improved when peer relationships were positive, supportive, and cooperative throughout the class (Jones & Jones, 1986). The cultural dimension of learning also has come to be better understood in recent years. Educators now are more aware that knowledge, skills, and understanding are constructed in different ways within the different cultural frameworks of their students (Crealock & Bachor, 1995). Understanding the importance of the classroom as a physical environment also has gained prominence in the last few decades. Many schools have moved to make classrooms more accessible, more flexible and more comfortable. In addition, new technologies have made learning more accessible to some students by partially compensating for their disabilities. The relationship between the emotional and cognitive dimensions of learning also has become better understood (Crealock & Bachor, 1995; Phillips, 1992). Modern educators understand that meeting students' needs for safety, belonging, responsibility, fun, freedom, and self-actualization must be combined with effective instruction to obtain high student achievement (Glasser, 1990). Finally, the importance of considering developmental factors in curriculum design and instruction has been accepted by contemporary educators (Seifert, 1991). Perceptive teachers know there is a wide band of variability in how students of the same age have matured physically, cognitively, socially, and morally. As a result, they provide learning opportunities for students at different stages of development.

Elements of Instruction

Holistic program planning involves more than attention to cognitive, behavioural, social, cultural, physical, emotional, and developmental variables in the interpretation and adaptation of curriculum and the design of instruction. Holistic program planning also involves a particular orientation to the instructional process that places great emphasis on six elements.

1. An inclusive philosophy in which student diversity is accepted and celebrated.

2. The creation of an open classroom where student learning is facilitated by parents, older student tutors, volunteers, mentors, and the in-class participation of support personnel such as teaching assistants, special educators, and counsellors working in collaboration with the classroom teacher.

3. An active instructional milieu in which students discover and construct knowledge on their own terms and are encouraged to self-regulate their own behaviour and learning.

4. The commitment to a child-centred approach to instruction that builds on students' prior knowledge, interests, and preferred learning styles.

5. A multifaceted instruction characterized by individualization, differentiation, adaptation, and variety.

6. The belief that learning occurs most productively through cooperative tasks that link essential facts acquisition, conceptual understanding, proficiency with process skills and the ability to make accurate, constructive self-evaluations.

Put concisely, holistic program planning involves two sets of ideas. First, the variables in how children learn, including the cognitive, behavioural, social, cultural, physical, emotional and developmental aspects of their learning. Second, the elements of how children are taught, with an orientation to instruction that is inclusive, facilitated, active, child centred, multifaceted, and cooperative.

To understand how elementary teachers are able to weave these diverse learning variables and instructional elements into a coherent program, let us visit two classes where teachers are practising holistic program planning and instruction. In the first class, the teacher's planning is described in terms of the learning variables each instructional element addresses.

◈ Two Case Studies

Grade 5 Language Arts: The Biography

Mr. K's class was smaller than the one he had taught last year. His school had a policy of reducing class sizes if students with special needs were coincidentally in the group. This year, Mr. K had 24 students. One student was hard of hearing. While she had hearing aids, she often could not use them due to chronic ear infections. She was going through a difficult year of transition because she and her hearing parents recently had switched from the oral approach (which stressed oral and auditory training, speech reading, and cued speech) to a total communications program with a new emphasis on the manual approach (which stresses American Sign Language or ASL). As a result, she and her parents were adjusting to a new language and to their initial contacts with the deaf community. Another student in Mr. K's class had Down's Syndrome. Due to the school's longstanding policy of inclusion, he had grown up with his classmates and was accepted by them. Academically, he was slightly below the expectations for grade 5. Nevertheless, he was a responsible and diligent student who was capable of grade-level work if his learning needs were met. With respect to writing, there also were three low achievers in the class. All three students were below average with respect to their reading fluency, sight vocabulary and reading comprehension. However, they were good listeners and talkers; especially with their peers and on topics other than those initiated by the teacher. The remaining 19 students represented the diversity that Mr. K had come to expect in over a decade of teaching.

Mr. K began program planning by using the Holistic Program Planning matrix represented in Figure 5.1. He jotted down ideas that he might use in his grade 5 Biography unit at the intersection of each learning variable and instructional element in the matrix.

Cognitive Instruction

Since this was his students' first formal introduction to biography, he decided to use direct instruction (see Freeze, 1989; Mercer & Mercer, 1989) to teach the biography format and the thinking and writing process he wished his students to learn. He chose direct instruction as a method because of the structure, modelling, and practice it would provide to the whole class, inclusive of his students with special needs. Mr. K's application of the seven steps in the direct instruction approach is summarized in Appendix 5A.

FIGURE 5.1
Holistic Program Planning: Grade 5 Biography

	Instruction Is...		
Learning Is...	**Inclusive**	**Facilitated**	**Active**
Cognitive	Direct Instruction	In-class Library Book Reports	Biographical Data Posters USSR
Behavioural	Group Rewards Class Meetings	Participation Checks Signal Direction	Self-Management
Social	Peer Conferencing	Study Buddy	Triple Pass
Cultural	Family Trees	Family Interviews Home Reading	Games of Other Cultures
Physical	Adaptive Technology and Materials	Communications Consultant	Interactive CD-ROM books
Emotional	Interest Inventory	Guests	Guest Receptions
Developmental	Task Analysis Chaining	Librarian Resource Teacher	Teacher Assistance Support

	Instruction Is...		
Learning Is...	**Child Centred**	**Multifaceted**	**Cooperative**
Cognitive	Annotated Model Biographies	Biography Portfolio	Peer Evaluation Checklist
Behavioural	Individual Recognition	Rewards Menu	Good Behaviour Game
Social	Authors' Chair	Book Report Displays	Cooperative Learning Groups

Cultural	Family Artifacts Show and Tell	Culturally Diverse Biographies	Choose A Culture
Physical	Private Work Areas	Computer Work Station	Family Night Presentation
Emotional	Student of the Week	Future Bio-data Project	Biographical Art, Song, and Dance
Developmental	Pre-Teach and Review	Repeated Reading Semantic Webbing	Mixed-Ability Groups

However, prior to teaching them how to write biographies, he decided to provide opportunities for them to read biographies. In consultation with the school librarian, he built an in-class library of biographies suited to the range of reading levels in his class and designed to facilitate their interest in biographies. Since all classes in the school have a period of Uninterrupted Sustained Silent Reading (USSR) every day (Tierney, Readence & Dishner, 1990) he decided to encourage his students to read biographies from the in-class library during USSR. In addition, he planned to assign daily home reading to be monitored by parents and linked to monthly book reports.

In order to help his students become actively involved in collecting information and relating the different elements of a biography, he intended to have them create posters of biographical data about the characters they were going to write about. The posters would be organized to relate the time line, setting, achievements, personality growth, and significant others in the highlighted parts of each character's life. A partially completed poster is illustrated in Appendix 5A.1. On display, the posters would act as models of the research data-gathering process for all students. Mr. K also had some annotated model biographies to post in the classroom and to give to students to guide their individual efforts.

Mr. K knew that there were many steps in the biography writing process: a) selecting a character to write about, b) finding sources and collecting biographical data, c) making an outline, d) composing a first draft, e) sharing the draft to obtain constructive feedback, f) editing and revising, g) writing a final draft, and h) publishing the biography. To help students organize and safeguard the various facets of their work, Mr. K decided to create a biography portfolio for each student to be kept in the class. He decided each portfolio would contain an evaluation checklist students could use to evaluate the work of their peers in cooperative groups and for teacher feedback) (see Appendix 5A.2).

Behavioural Management

Mr. K. knew that successful learning for his grade 5's could only take place if the class was well disciplined. He decided to base his behaviour management approach on three principles:

- Student participation in developing class behavioural expectations

- Student self-management in meeting those expectations

- Individual recognition and group rewards for good behaviour

Mr. K planned to hold a class meeting early in the year to develop some class-room rules including consequences for individuals and a menu of rewards for the class as a group. At the meeting, he intended to introduce the signal direction system he would use during the year to direct classroom behaviour. Signal direction involves hand signals, rather than spoken commands, to direct student behaviour (Freeze, 1989). In order to help his students cooperate in understanding the rules and earning rewards, he planned to play the Good Behaviour Game once a week. In the good behaviour game, each student is asked to quickly write down one good thing someone in the class did for him or her, one good thing he or she did for a classmate, and one good thing they saw a classmate do for another class-mate. After a few minutes, the teacher collects all the papers and reads out a few to the class. Each student can earn up to three points, one point for each good thing they wrote down. When the class total reaches 500, the whole class votes for a group reward from the rewards menu (e.g., popcorn party, learning games day, special guest, etc.). Students, in groups or individually, also can earn participation check points all week long. Whenever the teacher "catches" them doing good work he gives them a participation check. As much as possible, Mr. K planned to have the students record and graph the points they earn as a group.

Social Relations

To facilitate learning as a cooperative social experience, Mr. K planned to divide his class into six mixed-ability cooperative learning groups of four. He planned to teach them a general approach to cooperative learning and the roles they would be asked to play in the group (Freeze, 1989). As a first activity, the groups would work on creating the biographical data posters. Once the groups were up and running, he intended to introduce peer-author conferences and an author's chair. At a peer-author conference, the author is present while a peer reads and discusses the student-author's work with other students. In the case of the author's chair, the student author reads his or her own work and leads a discussion of it.

To assist students in making peer and self-evaluations Mr. K planned to teach them to use the Biography Evaluation Checklist (Appendix 5A.2) and the Triple

Pass proofreading strategy. The triple pass strategy involves the evaluator in three repeated readings of another's biography to check for ideas on the first pass; spelling, capitalization, and punctuation on the second pass; and organization, sentence structure, and paragraphing on the third pass. He hoped also to pair students as study buddies who would work on book report displays based on the biographies assigned for home reading.

Cultural Relevance

Mr. K was aware that there were students with a variety of cultural heritages in his class. He decided to use this diversity as a resource for developing his students' biographical research skills. In an effort to make his instructional activities child centred, he resolved to involve his students in constructing their own family trees going back three generations based on interviews with their parents and other family members.

Physical Supports

To assist the hard of hearing student, Mr. K had already been working with the resource teacher, a teaching assistant, and the divisional alternative communications consultant. He had been promised some adaptive technology, special materials, and personnel support for the upcoming year. The adaptive technology included a computer and speech synthesizer for writing and speaking, an FM transmission device and receiver for teacher-to-student oral communication, and an overhead projector and screen to provide visual cues with oral instruction. The special materials (Smith, Luckasson & Crealock, 1995; Crealock & Bachor, 1995) included the Multimedia Dictionary of American Sign Language, which allows the user to see a video clip of a signed word, captioned video "books" and interactive CD-ROM "books" for the in-class library and software designed to enhance reading fluency and comprehension. The personnel supports included the part-time availability of a teaching assistant fluent in ASL and the ongoing support of the communications consultant throughout the year. The teaching assistant agreed to pre-teach and review the biography unit on days when new concepts or routines were being introduced. The communications consultant agreed to meet with Mr. K and the parents to plan some home and community activities designed to help their hard of hearing daughter adjust to the change in her communications program. In particular, Mr. K hoped to involve the parents in helping their daughter develop and lead an informative family night presentation on alternative communications for the entire school. Mr. K planned to ask the parents and student to meet with him early in the year to seek their advice and familiarize them with the resources available.

Mr. K planned to create some other resources in his classroom including a computer work station and a quiet private work area. He hoped that these supports would provide options for students who needed alternatives to engage them in reading and writing. He also intended to use the CD-ROM books and the reading skills software with his low achievers.

Emotional Engagement

Mr. K knew that his students might need some motivation to get them engaged in reading and writing biographies. Consequently, he planned to invite some interesting guests to share their life stories. He also thought to engage the students at a personal level. He conceived a future bio-data project in which students would write imaginary futures for their lives containing the key elements of the biographical format. Each student's future biography would be presented along with his or her family tree and history during his or her turn as "student of the week." Finally, Mr. K decided to use interest inventories to help guide students in the selection of reading materials and biography characters to write about.

Developmental Adaptations

Several students in Mr. K's class needed individualized interventions with respect to reading and writing. He knew some of the strategies he would use for the whole class would benefit his low achievers (e.g., direct instruction, annotated model biographies, mixed-ability groups, study buddy, computer work station and software). However, he knew they would need continued academic support throughout the year if they were to become competent and confident learners. He met with the resource teacher and teaching assistant to design some additional academic supports for his low achievers. The resource teacher agreed to develop a daily precision teaching program based on repeated readings (Freeze, 1989) and a semantic webbing approach to teaching vocabulary and preparing book reports (Crealock & Bachor, 1995).

The precision teaching approach to repeated readings involves short daily repeated readings of the same materials until the assured speed and accuracy are dramatically improved and errors reduced to near zero. Semantic webbing illustrates the meaningful relationships between words by linking them diagramatically.

It was agreed that the materials for these activities would be drawn from books used in the classroom and the lessons would be taught in the classroom and available to all students who wished to improve their skills. Regular sessions with the communications consultant were established for the hard of hearing student. Additional instruction for the student with Down's Syndrome also was planned. The resource teacher promised to complete a task analysis (Smith, Luckasson &

Crealock, 1995) of the biography unit and then to use a "chaining" strategy to link the tasks together through positive reinforcement. Task analysis involves the breaking down of a task into small sequential steps that are then taught separately. After all the steps are mastered separately, they are linked together through additional instruction until the complete task is mastered as a chain of linked steps. The links in the chain of biography writing might include choosing a character, collecting information about the character, constructing a timeline, constructing a biography outline, writing a draft, conferencing to make improvements, making revisions, and publishing.

Epilogue

While Mr. K's holistic program plan may seem complicated, it included many strategies with which he was already familiar and put him in contact with the support personnel who could help him to make the year a success for all the students in his class. Nevertheless, he worried about the extra work and stress involved: learning about the voice synthesizer, getting used to the FM transmitter, meeting regularly with the teaching assistant and resource teacher. As a result he decided to approach a teacher at his school who was a friend and a technology buff. After the meeting, Mr. K felt relieved. His friend had agreed to help him with the new technology and had assured him that he would be available as an informal adviser throughout the year. Mr. K looked over his plan. Only one thing was missing: he decided to enrol in a summer course in American Sign Language.

Grade-2 Math: Number Concepts

In the second class, the teacher's planning is described in terms of the instructional elements that meet the learning needs of her students. Ms. D's class has 29 students. Although one student in her class is visually impaired, the kindergarten and grade-1 teachers already had trained him to use some adaptive technology, and he had kept up with the top students in the class academically. Ms. D also has an English as a Second Language (ESL) student in her class who is new to Canada and very shy. Ms. D's greatest concern is with four students from socially disadvantaged backgrounds. All are new to her school and none had completed a full year at their previous schools. One had received very positive evaluations in grade 1, at his previous school, but had changed his foster home placement recently. According to their files, the other three had records of poor attendance, low achievement, negligent parenting, and inappropriate behaviour. As a member of the Early Years Team at her school, Ms. D often met with the other kindergarten to grade-3 teachers to coordinate activities, sequence instruction, and focus on problem solving with respect to individual students. As a result, the remaining 24 students, who had come to Ms. D from the school's grade-1 program, were known to her. Like Mr. K, Ms. D began program planning by using the matrix represented in Figure 5.2.

FIGURE 5.2
Holistic Program Planning: Grade 2 Numbers

	Instruction Is...		
Learning Is...	Inclusive	Facilitated	Active
Cognitive	Precision Teaching	Parent Volunteer Support	Base Ten Blocks
Behavioural	Classroom Routines	Work Award Stickers	Activity Clock
Social	Choral Number Recognition	Cross-Grade Tutors	Math Activities Centre
Cultural	Braille Numbers	CNIB	Decorator Numbers
Physical	Adaptive Technology	Classroom Arrangement	Orientation and Mobility Training
Emotional	Home-School Partnership	Counsellor Teaching Assistant	Number Games
Developmental	Preview and Review	Consultant Support	Conceptual Prerequisites Activities

	Instruction Is...		
Learning Is...	Child Centred	Multifaceted	Cooperative
Cognitive	Number Stories	Multimodal Instruction	Problem-Solving Teams
Behavioural	Sticker Books	Sticker Store	Class Calendar
Social	Personal Numbers	Number Bingo	Group Number Puzzles

Cultural	Number Songs	Numbers in Different Languages	Number Books
Physical	Number Models	Number Line	Class Numbers
Emotional	Number Collections	Multimedia	Personal Numbers
Developmental	Number Experiences	Indefinite Number Concepts	Counting, Matching, and Memory Games

Cognitive Instruction

Ms. D knows that young children need to actively build numbers with base 10 blocks and other manipulatives in order to understand them. In addition, she knows they need to be able to say, read, and write numerals, visualize the number sets the numerals represent, and tell number stories that describe the everyday world. Ms. D built an important part of her classroom math program around three instructional ideas:

- Math activity centres

- Multimodal instruction

- Parent volunteers

Ms. D assigned two of her parent volunteers to the math activity centre and showed them how to mediate student learning using Cawley's (1985) multimodal instruction Cawley's approach involves the adult facilitator in displaying, building, saying, or writing a number so the student can identify, build, name, or write it in their turn. For example, the parent volunteer might say "seven" and ask the student to build it with blocks (say–build) or they might build seven for the student and ask the student to name it (build–name). In total, there are 16 combinations that address student learning at the concrete, representative, and abstract levels (Crealock & Bachor, 1995) in the multimodal approach.

To ensure student mastery of number–numeral correspondence, Ms. D developed a series of daily precision teaching (Freeze, 1989) activities. In precision teaching, the same one-minute activity is repeated daily for 7 to 10 days so that students gain automaticity (high speed and 100% accuracy) for their number–numeral facts. The correct responses and errors are graphed to measure and motivate individual achievement. Once the students are able to complete the activity quickly and without error, it is replaced by a second activity and the process is repeated for a new set of facts. The first page of a precision-teaching activity for number–numeral facts is shown in Appendix 5A.3.

Ms. D knew that her students also had to apply their understanding of number to everyday situations. To help them, she divided them into mixed-ability problem-solving teams that had to find examples of various numbers in a picture or story and who had to write personal number stories for homework. So, for example, the team assigned the number 4, would find as many sets of 4 as they could in a picture (4 wheels on the car, 4 clouds in the sky, 4 people in the picture, etc.) and write number stories about 4 in their own lives.

Behavioural Management

As much as possible, Ms. D designed her classroom routines around learning about numbers. She had an activity clock that showed daily activities next to times on the clock and a class calendar that highlighted daily, weekly, monthly, and annual events. A student timekeeper changed the activity clock with each transition during the day and the calendar also was updated by a different student each day. Other aspects of behaviour management also were linked to number concepts. In Mrs. D's class, students were awarded stickers for participation, correct work and good behaviour.

Social Relations

Aside from the math activities centre, Ms. D had several other strategies that encouraged students to work together. Three of these strategies were seen as games by the children: number bingo, choral number recognition, and group number puzzles. Number bingo requires students to accurately identify the numerals on their bingo cards. In choral number recognition, the teacher displays a picture of a number set (e.g., a collection of dots) and the class calls out the number as soon as they recognize it. Group number puzzles involve jigsaw puzzles that reveal a number when solved. They are solved by a cooperative team in competition with the other teams in the class. Ms. D involved cross-grade tutors from grade 6 in her math program each year. They facilitated her students' learning at the math activity centre and during the group problem-solving activities.

Cultural Relevance

Mathematics is a bridge to the world culture. Nevertheless, numbers have been understood and represented in different ways around the world. Ms. D decided to include number books, video clips, and number songs from different cultures in her in-class library of reading, viewing, and listening materials. Each cooperative group, for example, would learn to count to 10 in a different language. As well, the students would learn different ways to write numbers from different cultures and then would decorate their numbers as an art project called "decorator numbers." She intended to have all of her students learn Braille numbers so they could relate to their visually impaired peer.

Physical Supports

Appropriate adaptive technology for Ms. D's visually impaired student had already been secured by the school. A Xerox-Kurzweil PC with a scanner, page sensor, and Braille printer had been provided the year before to turn print into synthesized speech and Braille documents. Also, he had a variety of magnification devices and an electronic cane. With the help of the divisional visual consultant and the Canadian National Institute for the Blind (CNIB) the student would continue to receive orientation and mobility training at school.

Emotional Engagement

Over the years as an Early-Years teacher, Ms. D had designed several activities to engage her students in thinking and learning about numbers. This year, she planned to develop personal numbers (age, house number, number in family, number of pets, etc.) and then to collect them to develop a series of class numbers. In addition, she intended to invite students to bring collections (e.g., rocks, shells, troll dolls, sports hats, etc.) to school and to count the number in each collection. Finally, she hoped to introduce her class to computers and other multimedia technology using number games such as *Exploring Measurement, Time and Money* (Eduquest/IBM) or *Conquering Whole Numbers* (MECC).

To help meet the needs of her socially disadvantaged students, she planned to have the school counsellor meet with them weekly to talk about feelings, set behavioural goals, and to teach behavioural management. In addition, she planned to have a teaching assistant meet with them daily to *preview* upcoming instruction and *review* important concepts, tasks, and accomplishments. Ms. D decided to contact their parents on a weekly basis with positive anecdotes about their participation and behaviour to be proactive in creating the basis for a positive home-school partnership. Eventually, she hoped to invite their parents into the classroom as guests or volunteers.

Developmental Adaptations

To meet the needs of her low achievers, Ms. D planned to provide supportive instruction in the conceptual prerequisites to understanding numbers. These activities would be carried out at a centre during class time by the teaching assistant and would be open to all students. They would include activities to help students recognize numbers independently of the colour, size, shape, arrangement, or function of the things in the number sets. A variety of tactile number experiences also would be provided including counting, matching, and memory games. Indefinite number concepts (e.g., many, a few, some, most, etc.) also would be introduced through experiential activities.

Epilogue

Ms. D's planning had helped her to identify the people she needed to recruit to make her program successful for all her students. As well, it had helped her to choose the instructional strategies best suited to the learning needs of her students. She was especially pleased that many of the supports she had built up over the years (such as her parent volunteer program, the cross-grade tutoring arrangement with a grade-6 teacher, a good relationship with the school counsellor, and her competency with computer technology) would be paying big dividends again this year.

◈ Conclusion

In this chapter, a holistic program planning matrix has been introduced and two exemplars of its use have been explored. Several important themes relevant to elementary education emerge from this discussion. First, many of the instructional strategies highlighted in this chapter can be applied across the curriculum at any elementary grade level. Teaching strategies such as direct instruction, precision teaching, or multimodal instruction can be used whenever factual knowledge acquisition is an important objective. Organizational strategies such as mixed-ability cooperative learning groups, peer conferencing, peer tutoring, and study buddies can be used to engage students in shared work in any subject area. Adaptive technologies can be used to benefit disabled and nondisabled students who need multifaceted instruction. Strategies such as interest inventories, signal direction, participation checks, and student peer- and self-evaluation checklists can be adapted to any grade level or subject area.

Second, the recruitment of parents, student tutors, volunteers, and professional colleagues to work in the classroom are options available in most Canadian elementary schools. Holistic program planning requires professional educators who are open to consulting with others to obtain the information they need and to working with others, inside and outside their classrooms, to arrange the supports their students need (see also Chapter 3).

Third, holistic program planning is a way of thinking about the teaching endeavour. In a real sense, it is planning that translates learning theory into instructional practice by thinking about the variables that affect learning and teaching in a comprehensive and integrated way.

Finally, it is educators who develop the flexibility and creativity to adapt instructional methods, materials, and technologies in a continuing process of professional innovation and personal commitment to their students who will be the force in education as we cross the threshold of a new millennium.

APPENDIX 5A

Direct Instruction Applied to Writing a Biography

Steps	Application
1. Diagnose	A short quiz to assess students' prior experience and knowledge about reading and writing biographies.
2. Describe	Biography defined as the history of the life and character of an interesting person with the significant events of his or her life highlighted. Five elements of a biography explained: timeline, setting(s) of event(s), achievements, personality, significant others.
3. Model	Teacher demonstrates all the steps of writing a biography: a) completing interest inventory and brainstorming to choose a character, b) finding sources in the library, c) collecting biographical information on the five elements of a biography from the sources, d) making an outline, e) composing a first draft, f) conferencing with the teacher or a peer, g) editing and revising, h) composing a final copy, and i) publishing.
4. Copy 5. Practise	The students copy and practise the procedure modelled by the teacher as they complete their interest inventory, do library research, build posters, make outlines, and compose and revise their biographies.
6. Monitor	The teacher monitors the students by regularly reviewing their portfolios, conducting participation checks for group work, conferencing with students, evaluating book reports and posters, and mediating peer and self-evaluations.
7. Generalization	The students complete biographies independently.

APPENDIX 5A.1

Biographical Data Poster: Michelangelo

Time Line	Setting	Achievement	Personality Development	Significant Others
1475	Florence	birth	—	parents
1504	Florence	"David" -statue -biblical story	fame	patrons
1508–12	Rome	"Sistine Chapel" -ceiling difficult -self-portrait hidden in "Last Judgment"	conflict artistic independence	Pope Julius II

APPENDIX 5A.2

Biography Evaluation Checklist

Element	Evaluation
Introduction	
1. Written about a real character	
2. Character comes alive (anecdotes, quotes, etc.)	
3. Background information about character (birth, childhood, important early events, etc.)	
4. Writer states important issue(s) of character's life	

Biography Evaluation Checklist *(cont.)*	
Element	Evaluation
Time Line	
5. Constructed around a time line	
6. Sequence of events clear	
7. Significant events and times highlighted	
Setting	
8. Setting(s) detailed	
9. Setting(s) related to time line	
Achievements	
10. Focus on character's achievement(s)	
11. Achievement(s) noteworthy	
12. Factors enabling achievement(s) described	
13. Setting(s) for achievement(s) described	
14. Facts are accurate	
15. Quotations are accurate	
Personality	
16. Personality traits revealed	
17. "Drive" leading to achievement(s) revealed	
18. Achievement and personality development revealed	
Significant Others	
19. Influence related to personality development of character	
20. Influence related to achievement(s) of character	
21. Influence related to highlighted time line events	
Conclusion	
22. Lasting significance of character's achievement(s)	

Biography Evaluation Checklist *(cont.)*	
Element	Evaluation
23. Comment on important issues of character's life	
24. Final significance of achievement(s) to character	
Writing Process	
25. Activities to choose a character to write about	
26. Library search	
27. Biographical data poster	
28. Outline	
29. First draft	
30. Peer-editing conference	
31. Self-evaluation and revision	
32. Final copy	
33. Proofreading and publication	
TOTAL	

Source: Adapted from O.B. Toews & D.R. Freeze. *Writing Assessment: Grades 4–9* (Winnipeg, MB: River East School Division, 1992).

APPENDIX 5A.3

Precision Teaching Number Facts Activity

Directions: Circle the correct answers as quickly and accurately as you can. You have one minute.

• •
• •   2   5   9   (6)   4
• •

Precision Teaching Number Facts Activity (cont.)

• • • • • • • • •	2	5	9	6	4
• • • •	2	5	9	6	4
• • • • •	2	5	9	6	4
• •	2	5	9	6	4

Note: Normally students would be given 60 questions of this type for a one-minute activity.

SUGGESTED RESOURCES

Multi-Media Technology

Exploring Measurement, Time and Money. Eduquest/IBM, 3500 Steeles Ave. E. Markham, ON L3R 2Z1.

Conquering Whole Numbers. MECC. 6160 Summit Dr. N. Minneapolis, MN 55430-4003.

General References

Alberto, P.A., & Trontman, A.C. (1995) *Applied behaviours analysis for teachers*. Englewood Cliffs, N.J.: Merrill.

Andrews, J., & Lupart, J. (1993). *The inclusive classroom*. Scarborough, ON: Nelson Canada.

Bigge, J.L. (1991). *Teaching individuals with physical and multiple disabilities*. Toronto: Collier Macmillan Canada.

Bos, C.S., & Vaughn, S. (1994). *Strategies for teaching students with learning and behaviour problems*. Boston: Allyn and Bacon.

Charles, C.M. (1992). *Building classroom discipline*. White Plains, New York: Longman.

Crealock, C., & Bachor, D.G. (1995). *Instructional strategies for students with special needs*. Scarborough, ON: Allyn and Bacon.

Frank, M. (1979). *If you're trying to teach kids to write, you've got to have this book.* Nashville: Incentive Publications.

Freeze, D.R. (1989). *Achieving.* Winnipeg, MB: Peguis.

Jones, F.J., & Jones, L.S. (1986). *Comprehensive classroom management.* Toronto: Allyn and Bacon.

Lewis, R.B., & Doorlag, D.H. (1995). *Teaching special students in the mainstream.* Englewood Cliffs, N.J.: Merrill.

Liedtke, W.W. (1995). *Diagnostic interview and intervention strategies for mathematics.* Sherwood Park, AB: ECSI.

Mercer, C.D. & Mercer, A.R. (1989). *Teaching students with learning problems.* Toronto: Merrill.

O'Brien, J., & Forest, M. (1989). *Action for inclusion.* Toronto: Inclusion Press.

Salend, S.J. (1990). *Effective Mainstreaming.* New York: Macmillan.

Smith, D.D., Luckasson, R. & Crealork, C. (1995). *Introduction to Special Education in Canada.* Scarborough, ON: Allyn and Bacon.

Snell, M.E. (1993). *Instruction of students with severe disabilities.* Toronto, Maxwell Macmillan Canada.

Stainback, S., Stainback, W., & Forest, M. (1989). *Educating all students in the mainstream of regular education.* Baltimore: Paul H. Brookes.

Thomas, V. (1979). *Teaching spelling.* Toronto: Gage

Turnbull, A., & Turnbull, H.R. (1990). *Families, professionals and exceptionality: A special partnership.* Toronto: Merrill.

Wolery, M., Ault, M.J., & Doyle, P.M. (1992). *Teaching students with moderate to severe disabilities.* New York: Longman.

REFERENCES

Andrews, J., & Lupart, J. (1993). *The inclusive classroom.* Scarborough, ON: Nelson Canada.

Cawley, J.F. (1985). *Practical mathematics.* Rockville, MD: Aspen.

Charles, C.M. (1992). *Building classroom discipline.* White Plains, NY: Longman.

Crealock, C., & Bachor, D.G. (1995). *Instructional strategies for students with special needs.* Scarborough, ON: Allyn and Bacon.

Freeze, D.R. (1989). *Achieving.* Winnipeg, MB: Peguis.

Glasser, W. (1990). *The quality school: Managing students without coercion.* New York: Harper and Row.

Jones, F.J., & Jones, L.S. (1986). *Comprehensive classroom management.* Toronto: Allyn and Bacon.

Mercer, C.D., & Mercer, A.R. (1989). *Teaching students with learning problems.* Toronto: Merrill.

Phillips, G.L. (1992). *Classroom rituals for at-risk learners.* Vancouver, BC: EduServ.

Seifert, K. (1991). *Educational psychology.* Boston: Houghton-Mifflin.

Smith, D.D., Luckasson, R., & Crealock, C. (1995). *Introduction to special education in Canada.* Scarborough, ON: Allyn and Bacon.

Tierney, R.J., Readence, J.E., & Dishner, E.K. (1990). *Reading strategies and practices.* Boston: Allyn and Bacon.

Toews, O.B., & Freeze, D.R. (1992). *Writing assessment: Grades 4–9.* Winnipeg, MB: River East School Division.

Promoting Self-Regulation in the Inclusive Classroom

John Walsh
Dawn Howard-Rose

University of Victoria

Introduction

Whether you are a veteran teacher or a novice intern, you have undoubtedly been struck by the diverse characteristics of students in contemporary classrooms. Almost every classroom is a complex mosaic of individuals from differing cultures, linguistic backgrounds, and social strata. When differences in students' abilities, interests, motivational levels, and academic backgrounds are also considered, the task of teaching in today's schools has never been more complex, nor more demanding. Given this diversity, veteran and novice teachers alike question how the individual needs of students can be met? How can teachers adapt their instruction to the challenges of inclusive classrooms, which embrace students' wide range of needs?

We do not have a simple answer to this question—adapting instruction to students with diverse needs in the inclusive classroom is far too complex. After all, a comprehensive discussion of the ways of meeting student differences in the classroom would logically entail a complete analysis of the psychology of individual differences, a comprehensive review of curriculum and instructional approaches, as well as a full detailing of assessment techniques. This is a task only a lifetime of teaching experience and professional learning might begin to address adequately.

Our ambitions here are substantially more modest. What we offer in this chapter is a discussion of how teachers in inclusive classrooms might aid students in becoming more self-directed or self-regulated learners. We also aim to give an understanding of the psychology of student self-regulation. We believe firmly that educational practice ought to be well grounded in theory and research. Discussing the theoretical grounding of the prescriptions for practice that we offer will not only justify our recommendations, but it will permit readers to find some of their own implications from the research literature that we examine.

The importance of promoting student self-regulation should not be underestimated. In a broad sense, creating students who are autonomous learners is the foremost goal of education (Winne & Walsh, 1990). After all, students must leave school and guide their own learning in the workplace and elsewhere.

Promoting self-regulation is also becoming more important as a practical matter in contemporary education. Teachers are responsible for meeting the needs of an increasingly wide array of students in the inclusive classroom. This requires that some students work autonomously at the same time as others are receiving individual attention. The more students are self-regulated, the more teachers will be able to meet the challenges present in inclusive education.

Finally, the inclusive classroom is by definition composed partly of learners who have experienced difficulty in school learning. In bygone days, these learners might have been placed in segregated classrooms; today they are integrated into regular classrooms. Most low-achievers are hallmarked as inactive, inefficient, and ultimately, ineffective at mustering appropriate responses to classroom work (Walsh, 1992).

In general then, research and theory on student self-regulation aids educators in three ways.

1. Research in this area provides theoretical understandings and concrete suggestions about how education might ultimately create students who are self-directed and lifelong learners.

2. At the classroom level, research on self-regulation may inform teachers about ways to manage the diversity of needs in the classroom.

3. The literature on self-regulation can aid teachers in developing this much-needed skill in low-achieving learners.

Taking the foregoing points together, it is clear that instruction in self-regulation has something to offer every student, irrespective of ability or achievement levels.

◈ The Nature of Self-Regulation

We have mentioned some of the reasons why theory and research on self-regulation is important for educators. We have not, however, described the nature of self-regulation in specific terms. The psychology of self-regulation will be the focus of this section. Much of the discussion will rely on current cognitive accounts of student learning that have attempted to describe the mental and motivational activities of learners in classrooms.

At one level, most teachers require little explanation of the nature of self-regulation. The majority of teachers witness self-regulated learners daily in their classrooms. In simple terms, self-regulated learners are seen as motivated, strategic, and resourceful. They are goal directed, organized, and know how to "get the job done." In this way, they discriminate quickly essential from nonessential detail in academic tasks. Further, self-regulated learners appeal to appropriate resources when completing tasks, but they do not rely exclusively on such resources. When encountering obstacles, they think of ways to actively circumvent them. By doing so, self-regulated learners may overcome unclear directions, noisy peers, abstruse texts, and a myriad of other instructional impediments that inadvertently arise in classrooms.

While the preceding description may be useful as a rough guide to identifying self-regulated learners in the classroom, it does not identify the specific processes, skills, and knowledge that make students self-regulated. Without such explication, self-regulation would inevitably be viewed as a general traitlike disposition that is not easily influenced by instruction. Until the last decade, self-regulation had been viewed in precisely that way, as a relatively fixed characteristic of students (Zimmerman, 1990).

Much of the recent attention of cognitive psychologists who study classroom learning has been directed toward understanding the psychological features of student self-regulation. While theoretical approaches to self-regulation differ in emphasis, most share a common understanding of the major components of self-regulation. First, self-regulated learners systematically use a full repertoire of cognitive strategies as they engage in academic work. More importantly, self-regulated students understand the relationship between the strategies they employ and the academic goals at hand. Taken as a whole, this multifaceted component will be designated here as the **task enactive** component of self-regulation. The word "enactive" is used to emphasize that self-regulated learners bring into play or enact strategies as they accomplish classroom work.

Self-regulated learners are not only skilled; they are "willed." They persist in the face of academic challenge, they are confident in task execution, and they set even higher goals once current task goals are accomplished (Bandura, 1989, 1993). Most importantly, self-regulated students engage processes that enhance their motivation to learn. They evidence self-control strategies that both aid in their initial task engagement and benefit their continued task involvement. This component of self-regulation is referred to as **motivational and volitional control** (Corno, 1989).

The Task Enactive Learner

The two major components of self-regulation, task enactive and motivational and volitional control, will be described more fully to lay the theoretical and research background to the instructional recommendations that will close the chapter. Perhaps more importantly, we wish to show the **content** of instruction in self-regulation. Just as the teaching of a subject entails knowledge of the subject matter, the teaching of self-regulation requires the knowledge of its content. Unlike teaching in the subject areas, teaching students to be more self-regulated involves instruction in strategies for enhancing learning and self-motivation, rather than instruction in subject matter, per se.

Classroom Tasks

It is useful to begin a discussion of the task enactive component of self-regulation by focusing upon the nature of classroom tasks. This is a logical starting point because the classroom task is the object of self-regulated learning.

Classroom tasks are the **cognitive demands** placed on students in order to change the way they think. We use this phrase to emphasize two of the defining features of classroom tasks. By the word "cognitive," we hope to highlight the mental nature of classroom work. Second, tasks are said to be demanding inasmuch as they pose goals that must be met. In this sense, all classroom tasks require students to seek solutions. Finally, classroom tasks aim to change students in a cognitive way. Tasks set for students in classrooms must, at least in a general way, improve the minds of learners if they are to be of educative value.

Current views of the nature of students' work in classrooms have described the classroom task as being composed of three interacting components (Doyle, 1983; Marx & Walsh, 1988; Walsh, 1992, 1993). First, tasks occur under a set of conditions. These conditions refer to the setting, resources, social context, and other circumstances under which tasks are set by teachers and completed by students. From a cognitive purview, if conditions of tasks are changed, the cognitive demands of the task also change. For instance, if students are allowed to work on a task in pairs rather than alone, the cognitive demands of the task will be lessened, or at least changed.

Second, classroom tasks have goals toward which students direct their efforts. When students complete task goals they produce the myriad products of classroom work. For example, students produce endless mathematics worksheets, group projects, creative writings, narrative essays, and other products of their labour. These task products are the most obvious components of the classroom task, but they are neither the only ones nor the most important.

Third, students complete classroom tasks using cognitive plans. There are numerous ways to describe these plans, but in general they can be thought of as the mental steps and strategies that learners take to create task products. The cognitive plans that are found commonly in classrooms can be categorized and described in general terms as **memory, procedural and comprehension plans** (Doyle, 1983; Marx & Walsh, 1988; Walsh, 1992).

Many school tasks require students to memorize important pieces of information. When self-regulated students approach these kinds of tasks, they select from a large repertoire of memory plans to accomplish the tasks. For example, they may use mnemonic devices (Levin & Levin, 1990), imagery-based techniques (Levin, McCormick, Miller, Berry & Pressley, 1982), or any of a full range of orchestrated strategies or plans aimed at enhancing the verbatim recall of information.

Procedural plans are used when tasks can be solved by applying a multistep rule or formula. Much of mathematics requires this type of plan. Procedural plans are not limited to this domain however. Knowing how to find a word in a dictionary, how to write a letter to a friend, or how to load a program into a computer are all examples of procedural plans.

Students often use cognitive plans to understand or comprehend information they are trying to acquire. For example, while taking notes from a teacher's talk about a particular topic, self-regulated learners would rarely try to take notes verbatim. Instead, they would translate incoming information into their own words, using their prior knowledge to help them interpret it (Kiewra, 1988). Generative strategies such as this make links between old and new information, and have been found to be particularly effective learning strategies (Wittrock, 1974).

To summarize thus far, we have tried to emphasize that classroom tasks are more than simply "things" students do in schools. They are cognitive demands set under certain conditions and met by students' cognitive plans. Accomplishing classroom work involves a complex self-regulation of these cognitive plans, on the one hand, and task conditions and goals, on the other hand. The result of this complex interaction is the task product.

Learners' Strategies and Styles

With a better understanding of classroom tasks in place, the next goal is to describe how self-regulated learners engage in these tasks. Self-regulated learners are more strategic than their less autonomous peers. Zimmerman and Martinez-Pons (1986) have identified 14 strategies that self-regulated learners frequently employ when tackling classroom work. Among these, Zimmerman and Martinez-Pons note particularly that self-regulated students tend to engage in the strategic organization, transformation, rehearsal, and memorization of information. As they do so, self-regulated learners set goals, make plans, monitor their progress, and evaluate their performance.

Self-regulated students also have been described by the style of task engagement they evidence when confronted with academic challenges. In their seminal work on self-regulation, Corno and Mandinach (1983) suggest that self-regulated learning involves a global effort to make new associations between pieces of information and to deepen old associations. Making associations in order to acquire or better understand information requires strategies, to be sure, but it also requires an attitude and approach to learning. It is this approach, or style, that hallmarks the task engagement of self-regulated learners.

It may be instructive to contrast a self-regulated learning style of task engagement with two other styles that typify less effective classroom learning. Corno and her colleagues (Corno & Mandinach, 1983; Corno & Rohrkemper, 1985; Rohrkemper & Corno, 1988) have found that students doing poorly in school frequently do *not* think deeply about the content they are learning or the tasks they are trying to accomplish. In this sense, these students evidence low levels of cognitive engagement when confronting classroom work. These students, referred to as **recipient learners**, generally take a passive approach to school tasks, making little use of their own cognitive resources (e.g., strategic knowledge or skills) and of the outside resources available to them, such as reference books, teacher assistance, or the ideas of peers. Recipient learners have little will to engage in classroom work and, therefore, are unlikely to develop high levels of skill.

The second style of task engagement contrasted with a self-regulated learning approach is that of **resource management**. Resource managers acquire and transform information only to the extent necessary to produce an adequate product, but rely heavily on outside resources, such as peers' ideas, to do so. This approach may lead to reasonably high achievement in elementary school and, when used in moderation, can be adaptive for long-term learning objectives. However, when students come to rely on others for the bulk of their thinking during classroom tasks, they short-circuit the cognitive work that will result in learning. Thus, while the task at hand is accomplished, learning suffers over the long term.

The task enactive component of self-regulation is thus composed of two important features. First, self-regulated learners exhibit a particular style of task engagement. This style or approach to classroom learning is active and planful, and is coordinated with an aim to increase the associations between and within information. Second, self-regulation involves the strategic deployment of cognitive plans aimed at meeting task demands. This is the "know how" part of self-regulation.

Student Motivation

Self-regulated learners are not only skilful, they are also wilful. While other students might resign their efforts when classroom work is difficult, self-regulated students are tenacious, self-disciplined, and generally highly motivated. This desire to meet academic challenge can be taught. Modern accounts of motivation have emphasized that motivation in the face of challenge is as much a result of the motivational strategies that are employed by learners, as it might be the result of an inherent disposition. Indeed, the motivational part of self-regulation is the result of self-directed learners orchestrating strategies that induce and control motivated action (Ames & Ames, 1984; Bandura, 1986, 1993; Weiner, 1986).

Before detailing how self-regulated students are more motivated, it is helpful to distinguish motivation and volition. Motivation to learn in school is a collection of states and self-perceptions that give rise to the intention to act (Corno, 1989; Kuhl & Beckmann 1985). Students' interests, views of themselves as learners, expectations about consequences of their actions, and so forth, are all important determinants of students' intentions to engage in academic work. When they are effective, all of these perceptions call students into action; they motivate learners to initiate action.

Even the best intentions to accomplish academic work often are not sufficient to carry students to the end of highly challenging classroom tasks. Academic work is hard work and it is often done in the midst of far more desired activities. Moreover, academic tasks frequently require diligence over many hours and sometimes even months. Students who sustain intense effort in these situations demonstrate **volitional control**. They are highly wilful. Self-regulated students, in particular, possess strategies that sustain and control their efforts. These learners know how to protect the course of their chosen action from the myriad distractions present in classrooms and elsewhere.

A complete discussion of contemporary psychological theory about the nature of student volition and motivation is well beyond the aims of this chapter and is handled well by others (Ames & Ames, 1984; Zimmerman & Schunk, 1989). A brief look at some of this research, however, will show how self-regulated learners' self-perceptions influence their motivation and how they apply strategies to enhance their own volition.

Student Self-Perceptions

Recent accounts of student motivation have emphasized the role that self-perceptions of competence play in motivating classroom learning. The research of Schunk (see Schunk, 1989 for a review) has shown in particular that students' judgments of their ability at specific tasks are related strongly to their performance and persistence on these tasks. Learners' judgments about their capacity to perform, their

self-efficacy, is not just a simple reflection of their past performances on a set of similar tasks. Some learners consistently undermine their efforts by having lower self-efficacy than their past performances might suggest. Other learners may highly overestimate their self-efficacy and engage in tasks for which they are ill prepared. The resulting failure in either case may ultimately lead them to believe that the task was simply too difficult and that they should resign their efforts.

Self-regulated learners would be expected to possess higher general levels of self-efficacy for academic work. Moreover, these learners are generally better at processing information that permits an empowering sense that they can be successful at classroom work. In the same way that self-regulated individuals may be particularly attentive to task information, they are also attentive to motivational information. They process information from their experience with tasks, from witnessing others perform similar tasks, and from listening to the encouragement of others (Bandura, 1986). Armed with this information, they make informed judgments about their competencies. Moreover, when they face a task for which they are not equipped, they assess what they need to learn first in order to eventually succeed. In this way, their overall sense of self-efficacy for academic work does not suffer.

Students who are achieving poorly are less attentive to information that might imbue them with a strong sense of self-efficacy for academic tasks. Even when presented with information that affirms competence, such as significant success experiences with a given task, these learners readily discount the information by attributing their success to factors other than their ability and effort. If success is not personally attributed, it cannot influence students' self-efficacy (Bandura, 1986). Armed with intractably low levels of efficacy, underachieving students persist less in the face of academic challenge and fail to achieve as a result. Indeed, they may not engage in academic tasks at all.

Volitional Control Strategies

As noted earlier, not all of the motivated learning that is evidenced by self-regulated learners is the result of self-perceptions, such as self-efficacy. Self-regulated students know how to stay on task. In other words, they implement strategies that aid their wilful or volitional control of their own learning. A brief look at some of these strategies will help to illustrate this aspect of self-regulation.

One of the most powerful means of enhancing volitional effort is by teaching students to set goals for their learning. The last two decades of research in a number of applied fields has shown that when learners set short-term goals of moderate difficulty, motivation is enhanced (Zimmerman, Bandura & Martinez-Pons, 1992). Task persistence and achievement is enhanced further when individuals monitor their progress toward self-imposed goals and reward their own accomplishments (Mace, Belfiore & Shea, 1989).

The volitional control of learners can also be enhanced by the pattern of inner speech or **self-talk** that they engage in during task completion (McCaslin-Rohrkemper, 1989). While the specific content of this guiding inner speech may differ widely, the pattern of inner speech reported by self-regulated learners tends to be task-focused and self-encouraging. For example, the inner speech used by these learners may draw their attention back to a task when concentration has waned, or it may remind them of an impending deadline when peristence has diminished. These kinds of self-statements are highly related to classroom achievement (Peterson, Swing, Braverman & Buss, (1982). Moreover, experimental studies have demonstrated that changing students' self-statements can produce large improvements in the achievement and behaviour of underachievers (Meichenbaum, 1977; Zivin, 1979).

Self-regulation involves students' deployment of strategies that aid students in completing classroom tasks. These strategies are not limited to cognitive ones that relate directly to solving tasks. Self-regulation also includes strategies that are directed both at learners' motivation to engage in academic work and their volition to continue effort. An underlying theme of our discussion is that student self-regulation can be enhanced by instruction. Students can be taught to be more active, independent, and motivated. How the teacher can accomplish this is the focus of the next section.

▩ Guidelines for Practice

In the closing section of this chapter, some of the ways that teachers might instruct their students to become more self-regulated are outlined.

Modelling Task Directions

Perhaps one of the easiest and most obvious occasions to teach students how to be more self-regulated is when teachers give instructions for classroom or homework tasks. This is a time when students will, or should, begin to plan how they will work on the tasks assigned to them. At this point, teacher suggestions for cognitive strategies and motivational approaches to the task will be most useful to learners.

This time also provides an opportunity for teachers to **model** the precise cognitive skills, approaches, and attitudes they wish students to develop. Modelling task plans for students accomplishes two goals. First, it helps all students to see how self-regulated learning can be used in planning an approach to a task.

Modelling how students might complete the cognitive requirements of a task is most important in helping those who often have difficulty understanding fully what they must do to complete the task (i.e., the necessary cognitive plans). In many classrooms, instructions for assigned tasks typically focus on features such as format, length, and scope of topics to be covered. Discussion of these aspects are, of course, helpful in setting the conditions under which tasks must be completed by students. Such instruction does not, however, illustrate how the task is to be done.

Observational research conducted recently in British Columbia (Howard-Rose & Rose, 1994) has found that students who are integrated into inclusive classrooms are frequently confused by task instructions and that such confusions seriously hamper their ability to complete classroom work. Further, observation has revealed that when students are given more comprehensive instructions about the cognitive requirements of the task, often they are able to complete the task without difficulty.

A good example of how one teacher presented instructions concerning a "report card" assignment shows how she engaged students cognitively in the task by focusing on its substantive content rather than its format. In this assignment, students were asked to evaluate their skills in listening, speaking, reading, mathematics, hand-writing, and work habits. During one of several presentations related to this self-eval-uation task, the teacher was observed clarifying to students that she did not want simple "yes" or "no" responses to questions she had asked them to address in their report cards, but would like them to contemplate the questions fully by imagining themselves in a math or reading class and picturing their performance and work habits. She then wrote part of a sample report card on the blackboard and modelled self-talk about her own writing skills as she completed the information on the board. On another occassion, this teacher interrupted a group activity to announce that this was a good opportunity for students to pay attention to their own listening and speaking so that they would be able to remember how they were doing when they worked on their report cards (Howard-Rose & Rose, 1994).

Self-regulated learning can be modelled during the presentation of task instructions, and this is one of the best times to draw students' attention to self-regulatory behaviours. In order to teach students to be more self-regulated, the presentation of task instructions should be more of a substantive lesson. The con-tent of the assignment, including concepts and ideas to be addressed, as well as the ways students should think about their task, should be emphasized. The teacher can accomplish this by talking aloud while working through examples.

Participant Modelling

A central issue in the instruction of self-regulation concerns how teachers can gradu-ally shift control of learning from themselves to the student. If such control is shifted too quickly, students will inevitably flounder. This experience can undermine stu-dents' perceptions concerning their ability to regulate their own learning and increase students' reliance on teacher-led instruction. If teachers steadfastly maintain their reg-ulation of tasks, they short-circuit the need for students to regulate their learning and, as a consequence, reinforce a passive approach to learning. How then, can an orderly and timely transfer of task control from teachers to learners be accomplished?

Over the last decade, a number of instructional models have been developed that attempt to meet this need. Among these, participant modelling is prototypic (Bandura, 1986; Corno, 1989, Marx & Walsh, 1988; Walsh, 1992). Participant modelling involves three distinct steps. First, the teacher **models** aloud the components of self-regulation. In other words, the teacher would model the procedures for doing a task and, in doing so, also model any motivational self-talk that might be important.

The second step in participant modelling, **guided practice**, is designed to transfer task control gradually from the teacher to the learner. At this step, a student is called upon to perform aloud the task strategies and motivational thoughts that were modelled previously. As the student does this, the teacher guides and corrects strategy use.

In the last step of participant modelling, the transfer of task regulation is completed. The student **practises** the task and supporting strategies independently. The teacher's role is to provide feedback on the completed task, that is, the task product and on the strategies that were used to complete the task.

Although participant modelling appears to be a straightforward instructional model, its implementation is not without challenges. As has been noted in Walsh (1992, 1993), research indicates that teachers often have difficulty illustrating strategies that can be useful to solve tasks and regulate learning. In part, this is because much of the lesson planning that teachers do is concerned with the content and practice activities of lessons, and not with the strategies and self-regulatory thinking that are important in teaching self-regulation. This may simply be because teachers have not understood how self-regulation might be taught.

Even when teachers have been taught to demonstrate strategies and motivational thinking during lessons they often abandon such an approach quickly. They frequently go back to emphasizing the content of a lesson, without attending to strategies for accomplishing tasks. This observation may simply suggest that teachers need more practice incorporating strategy instruction so that it takes less effort. After all, teaching is demanding. Paradoxically, it may also be that the same content expertise that makes teachers knowledgeable instructors may make them less able to demonstrate the strategies and motivational thinking that are useful in teaching self-regulation. Expertise makes many strategies automatic, and it is often frustrating to make apparent what has become automatic. For example, part of the frustration in teaching someone to drive a car is trying to explain such an automatic set of behaviours.

Despite some difficulty, participant modelling is useful for directly teaching self-regulation. In particular, it provides a systematic way of transfering task control from the teacher to the student. It also provides a number of opportunities for teachers to draw students' attention to the importance of self-regulation.

Self-Regulation and the Classroom Environment

There are a number of ways in which the classroom environment influences students' motivation and approach to assigned tasks. One of these is the extent to which there are opportunities for student decision making and self-management. Another environmental factor is the social risk that students perceive is present when they make a mistake. For students to be actively and cognitively engaged in attempts to learn, they must feel they can make mistakes along the way without facing dire social consequences. A third way in which the classroom environment influences self-regulation concerns the views that teachers have about student ability. Whether teachers conceptualize student ability as a single, static quality or as an array of strengths and weaknesses subject to instructional change has important implications for the learning environment that teachers create in the classroom.

Opportunities for Student Self-Management

To promote self-regulation, the classroom environment should be one that encourages self-management and self-responsibility, at least as much as possible without teachers abdicating their responsibilities. Placing students in charge of some aspects of their own learning should not be viewed as a simple matter; it is not. Teachers must choose carefully how much and which aspects of instruction should be controlled by students.

A consistent theme in many approaches to classroom management suggests that if students have some say in setting classroom goals, behavioural rules, and consequences, they will cooperate more. Indeed, students are often more stringent than teachers when they set their own learning and behavioural goals.

Given the preceding approach, teachers who involve their students in decision making about classroom rules, particularly during the beginning of the school year, can set a classroom environment that encourages self-regulation. Teachers who are effective classroom managers also teach their students procedures and routines to use in the classroom (Emmer & Evertson, 1982). These procedures can evolve with student input in exactly the same way that classroom rules can be set jointly. Of course, there are some classroom rules and procedures that teachers would want to ensure are adopted by students, such as rules concerning safety, aggression, and so forth; nevertheless, the process of permitting students to shape classroom regulations can be the beginning of setting an atmosphere of self-regulation in the classroom.

Research on motivation and student learning suggests that students vary in their motivational orientations toward school tasks (Ames, 1992; Meece, 1991). Some students appear to be concerned chiefly with developing mastery. They seek intellectual challenges to garner a greater sense of accomplishment. Other students are concerned mostly with how they perform in relation to others. These learners are motivated to attain high grades and other forms of recognition, often by investing the minimum amount of effort. Learners with this type of orientation hold a performance, rather than a mastery, orientation toward their classroom work (Ames, 1992; Ames & Archer, 1988; Marshall, 1988; Meece, Blumenfeld & Hoyle, 1988; Meece, 1991).

In terms of approach to classroom work, performance-oriented learners try to avoid challenging tasks. They tend to give up easily and often attribute their failure to a lack of ability. In contrast, mastery-oriented individuals are likely to pursue challenge. They persist in the face of difficulty, engage in learning for its intrinsic value, and attribute failure to insufficient effort or ineffective strategies (Ames, 1992; Dweck & Leggett, 1988). Mastery learners also have been found to be more cognitively engaged in learning tasks and to use more effective learning strategies than performance-oriented students (Meece et al., 1988).

Obviously, most teachers would prefer to have mastery-oriented students in their classes. While changing goal orientation is not easy, it can be done. Students' goal orientations are not permanent characteristics. They are influenced, at least in part, by the classroom environment created by the teacher.

One factor in the learning environment that influences students' orientations toward classroom work is the risk for failure that is implicitly communicated by teachers. Students' perceptions of classroom failure will be discussed more fully in the next section of this chapter. For the present, however, it is important to note that in classrooms where errors are costly in terms of students' anxiety and where rewards such as high grades are given only to the few best performers, students are likely to concern themselves exclusively with their relative achievement. On the other hand, when teachers acknowledge student effort, improvement, unconventional speculations or approaches, and where student mistakes are seen as a natural part of learning, mastery goals orientations are developed.

Students are also more likely to develop a mastery orientation when they are given some choice among a set of subject topics and learning tasks. Such choice *must* be made on the basis of students' interests and not to avoid effort or risk (Ames, 1992). Students who are performance oriented may need to be encouraged to accept challenging tasks by reducing the personal and social costs of failure. This will create an atmosphere where they can select personally relevant tasks, rather than ones that simply permit high relative achievement.

Making Failure Constructive

Imagine that you were able to create a classroom environment in which all of the activities and tasks were "perfect" for students. What would this mean? Would tasks be matched perfectly to each student's ability so that students would always succeed? As educators, we naturally tend to value success and devalue failure; after all, we are not in the teaching profession to help students fail. For a number of reasons, which will soon become apparent, we invite you to examine more deeply the role played by task difficulty and failure in promoting learning. We argue that the perfect instructional task may not be the one that permits only success, and that part of self-regulation involves students making failure a constructive part of learning.

As with all aspects of self-regulated learning, success and failure must be considered in terms of their motivational and cognitive influences on students. We said earlier that, in classrooms where students' mistakes are viewed as part of learning and where relatively little risk is involved in failure, students are more likely to hold a mastery orientation. This sentiment is often conveyed by teachers with statements such as: "There are no wrong answers in my class." While the good intentions behind this kind of statement are clear, this is not the way research on motivation would suggest teachers ought to promote a mastery orientation and self-regulation in the classroom. On the contrary, it is very important to point out to students both the incorrect and correct aspects of their work or responses in class, otherwise inappropriate or incorrect information will be reinforced (Brophy 1981, 1983). What is critical, however, is to give feedback in an atmosphere of cooperation, acceptance, and shared learning.

Let's return for a moment to the question posed at the outset of this section: what might a classroom environment with perfect tasks and activities be like? Most novice teachers would imagine this environment as one where every student succeeds most or all of the time. There is good evidence, however, to support a view of the optimal environment as one where obstacles, difficulties, errors, and failures are not avoided as undesired side effects of an imperfect classroom, but are acknowledged as realistic and positive opportunities for developing adaptive skills. Rohrkemper and Corno (1988) propose that constructive failure experiences can, in the long run, enhance self-regulated learning, both in and outside the classroom. Self-regulation is enhanced particularly in classroom environments where students are challenged with moderately difficult tasks (Bandura, 1993), and where students are helped to learn and practise strategies for adapting to difficulties. Students' adaptive responses might include changing the task (e.g., breaking larger tasks down into more manageable units), changing themselves (e.g., learning more facts before completing the task), or changing the situation (e.g., seeking assistance from others) (Rohrkemper & Corno, 1988).

A recent descriptive study of students working in an inclusive classroom illustrates nicely the classroom norms that aid students in viewing failure constructively and in becoming more self-regulated (Howard-Rose & Rose, 1994). In this classroom, students regularly checked their answers with their peers. Indeed, in some skill areas, such as computer work, spelling, and math, certain students served as class experts for the entire class. This system created an atmosphere of cooperation, where students actively helped one another master their learning objectives. In such a classroom, difficulties, mistakes, and failure were viewed as challenges to be overcome by the active use of strategies, rather than as events to be avoided.

Another way in which teachers can reduce the negative effects of failure is by creating a multidimensional rather than unidimensional value system in the classroom (Rosenholtz & Simpson, 1984). In a multidimensional classroom, the teacher promotes the idea that students have differing strengths and that many kinds of abilities are valued in the classroom. In contrast, teachers who subscribe to a unidimensional classroom value system hold that there is only one standard of success, usually academic performance. In these classrooms, student performance is judged relative to one standard. This type of classroom invites invidious comparisons among students and results in students adopting a performance orientation toward classroom work (Marx & Walsh, 1988).

Given the diversity of abilities found in inclusive classrooms and the desire to produce mastery-oriented self-regulated students, teachers are advised to create multidimensional classrooms. This is not a simple matter. It requires that teachers possess a genuine respect for the diverse qualities offered by each student in the class, which may involve actively searching for students' talents and interests that are not typically manifested by classroom work.

Finally, and perhaps most importantly, teachers must know their students so that feedback, whether indicating success or failure, can be tailored to the student. An excellent example of such an understanding is found in the following statement extracted from a recent interview with a teacher.

> The last thing (Julie) wants to be told is that "This is a little tough on you, maybe you shouldn't try it." You just don't say that to her; she just wants to try it and she isn't upset or doesn't hide her paper if there are only four questions filled out on it, or it is not complete. She just comes and asks for more time or a little extra help. She doesn't want to impose, but when she does get it done, she's just thrilled (Howard-Rose & Rose, 1994).

◈ Summary and Conclusion

Recapping the themes discussed in this chapter will serve to highlight our major messages. First, it must be emphasized that the inclusive classroom makes heavy demands on students' skills at regulating their own learning. Students experiencing academic difficulty almost always lack the skills involved in self-regulation. Moreover, adequately achieving students can usually also benefit from enhancing their self-regulatory skills. With these points in mind, our first message is a simple one: the explicit instruction of self-regulation must be part of teaching in inclusive classrooms.

Enhancing self-regulation is not a simple task, but research and theory point to several ways that self-regulation can be enhanced. As we have noted, teacher modelling is a particularly powerful way of building students' skills at regulating their own learning. Modelling how to do a task rather than simply giving students broad directions can help them understand the skills and strategies they might use to complete the task. It can also be an occasion to demonstrate how they might regulate their own learning and motivation. For example, in terms of the latter, teachers might demonstrate how to set goals.

If self-regulation is to blossom in inclusive classrooms, an instructional climate that encourages student self-regulation must be present. Teachers who involve students in setting classroom rules, goals, and routines help to produce self-regulated learners. Teachers who help students view failure as constructive experiences also produce self-regulated learners. Finally, teachers who offer genuine respect for the diverse accomplishments of students can create a climate that encourages student mastery and self-regulation.

SUGGESTED RESOURCES

Blumenfeld, P.C., Pintrich, P.R., Meece, J., & Wessels, K. (1982). The formation and role of perceptions of ability in elementary school classrooms. *The Elementary School Journal, 82,* 401–20.

Howard-Rose, D., & Rose, C. (1994). Students' adaptions to task requirements in regular and resource room class settings. *Journal of Special Education, 28,* 3–26.

Paris, S., & Winograd, P. (1990). Promoting metacognition and motivation of exceptional children. *Remedial and Special Education, 11,* 7–15.

Rohrkemper, M., & Corno, L. (1988). Success and failure on classroom tasks: Adaptive learning and classroom teaching. *Elementary School Journal, 88,* 297–312.

Walsh, J. (1993). The promise and pitfalls of integrated strategy instruction. *Journal of Learning Disabilities, 26,* 438–42.

Zimmerman, B.J., & Schunk, D.H. (1989). *Self-regulated learning and academic achievement: Theory, research and practice.* New York: Springer Verlag.

REFERENCES

Ames, C. (1992). Classrooms: Goals, structures, and student motivation. *Journal of Educational Psychology, 84,* 261–71.

Ames, C., & Ames, R. (1984). *Student motivation.* New York: Academic Press.

Ames, C., & Archer, R. (1988). Achievement in the classroom: Student learning strategies and motivational processes. *Journal of Educational Psychology, 80,* 260–67.

Bandura, A. (1986). *Social foundations of thought and action: A social cognitive theory.* Englewood Cliffs, NJ: Prentice-Hall.

Bandura, A. (1989). Human agency in social cognitive theory. *American Psychologist, 44,* 1179–84.

Bandura, A. (1993). Perceived self-efficacy in cognitive development and functioning. *Educational Psychologist, 28,* 117–48.

Blumenfeld, P.C., Mergendoller, J.R., & Swarthout., D.W. (1987). Task as an heuristic for understanding student learning and motivation. *Journal of Curriculum Studies, 19,* 135–48.

Brophy, J. (1981). Teacher praise: A functional analysis. *Review of Educational Research, 51,* 5–32.

Brophy, J. (1983). Conceptualizing student motivation. *Educational Psychologist, 18,* 200–15.

Corno, L. (1989). Self-regulated learning: A volitional analysis. In B.J. Zimmerman & D.H. Schunk (Eds.), *Self-regulated learning and academic achievement: Theory, research, and practice* (pp. 109–41). New York: Springer-Verlag.

Corno, L., & Mandinach, E.B. (1983). The role of cognitive engagement in classroom learning and motivation. *Educational Psychologist, 18,* 88–108.

Corno, L., Rohrkemper, M.M. (1985). The intrinsic motivation to learn in classrooms. In C. Ames & R. Ames (Eds.), *Research on motivation in education: The classroom milieu* (pp. 53–90). Orlando, FL: Academic Press.

Doyle, W. (1983). Academic work. *Review of Educational Research, 53,* 159–99.

Dweck, C., & Leggett, E. (1988). A social cognitive approach to motivation and personality. *Psychological Review, 95,* 256–73.

Emmer, E.T., & Evertson, C. (1982). Effective classroom management at the beginning of the school year in junior high school classes. *Journal of Educational Psychology, 74,* 495–98.

Howard-Rose, D., & Rose, C. (1994). Students' adaptions to task requirements in regular and resource room class settings. *Journal of Special Education, 28,* 3–26.

Kiewra, K.A. (1988). Cognitive aspects of autonomous note taking: Control processes, learning strategies, and prior knowledge. *Educational Psychologist, 23,* 39–56.

Kuhl, J., & Beckmann, J. (Eds.). (1985). *Action control: From cognition to behaviour.* West Berlin: Springer-Verlag.

Levin, J.R., McCormick, C.B., Miller, G.E., Berry, J.K., & Pressley, M. (1982). Mnemonic versus nonmnemonic vocabulary learning strategies for children. *American Educational Research Journal, 19,* 121–36.

Levin, M.E., & Levin, J.R. (1990). Scientific mnemonics: Methods for maximizing more than memory. *American Educational Research Journal, 27,* 301–21.

Mace, C.F., Belfiore, P.J., & Shea, M.C. (1989). Operant theory and research on self-regulation. In B.J. Zimmerman & D.H. Schunk (Eds.), *Self-regulated learning and academic achievement: Theory, research and practice* (pp. 27–50). New York: Springer-Verlag.

Marshall, H.H. (1988). In pursuit of learning-oriented classrooms. *Teaching and Teacher Education, 4,* 85–98.

Marx, R.W., & Walsh, J. (1988). Learning from academic tasks. *Elementary School Journal, 88,* 207–19.

Marx, R.W., & Walsh, J. (1991). Recitation, lecture and direct instruction: Possibilities and limitations. In R. Short, L. Stewin, & S. McCann (Eds.), *Educational psychology: Canadian perspectives* (pp. 254–76). Mississauga, ON: Copp Clark Pitman Ltd.

Meece, J.L. (1991). The classroom context and students' motivational goals. In M. Maehr & P. Pintrich (Eds.), *Advances in achievement motivation research* (Vol. 7, 261–86). Greenwich, CT: JAI Press.

Meece, J.L., Blumenfeld, P.C., & Hoyle, R.H. (1988). Students' goal orientations and cognitive engagement in classroom activities. *Journal of Educational Psychology, 80,* 514–23.

McCaslin-Rohrkemper, M. (1989). Self-regulated learning and academic achievement: A Vygotskian view. In B.J. Zimmerman & D.H. Shunk (Eds.), *Self-regulated learning and academic achievement: Theory, research, and practice* (pp. 109–41). New York: Springer-Verlag.

Meichenbaum, D. (1977). *Cognitive behaviour modification.* New York: John Wiley & Sons.

Peterson, P.L., Swing, S., Braverman, M., & Buss, R. (1982). Students' aptitudes and their reports of cognitive processes during direct instruction. *Journal of Educational Psychology, 74,* 535–47.

Rohrkemper, M., & Corno, L. (1988). Success and failure on classroom tasks: Adaptive learning and classroom teaching. *Elementary School Journal, 88,* 297–12.

Rosenholtz, S.J., & Simpson, C. (1984). The formation of ability conceptions: Developmental trend or social construction? *Review of Educational Research, 54,* 31–63.

Schunk, D.H. (1989). Self-efficacy and cognitive skill learning. In C. Ames & R. Ames (Eds.), *Research on motivation in education Vol. 3: Goals and cognition* (pp. 13–44). San Diego: Academic Press.

Walsh, J. (1992). Promoting self-regulation in the learning disabled. *Exceptionality Education Canada, 2,* 41–58.

Walsh, J. (1993). The promise and pitfalls of integrated strategy instruction. *Journal of Learning Disabilities, 26,* 438–42.

Weiner, B. (1986). *An attributional theory of motivation and emotion.* New York: Springer-Verlag.

Winne, P.H., & Walsh, J. (1990). Instructional psychology and teaching. In E.O. Miranda & R. Magsino (Eds.), *Teaching, schools and society* (pp. 231–47). London: Falmer Press.

Wittrock, M.C. (1974). Learning as a generative process. *Educational Psychologist, 11*, 87–95.

Zimmerman, B.J. (1990). Self-regulated learning and academic achievement: An overview. *Educational Psychologist, 25*, 3–17.

Zimmerman, B.J., & Martinez-Pons, M. (1986). Development of a structured interview for assessing student use of self-regulated learning strategies. *American Educational Research Journal, 23*, 614–28.

Zimmerman, B.J., & Schunk, D.H. (1989). *Self-regulated learning and academic achievement: Theory, research and practice.* New York: Springer Verlag.

Zimmerman, B.J., Bandura, A., & Martinez-Pons, M. (1992). Self-motivation for academic attainment: The role of self-efficacy beliefs and personal goal setting. *American Educational Research Journal, 29*, 663–76.

Zivin, G. (Ed.). (1979). *The development of self-regulation through private speech.* New York: John Wiley & Sons.

Classroom Management in the Elementary School

Don Dworet

Brock University

Clint Davis

Hamilton-Wentworth Roman Catholic Separate School Board

Janice Martin

Board of Education for the City of Etobicoke

Introduction

There is little doubt that classroom management, defined as the ability of the teacher to make maximum and effective use of student and teacher time, is one of the highest priorities of both the new and experienced teacher. Some teachers experience great success in this area. Some, unfortunately, do not. This chapter is about how to plan for success and ensure that strategies that maximize the changes for a smooth-running classroom and minimize class disruption are appropriately considered and implemented. It begins with the teacher. In as much as the principal sets the tone for the school, the teacher sets the tone for the classroom.

The following two examples illustrate the dramatic impact teacher behaviour or style has on student behaviour. One teaching style focuses on curriculum content and views the behaviour of the students as an impediment to that goal. The other teaching style views the education of the child as a combination of academic and social skills.

CASE STUDY 1

The class straggled down the hall towards the closed classroom door. They waited impatiently and noisily. After a minute or two the door was opened by the teacher, who began to verbally assault the students for being noisy. This "inclusive" grade-five class of 28 culturally and academically diverse students paid little heed as they chaotically entered the class-room. The teacher angrily slammed the door and continued the verbal barrage. The classroom itself was notable for its absence of instruc-tional materials. There were few dis-plays on the walls, textbooks were loosely formed in piles on the counter, and there did not appear to be a teacher's desk. Instead, there was a table heaped high with papers and notebooks. The class continued to make noise with the screeching teacher barely heard over the din. Later the teacher was heard to com-plain bitterly of disrespectful students and the difficulties she continually endured. Was this a novice teacher? On the contrary, this, was a teacher with some 20 years' teaching experi-ence—20 years of screeching and frus-tration on the part of the teacher and the students.

Classroom management is affected largely by the approach and attitude of the individual teacher. Classroom management concerns have always been chal-lenging. In the classrooms of the nineties teachers must also deal with the addi-tional effect of the inclusive setting. There is a great diversity of students currently placed in regular education classrooms and the effect of this is keenly felt. Michael Valpy, writing a series on education in the nineties for the Toronto *Globe and Mail*, states that "superintendents, principals and teachers accept as a rule of thumb that four out of ten children they have on their roles tote the baggage of some sort of subjective dysfunction" (*The Globe and Mail*, October 2, 1993). He goes on to define "subjective dysfunction" as physically and emotionally unhealthy children, neglected children, children whose parents lack the time and energy to be with them, substance-abusing children, children with minimum social skills, children from a vast range and variety of bruised, stressed, and fragile families. Even if we were to reduce that figure of 40 percent by half, there is little doubt that educators today are facing classes containing several students whose ability to interact appro-priately, achieve and/or respond physically to regular classroom expectations is quite limited.

Down the hall, another teacher waits for the arrival of her grade-six inclusive class. She uses these few moments to mentally review those students who had shown improvement, those requiring extra encouragement, and those needing specialized attention. The upcoming lesson was planned, materials prepared, teaching strategies rehearsed and refined. The students lined up in an orderly and expectant fashion. They knew from experience what their responsibilities were. As they filed into the classroom, the teacher was heard to comment to several of them. Remarks ranging from a simple greeting to a well-placed word of encouragement or recognition for extra effort were given. The room was organized into an eclectic mix of seating arrangements that encouraged and accommodated individual learning styles. Some desks were grouped to allow for the free-flowing interchange of discussion, some were put together into short rows of three that allowed those students to participate as a group but also allowed for the needed structure of individual study; some sat singly but were part of the class as a whole for these students had not yet reached the level of independent study that would facilitate learning in a group. Student work was creatively displayed interspersed with a colourful array of motivational posters, relevant curriculum materials, and student responsibility reminders. The teacher had an immediate and gentle command of the class and moved easily about as her charges actively engaged themselves in the lesson. The lesson plan was readily accessible and formed part of a carefully planned continuum that would culminate at the close of the school year. Each lesson was a logical progression through this continuum and held importance for the students. The teacher enjoyed working with the students as much as the students enjoyed working with her. Again, this was a teacher who had over 20 years of teaching experience—20 years of engaging, challenging, and rewarding experiences for both the teacher and her students.

The multicultural nature of our classrooms requires that classroom management approaches not only reflect the needs of those students who have learning and/or behavioural difficulties, but also those students whose ethnic background may differ from that of the dominant society. Failure to consider the needs of these students may well cause an otherwise effective program to fail. Planning for the inclusive classroom involves a sensitivity to diverse learners to ensure that no lesson, unit, or assignment impinges on the cultural, religious, or ethnic beliefs held by the students.

It is not surprising, given all the above, classroom management concerns are at the top of the list of priorities for most teachers. The successful inclusion of children with diverse learning needs and abilities in the community elementary school is a complex task requiring the coordination of a number of key elements within the school (Blankenship & Lilly, 1981). The most important of these elements is the approach taken by the teacher to organize and manage the class. Classroom management continues to be a popular topic in elementary textbooks (Charles, 1992; Collis & Dutton, 1990; Cooper, 1990, Shalaway, 1989). This is due in large part to the fact that for most teachers classroom management issues can well be one of the most challenging aspects of teaching. Teachers can no longer assume what the educational, social, physical and behavioural abilities of their students will be. Teachers are expected to assess their students' abilities in these areas and to adjust their programs accordingly. Social and behavioural skills need to be taught, not simply expected, alongside the academic program.

This chapter will describe a proactive and preventative model for classroom management. There are two sections to the approach that when employed one with the other will form an effective classroom management system. The first section will describe the model with its three stages: planning, implementation, and maintenance. The second section will describe intervention strategies and tools that can be employed within this proactive model when dealing with specific behavioural concerns.

⊠ Section I: A Proactive Approach to Classroom Management

The variety of management systems based on a number of widely divergent theoretical orientations have been developed to assist the regular education classroom teacher with the task of establishing the structure of the classroom (Doyle, 1986; Dreikurs et al., 1982; Jones & Jones, 1986; Rinne, 1984). When we study examples of successful classroom management systems we find commonalities. Effective classroom management systems are proactive in nature. They focus on preventing problems from occurring rather than reacting to problems once they have already occurred (Evertson et al., 1984). It is clear that in the inclusive classroom with diverse student needs, proactive and preventative measures are crucial (Bos & Vaughan, 1988; De Luke & Knoblock, 1987). Effective classroom management reflects teachers' abilities to organize their environment to make maximum use of space, to account for theirs and the students' physical presence, and time. The efforts expended to thoroughly organize the program, including making effective use of professional and volunteer personnel, will alleviate many management concerns currently facing teachers.

The Model

Proactive classroom organization and management systems involve three distinct stages: planning, implementation, and maintenance (see Figure 7.1). Planning the system occurs before the school year begins. Implementation of the system is done during the first weeks of school. Maintaining the system is ongoing and occurs throughout the school year. All three stages are critical to the success of the system as a whole. The planning stage entails the reflective examination by the teacher of everything related to the educational setting ranging from the use of classroom space and movement of people in it to procedures and routines. Additionally, given the diversity of the inclusive classroom, special attention must be given to the effective use of support personnel, both professionals as well as volunteers. Planning a classroom management system is critical to the successful classroom. Without it teachers will have no management strategies and will then have little to use other than reactive measures. Often these are punitive in nature and may well result in the exclusion of students when such students are banished to the hallway or the office. Reactive management is nonproductive and leaves both the teacher and the students frustrated and angry. Teaching and learning cannot take place with the teacher and students involved in an on-going power struggle. This situation puts the teacher and students in an adversarial situation rather than one of partnership. Once the critical stage of planning is completed, then the teacher is prepared and confident, ready to put the planning into action through a deliberate process of implementation.

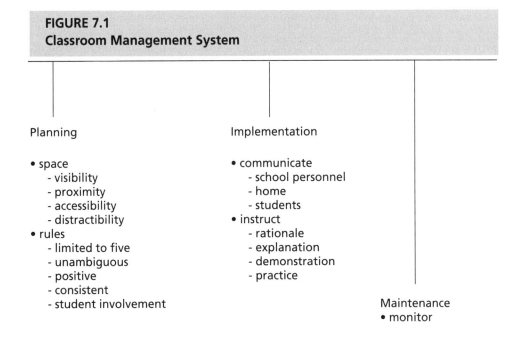

FIGURE 7.1
Classroom Management System

Planning

- space
  - visibility
  - proximity
  - accessibility
  - distractibility
- rules
  - limited to five
  - unambiguous
  - positive
  - consistent
  - student involvement

Implementation

- communicate
  - school personnel
  - home
  - students
- instruct
  - rationale
  - explanation
  - demonstration
  - practice

Maintenance
- monitor

Planning (*cont.*)
• procedures
   - specific routines
   - student accountability
   - student involvement
• support
   - personnel
   - who will work with whom
   - degree of assistance
   - absences
   - information management

Maintenance (*cont.*)
• reinforce students
• deal effectively
  with students
• evaluate
• modify

Implementation is a careful, contrived, and deliberate process. It is the teaching of the planned system to the class. Through instruction, modelling, and practice of the planned system two things should occur: the teacher can see the plan in action and can make any modifications necessary (get the bugs out), and the students have no ambiguity as to teacher/classroom/school expectations academically as well as behaviourally.

Once implemented, the classroom management system must be carefully maintained. Without careful maintenance, the system will gradually dissolve leaving the classroom in a state of increasing confusion and not a little frustration for both the teacher and the students. It is through careful maintenance that the teacher is afforded the flexibility necessary to make changes to the system as student needs change throughout the school year. With the above rationale in mind, what follows is a more in-depth study of the three stages of designing and effecting a classroom management system.

Planning

A well-managed classroom does not come easily. It requires time, effort, and commitment. In the planning stage teachers must consider the modifications required by special-needs students and how these modifications can be implemented. Should the use of support personnel and/or special materials be required (i.e., educational assistants, volunteers, peer tutors), the teacher may have to provide for a delay in implementation until such supporting structures are in place.

Getting Started

Collaborative planning with others such as resource teachers and other teacher team members can prove to be very helpful. It takes creativity to design a program that will meet the needs of all pupils regardless of ability/disability. Planning with grade-level teams or with individual colleagues will go far in determining solutions to difficult problems. As the range of academic and behavioural difficulties in classrooms increases, the more support colleagues must provide for each other emotionally as well as professionally. For example, when a student displays behavioural difficulty the reactive response may be to send the child to the office. Through cooperative planning another teacher may be willing to accept that child into their class and to provide a more proactive and preventative solution to the behavioural difficulty. Both the sending teacher and receiving teacher, however, need to discuss beforehand how this will work and what will happen when the student arrives at the other teacher's classroom.

Curriculum content is no longer the exclusive domain of the planning function. Planning specifically to academic domains with the focus on learning outcomes must go well beyond the prescribed knowledge-based curriculum. Planning must also take into account the behavioural, social, and academic needs of the diverse learners and how modifications may affect the implementation of the lesson.

While the inclusion of students with special instructional needs certainly adds to the responsibilities of the teacher, it is important to note that the strategies that regular classroom teachers have found to be effective for students without special needs are equally effective for students whose instructional needs differ from the regular student population. Teachers who have developed effective classroom organization and management systems have as their objective the prevention of difficulties in the classroom (be they academic or behavioural in nature), as opposed to reacting to problems after they have occurred. These effective teachers are best described as being proactive rather than reactive.

Knowledge of the students is key to the preventative system. An examination of previous school records is essential in getting to know much about the students prior to the school year beginning. Through a careful examination of the records teachers will become aware of students' strengths and weaknesses, effective approaches and those that failed, family issues, and cultural issues. School individuals who experience success with those students with disabilities are identified. By becoming aware of as many issues as possible, the teacher can develop a seating arrangement, a timetable, initial work assignments, and even a "first day" routine that will minimize the opportunities for management problems to develop. Without such knowledge the teacher will be virtually unprepared for the class. The first few weeks may well set the tone for the entire year. Much careful thought and consideration must go into preparing for this period.

Planning the Classroom Organization and Management System

There are four components of the classroom organization and management system that require advanced planning on the part of the teacher:

- Use of space
- Classroom rules

- Classroom procedures and routines
- Educational assistants and the use of volunteers

It should be noted that this type of planning may require a large investment of time. The result of such an investment will be the smooth operation of the classroom that will afford the teacher the time essential for the task of *teaching*.

Use of Space

Physical space and its organization is a crucial component of effective classroom management. How the space within the classroom is organized can either enhance or detract from the attainment of the instructional objectives. When designing a classroom layout the teacher needs to take the following into consideration: visibility, proximity, accessibility, and distractibility.

1. *Visibility.* The teacher must be visible to all of the students and the students must be visible to the teacher. This is an especially important factor when one is considering the inclusion of deaf and/or hearing impaired students, or students with auditory-processing problems in the regular classroom. Clear visual fields allow the teacher to be aware of students who are not attending and focusing appropriately and to intervene when necessary. For example, a teacher who chooses to work with various students at the student's desk may be well advised to ensure that all students know his or her location and can readily see him or her. A teacher who has to move out from behind a teacher's desk blocked from view by a row of binders and/or resource materials and navigate a virtual obstacle course to reach his or her students will prove to be highly ineffective.

2. *Proximity.* The organization of the physical space of the classroom should allow the teacher to move easily about the room. Close physical proximity to the students is important for two reasons; first, physical proximity can be a powerful behaviour management strategy and second, it allows the teacher to effectively monitor the activity of the students from both an academic and behavioural perspective.

3. *Accessibility.* Classroom materials and supplies need to be placed and arranged so that they are easily accessible by all students. Physically challenged students need to have their special equipment in a part of the room that can be easily accessed. High-traffic areas of the classroom (pencil sharpener, trash can, etc.) should be free of congestion.

4. *Distractibility.* Today's classrooms are very active, stimulating places. Many students may find the abundance of visual and auditory stimulation to be highly distracting and overwhelming. This can be especially true for students with auditory-processing problems and Attention Deficit/Hyperactivity Disorders. Specific

adaptations may be needed for students who experience these difficulties in terms of seating arrangements, the use of study carrels for quiet work, or a designated quiet area within the classroom. Students with visual impairments often find the glare of the sun distracting and will require special consideration when the seating arrangements of the classroom are established. The effective use of the physical space within the classroom can prove to be highly beneficial to the preventative classroom management system.

Classroom Rules

The second component of the planning stage is the establishment of classroom rules. Rules reflect the general expectations and standards of behaviour for students and teachers. While some students have a clear understanding of how to behave appropriately within the classroom context, many do not. Students with special needs are often unsure or unknowledgeable as to what is appropriate behaviour in the classroom.

Each teacher must decide on a set of rules for the classroom. This decision will be affected by the teacher's instructional objectives, the developmental level of the students, as well as societal and cultural expectations (the latter two factors are often reflected in Board/District policy). If the classroom rules are to be an effective support to classroom management, the following guidelines should be kept in mind.

1. There should be no more than five rules. All students have a limited ability to retain lengthy lists of rules and regulations. Students with a memory impairment will have added difficulties coping with a long list. The more rules a classroom has, no matter how well stated and logical they may be, the more likely it is that the students will begin to feel over-regulated and antagonistic.

2. Rules should be stated in terms that are so clear that students will know precisely what is expected. Ambiguously stated rules create more problems than they prevent.

3. Rules should be stated in positive terms. The rules of the classroom should be supported by logical rationales that are explained to the students. A negatively stated set of rules conveys negative expectations and precipitates rather than reduces teacher-student conflict.

4. Classroom rules should be consistent with school rules.

5. Finally, effective teachers involve their students in the development of the classroom rules. This approach can promote student responsibility and encourage ownership in helping the class function optimally.

Classroom Procedures and Routines

The third component of the classroom organization and management system is to establish procedures and routines to utilize in the classroom. There are two sets of required procedures and routines in a classroom—procedures and routines for specific activities, and procedures and routines for student accountability.

1. *Specific activities.* In order for the teacher to maintain lesson flow, student engagement in academic work, and smooth transitions between activities, carefully planned procedures and routines are essential. Procedures and routines for specific activities allow for a minimum of disruption in the classroom thereby ensuring that learning can take place. In the elementary classroom the following considerations require the development of planned procedures and routines:

- Student use of classroom space and facilities
- Procedures during whole class activities
- Procedures during small group and learning centre activities
- Transitions from one activity to the next
- Procedures that apply to other areas of the school and playground

A typical set of procedures and routines for activities in an elementary inclusive classroom may be found in Figure 7.2.

FIGURE 7.2
Classroom Procedures and Routines for Specific Activities

Student Use of Classroom Space

- Desks, Tables: Storage Areas
  - Cleanliness and neatness
  - Reorganizing materials at the end of the day
- Learning Centres
  - Access to centre
  - Behavioural expectations
  - Care of materials
  - Coming and going procedures
- Shared Materials
  (Bookshelves, Cabinets, Drawers)
  - Access to materials
  - Use of materials

- Teacher's Desk and Storage Area
  - Teacher permission
- Bathroom, Drinking Fountain, Pencil Sharpener, and Sink
  - When and how to be used
  - Turn-taking procedures

Student Use of Other Areas of School

- Coming To and Going From Classroom
  - Lining up procedures
  - Hallway travel procedures
- Out-of-Classroom Bathrooms, Drinking Fountains, Library, Office, Resource Centre
  - Coming and going procedures
  - Behavioural expectations
- Lunchroom
  - Behavioural expectations
  - Noise level
  - Table manners

Procedures For Whole-Class Activities

- Student Attention
  - Listen to person speaking
- Student Participation
  - Nonverbal signal to speak (Raise hand)
- Assignments
  - Record assignments on chalkboard and students copy into assignment notebook
- Talk During Seat Work
  - Noise level expectation
  - Nonverbal signal to ask for quiet
  - Nonverbal signal for teacher's assistance
- Distributing Materials
  - Who, when, how?
  - What do students do while they wait?
- Submitting Completed Assignments
  - Where, when?

- Returning Graded Assignments
  - When, where?
  - Student storage of graded assignments

- Make-Up Work
  - Notification of missed assignments
  - Time line for completion

- Seat Work Completed
  - Extra-credit assignments
  - Enrichment activities

Procedures For Small Groups

- Student Transition to and from Group
  - Nonverbal signal from teacher

- Materials For Group Work
  - Post list of materials along with assignment

- Behavioural Expectations
  - Roles of group members

Other Procedures

- Beginning and Ending Each Day
  - Overview of day's activities
  - Clean-up routines

- Administrative Procedures
  - Attendance reporting and other record keeping
  - Collection of permission forms, money, etc.

- Fire Drills and Other Emergencies
  - Specific exit procedures

- Student Helpers
  - Procedures for choosing and rotating responsibilities

These procedures and routines apply to all students in the classroom. However, teachers in inclusive classrooms will also have to consider the specific needs of individual students who have special needs. Students with learning disabilities may require additional visual cues in the form of a chart or checklist to assist them to recall the time, place, and steps of a particular procedure or routine. Adaptations are clearly prescribed by the special needs of individual students.

2. *Student accountability.* Students should be clear about the teacher's expectations concerning the quality and quantity of academic work along with time lines

for completion and procedures to be followed when a student encounters difficulty. If the procedures and routines regarding accountability are understood and internalized at the beginning of the school year, future problems may be prevented. Figure 7.3 provides some suggestions for accountability in the inclusive classroom. Again, some adaptations may need to be made in the accountability procedures and routines for students with special instructional needs.

FIGURE 7.3
Classroom Procedures and Routines for Student Accountability

- Quality of written assignments
- Use of manuscript or cursive writing
- Use of pen or pencil
- Heading for papers
- One side of page or two sides
- Incomplete work/Late work
- Notification of assignments
- Posting of assignments
- Explanation of assignments
- Sequencing of assignments
- Monitoring of assignments
- Monitor work of all students
- Identify errors in student work
- Submission of completed work
- Record keeping for completed assignments
- Evaluation of completed work
- Work not turned in on time
- Feedback from teacher—grades and written comments
- Student self-evaluation
- Criteria for displaying work
- How and when to return completed work to students
- Students correct their work
- Teacher checks and returns corrections

Physically challenged as well as learning-disabled students may have difficulty meeting the accountability requirements. Adaptations to the amount of work completed or the length of time allowed to complete it should be considered by the teacher. Absolute standards may have to be replaced by the **Total Quality Management** concept of continuous improvement (Deming, 1991; Glasser, 1990). This concept suggests that the current establishment of arbitrary standards is inappropriate for most learners. A more effective approach advocated by Deming and Glasser states that learning should be continuous, and set at rates appropriate to the individual learners.

Educational Assistants and the Use of Volunteers

The current demands on teachers to provide a thorough academic program incorporating various educational methodologies (i.e., active learning, learner-centred learning, critical thinking strategies, etc.) means that teachers cannot be "all things to all people." Teachers should make effective use of educational assistants, community volunteers, student teachers, secondary level students, peer tutors, and others who are willing to provide schools with additional assistance. The role of the educational assistant must be clearly defined but must also have an element of flexibility. When planning for the use of the educational assistant, the teacher should bear in mind that it is the teacher's role to be responsible for the management of the classroom personnel. Additionally, the teacher bears the responsibility for the successful use of such employees within the context of the classroom. Although the educational assistant cannot take on duties of programming and strategy development, they can help with implementation and evaluation of the programming strategies. A close working relationship with a good educational assistant will advance the progress of the students as well as going far to secure the success of the program.

When a teacher welcomes volunteers into the classroom, the teacher would be well advised to have a predetermined plan for the effective use of these people. It is important to note that the volunteer is often a parent of a student who is in attendance at the school, if not in the teacher's class. The teacher should consider carefully if the presence of the volunteer is beneficial or detrimental to the overall success of the classroom. The use of volunteers need not be limited to just assisting the teacher in various clerical or administrative tasks or to listening to the children read. Glasser (1990, p. 130) extends the concept of volunteers to include volunteer "friends." Glasser writes: "In my opinion these students need more personal attention in a school than it is possible for the staff to give them. They need adults who have the capacity to approach them in such a warm and friendly way that they will be accepted as friends." He goes on to suggest that some students having difficulty in school may need additional emotional support and, if given, these students may be able to cope much more easily.

When planning for the use of additional personnel in the classroom, consideration of the following issues should be made:

1. *Who will work with certain students and who will work with the regular class.* Flexibility of personnel throughout the day must be permitted and determined by student need. Teachers should regularly review how individuals, including themselves, are being used to provide instruction in the classroom. Often, when volunteers present themselves, the volunteer is used to provide tutorial assistance for the special-needs learner. It may be more appropriate for the volunteer to work with the whole class, perhaps to read to them or to supervise an independent activity and for the teacher to work with the particular student requiring individual assistance.

2. *The degree of assistance offered by the various individuals working with the students.* It is important that communication among all those working with particular students is frequently maintained. The student must receive a strong level of consistency regardless of who he or she may be working with. It is the classroom teacher's responsibility to monitor this and ensure that the student is not able to take advantage of those willing to provide more assistance than required.

3. *Arrangements for absences of support personnel.* The assumption that all available personnel will always be able to provide instructional assistance is erroneous. There will be times when assigned assistants, volunteers, etc., are not able to carry out their assigned responsibilities. The teacher's management plan must take into account the absence of such personnel and contingency plans should be in place when this occurs. These contingency plans may include the use of senior-grade students, resource teacher personnel, or a change in program to permit more direct teacher assistance for the special-needs students. In some cases, the special-needs students may have to be taught outside of the class if maintaining the student in the class without additional assistance is detrimental to either the student or other members of the class.

4. *Transmission of relevant information.* All individuals working in a classroom must be aware of pertinent information concerning student need, academic programming, and behavioural management strategies. The teacher must be aware of confidential issues and only share with nonprofessional personnel information relevant to the situation.

Implementing the System

Implementing the classroom management system has two key components. The first is communicating the system to others, the second is the teaching of it to the students. Both components are important to facilitate the successful implementation of the management system. Implementation of the planned system occurs in the first two to possibly three weeks of the school year. The time is well spent as the successful implementation of a carefully and well-prepared plan makes for the smooth operation of the classroom, which enables the teacher to make the best use of the instructional time once implementation is complete.

Communicating the System

The communication of the system involves communication with school personnel, the home, and the students. This eliminates ambiguity on all fronts and provides a strong and consistent base on which the teacher can rely for support.

1. *School personnel.* For the effective implementation of the classroom management system, it is important that all school members including administrative personnel are supportive of the strategies being employed. Hopefully, the various strategies used are discussed among staff members and these members are supportive of one another. Interventions and reinforcement procedures need to be carefully planned for, particularly as they may involve other school personnel beyond the confines of the classroom. For example, if a child with a behavioural disorder responds well to the positive reinforcement of reading to younger grade children, this should be arranged with the teacher of the younger grade prior to it being offered as a positive and rewarding consequence for the student in question. Since many students frequently interact with more than one teacher either due to rotary programs or different supervisors during recess or lunch breaks, consistency of response is necessary. It is incumbent on school administration to ensure that some common elements of classroom management are evident throughout the school and that any disagreement among school personnel regarding behavioural, academic, and physical expectations of particular students is clearly resolved before students interact with school personnel. Further, the primary individual responsible for the student's program (usually the classroom teacher) should be identified. In those instances when the student has difficulty with related personnel this individual should be notified and involved in any conflict resolution.

2. *Home.* Communication between the school and the home needs special consideration. Strategies for effective and ongoing communication with parents should be developed. Parents are concerned about what happens in the classroom. This concern becomes heightened when the classroom of concern is an inclusive one. Parents should be kept informed about their child's progress and should be involved in the decision-making process regarding any adjustments to the academic expectations and programming that need to be made in order to successfully include their child. Parents need to have confidence that their child's teacher has the best interests of their child at heart. Though educators would like to believe that a level of confidence already exists, it is frequently not an accurate

assumption. Teachers must accept that along with inclusive practices there is a need to expend more effort in keeping parents informed and involved.

Parents believe that "no news is good news." Teachers who delay in contacting parents regarding their child's progress until difficulties arise often find parents defensive and angry. The positive way to avoid this is to establish a routine early in the school year, which encourages the informing of parents about their child's growth, behaviourally and academically, and how they may help to maintain these gains.

3. *The students.* Students need to be involved. Both those students who have traditionally been excluded from the regular education classroom as well as the regular education student benefit by being part of the classroom management implementation process. Of special note is the need to have the involvement of the special needs student in the establishment of the procedures and routines of the class as well as involvement in any modification required as a result of their particular educational/behavioural need.

As we have seen, effective teachers in the inclusive elementary classroom spend a great deal of time before the school year begins in planning their classroom organization and management system. Usually they spend much more time involved in this planning than their less effective colleagues. There is, however, another way that effective classroom managers may be differentiated from their less effective colleagues and that is in the way they implement their classroom management system. Effective teachers in the inclusive classroom teach their classroom management system to the students. They do not merely tell the students what the procedures and routines are, they teach these procedures and routines in the same manner in which they teach subject matter (Leinhardt, Weidman & Hammond 1987).

Teaching the System

Teaching the classroom management system involves four steps:

- Providing a rationale for the procedure or routine
- Explaining the procedure or routine
- Demonstrating the procedure or routine
- Practising the procedure or routine

1. *Rationale for procedures and routines.* Students need to understand why a procedure or routine is important in terms of the day-to-day functioning of the classroom and in terms of attaining the instructional objectives of the class. Students who experience behavioural difficulties need detailed explanations concerning the rationale for various routines because they attribute negative motives to those whom they perceive to be in control of their lives.

2. *Explanation of procedures and routines.* If the students are to comply with a procedure or routine they must know the limits or boundaries of the procedure and the specific steps of the routine. Effective teachers spend a considerable amount of time explaining the various aspects of the procedures and routines to the students including the meaning of abstract concepts that are open to a variety of interpretations such as "respect," "quality," or "on time." Students with language disabilities need precise explanations of such concepts if they are to learn the system.

3. *Demonstration of procedures and routines.* Students learn in a variety of ways. Many students learn by receiving verbal messages while others require visual demonstrations. Effective teachers realize this and provide ample opportunities for the demonstration or modelling of the procedure or routine that is being learned. These demonstrations are first provided by the teacher and then by the students. Hearing-impaired students and students with various types of language-based learning disabilities require this type of visually presented information in order to successfully understand the procedure or routine being taught.

4. *Practice of procedures and routines.* Drill and repetition are crucial components of any learning situation. Without practice there is no mastery and no consolidation of skill. Effective teachers have learned that if students are to internalize the procedures and routines of the classroom, they must practise these procedures and routines on a regular basis. It is important for the teacher to understand that many children who are currently being placed in regular classrooms—who formerly may have been in a special classroom—have had limited opportunity to learn and practise appropriate social and behavioural skills. Research evidence suggests that the most highly effective teachers spend a large part of the first two weeks of the school year introducing, practising, and consolidating the procedures and routines of the classroom management system with their students.

Maintaining the System

While careful planning and conscientious implementation of the classroom management system are important to the prevention of problems in the classroom, they are not sufficient to guarantee that the system will be effective. The third component of the proactive/preventative approach to classroom management is the consistent maintenance of the system throughout the school year. There are four elements to the maintenance of the system:

- Monitoring behaviour

- Reinforcing compliance

- Dealing with inappropriate behaviour

- Evaluating and modifying the system

1. *Monitoring behaviour.* Monitoring of student behaviour requires that the teacher routinely survey the classroom for signs of confusion concerning a procedure or routine. It also involves checking for understanding through questioning, examination of assignments, and direct observation of student behaviour. It is important for teachers to engage in "MBWA," which is an acronym for "management by walking around."

2. *Reinforcing compliance.* Students need to be made aware of those situations in which they are complying with the procedures and routines of the classroom if their behaviour is to become consistent with the teacher's expectations (Brophy, 1981). Effective reinforcement by teachers focuses on a description of what the student did that was in compliance and how that behaviour positively affects the other students and/or teachers.

3. *Dealing with inappropriate behaviour.* Students who are not complying with the procedures and routines of the classroom must be dealt with promptly to avoid continuance and possible contagion effects of other students. Redirecting students back to the task, eye contact, moving closer to the student as well as gentle reminders of the procedures or routines that have been avoided all serve to help the student "get back on track." Reteaching of the procedure or routine may be indicated by a student's noncompliance.

4. *Evaluating and modifying the system.* Persistent difficulties with student compliance may indicate that the teacher needs to re-evaluate the classroom management system, modify it, or possibly reteach a particular procedure or routine to the student or students who are experiencing difficulty.

There are a multitude of teaching styles and classroom management techniques. Some teachers are seemingly blessed with the ability to teach constructively, positively, passionately, and invitationally while others find that they are in a continual power struggle with their students (as was seen in one of the case studies at the beginning of this chapter). This latter group of teachers are the ones who are heard to complain that their classes would be so much better if only they had better equipment, less students, more room, a newer facility, no "bad" students, more administrative support, and so on. These are the teachers who mirror student behaviour rather than manage it. The students are left with little recourse but to hope that in the next school year they will have the good fortune of being placed with a different type of teacher— one who is more proactive and engaging.

▣ Section 2: Strategies for Specific Behavioural Concerns

Teaching is an art, a combination of drama, craft, business skill, curriculum knowledge, personality, and energy melding together in a flexible, cohesive, yet ever-changing form that reflects student need and teacher motivation and results in a positive outcome from which emerges the growth and development of all participants. Theoretically, given the above description, every lesson should progress smoothly to a logical and positive conclusion.

Unfortunately, there comes a time when, for whatever reason, be it personal or social, a behavioural difficulty will surface. This is a fact of life in teaching. Even the most experienced and professional teacher will have to deal with behaviour that is not productive to learning. This behaviour is often termed "misbehaviour" or "inappropriate behaviour." These terms are misnomers. No behaviour is inappropriate, certainly not in the eyes of the student producing it! The truly professional teacher will recognize acting-out behaviour for what it is. It is the student acting out their frustration; a reaction on the part of the student to a stimulus or an antecedent of some kind. The stimulus may be that a concept of the lesson is too difficult for that student to deal with, or it may be a reaction to a stimulus that has occurred outside of the classroom or even outside of the school. Regardless, the teacher must deal with it effectively and quickly with as little disruption to the learning otherwise taking place in the room.

There are many tools available to the art of teaching—choosing the right one and employing it well forms part of the craft. When working with challenging behaviours in the classroom the most powerful tool at the disposal of the teacher is the teacher's attitude. Challenging behaviours are presented in the classroom from an emotional base on the part of the student. The attitude of the teacher must be one of acknowledgement of the student's emotions. The student's emotional action must not be dealt with by an emotional reaction by the teacher. Such a reaction will only serve to escalate the student behaviour to the detriment of all concerned. The behaviour must be viewed as a symptom of the student and should not become a symptom of the teacher. With this in mind, student behaviour becomes a part of teaching rather than a barrier to it. The behaviour then can be "read" more appropriately and an effective consequence can be implemented quickly. Students acting emotionally are displaying a reaction to a stimulus but are unable to express it in socially acceptable terms. Do not expect a student to approach quietly and explain that they haven't eaten yet today because there was an argument at home and they are feeling pressure to perform academically when really they'd rather call it quits for the day if that's all right. Our students simply don't possess the skills to express their needs in such a rational manner. For example, any one behaviour can be effectively consequenced in many different ways. The consequence that is ultimately implemented would be the one that is prescribed for the situation as a whole, not in isolation. Variables such as student history (academic as well as social); special needs of the student; ethnic background; curriculum; student personality; as well as what the long-range goals are for the individual student will affect the decision of the teacher to employ one particular strategy or consequence over another. The art of teaching in such a situation is for the teacher to be able to do this in a very short space of time. The following list of points is for teachers to remember when faced with challenging behaviours.

- "Read" the behaviour—what need is the student really indicating?
- Is the student in crisis and therefore requires privacy outside of the classroom in order to be assisted?
- Is there a safety issue for the student and/or others?
- Allow the student to "own" their behaviour: do not take it as a personal affront or insult.
- The student is looking to you, the teacher, for help and guidance—choose an intervention and a consequence that will best serve this purpose.
- What is the long-range plan or goals for the student?
- Punishment is not an intervention.

With these points in mind, what follows is a suggested procedure for implementation of behaviour intervention:

- Read the behaviour.
- Redirect the student's focus.
- Acknowledge the child and the behaviour calmly and directly.
- Meet the student's need as determined by reading the behaviour.
- Support the student through caring concern.
- Refocus the student.
- Follow through.
- Consult and collaborate as required.
- Adjust the student's short-term plan and possibly long-term plan as necessary.
- Support and follow through.

In a classroom, the procedure can be demonstrated through the following scenarios: a grade-five class is working on math. The students have been asked to complete a review test for evaluative purposes. The students are working well with the exception of Susan, who has experienced some degree of difficulty with math on previous occasions. Susan turns her paper over and slams her pencil down on her desk, breaking it in two, and announces loudly and rudely that she hates math, doesn't understand why she has to do this stupid test, the teacher is stupid, the school is stupid, and she can't be made to do it. The teacher can deal with this in two ways. The teacher, Mr. Matthews, can react to the language or he can act with the student. In reacting to the language, an argument is sure to ensue. The student will say she doesn't care and may well run out of the class, stating she hates the teacher and all teachers before him. In taking action with the student, the teacher may choose the following path. The teacher quickly but calmly moves to the student and quietly states the obvious, "Susan, you're quite upset about this math work" (reading the behaviour/acknowledgement). "You're not one to get like this so there must be some problem with the test (redirect), what can you tell me about it?" (support). "It's stupid because I can't do it, and now I'm going to fail!" At this point Susan starts to cry. "No, Susan, you're not going to fail, certainly not because of some stupid math test that some stupid teacher in a stupid school made you do when you don't understand the questions. Tell you what, you may go the washroom, rinse your eyes, get a drink from the water fountain and when you're ready to come back, I'll give you some pointers on how to deal with these stupid questions (refocus/support). Would you like Joanna to go with you?" (meeting the student's need to feel worthwhile and successful, supporting the student through caring concern). Upon the student's return, Mr. Matthew modifies the test expectations for her, works with her as required so that Susan meets expectations successfully (refocus).

Later in the day when Susan has fully recovered from her emotions, Mr. Matthews suggests several options to Susan that would help her—a study buddy, extra help at lunch or after school, or a tutorial partner from a higher grade level. The teacher talks to Susan's other teachers to determine if this behaviour is common in other class situations and asks for input on how he might best deal with her anxiety in math class (consult and collaboration). Mr. Matthews makes adjustments to Susan's short-term goals until she gets over this particular "hurdle" but keeps his options open for long-term adjustment should Susan continue to experience difficulty (short-term/long-range planning). During the next several weeks, he ensures that Susan will feel better about her math work through the judicious use of praise and encouragement as well as some orchestrated successes to provide Susan with empirical evidence that she could be successful in math (support, follow through). It should be noted that Mr. Matthews will move through the suggested procedure as required. This may not follow the order suggested, which is indicated by student need as evaluated by the teacher.

For the sake of demonstration, let's examine a more difficult scenario where the situation is threatening to become violent. The class is a grade-seven math class. The class has been working fairly well with little disruption when Ralph, with one swipe of his arm, clears his books from his desk onto the floor and violently pushes his desk over, folds his arms over his chest and yells "I'm not doing any more of this ******* work and no ******* teacher's gonna make me!!!" This is a potentially dangerous situation where the safety of students could easily become a concern. Should the teacher choose to react to the behaviour rather than act with the student, the student may feel further challenged and thus engage in a power struggle that could result in him throwing the desk chair across the room and possibly hurting others as he storms out. A more proactive and thus effective approach would be to follow the procedure outlined above. The teacher might say, "Ralph, you're really angry and I can't believe it's at me or the math work, because you're not one to act like this" (reading the behaviour/acknowledgement). "Are you feeling OK? You don't look so good, your face is flushed and you look positively ill" (redirect, caring concern). During this time the teacher approaches the student cautiously and slowly, appearing calm and relaxed, arms held loosely at sides, open palms and nonthreatening. "How can I help you?" (support, caring concern). "Let me feel your forehead to see if you have a temperature." (support, caring concern). "I believe you should go down to the office to see the nurse, I'll come with you" (redirect, caring concern, support). The teacher accompanies the student to the office expressing concern for his welfare along the way, or she may enquire once the student is out of the class, what all the anger was about and simply listen to what the student has to say (caring concern, support, refocus). The teacher may also offer the student time for self-evaluation with the goal of collaboration with the student to find a solution to his difficulty (support, caring concern, refocus, adjustment of short- and possibly long-term goals, as required). Once at the office the teacher may briefly consult with administration before returning to class. Later, the teacher should consult with other staff members and possibly students to assist in meeting Ralph's needs (follow through, adjustment). Regardless of whether or not support staff is used, the teacher works with Ralph to build self-esteem and self-control (collaboration, follow through, support, caring concern). It is important to note that the more challenging the behaviour, the more the teacher needs to demonstrate support for the student in a caring concerned, nonpunitive manner. Also of note from this scenario is the need for a school plan for dealing with students in severe difficulty. In this situation the teacher had to escort Ralph to the office, and leave the class unattended during this time. Part of the behaviour intervention plan in the school will have to include such contingency plans that would support staff as necessary. In this case, a neighbouring teacher could be asked to supervise.

The foregoing illustrations serve to demonstrate how a teacher may effectively deal with behavioural difficulties while at the same time maintaining a positive relationship with the student. The student is shown caring concern. The student's dignity is maintained and he or she is treated with respect. It has been said that a teacher should always deal with students as if the student's parents were watching. This may well be a powerful caveat from which teachers should operate.

Tools for Behaviour Intervention

The following is a list of basic behaviour intervention strategies or tools that can be employed by teachers. It is important to note that to be effective, teachers should have a repertoire of strategies that are varied and avoid using the same strategy repeatedly. The list that follows is not exhaustive but serves as a guideline to demonstrate some of the variety of strategies available to teachers.

1. *Activity–Time out.* The student is removed from an activity for a period of time for inappropriate behaviour. This is done in the classroom. Before returning to the activity, the student must be able to identify the reason for removal, alternative ways of handling similar situations in the future, and state plans for behaviour upon the return.

2. *Behaviour modification.* A behaviour management system whereby behaviour is strengthened or weakened through the use of positive reinforcers. These reinforcers often take the form of rewards for appropriate performance. A **fade program** forms part of this system. Fading refers to a gradual withdrawal of the reinforcers used in behaviour modification to reward target behaviours.

3. *Behaviour rehearsal (role playing).* Role playing allows students to be exposed to hypothetical situations in dramatic terms without experiencing real consequences for their expressions or actions. In such nonthreatening situations, students are able to examine the consequences of various behaviours.

4. *Logical consequences.* The setting up of a consequence for a misbehaviour should be logically related to what has occurred. For example: books strewn on the floor should be cleaned up by the student who created the mess.

5. *Cueing (physical and/or verbal).* Used to teach a student to remember to act appropriately at a specific period of time (often this may be done with a secret cue known only to the teacher and student).

6. *Imagery techniques (relaxation techniques).* Used to teach students to control feelings of anxiety in stressful situations. Imagery involves the visualization of pleasant scenes or situations to assist the student to redirect his or her attention from a stressful or anxiety-producing situation. Ultimately, the student would employ this strategy independently.

7. *Instructional detention.* The child remains after school to make up for time lost during instruction time. As a logical consequence, the student completes assignments missed during class time due to behavioural concerns. It is presented as a result of lost class time during the day but must not be used or perceived as punishment.

8. *Self-talk training.* The student identifies the problem and self-explores all alternatives with the goal of eliminating those alternatives that hold negative consequences. The student shares his or her findings with the teacher. The student negotiates with the teacher for a contractual agreement. This procedure shifts the responsibility from teacher to student.

9. *Modelling.* Teaches more positive behaviours through observation of others performing them in structured situations. If a teacher expects to teach appropriate behaviours, it is imperative to model those behaviours.

10. *Proximity control.* The teacher uses physical distance between self and student to manage behaviour. The close proximity of the teacher reminds students that adults care and will help.

11. *Redirection.* The teacher guides a student back to a task through an alternative motivation, as a way of showing the student a more productive and positive response than the present course of action.

12. *Reinforcers.* Reinforcers are used following a stimulus and strengthen or increase the future occurrence of the response. There are three groups of reinforcers: social reinforcers, token reinforcers, and activity reinforcers. These are usually used in conjunction with a program of behaviour modification.

13. *Response cost.* This technique involves the loss of reinforcers as a result of undesired behaviour. It equates to the cost of the behaviour. This could involve loss of activity time, points, tokens, or a portion of free time.

14. *Self-monitored program.* A systematic charting and/or reinforcement program to eliminate undesirable behaviours (or to instil positive ones) that are managed and controlled by the student, thus, promoting self-control. The teacher, in consultation with the student, sets out the program but it is the student who implements it.

15. *Time out.* The student is temporarily removed from a reinforcing situation immediately following the occurrence of an inappropriate behaviour. This method can be effective but can also be easily abused, therefore it is important to establish guidelines for its use. This differs from activity time out, where the time out is implemented within the confines of the classroom. This time out will necessitate the removal of the student from the classroom to a school designated time out location under the supervision of school personnel. For the student to re-enter the classroom, the student must devise and present a plan for behavioural control that is acceptable to the classroom teacher. This may be done with the support of additional school personnel such as a resource teacher.

All of the above tools involve working *with* the student. The inventive teacher will often devise new tools for use with a particular student in a particular situation. The key word in working with behaviour is flexibility. If one approach does not work, then others should be tried. Behavioural intervention is dictated by student need and is limited only by teacher imagination and creativity. All of this takes time, planning, and careful consideration. It demands that the teacher know the students, their weaknesses as well as their strengths. Many educators simply level punishment upon their "errant pupils" and cloak such actions under the guise of "logical consequences" and "time out." Punishment results from a reaction of anger and lack of skill on the part of the teacher.

▣ Conclusion

Effective behaviour management is the result of careful consideration through planning, application through implementation, and follow through and maintenance. The development of an effective classroom management system requires careful planning with particular consideration given to those students with specific disabilities. It involves collaboration and communication with school and support personnel, the home, and the students. This investment will be realized in the free flowing of learning and positive interactions that take place in a secure and well-managed classroom. The implementation of the plan should happen in the first weeks of the school year and is taught as an important part of the curriculum. Maintenance of the system ensures that the teacher and the students will continue to enjoy a dynamic and creative learning and growth experience throughout the year. In the elementary classroom of the nineties, where students of varying abilities and specific learning and behavioural disabilities are included, it is crucial that the teacher realize the importance and necessity of developing an effective proactive and preventative classroom management system. It is hoped that this chapter will facilitate teachers in this endeavour.

SUGGESTED RESOURCES

Albert, I. (1989). *A teacher's guide to cooperative discipline: How to manage your classroom and promote self-esteem.* Circle Pines, MN: American Guidance Service.

Crealoch, C., & Bachor, D. (1995). *Instructional strategies for students with special needs* (2nd edition). Scarborough, ON: Allyn & Bacon.

Deiner, P.L. (1983). *Resources for teaching young children with special needs.* New York: Harcourt Brace Jovanovich.

Eggert, L.L. (1994). *Anger management for youth: Stemming aggression and violence.* Bloomington, IN: National Education Service.

Glasser, W. (1990). The quality school. New York: Harper & Row.

Nichols, E. (1994). *Tools for transitions: A counsellor's guide to learning disabilities.* Toronto: Learning Disabilities Association of Ontario.

Rockwell, Sylvia. (1993). *Tough to reach, tough to teach.* Reston, VA: Council for Exceptional Children.

Schwartz, S., & Pollishuke, M. (1990). *Creating the child-centred classroom.* Toronto: Irwin.

Winzer, M. (1993). *Children with exceptionalities: A Canadian perspective.* Scarborough, ON: Prentice-Hall.

REFERENCES

Blankenship, C., & Lilly, M.S. (1981). *Mainstreaming students with learning and behavioural problems.* Toronto: Allyn and Bacon.

Bos, C.S., & Vaughan, S. (1988). *Strategies for teaching students with learning and behaviour problems.* Toronto: Allyn and Bacon.

Brophy, J. (1981). On praising effectively. *The Elementary School Journal, 81,* 269–78.

Charles, C.M. (1992). *Building classroom discipline,* (4th edition). New York: Longman.

Collis, M.,& Dutton, J. (1990). *Becoming responsible learners: Strategies for positive classroom management.* Portsmouth, OR: Heinemann.

Cooper, J.M. (Ed.). (1990). *Classroom teaching skills* (4th edition). Toronto: D.C. Heath.

De Luke, S.V., & Knoblock, P. (1987). Teaching behaviour as preventative discipline. *Teaching Exceptional Children, 18–24.*

Deming, W.E. (1991). *Out of crisis.* Cambridge, MA: MIT Press.

Doyle, W. (1986). Classroom organization and management. In W.C. Wittrock (Ed.), *Handbook of research on teaching* (3rd edition). New York: Macmillan.

Dreikurs, R., Grunwald, B., & Pepper, F. (1982). *Maintaining sanity in the classroom: Classroom management techniques* (2nd edition). New York: Harper & Row.

Evertson, C., Emmer, E., Clements, B., Sanford, J., & Worsham, M. (1984). *Classroom management for elementary teachers.* Englewood Cliffs, NJ: Prentice-Hall.

Glasser, W. (1990). The quality school. New York: Harper & Row.

Jones, V., & Jones, L. (1986). *Comprehensive classroom management: Creating a positive learning environment* (2nd edition). Toronto: Allyn and Bacon.

Leinhardt, G., Weidman, C., & Hammond, K.M. (1987). Introduction and integration of classroom routines by expert teachers. *Curriculum inquiry,* 17, 135–76.

Rinne, C.H. (1984). *Attention: The fundamentals of classroom control.* Columbus, OH: Merrill.

Shalaway, L. (1989). *Learning to teach not just for beginners.* New York: Scholastic.

Valpy, M. (October 2, 1993). The 40% factor. *The Globe & Mail.*

Promoting Social Development and Acceptance in the Elementary Classroom

Kimberly A. Schonert-Reichl

Shelley Hymel

University of British Columbia

Introduction

The creation of educational environments that foster peer acceptance among all children, regardless of their differences, has become a significant concern to educators interested in nurturing the development of the whole child. Although the socialization of children has traditionally been seen as the primary responsibility of parents and family, in today's changing society schools are faced with increasing demands to provide children not only with traditional academic resources, but with opportunities that promote social development (Anderson, 1994; Durlak & Jason, 1984; Elias & Clabby, 1988; Johnson, Jason & Betts, 1990; Yeates & Selman, 1989). As the following case illustrates, the boundaries between social and academic problems can often become blurred, and failure to address social adjustment difficulties may seriously impede academic progress and educational success.

Fred, an 11-year-old boy, had experienced academic problems in school for several years, and the beginning of grade 6 brought new difficulties. Fred lived with his mother, stepfather, and seven brothers and sisters in a small, two-bedroom apartment. His family was on public assistance and no one in his immediate family had ever graduated from secondary school. Fred's appearance was unkempt—his clothing had not been washed for some time and he often smelled. Classmates often made fun of the way that Fred was dressed and the thick glasses that he wore. Fred was also shy and withdrawn in class, and the kids in his class made fun of that. He also had a learning disability, and his classmates teased him whenever he had to go to the resource room for help.

Fred stopped attending school at the beginning of October. The school's attempts to reach Fred's mother were difficult because the family's telephone was frequently disconnected due to the family's inability to pay. By mid-December, Fred had not attended school for three months. The precipitating event to his truancy had been an altercation between him and several classmates. During class one day, several boys had taken his glasses and written on them with markers. These students had also taken Fred's jacket and put a note on it that said "kick me." Mr. Smith, Fred's teacher, was frustrated and overwhelmed with the entire situation. He felt that Fred was being used as a scapegoat by the class. Mr. Smith commented, "These students are just not accepting of any differences in their peers' behaviours or appearance. I want to help Fred, but I just don't know what I can do."

Recent empirical research suggests that children's social interactions and behaviours in the classroom are stronger predictors of their grades than are their standardized test scores (Wentzel, 1993). Moreover, whereas interventions designed to develop positive social behaviour at school have frequently resulted in higher levels of academic achievement, interventions designed to improve academic achievement do not always lead to corresponding improvements in classroom social behaviours (Cobb, 1972; Coie & Krehbiel, 1984; Hops & Cobb, 1974). Thus, for both ideal and practical reasons, creating educational environments that foster positive social development in children has become a critical educational focus, important for ensuring *both* academic success *and* social competence among students.

Schools provide a unique opportunity for encouraging social growth because many of students' interpersonal interactions often occur in a setting in which adults can intervene and guide positive development. Despite the infinite number of occasions in which social interventions can occur in school environments, teachers often feel ill equipped and unacquainted with the strategies necessary for promoting both social development and acceptance among their students. Providing teachers with information and techniques for fostering socialization becomes particularly salient as schools move to merge regular and special education into one unified system—a system that is noncategorical and attends to the individual needs of students. One goal of the inclusive education movement is the creation of school environments that promote both social competence and development among *all* students (Gartner & Lipsky, 1987; Stainback & Stainback, 1985). A motivating factor behind inclusive education is the belief that the social integration of students, regardless of differences in such things as ability or behaviour, will foster interaction and acceptance among children and therefore promote both their social and moral growth. As stated by Snell (1991, pp. 137–38): "Probably the three most important and reciprocal benefits from integration ... are (a) the development of social skills ... across all school age groups, (b) improvements in the attitudes that nondisabled peers have for their peers with disabilities, and (c) the development of positive relationships and friendships between peers as a result of integration."

Despite the compelling nature of these arguments, promoting interpersonal acceptance among students is often quite difficult to achieve in practice. As researchers have noted, social integration requires more than mere physical integration to ensure success (Certo, Haring & York, 1983; Johnson, Johnson & Maruyama, 1983; Simpson, 1980). If one goal of inclusive education is to promote social acceptance and development among students, then direct interventions designed to facilitate positive social interactions between all students is necessary, especially in an inclusive setting.

Over the years, a plethora of intervention programs have been developed specifically to improve contact between students with and without special needs. These methods have often yielded successful outcomes and have included such programs as cognitive information sessions or curricular infusion, designed to change the attitudes and beliefs of peers without special needs (Donaldson & Martinson, 1977; Fiedler & Simpson, 1987; Simpson, 1980), direct training of social skills (Asher & Hymel, 1986; Nelson, 1988; Sasso, Simpson & Novak, 1985), and specific activities designed to increase the frequency of positive social contacts among all students (Strain, 1981). Despite the ubiquitous success of such intervention techniques, we argue here that teachers in inclusive settings must attend to promoting the acceptance and social development of *all* children and not just target intervention efforts to those students identified with special needs. Indeed, all children would benefit from experiences that facilitate healthy social adjustment.

In this chapter, we consider the social development of elementary school-age children and suggest ways in which teachers can facilitate such development in the inclusive classroom setting. Although education has traditionally emphasized the three "R's" of reading, writing, and arithmetic, we suggest that a fourth "R" of schooling—relationships—is also an important consideration in our education system. Over the past decade or two, researchers have increasingly recognized the importance of children's interpersonal relations, especially with agemates, for overall development (see Asher & Coie, 1990; Parker & Asher, 1987 for reviews). Furthermore, educators have increasingly called for assistance in developing procedures for maximizing the social abilities of their students. Although enhancing social development has to date been primarily implicit in the school curriculum, it is time to consider how this can explicitly be fostered within the inclusive classroom setting.

▣ Social Problems in the Inclusive Classroom

Research suggests that children and adolescents with learning and behavioural difficulties experience a multitude of social and emotional difficulties relative to their nondisabled agemates, including low self-esteem (Black, 1974) and poor self-concept (Pearl & Bryan, 1979), inadequate social skills (Bender & Smith, 1990; Gresham, 1982; Hollinger, 1987; Selman & Demorest, 1984), egocentricity and lower empathy (Chandler, 1973; Chandler, Greenspan & Barenboim, 1974; Dickstein & Warren, 1980; Kaplan & Arbuthnot, 1985), fewer friendships and lower overall acceptance among their classmates (Armstrong, Rosenbaum & King, 1992; Asher & Taylor, 1981; Drabman & Patterson, 1981; Ray, 1985; Sabornie & Kaufmann, 1985; Stone & LaGreca, 1990; Vaughn, Hogan, Kouzekanani & Shapiro, 1990); (see Bryan, 1991 for a review). Not only are students with special needs perceived more negatively by their nondisabled classmates, but teachers do not uniformly accept these students either (Gans, 1985; Garrett & Crump, 1980). For instance, Center and Wascom (1987) compared teachers' perceptions of the social behaviours of students with and without behavioural disorders. Their findings revealed that teachers perceived less prosocial and more antisocial behaviour in those students with behavioural disorders than in those students without behavioural disorders.

The attitudes of teachers undoubtedly have a significant impact on the attitudes of students in the elementary classroom setting. Research indicates that if teachers possess negative feelings toward students with special needs, these feelings can be clearly communicated to students (Cartledge, Frew & Zaharias, 1985; Simpson, 1980). Moreover, teachers can have an impact on how children with disabilities are perceived by classmates (Armstrong, Rosenbaum & King, 1992). Even the way teachers respond to a student's misbehaviour has implications for how the child comes to be perceived by his or her classmates (White & Kistner, 1992). The lack of acceptance by both peers and teachers that the special needs child may face not only affects self-concept and self-esteem, but may also have a negative impact on school performance and achievement (Heron & Harris, 1987; Schumaker & Hazel, 1984).

At the same time, it is also important to recognize that such negative effects are not inevitable, and that the development of positive peer relationships can play a significant role in determining social and academic success (versus failure) within the inclusive classroom (Plumb & Brown, 1990; Westervelt & McKinney, 1980). Indeed, previous research on mainstreamed settings suggests that regular education students can help students with special needs feel both accepted and supported (Stainback, Stainback & Wilkinson, 1992). Thus, the inclusive classroom, if designed with explicit consideration of the social developmental needs of its members, can positively influence student outcomes.

Appropriate structuring of the inclusive classroom becomes particularly important when one considers that it is during the school years that we come to acquire our most basic social skills and learn to negotiate our way in a social world. In his book, *Friendship Development Among Children in School*, Rizzo (1989) asks us to consider an ecological perspective on children's interpersonal adjustment, in which social adjustment in the classroom is seen as a complex and dynamic interchange between the child and the social environment. For example, after spending many months observing a group of first graders as they learned about the social world of the school, Rizzo suggested that the relatively intimidating nature of the recess playground itself encouraged children to develop partnerships and friendships with classmates, so at least they would not be alone during recess. As educators, then, we can facilitate or enhance the ongoing process of social development by structuring the environment of the classroom and school, but only if we understand the nature of social development during the elementary school years.

◈ Social and Emotional Development During the Elementary School Years

If teachers wish to provide an optimal environment for encouraging children's progress toward higher levels of social maturity, they first must be aware of what is "typical" of children at various stages of development, and what characterizes the logical "next step" in development. That is, educators should be knowledgeable about children's emotional and social development prior to implementing strategies designed to foster social growth. Accordingly, in the following sections, we outline domains of social and emotional development that we believe to be particularly important within the inclusive classroom. Our discussion brings together various lines of developmental research and is intended to provide teachers with some of the necessary information for determining whether students are displaying age-appropriate levels of emotional and/or social development. Although general age-related trends are highlighted here, it is important to emphasize that the development of individual children may proceed at a slower or more rapid pace than suggested by the age-norms provided, although the specified order of acquisition of each milestone should nevertheless be observed.

Development of Social Participation

Educators sometimes assume that children learn naturally to interact with one another, and that social interaction experiences are one area in which children develop prior to school entry. However, truly interactive social involvement is not a dominant form of social participation until the early elementary school years. Specifically, research on the development of social participation or children's play (Parten, 1932; Rubin, Fein & Vandenberg, 1983) has shown that over the preschool years children primarily engage in solitary forms of social participation with solitary and parallel play (playing near other children and often with the same materials, but not truly interacting) predominating. By the kindergarten year, five-year-olds are increasingly likely to engage in truly interactive exchanges with their peers (what is referred to as associative or cooperative play), although more solitary forms of social participation are still quite common. Thus, during the early elementary school year, children become increasingly likely to engage in true interaction with their peers. And it is through these social experiences that children learn to cooperate, negotiate, and compromise, effectively deal with conflict, and learn to solve social problems in an acceptable manner. The process is a very gradual one because children are continuing to develop cognitively. Indeed, how children *think* about social relationships evolves more slowly, as a result of both their ever-increasing cognitive capacities and their social experiences with others (Higgins & Parsons, 1983).

Development of Empathy

Empathy—defined here as an individual's emotional responsiveness to the emotional experiences of another—has been increasingly recognized as an important dimension of social competence because it is assumed that one's emotional responsiveness to others plays a significant role in enhancing or diminishing the quality of one's social relationships (Bryant, 1987; Clark & Bittle, 1992; Hoffman, 1982; Schonert-Reichl, 1993). Furthermore, beginning in the preschool years, empathy is seen as an important motivator of prosocial or altruistic behaviour (Eisenberg & Miller, 1987). However, the ability to empathize or sympathize with others appears to develop gradually throughout the childhood years and even into adolescence.

Hoffman (1982, 1988) suggests that there are four distinct stages that characterize the development of empathy. Even very young children (e.g., one-year-olds) are capable of a rudimentary empathic response, such as crying when another person cries. Hoffman characterizes this early stage as one of **global empathy**. By two years, children appear to want to help or "cure" a distressed person, although their "help" usually involves things that *they* would like (such as getting their *own* mother, or offering *their* favourite stuffed toy). Hoffman describes this stage as characterized by **egocentric empathy**, since young children have a very limited ability to consider what the other person wants or needs. Throughout the preschool and elementary school years, children move through a third stage in which they gradually become able to **empathize with another person's feelings**. During this stage, children become better at recognizing the more subtle emotional cues and indicators of distress (Pearl, 1985; Radke-Yarrow & Zahn-Waxler, 1984; Radke-Yarrow, Zahn-Waxler & Chapman, 1983). According to Hoffman, children also become better able to figure out what the *other* person might need by way of comfort or help, and are less likely to assume that the other person would want what they want. Still, during the elementary school years, children are pretty much tied to the immediate situation. It is not until late childhood or even early adolescence that children are able to empathize with another person's general condition or plight, which constitutes Hoffman's fourth stage of **empathy for another's condition**.

Given these gradual developmental shifts, it becomes important to recognize that younger children would not be expected to readily interpret emotional cues of distress, although attention to such cues can be fostered. Moreover, younger children would be less able to empathize with the other person's feelings, let alone their condition. This last point is particularly salient in the inclusive classroom setting because teachers may try to promote acceptance among all children by appealing to their empathy. Such attempts may induce frustration for both teachers and students if the teacher does not first realize that the children have not yet achieved the cognitive level of empathy necessary for understanding their classmate's condition. At the same time, although such appeals may not be readily understood by all children, they model a higher level of empathic maturity, and such experiences may indeed help to promote further empathic development. Thus, understanding students' varying empathic abilities may be particularly important in the inclusive classroom, as teachers attempt to promote understanding of others' feelings and experiences among students with and without special needs.

Research has found that parents play a key role in the developing empathy in their children. For example, parents who are nurturing and supportive and who themselves demonstrate empathy and sensitivity to others, have children who also respond more empathically to the distress of others (Radke-Yarrow & Zahn-Waxler, 1984). Modelling empathic reactions, however, is not sufficient for developing empathy in children. Parents (and teachers) must set clear limits for children and intervene when children display inappropriate emotions and reactions. Such interventions have been found to be associated with higher levels of empathy in children (Eisenberg et al., 1991). In their book, *Bringing Up the Moral Child*, Schulman and Mekler (1985, p. 67) suggest a number of strategies for parents who wish to develop empathy in their children. The following recommendations adapted from their book can be particularly useful for teachers interested in encouraging empathy development in students:

1. Draw children's attention to the feelings of others. Ask them to see situations from the other person's perspective.

2. Tell children how their behaviour affects the feelings of others, including yourself.

3. Talk about feelings and discuss "why people feel the way they do."

4. Make explicit the actions a child can take to demonstrate consideration for others' feelings.

5. Emphasize the importance of consideration and respect for others. Tell the child that it is important to you that *your* students show consideration for one another.

6. Tell children that you care about their feelings too.

7. Children do not implicitly know what your expectations are. Remember to take time to explain to them what types of behaviours you expect.

8. Help children understand other people's feelings by encouraging them to remember a time when they might have felt the same way.

9. Encourage consideration of others by giving your approval to children who demonstrate caring behaviours.

10. Model empathy and tell children of your own empathic reactions.

11. Identify specific examples of people who are empathic.

12. Tell children about the positive feelings one experiences when one shows care for others.

These suggestions can serve as guidelines for teachers to create opportunities for empathy development within the context of the inclusive classroom. Undoubtedly, a number of occasions arise in school where such strategies can be utilized. For example, a teacher may want to bring in newspaper or magazine articles that illustrate an adult's or child's prosocial behaviour (e.g., helping others in distress during an emergency, volunteering time to help others, donating clothing or money to charity). A teacher should also make a concerted effort to point out the importance of empathy for others, particularly among students in the classroom. In a book entitled *Educating for Character*, Thomas Lickona (1991, p. 99) provides several illustrations for promoting empathy and prosocial behaviours among classmates. For example, he describes a strategy utilized by a fifth-grade teacher in New York who promotes positive affirmation among classmates by scheduling **appreciation time**. "Three times a week, the teacher gathers her students into a circle and invites them to 'tell something that someone else did that you appreciated.'" Lickona reports that this teacher has found appreciation time to be one of the most popular activities among students.

Lickona (1991) describes another activity utilized by a sixth-grade teacher in Canada, designed to acknowledge and reinforce positive interpersonal acts through use of a **good deeds tree**. On one of the bulletin boards in the classroom, a tree with bare branches was drawn by the teacher. Next to the tree was a box filled with "leaves" made from green construction paper. At the beginning of the school year, the teacher asked students to report any good deed that a classmate did for them or a good deed that they had observed. A leaf with the student's name who had performed the good deed was then prepared by the teacher and affixed to the tree. A brief description of the good deed might also be provided on the leaf, offering specific examples or models of positive interpersonal acts for the students. As the number of reported good deeds increased over the school year, the tree appears to grow, providing a visible and concrete symbol in the classroom of students' increasing acts of kindness to one another. In fostering empathy, per se, it may be beneficial to discuss each good deed with the class, emphasizing the feelings that likely arise in response to such actions on the part of both the recipient and the actor. These are just a few concrete examples of how teachers can provide opportunities within the classroom that promote empathy and acceptance among all students. Such techniques enhance the development of prosocial behaviours by demonstrating specific examples of students' caring and respect for one another.

Development of Perspective Taking

What appears critical to the development of empathy and altruism is the development of perspective-taking or role-taking ability—the ability to "put oneself in another's shoes." Robert Selman (1976, 1980) has studied the development of perspective taking for many years now and suggests that there are five distinct levels of development in this area, levels that emerge gradually over the school years.

According to Selman, preschool and kindergarten children (three to six years) are basically egocentric and fail to distinguish between their own interpretation of an event and someone else's. Selman refers to this as Stage 0, characterized by an **egocentric viewpoint**. At this age children do not appear to realize that someone may have a different perspective or point of view from their own. The early elementary school age child (four to nine) is typically found to be in Stage 1, which Selman calls **social-information role taking**. In this stage, the child *does* recognize that other people can see things differently than they do, but they think that this only happens because the other person has access to different information. If they both had the same information, surely the other person would see it their way. It is not until 8 to 10 years, when children enter Stage 2, **self-reflectional role taking**, that they can understand that another person *can* have a different perspective from them, even if they have access to the same information. The second- to fourth-grade child can also understand that the other person can take *their* perspective, just as they can take the other person's perspective (what Selman refers to as "mutual awareness"). One limitation here is that the child of 8 to 10 years is not very good at considering both of these perspectives simultaneously. They can consider one or the other, but not both at the same time. By 10 to 12 years, at the stage of **mutual role taking** (Stage 3), the child can consider multiple perspectives simultaneously, and knows that the other person can do the same. At this age, the child also becomes capable of taking the perspective of a separate third party, someone not involved in the situation, and can figure out how each party, participants and non-participants, might react. A final stage of **social and conventional system role taking** (Stage 4) emerges in early adolescence, when children come to realize that members of a group can share a common perspective, and can consider or assume another's perspective by thinking about the "typical" perspective of that group.

Development of Prosocial Reasoning

Perhaps as a result of the development of perspective taking, children's ideas about helping others also change with age. Relevant here is research by Nancy Eisenberg (Eisenberg, 1986; Eisenberg & Mussen, 1989) on the development of prosocial reasoning. Eisenberg interviewed children from preschool age through adolescence, asking them to respond to prosocial dilemmas in which the children had to decide whether or not to help another person who was in trouble, when helping would be costly to themselves. She was interested in whether or not the children would decide to help the other person, and also in their reasons for helping or not helping. For example, in one dilemma, the child is walking to a friend's birthday party. On the way, the child comes upon another child who is hurt from a fall. If the child stops to help, he or she will miss the cake and ice cream at the party. The children were asked what they should do and why. On the basis of children's responses to such dilemmas, Eisenberg suggested five distinct stages of prosocial reasoning.

Briefly, Eisenberg found that preschool and early elementary school-age children were basically hedonistic and were most concerned with consequences for the self—Level 1, **hedonistic and self-oriented reasoning**. They often would not help, since it was costly to them, and if they would agree to help, it was because they saw some direct gain for the self, or figured there would be future reciprocity (e.g., the other child would help them later). They might also be willing to help if the person in trouble was someone that they especially liked or needed. Elementary school-age children were most often in the second level, reflecting a **needs orientation**. These children did show concern for the needs of others, even if it might conflict with their own needs, and would be willing to help. However, there was seldom any reference to how the other person would feel (self-reflective role-taking), sympathy, or internalized affect such as guilt.

By later elementary school and sometimes high school—Level 3, **approval and interpersonal orientation** or **stereotyping orientation**—the children appeared to have developed very stereotypic ideas about what was "good" versus "bad" behaviour or a "good" versus a "bad" person. They often talked about gaining the approval or acceptance of others as a reason for helping someone. So, at this stage, children would help because others would like them if they did, and because it was expected or a "social rule." It was not until high school age—Level 4, **self-reflective/empathic orientation**—that children were capable of truly empathic responding and considered how the other person would feel (self-reflectional role taking). At this point child would say things like "I'd feel sorry for her," or "I'd try to put myself in her shoes." Some children at this level even talked about feeling guilty if they did not help or feeling good if they did help. It is important for teachers in the elementary classroom to remember that such an orientation was seen primarily among high school students, and was not typical of elementary school-age children. Moreover, only at the last level—Level 5, **strongly internalized orientation**—did children express truly internalized values of helping, concern for the rights and dignity of others, and concern with maintaining self-respect. Now students might suggest that "I'd feel it was my responsibility to help," or "If everyone helped, society would be a lot better." Eisenberg never observed this last level in elementary school-age children, and observed it only rarely in high school students.

By understanding the factors that appear to underline help giving at different stages of social development (according to the children themselves), teachers may be able to "capitalize" on effective motivators in encouraging help giving in their students. For example, appeals to likely future reciprocity or existing friendships may be particularly useful with early elementary school-age children, while appeals to stereotypes of "bad" versus "good" behaviour or persons or to established social rules may be more effective with middle elementary school-age children. By later elementary school, students may be more likely to respond to appeals to empathy or perspective taking in encouraging help giving. At the same time, it remains important for teachers and other adults to also verbalize and model *higher* levels of prosocial reasoning in order to guide students to the next likely level of social cognitive development. Even though such appeals may not always be effective (given the limits of children's current levels of prosocial reasoning), repeated exposure to higher level reasoning begins to set the stage for the gradual process of development toward greater social maturity.

Development of Person Perception

It is also important to consider developmental changes in the way children think about other people, and the way they think about relationships in general. Conceptions of others, or person perception, change drastically over the school years. Livesley and Bromley (1973) and Barenboim (1981) have outlined several broad shifts in the development of children's perceptions of others. When asked to describe others, young children (two to six or eight years) focus primarily on external, concrete, observable characteristics and physical features such as appearance, possessions, proximity, and overt behaviour (Livesley & Bromley, 1973; Peevers & Secord, 1973). Young children seldom make reference to internal states, and if they do, they are typically limited to global descriptors (nice, good, bad, mean) and are not necessarily viewed as lasting or stable qualities (Rholes & Ruble, 1984). Moreover, such descriptions are generally provided in absolute terms, rather than involving comparisons between others. At about six to eight years, children begin to emphasize comparisons between others, but these comparisons are limited to external, concrete, behavioural characteristics. Such behavioural comparisons peak at about age eight to nine (Barenboim, 1981). After the age of seven or eight, children begin to focus more on abstract, internal qualities in others and on dispositional characteristics (Livesley & Bromley, 1973; Peevers & Secord, 1973). Beginning at about the age of 8 to 10, and peaking at about age 14, children tend to describe others primarily in terms of psychological qualities, internal characteristics, motives, and personality traits (Barenboim, 1981). At first, these psychological descriptors are offered in absolute terms, but later, at 10 to 12 years, children begin to compare and contrast others in terms of psychological qualities. It is only in later childhood and adolescence, then, that children begin to spontaneously consider internal motives, attitudes, and beliefs when describing others and begin to recognize inconsistencies and exceptions in characteristics of others (Livesley & Bromley, 1973).

We also know that during the elementary school years, children's descriptions of others tend to be evaluatively consistent and univalent, with liked others described primarily in positive terms and disliked others described primarily in negative terms (Livesley & Bromley, 1973; Peevers & Secord, 1973), regardless of actual (observed) behaviour (Yarrow & Campbell, 1963). The ability to consider bivalent (positive as well as negative characteristics in the same person) qualities in others increases gradually with age, although even among older children it is not very common.

Development of Friendship Conceptions

Changes in how children conceptualize others parallel their emerging ideas about friendship, as documented in numerous studies on the development of children's understanding of friendships (Berndt, 1986, Bigelow, 1977; Bigelow & LaGaipa, 1975, 1980; Damon, 1977, 1983; Selman, 1980; Smollar-Volpe & Youniss, 1982; Youniss, 1980). For the preschool child, friends appear to be momentary physical playmates (Rubin, 1980), whoever they are playing with at the time. The young child's understanding of friendship emphasizes concrete, physical, and observable aspects of the relationships, such as proximity ("He lives near me."), the sharing and exchange of goods ("She gives me things." "We share recess snacks."), and common activities ("We play together."). At this age, friendships are both easily established and easily terminated.

By middle childhood, children's conceptions of friendships rely less on concrete, physical characteristics and more on internal qualities. By grade 4 or 5, friends are expected to share similar values and attitudes. The concept of mutual trust in a friendship emerges at about this time, and such things as shared interests, cooperation, and reciprocity become critical. Friends are now expected to help and trust one another and are viewed as special people with desirable psychological qualities (e.g., helpfulness, kindness). Concepts such as loyalty and commitment (relatively rare among young elementary school-age children) are increasingly emphasized during the middle elementary school years, reaching a peak at about the seventh-grade level. By the early adolescence (ages 12 to 13), friendship conceptions come to include such things as mutual understanding and intimate exchange. Now friends are seen as people who understand one another and, as a confidant, can self-disclose and share their innermost thoughts and feelings.

Friendship conceptions are not fully developed by early adolescence, however. Youniss and his colleagues suggest that the perceived obligations of friends continue to change during adolescence. For example, while most 10- to 11-year-olds believe that the central obligation of friendship is to be nice and help one another, the majority of 16- to 17-year-olds emphasize emotional support as a primary obligation of friendship, a concept suggested by few 10- to 11- year-olds. Moreover, Damon (1983) finds that it is not until later adolescence or even adulthood that we recognize the dynamic nature of relationships, that friendships change over time, and that even a best friend cannot fulfil every need.

Development of Biases and Prejudice

One other important consideration in understanding the nature of social relations among school children in the inclusive classroom setting is to recognize the existence of biases and prejudice that makes the social world of the school, just like that of the larger society, a sometimes unfair learning situation. In a compelling and thought-provoking article, Ervin Staub (1988) argues that perhaps one of the greatest obstacles to positive interpersonal relations in schools and in society in general comes from the basic human tendency to categorize other people, and to differentiate between "us and them," members of an ingroup and members of an outgroup. In many ways, this differentiation process is quite adaptive, allowing us to distinguish the "good guys" from the "bad guys." But it has an unfortunate side-effect of making us fearful and skeptical of others, particularly if they are somehow different from us.

Staub (1988) suggests that this fear of the unknown, or fear of what is different from the known, often results in the devaluing of outgroups, of "them," in stereotypes and in prejudice. And the research indicates that particular stereotypes and prejudices become deeply embedded in our culture, expressed in our literature, art, media, in our societal institutions and practices, and thereby maintained within the culture and perpetuated across generations. Research tells us that by the elementary school years, children will have developed very clear stereotypes, although the nature and target of these exaggerated beliefs will depend on the culture in which the child is raised (see Aboud, 1988 for a review). Moreover, adult research by Tajfel and others (Festinger, Schacter & Black, 1950; Tajfel, 1978, 1982) suggests that the tendency to differentiate others into "us and them" will be formed on the basis of very minimal information, even trivial or meaningless distinctions. However, once people form such an ingroup-outgroup distinction, they behave in ways that maintain and even exaggerate the differences, and begin to show ingroup favouritism and outgroup discrimination and devaluation. The resulting stereotypes about "them" have been shown to lead to selective memory, selective attention, and biased interpretations of the behaviour of others.

In light of these arguments, it is important to keep in mind that children, like adults, learn to make first impressions based on a fairly limited set of information. They can categorize, "pigeon-hole," and stereotype others, and show biases against people who are somehow different. Ultimately, such biases contribute to interpersonal antagonisms, and may lead to negative interpersonal behaviour, even aggression and violence. Recognizing that such biases exist, even among elementary school-age children, is important in trying to foster positive social development in our children and in understanding why children, like adults, may not always be fair in their evaluations of others.

Development of Moral Reasoning

Morality concerns standards or guidelines that direct what people *should* do in their interactions with one another—in particular, how rights, duties, and benefits are to be appropriated and coordinated among individuals (Rest, 1983). More generally, moral development refers to the process through which a person progresses from an egocentric, externally directed individual, to a self-directed and other-focused, socially responsive, and responsible person. Although over the years theorists have conceptualized moral development and moral behaviour in different ways (Bandura, 1977; Freud, 1933), for the purposes of the present review we rely primarily on the theory put forth by Lawrence Kohlberg (1969). Drawing on the work of Piaget (1932, 1965) and Dewey (1964), Kohlberg considered the development of moral reasoning to be an important part of social and cognitive growth in children and adolescents because it provides a basis on which moral behaviours are constructed and accomplished (Kohlberg, 1976). Within the education literature, researchers have called for the development and implementation of moral reasoning interventions for children and adolescents with behavioural problems (e.g., Maag, 1989; Schonert & Cantor, 1991; Swarthout, 1988) because research findings suggest that deficits in moral reasoning are related to antisocial behaviours (e.g., Bear & Richards, 1982; Schonert-Reichl, 1994) and adult adjustment difficulties (Kohlberg, LaCrosse & Ricks, 1972). Moreover, other evidence suggests that interventions that elevate the moral reasoning ability of students also decrease problem behaviours, such as truancy, tardiness, and police/court contacts (Arbuthnot & Gordon, 1986). In order for educators to facilitate positive moral development, however, it is important to understand the gradual process through which mature moral reasoning emerges across the school years.

Kohlberg (1969) delineated a six-stage sequence of moral reasoning development that characterizes each stage of moral development as more advanced and more adequate than the preceding stage. Specifically, Kohlberg's cognitive developmental theory of moral reasoning is an attempt to explain the ways in which an individual's reasoning about moral issues—that is, issues of right and wrong change during childhood and how the individual will deal with moral issues as he or she develops toward adulthood. Kohlberg distinguishes three basic levels of moral development—the pre-conventional or pre-moral level, the conventional level, and the post-conventional or autonomous level, with two distinct stages evident within each of these three levels.

To assess an individual's level or stage of moral reasoning, Kohlberg developed the **Moral Judgment Interview** (MJI) (Colby & Kohlberg, 1987; Kohlberg, 1958). In the administration of the MJI, an individual is first presented with a hypothetical dilemma and is then asked to indicate what he or she thinks the main character in the dilemma should do and why. Next, the individual is asked to respond to several probe questions that are designed for understanding his or her underlying reasoning. In assessing both the behaviour (what is to be done) and the reasons behind it, Kohlberg distinguishes between "content" and "structure." Specifically, content refers to what the person thinks should be done, while the structure refers to the person's justifications and underlying reasoning as to *why* it should be done. An example of a moral dilemma from the MJI is as follows:

> Joe is a 14-year-old boy who wanted to go to camp very much. His father promised him he could go if he saved up the money for it himself. So Joe worked hard at his paper route and saved up the $100.00 it cost to go to camp and a little more besides. But just before camp was going to start, his father changed his mind. Some of his friends decided to go on a special fishing trip, and Joe's father was short of the money it would cost. So he told Joe to give him the money he had saved from the paper route. Joe didn't want to give up going to camp, so he thinks of refusing to give his father the money (Colby & Kohlberg, 1987, p. 3).

The individual's moral reasoning about the moral dilemma is solicited through a series of questions, including:

> Should Joe give his father the money? Why or why not?

> The father promised Joe he could go to camp if he earned the money. Is the fact that the father promised the most important thing in the situation?

> What do you think is the most important thing a father should be concerned about in his relationship to his son? (Colby & Kohlberg, 1987, p. 3)

Each of Kohlberg's dilemmas presents a moral crisis that pits one moral concern against another. In the above dilemma ("Joe and his father") the moral conflict is between authority (i.e., Joe's father telling him to give over the money) and contract (i.e., the promise made to Joe by his father). It should be noted that an individual's initial moral judgment (i.e., whether or not Joe should give his father the money) is not what is evaluated in determining one's stage of moral reasoning. Instead, what is important is the person's *justifications* or reasoning underlying his or her response. So, for example, an individual can respond in the affirmative to either moral response—that is, he or she can say that Joe *should* give his father the money or he or she can say that Joe *should not* give his father the money. Either response does not necessarily reflect higher moral reasoning, since this is evaluated on the basis of the reasons behind the action, and either response could be accompanied by reasoning reflective of any of Kohlberg's stages of moral reasoning.

According to Kohlberg, preschool and primary elementary school-age children are typically characterized by "pre-conventional" levels of moral development, and will reason about moral issues primarily in an egocentric manner. Within the pre-conventional level, a child reasoning at the first stage of moral reasoning (early to middle childhood), exhibits a **punishment and obedience orientation**. Children at this stage find it difficult to consider two points of view and do not recognize internal, psychological motivations or intentions. What decides what is right or wrong for children at this stage is determined by either blind obedience to authority or the avoidance of punishment. For example, in response to the above dilemma, a typical Stage 1 response would be "[Joe should give his father the money] because you should do what your father or parents tell you to do." (Colby & Kohlberg, 1987; p. 235). At this stage, the child does not make any reference to the consequences of his or her actions on the well being of others. At Stage 2 (late elementary and middle school years), children move to an **instrumental purpose orientation** in their moral reasoning. By this time, they possess rudimentary skills in stepping out of their own perspective to consider the viewpoints of others—separating their own interests from the interests of others. However, what is right is determined by what satisfies their own personal, concrete needs. Reciprocity is understood as an equal exchange of favours—"I'll scratch your back if you'll scratch mine." A response to the above dilemma reflective of Stage 2 reasoning would be "[Joe should give his father the money] because his father will pay him back later, or do favors for him" (Colby & Kohlberg, 1987, p. 236).

It is not until early adolescence that children typically enter the **conventional level** of moral development, the level that focuses on meeting the needs of others rather than just meeting the needs of oneself. At Stage 3 (early to middle adolescence), children exhibit an **interpersonal cooperation orientation**, in their moral reasoning. Here, children are able to consider others' needs and focus on promoting harmony among individuals in the context of close personal ties within their own social context. Thus, doing right is motivated by wanting to maintain affection and approval of parents, friends, and teachers by being seen as either a "good boy" or "nice girl." Individuals at this stage are able to understand reciprocity in terms of the Golden Rule. ("Do unto others as you would have them do unto you.") In response to the "Joe and his Father" dilemma, a Stage 3 reasoner might say, "[Joe should give his father the money] out of love, to show his father how much he loves him, or to preserve their relationship" (Colby & Kohlberg, 1987, p. 238). By later adolescence and adulthood, individuals typically reason at the fourth stage of moral development. The reasoning that characterizes Stage 4 of moral development is a **law and order orientation**, which takes into account a social system—that of societal laws—and emphasizes the importance of maintaining the functioning and existence of the system as a whole. Individuals reasoning at this level believe that laws cannot be disobeyed because they are vital for maintaining social order and without them there would be chaos. A response typical of a Stage 4 moral reasoner in response to the above dilemma would be as follows: "[Joe should give his father the money] because if there is to be family unity there must be an authority in the family" (Colby & Kohlberg, 1987, p. 241).

Research findings indicate that the majority of adults reason at Stage 4 of moral reasoning (Rest, 1986).

Some adults, however, are able to move on to a post-conventional level of moral development. At Stage 5, reflecting a **social contract/intrinsic rights orientation**, individuals emphasize fair procedures and individual rights and suggest that laws should be changed when they are not meeting the needs of the majority of society. What is right is determined by what protects the intrinsic universal rights endemic to all human beings. In response to the "Joe and Father" dilemma, these individuals might say, "[The most important thing a father/son should consider] is that both persons are individuals with equal rights or persons who should have respect for one another's rights" (Colby & Kohlberg, 1987, p. 243). In Kohlberg's research, Stage 5 moral reasoning was found in only 10 to 15 percent of individuals and was rarely found in adults before their mid-20s (Colby & Kohlberg, 1987). Finally, Stage 6 individuals reason about moral issues in terms of **universal principles of morality**, based on self-chosen ethical principals of conscience that are valid for humanity. Issues such as respect for the dignity and worth of each person are emphasized. In Kohlberg's 20-year longitudinal study, however, no Stage 6 individuals were found. Colby and Kohlberg suggest that this may be due, in part, to the inability of their scoring system to adequately distinguish between Stage 5 and Stage 6 reasoning. According to Colby and Kohlberg, some of those individuals hypothesized to be at Stage 6 include Ghandi, Socrates, Martin Luther King Jr., and Abraham Lincoln.

Kohlberg's stages of moral reasoning provide a systematic framework for understanding how individuals "think" about moral issues and how such thinking changes with age. Presumably, such thinking has direct implications for behaviour, but the links between moral reasoning and moral behaviour are not always that clear. For example, in a recent Canadian study investigating the relationship between social behaviour and moral reasoning among students in grades 5, 6, and 7, Schonert-Reichl (1994) found that moral reasoning was significantly and positively related to several dimensions of peer-rated pro-social behaviour in the classroom (e.g., cooperating, helping, sharing, trustworthy) but was not significantly related to peer-rated antisocial behaviours in the classroom. These findings support the view that more mature moral reasoning is associated with prosocial classroom behaviours. Although not evidenced in Schonert-Reichl's study, most researchers have found a negative relationship between moral reasoning and moral misbehaviour, in which students reasoning at lower levels of moral reasoning are more likely to display antisocial behaviours in the classroom than those students reasoning at higher levels (Bear & Richards, 1982). Others, however, have found more complex associations between moral reasoning and moral misbehaviour. For instance, results of a recent study by Richards et al. (1992) investigating moral reasoning and behaviour in children in grades 4 and 8, suggests a curvilinear relationship between moral reasoning and moral behaviour. Specifically, they found that conduct problems were lowest among those students demonstrating Stage 1 *or* Stage 3 reasoning, whereas conduct problems were highest among those students reasoning at Stage 2. These researchers concluded that "Conduct deteriorates as youngsters advance from Stage 1 to Stage 2, then improves again as they consolidate their thinking at the conventional level" (1992, p. 186). Thus, teachers should keep in mind that advances in children's moral reasoning do not always result in improved classroom behaviour. As noted earlier, moral behaviours also appears to be influenced by other factors, such as empathy. What is important, then, is for teachers to consider the reasons behind children's behaviour, in addition to the behaviour itself, and to be cognizant of the factors that facilitate the development of moral reasoning so they can utilize classroom practices that foster the development of moral reasoning in their students.

Despite the fact that moral reasoning and moral behaviour do not always coincide in a systematic and predictable fashion, Kohlberg (1976) argues strongly that the ability to make competent moral decisions is based *partly* on the attainment of certain levels of cognitive and social perspective-taking development (Kohlberg, 1969). That is, achievement of a certain level of cognitive development or perspective taking is *necessary but not sufficient* for a particular stage of moral development.

In identifying the determinants, conditions, and mechanisms for change in one's level of moral reasoning, Kohlberg, drawing on the research of Piaget (1932, 1965), believed that two aspects are necessary for advancing moral understanding—**cognitive disequilbrium** and **social interaction** (Turiel, 1974; Walker, 1983). Cognitive disequilibrium occurs when an individual cannot fit a new experience into his or her own existing structure or perception of the world. Subsequently, the person in a state of cognitive disequilibrium searches for new cognitive structures to re-establish cognitive equilibrium. Cognitive disequilibrium may result from conflicts existing within the individual or from socially derived conflicts. Whereas the former may involve situations in which the individual is reflecting on personal experiences, the latter may involve situations in which a social interaction accentuates formerly unnoticed inadequacies in one's approach to a moral problem. Both Piaget and Kohlberg have suggested that cognitive disequilibrium is primarily stimulated by the child's interaction with the social environment via peer interactions. Indeed, researchers and theorists have emphasized that moral development is dependent upon the stimulation of cognitive development via social interaction.

Results of several studies have suggested that parents can play a significant role in the development of moral thinking in their children. For example, more mature moral judgments (as well as more self-controlled behaviour) have been found in children whose parents use consistent discipline techniques and who a) emphasize reasoning and explanations in their discipline (inductive discipline) (Aronfreed, 1976;

Parke, 1977), b) initiate discussions about the feelings of others (Hoffman, 1984), and c) utilize democratic forms of family discussions (Edwards, 1980; Walker & Taylor, 1991). Presumably, these same discipline practices, when used by teachers, would also foster positive moral development in students.

The role of peers in the development of moral reasoning, however, may be even more critical. For example, Kruger (1992) had 7- to 10-year-old girls discuss two different moral dilemmas with either their mothers or with a female agemate and found that the girls paired with peers subsequently demonstrated more sophisticated moral reasoning than did the girls paired with adults. What appeared critical here was the nature of the conversations that emerged in each case. The moral reasoning statements observed among girls paired with adults tended to be "passive," emerging in response to adult elicitation efforts, while the moral reasoning statements observed among girls paired with peers tended to be more "active," in that the girls spontaneously generated their *own* moral reasoning statements. In peer-peer moral discussions, then, children may be better able to "figure it out on their own." According to Kolhberg (1969), social interactions with peers facilitate moral reasoning development because these interactions provide opportunities for role taking in which they can take the perspective of another person who may reason differently about a moral dilemma, thus invoking cognitive conflict. Such opportunities may be more likely among equals (i.e., peers) than among nonequals (i.e., adult-child interactions).

In light of these findings, it is not surprising that the educational applications of Kohlberg's theory have strongly emphasized the promotion of classroom discussion of moral dilemmas among students for the purpose of stimulating moral growth (e.g., Berkowitz & Gibbs, 1983; Blatt & Kohlberg, 1975) and restructuring the school environment (Higgins, Power & Kohlberg, 1984). Specifically, Kohlberg proposed that both direct and indirect conditions are needed for moral growth to occur in educational settings. The *direct* conditions needed for moral growth to occur address issues of the quality of classroom interactions and discussions and include a) exposure to cognitive moral conflict—that is, exposure to situations or experiences that contradict students' current moral structures, b) role-taking or perspective-taking opportunities, c) the consideration of fairness and morality, and d) exposure to the next higher stage of moral reasoning (also known as +1-stage modelling).

With these conditions in mind, Blatt and Kohlberg (1975) found that moral development could be stimulated in classrooms through a group process known as the moral discussion group (MDG). The MDG as conceived by Blatt and Kohlberg involved the presentation of moral dilemmas by a teacher who promoted interaction among students whose goal was resolution of the dilemma. In addition, during such moral discussions, the teacher utilized Socratic methods of questioning (e.g., eliciting the students' opinions, asking clarifying questions, paraphrasing, and checking for understanding), provided opportunities for students to take one another's perspective, and stimulated development by presenting moral reasoning one stage above the students' own. As a result of Blatt and Kohlberg's findings suggesting that moral dilemma discussions among students lead to increases in moral reasoning, many educators have utilized the MDG as a means of facilitating moral growth. Indeed, educators and researchers interested in stimulating moral reasoning have devised curriculum guides that emphasize the discussion of hypothetical and real-life moral dilemmas within the context of the classroom environment and school curriculum (see Arbuthnot & Faust, 1981; Galbraith & Jones, 1976; and Reimer, Paolitto & Hersh, 1983 for examples of moral dilemmas and moral education lesson plans).

Although the discussion of hypothetical moral dilemmas within the classroom was found to be effective in stimulating moral reasoning, Kohlberg believed that moral discussion constituted only one portion of the conditions necessary for stimulating moral growth. Indeed, Kohlberg felt that if educators desire to promote the moral development and moral behaviours of their students, they must also be cognizant of the indirect conditions necessary for moral growth. Specifically, the *indirect* conditions refer to the general moral atmosphere of the classroom or school, and emphasize the need for a moral climate that provides a number of contexts in which students are encouraged to voice their opinions and listen to the opinions of others. The building of a positive moral atmosphere not only facilitates the creation of interindividual cooperation and communication among students and teachers, but also facilitates the development of reasoning that takes into account the needs of others rather than just the needs of the self. Because teachers in inclusive classrooms are particularly concerned with providing educational environments that foster acceptance and caring among *all* students regardless of their differences, we believe that they should be knowledgeable about strategies and classroom practices that foster the creation of a healthy and positive moral climate.

Summary

Developmental research has provided compelling evidence concerning the many and varied aspects of social behaviour and social cognition that develop gradually during the time that children are in school. Although social experiences that enhance social growth are available across a variety of contexts, we argue that in our culture, many, if not most, of these occur within the context of the school. Thus, it is important that educators be aware of the nature and direction of children's social development so that we can be in a better position to facilitate such growth. Although to date such efforts have been largely implicit within the school setting, the time has come to recognize these opportunities and our influence on the social growth of our children. In creating a school environment that maximizes the social development of our students, we believe it is important to keep in mind the developmental level of the children you are dealing with in setting up any kind of classroom intervention program. You have to know the level of social development and cognitive understanding of the participants so you can pitch your program appropriately, not expect more than is possible, and be able to recognize what the next level is likely to be, so you can foster development in that direction.

Fostering positive social development is a goal that can be approached on many levels. Much of the research on children's interpersonal relations to date has emphasized an individualized approach to the enhancement of social skills, aimed at improving the social behaviour and peer acceptance of particular children (Asher & Coie, 1990). Some children may be particularly lacking in socials skills and, for them, an individualized social skills training program may be necessary. Over the past few decades, there has been considerable progress in developing individualized social skills interventions for children who are generally rejected by their classmates. In particular, recent research has documented the effectiveness of a coaching intervention procedure in which rejected children can be taught to interact more effectively with their peers. If individualized social skill training is deemed appropriate, the interested reader is directed toward a recent paper by Asher and Hymel (1986), which describes this coaching intervention procedure. Although there is clearly a need for such individualized programs, such interventions are not the primary focus of the present chapter.

Our hope is that as the importance of peer relationships becomes a recognized part of the educational process that occurs in our schools, we may be able to enhance the social development of all of our children, and, in doing so, improve social functioning in our society more generally. In addition, by enhancing interpersonal relations at this more general level, we can at the same time help ameliorate the problems of particular rejected children. Although a given rejected child may well be in need of particular social skills training, such a focus on the individual may not be enough. Recent research suggests that even if a child receives appropriate social skills training, it is no guarantee of improved peer relations, since the child will still need to be accepted within an established peer group, one which has come to view him or her in a particular way (Hymel, Wagner & Butler, 1990). Thus, even within an individualized focus, it may be important to address the receptivity of the classroom environment, as well as the particular deficits of the child. By fostering positive interpersonal relations at the classroom and school level, we may be able to both enhance the adjustment of particular rejected children, and at the same time, facilitate the interpersonal development of all children.

With this in mind, we now turn to a review of a number of strategies that can be used to facilitate positive social adjustment in *all* children by adopting various practices at the level of classrooms and entire schools. Many of the procedures we discuss have been designed by developmental, clinical, and educational psychologists over the past 10 to 15 years. At the outset, however, we want to suggest that such programs may be most successful when conducted consistently within a schoolwide context that fosters positive relations in a number of different ways simultaneously.

▦ Classroom Strategies for Promoting Social Acceptance

Considerable evidence now exists suggesting that the school climate or school "ethos" is related to characteristics such as disruptive classroom behaviour and attendance (Rutter, Maughan, Mortimore, Ouston & Smith, 1979), truancy (Reynolds, Jones, St. Leger & Murgatroyd, 1980), students' sense of well being and attitudes toward learning (Minuchin, Biber, Shapiro & Zimiles, 1969; Moos, 1979), student self-concept and self-reliance (Brookover, Beady, Flood, Schweitzer & Wisenbaker, 1979), and student mental health and adjustment (Kasen, Johnson & Cohen, 1990). Taken together, these studies indicate that the school environment plays an important role in facilitating positive development in students.

One of the most difficult tasks with which teachers are frequently confronted is finding ways to help students to understand and get along with one another. If teachers cannot create an atmosphere of acceptance among students, the classroom will seldom be a place where students can learn to their optimal abilities. Therefore, in order for the inclusive classroom to be successful, we believe that the first step in promoting acceptance among students is through the creation of a classroom environment where students respect and care for one another. Activities and classroom practices that promote self-esteem, autonomy, positive teacher-student and student-student collaboration need to be provided so that students will develop into responsible and caring adults. Therefore, it is imperative that teachers make concerted efforts to create a classroom environment that facilitates positive social development.

Creating a Positive Moral Atmosphere in the Classroom

Educators develop rules and obligations, they discipline students, and serve as models of ethical or unethical behaviour. Classroom rules and teacher-student and student-student interactions transmit attitudes and beliefs about cheating, lying, and consideration for others. This is the hidden curriculum and refers to the general moral atmosphere of the school and classroom (Jackson, 1968). Designing school environments to facilitate social and moral development has been advocated by many educators and researchers (Higgins, Power & Kohlberg, 1984). In order to appropriately reach a diverse range of students, teachers need to engage *all* students in the social milieu of the school and classroom by creating a moral community that promotes both social development and acceptance and takes into account the importance of developing the academic, social, and moral potential of individual learners. Building a sense of community in the classroom is a necessary first step toward developing an environment that promotes not only academic success but also social acceptance.

Lickona (1991, p. 91) suggests that three conditions are necessary for the creation of a moral community in the classroom: "(1) Students know each other, (2) Students respect, affirm, and care about each other, and (3) Students feel membership in, and responsibility to, the group." According to Lickona, from the first day of school, teachers should provide activities that help students get to know one another because "it's easier to value others and feel an attachment to them if we know something about them." Indeed, providing opportunities that help students get to know one another is seen as the first step in creating a sense of community and connectedness in the classroom. From a series of observations of teachers across the United States and Canada, Lickona has outlined several useful activities designed to facilitate the development of a moral community in the classroom.

In the **Partners activity**, the teacher pairs students who do not know one another and has them list "ways we are different" and "ways we are alike." Students are also asked to interview one another about their background (e.g., number of bothers and sisters) and their favourite things (e.g., favourite food, favourite color, favourite subject in school). At the completion of their "interviews," students are invited to share their lists with the group. In the **Treasure Bag activity**, the teacher asks students "to bring in a bag containing five things that tell something about you." Students share their contents with the rest of the class and the reason behind their choices. Finally, in the **People Hunt activity**, the teacher provides students with a list of 20 items and instructs them to fill in people's names for as many items as they could by going around the room and talking to classmates. Sample items include (Lickona, 1991, p. 91):

1. A person who can whistle _____

2. Likes pizza _____

3. Enjoys reading _____

To help improve the moral atmosphere of the classroom and facilitate opportunities for social development, teachers must also provide an environment in which students feel free to express their opinions and ideas with one another and with the teacher. Indeed, both students and teacher must share responsibility for making the classroom a place in which learning can take place. One way that teachers can foster greater participation in class discussions is to have an exercise that helps students feel more comfortable with each other and gets them to think about their responsibilities as a class member. One such activity is called **Good feelings/Bad feelings**. To complete this activity, "students are asked to write 'two things other people can do that give you good feelings in a group discussion' and 'two things people sometimes do that give you bad feelings in a group discussion'" (Lickona, 1991, p. 95). After completing their lists, students, in groups of three, share their lists with one another. Next, students form a circle in the room and do a "circle whip" with each student telling one of his or her positives, and then, another time around, each telling one of his or her negatives. Students keep a list of what is mentioned. At the completion of the activity, each student chooses one suggestion that they feel would make him or her a better member in group discussions. Because these suggestions are generated from the students rather than the teacher, students feel more committed to following through on the behaviours they suggested. Giving students a voice in the classroom as well as providing them with opportunities to learn about one another helps create a classroom in which students feel that they are an integral part of the community of learning.

Developing a Prosocial Value Orientation

Staub (1988) suggests that in order to foster positive social development in our children, we have to help them to develop a prosocial value orientation. One of the characteristics of this prosocial value orientation is the tendency toward positive rather than negative evaluations of others. Other characteristics include concern for other people's welfare (e.g., sympathy, empathy), and a feeling of personal responsibility for others' welfare. Research has shown that such a prosocial value orientation is positively related to one's willingness to help others who are in distress (see Staub, 1988). However, it is important to remember that, given the developmental changes reviewed earlier, the willingness to help others as a result of feelings of responsibility and respect for other's rights is not likely to be found in elementary school-age children. Therefore, it is necessary that teachers utilize explicit strategies in the classroom so these skills can be taught and encouraged.

The research literature also provides some ideas about how such a prosocial value orientation can be fostered and enhanced by both parents and teachers. Staub (1988) argues that we must provide a context, in the schools, in which children can develop the necessary skills for good interpersonal relations. We would argue further that unless the entire school provides such a context consistently, specific lessons may be of limited value. Staub has identified several different ways in which the schools can contribute to the development of a prosocial value orientation: a) positive discipline practices, b) democratic and autocratic modes of operation, c) guided participation in prosocial activities that benefit others, d) content of knowledge (i.e., valuing differences and emphasizing commonalities) and, e) cooperative versus competitive learning.

Positive Discipline Practices

As is the case with parental discipline practices, it is important that schools also employ positive discipline practices, as opposed to power-assertive or physically aggressive methods of discipline. Teachers who exhibit love, warmth, and nurturance in their classes, who show respect for their students and their opinions, who use noncoercive discipline, and who rely heavily on reasoning and explanations in their discipline should facilitate positive social development in their students, as compared with teachers who are more business-like in their classes or who use power-assertive and physically coercive discipline practices.

The research tells us that inductive discipline, which provides children with reasons and explanations for prohibitions, is particularly important in fostering moral development (Aronfreed, 1976; Parke, 1977). Inductive discipline techniques are also typically other-centred, including references to others and stressing the impact of a child's behaviour on others. Other-centred discipline, in which the impact of behaviour on the other person is repeatedly emphasized, may be particularly important in promoting the development of empathy in children.

Another important ingredient is giving children opportunities to provide input into the system as a means of fostering independence, taking responsibility, and developing self-control. For example, students need to be given the opportunity to directly participate in rule setting and decision making within the classroom and work through problems together, rather than placing the teacher in the exclusive role of "judge and jury." At a most basic level, students and teachers should work together to determine their own rules for classroom behaviour. In developing these classroom rules, opportunities for discussion of why a proposed rule is important may foster the development of more mature social and moral reasoning. There are other ways that students can participate in classroom rules and evaluation procedures, however. The practices of one grade-6/7 teacher, Ty Binfet, in Western Canada provide one illustration of how to implement these guidelines into classroom practice. For example, every time Mr. Binfet writes report cards for his students, he asks his students to write reports on his progress as a teacher. Their suggestions and comments provide insight into how students perceive the classroom—what they value in teachers and teaching practices. Following is an example of a student's comments to Mr. Binfet.

> Ty Binfet has taught progressively this past term. Teaching slowly but properly, Ty has upgraded almost all the students' academic capability. His

patience and understanding is noted, however, his judgment towards who he punishes and for what reason is sometime uncalled for and incorrect. His teaching arguments in all subjects are all thought out and well presented, although, his ability to reason and listen to children has decreased in this past term. I look forward to a better term ("Who Says Students Don't Have Critiques," 1993, p. 10).

The basic goal here is to increase students' responsibility for their own behaviour by making them a part of deciding the rules and regulations in the classroom. Such practices help to improve the moral atmosphere of the classroom—creating an environment that students perceive as fair. This focus on student involvement and input is related to the next area considered: democratic and autocratic modes of operation.

Democratic and Autocratic Modes of Operation

In the 1930s, Kurt Lewin and his associates (Lewin & Lippitt, 1938; Lewin, Lippitt & White, 1939) conducted several classic studies concerning the influence of social climate and leadership style on the interpersonal relations of 10-year-old boys. In these studies, groups of boys were set up with an adult who adopted either: a) an authoritarian, b) a democratic, or c) a laissez-faire style of leadership. Every six weeks, the leader and the leadership style was changed, so that in the end, each group had been exposed to each of the three leadership types. (Leaders and leadership styles were varied so that differences were not attributable to the personalities of the particular adults.) The activities engaged in were structured to reflect the particular leadership style at the time. For example, in the democratic group, the boys were presented with a list of activities as a basis for discussion and they decided on the activities by voting. In the authoritarian group, the same activities were launched by the leader without any choice by the group members. In the laissez-faire groups, the students were shown the available materials, but were left to choose their own activities. Lewin and his colleagues examined the effects of these different leadership styles in a variety of ways. They found that the boys almost unanimously indicated that they liked the democratic leader the best, and there was also a slight preference for the laissez-faire leader over the authoritarian leader. This was not just a case of preferring particular adults, since each leader adopted various leadership styles, and the boys' opinions of them varied with the style of leadership used, not the leader, per se.

Particularly interesting was the boys' reactions to the authoritarian leadership setting. There were two distinct reactions. In some cases, the boys reacted with a high frequency of aggression, sometimes focused on a single child (a scapegoat), and other times more equally distributed. The other reaction was a high degree of apathy. In this case there was a fairly low frequency of aggression when the leader was present, but when the leader left the room, aggressive behaviour increased considerably. In contrast, in the democratic leadership condition, the boys exhibited moderate amounts of aggression. In the laissez-faire condition, there was moderate to high aggression.

The point here is that the social behaviour of the boys was clearly influenced by the climate and leadership style of the group. The same groups of boys changed their behaviour, after a short reaction period, when the climate of the group changed. What we can take from this research is the idea that democratic modes of operation can reduce negative interpersonal behaviour and aggression. As well, when children are given the opportunity to participate in the decision making of the class, they can develop a sense of control and autonomy. Also, the children are provided with positive role models for how disputes and disagreements can be settled fairly.

Guided Participation in Prosocial Activities that Benefit Others

Whiting and Whiting (1975) conducted a study of childrearing practices in six cultures, attempting to identify those practices most likely to foster altruism in the children. They found that the one factor most strongly related to altruistic behaviour was the degree to which children were assigned responsibilities that benefited others and contributed to the maintenance of the family (e.g., caring for younger siblings or tending animals). Giving children responsibility for things alone (e.g., keeping one's room in order) was not enough, however. What was important was that these responsibilities led to benefits for others. Staub (1988, p. 89) notes that "the children showed the least altruism in a 'Yankee' town, where their only responsibility was to keep order in their own room."

Applying this to the school setting, Staub suggests that schools have the opportunity to involve students in activities that benefit others with similar positive effects. In such classrooms, students can learn from their own participation in such activities, as well as through the role models provided by the school staff. As part of the school experience, students can collect money for charity or sponsor a foster child in a third world country, rather than selling candy bars for a class trip. As another example, children can help elderly people in the community, perhaps spending time reading to them or just visiting on a regular basis. Or students can engage directly in various types of community service, perhaps with activities focused on poverty, the elderly, the environment, or any appropriate concern within the local community.

Within the schools, there exist many opportunities to help others, including peer tutoring, either within a classroom or across grades. For example, many schools have established **reading buddy programs,** in which older students are paired on a regular basis with a younger student to engage in various reading activities. Also, students can be given full responsibility for maintaining or improving aspects of their classroom or school. One example here is student-initiated and maintained programs for environmental awareness and conservation within their schools. Such participation can also be highlighted in the content of reading and writing assignments, which could easily emphasize prosocial values, behaviours, and practices rather than "what I did on my summer vacation."

Content of Knowledge (Valuing Differences and Emphasizing Commonalities)

This aspect of prosocial value orientation focuses on teaching students about what Staub calls the "shared humanity of all persons" (Staub, 1988, p. 90). Special learning activities can be geared to learning about differences in customs, beliefs, and values of different groups of individuals, both within and outside of the mainstream culture. It is important, however, in all such efforts, to make sure that such activities do not lead to greater categorization and differentiation. The goal here is not to contribute to our tendency to categorize others and perpetuate stereotypes, but to concretize and particularize individuals, learn to appreciate and value these individual differences, and thereby make children empathetic and responsive to a wider range of people. Activities must be designed to help children appreciate the commonalities among people, in desires, feelings, and needs, despite the often superficial differences. Children should be guided to discover for themselves the benefits of individual variation, and the appreciation of individual differences.

Cooperative Learning

Providing opportunities for students to work cooperatively is undoubtedly an important component of a classroom that promotes acceptance among all students. Research has demonstrated that cooperative learning, as compared with competitive and individualistic learning strategies, may be particularly useful in promoting positive academic achievement (see Hymel, Zinck & Ditner, 1993 for a review). In addition, however, cooperative learning practices may also facilitate social development and interpersonal acceptance among students. Most relevant to our present discussion is a meta-analysis conducted by Johnson, Johnson, and Maruyama (1983), examining the effect of cooperative learning strategies on outcomes of interpersonal attraction and interdependence, rather than achievement. The purpose of their analysis was to consider how different types of learning structures (cooperative, competitive, and individualistic) might impact on interpersonal relations of children who were either heterogeneous (that is, children of different ethnic backgrounds, or children who are handicapped versus not handicapped) or rather homogeneous.

Johnson et al. (1983) point out that school desegregation and mainstreaming efforts have been based on the assumption that if you place heterogeneous children together in a classroom situation, positive relationships and attitudes among these students will be enhanced. These notions are derived in part from arguments put forward in the 1940s and 1950s that by increasing the physical proximity of heterogeneous students, positive interrelations will result. However, in their review of research on the effects of increasing physical proximity or contact among heterogeneous students, Johnson et al. found that these efforts have yielded mixed and often disappointing results. It appears that physical proximity is necessary, but not sufficient to reduce biases and prejudice, and ensure positive attitudes and relations among these groups.

Theoretically, Johnson and his colleagues (Johnson, Johnson & Holubec, 1986; Johnson et al. 1983) argue that the effects of increasing physical proximity on interpersonal attitudes and relationships will vary depending on the structure of the situation, specifically the degree to which the students are made to be interdependent on one another. First, they argue that "physical proximity among heterogeneous students is the beginning of an opportunity, but like all opportunities, it carries a risk of making things worse as well as the possibility of making things better." Prior to interaction, one might assume that negative attitudes exist between students from different ethnic backgrounds and between handicapped and nonhandicapped students, attitudes that are prevalent within the culture or society in general, making their strength determined by existing family, community and cultural standards of that particular time and place. Second, Johnson et al. suggest that whether a process of acceptance or rejection results from increasing physical proximity will depend on the nature of the interactions that take place between the students. Specifically, they are referring here to whether positive, negative, or no goal interdependence is required of the students in their interactions. Finally, Johnson et al. (1983) suggest that acceptance and positive attitudes and interrelations will result from positive goal interdependence, while rejection and negative attitudes and interrelations will result from negative or no goal interdependence. Based on their definitions of cooperative, competitive, and individualistic learning structures, it is argued that cooperative learning settings, which require positive goal interdependence among students within a group, would be most likely to facilitate positive attitudes and relationships among heterogeneous students. Competitive learning situations, which require negative goal interdependence, and individualistic learning situations, which require no goal interdependence between students, would be less likely to enhance interpersonal relations among heterogeneous students.

Johnson et al. (1983) conducted a meta-analysis of studies comparing the types of learning structures in terms of interpersonal outcomes in either cross-ethnic relations, mainstreaming (handicapped and nonhandicapped students), or rather homogeneous groups. Interpersonal relations were assessed by means of indices of interpersonal attraction (sociometric measures of liking, attitude questionnaires) and observations of positive interactions during instruction and/or free time. In this analysis, they considered 251 findings derived from 98 studies conducted between 1944 and 1982. Results were the same regardless of the type of groups compared (cross-ethnic, handicapped, or homogeneous), and regardless of the particular meta-analytic procedures used. Overwhelmingly, cooperative learning experiences were found to promote more positive relations between individuals from different ethnic backgrounds, between handicapped and nonhandicapped individuals, and among homogeneous individuals than did either competitive or individualistic learning experiences, or cooperative learning situations that included intergroup competition. As well, cooperative learning with intergroup competition tended to promote more positive relationships than did competitive or individualistic experiences. Finally, there seemed to be little difference between competitive and individualistic learning experiences of interpersonal outcomes. In subsequent analyses, they went on to consider other factors that might have influenced the attraction process within these different learning structures. Briefly, they found that interpersonal attraction was enhanced by a number of variables, virtually all of which are more likely in cooperative rather than competitive or individualistic learning situations. Thus, it appears that cooperative learning strategies offer an optimal setting for facilitating positive interpersonal interactions and more positive attitudes among students, and one that, importantly, does not appear to jeopardize academic progress.

In discussing the utility of cooperative learning strategies, it is also important to consider the issue of whether these positive effects generalize to settings other than the instructional situation. If cooperative learning situations do indeed promote more positive interpersonal relations within the group, do these effects show up in other settings? The answer is yes. Several studies have been conducted by Johnson et al. (1983) that demonstrate that when students who had participated in cooperative learning situations, as compared with competitive and individualistic learning situations, were later placed in free-choice, post-instructional settings, they were more likely to exhibit more of both cross-ethnic and cross-handicap interaction.

Although these research findings certainly provide strong support for the use of cooperative learning in the classroom, it is important to recognize that cooperative instruction does not simply mean having children sit together at the same table and talk to each other while doing individual assignments or putting students together to work on a project. Many teachers (and students!) report having tried cooperative learning activities in class, but regard these efforts as miserable failures. Thus, despite encouraging research evidence, the actual experience of cooperative learning appears to result in less positive outcomes. In a recent review of cooperative learning practices, Hymel, Zinck and Ditner (1993) suggest that the success of cooperative learning efforts depends on careful implementation of several basic, necessary components. After many years of experience and research with cooperative learning situations, Johnson, Johnson, and Holubec (1986) have identified five critical elements, without which cooperative efforts are likely to fail. The first critical element is establishing positive interdependence among students. Students must perceive that they "sink or swim together" and that they cannot succeed (individually) unless all members of the group succeed, and, as a result, they are dependent on one another for success. A second critical element is face-to-face interaction. Without direct interaction and verbal interchange between students, the affective outcomes of cooperative learning may never be realized. Third, effective cooperative learning requires individual accountability, such that each student in the group is accountable for mastering the assigned material. Although students can learn with the assistance and support of their group partners, each individual must learn and be accountable. A fourth component is interpersonal and small group skills. In order for students to work effectively together, they must be given the social skills necessary for collaboration and be motivated to use them. As one example, students must learn the skill of criticizing ideas without criticizing the individual. Thus, direct training in relevant social skills may be required. Fifth and finally, it is imperative that students be provided with group processing evaluative opportunities. Following a cooperative group activity, students must be given the time and opportunity to evaluate how well their learning groups are functioning and the extent to which group members effectively used the social skills necessary to maintain effective working relations within the group. Such evaluative opportunities may be particularly important when the cooperative experience has *not* been a successful one, providing the opportunity for students to recognize and learn from their "mistakes," and try to suggest ways to improve group functioning next time. For details as to the variety of ways in which each of these critical elements can be achieved, the interested reader is referred to Hymel, Zinck, and Ditner (1993) and especially to Johnson, Johnson, and Holubec (1986).

Direct Training in Social Interaction Skills

In addition to the general principles outlined by Staub (1988) for structuring the classroom and school setting, it is also important to recognize that teachers can play a critical role in the direct training of social skills in their students. Over the past decade, numerous programs and curriculums have been developed for educators that emphasize the direct training of interpersonal skills, but a complete review of these materials is beyond the scope of this chapter. Instead, we will consider one broad area of social skills training—the ability to effectively solve social problems—and highlight some of the curriculum materials that may be useful.

Throughout a given school day, a student will encounter a countless variety of social or interpersonal problems that he or she must solve. The ability to solve social problems in an acceptable, nonaggressive manner constitutes a major developmental task for the elementary school child. Until recently, these social lessons have generally been learned primarily through "trial and error" or experience. However, in recent years, based on pioneering work by George Spivak and Myrna Shure, several different authors, educators, and researchers have developed extensive programs for the training of social problem-solving skills in school-age children (Elias and Clabby, 1989, 1992; Greenberg & Kusche, 1993; Weissberg, 1985; Weissberg & Gesten, 1982). Each of these programs appears to share a common goal—that of providing children with a general framework for effectively and appropriately dealing with social problems and interpersonal difficulties without having to rely on adults for help. The children are not taught specifically what to think or do when faced with a social problem. Instead, they are taught how to think when they encounter a social problem. Although the specifics of these programs vary, each includes training in a number of prerequisite skills (such as identifying feelings or emotions experienced by self and others in any social dilemma, or developing self-control to inhibit initial and aggressive reactions in favour of more reasoned approaches to the problem), followed by direct training on how to best handle social problems, including the ability to generate many different or alternative ways that the problem could be solved, and the ability to anticipate and evaluate the consequences of their proposed solutions, both for themselves and others. For the most part, these programs are cognitively based approaches to the training of social problem solving, and rely a great deal on verbal discussion. The particular activities involved in these programs are often varied according to the developmental needs of the children involved. For example, the PATHS (Providing Alternative Thinking Strategies) curriculum originally developed by Greenberg and Kusche (1993) for use with deaf children, is also designed for use with young elementary school-age children (up to grades 1 and 2), (see also Greenberg, Kusche, Cook & Quamma, in press) while the Rochester Social Problem Solving (SPS) program includes two separate curriculums, one designed for use with second- through fourth-grade students and the other designed for use with fifth- through eighth-grade students.

As one example, Weissberg and colleagues (1982, 1985) outline and train a six-step framework for solving social problems:

1. Problem Definition   (Say the problem and how you feel.)

2. Goal Statement   (Decide on your goal.)

3. Impulse Delay   (Stop and think before you act.)

4. Generation of Alternatives   (Think of as many solutions as you can.)

5. Consideration of Consequences   (Think ahead to what might happen next.)

6. Implementation   (When you have a really good solution, try it.)

In the curriculum for second- through fourth-grade students, this six-step procedure is developed gradually, in 34 teacher-directed problem-solving lessons, each about 20 to 30 minutes in length, and utilizing a variety of techniques including discussion, skits, stories, crossword puzzles, and so forth. The children are gradually moved through each of the steps in the framework, with opportunities to practise each skill, both cognitively (in verbal discussions and dialogues with the teacher) and behaviourally (in role plays, skits, etc.). Research on the effectiveness of these social problem-solving training programs has been generally positive, with children trained in social problems solving skills consistently found to improve in their problem-solving abilities in terms of both cognitive and behavioural outcomes (Weissberg and Gesten, 1982). However, Weissberg and Gesten note that more positive outcomes tend to be obtained with each successive implementation of the program. Presumably, greater success comes with greater experience.

Similar efforts to train social problem solving in school-age children have been developed with specific attention to conflict resolution or peacemaking skills. For example, the Community Board Program of San Francisco has developed a Conflict Resolution Program for use with elementary as well as secondary school students (see Suggested Resources). In this program, certain students are selected and trained as conflict managers, with extensive training in such things as leadership and communication skills, problem-solving skills, and taking responsibility for their own actions. Once trained, these students work in pairs to help other students to get along together at school and to settle their own disputes. These trained conflict managers do not "settle" the disputes of others, rather they are trained to calm intense situations and then facilitate the resolution process. By helping disputing students to identify and express their concerns and come to their own resolutions, the students' responsibility for handling their own problems is increased. Although the training and commitment necessary to effectively establish this Conflict Managers Program is extensive (and somewhat expensive) and generally requires the commitment of an entire school, initial evidence supports the effectiveness of such programs. Moreover, in one school district in Ontario, a variation of this peacemaker program has been effectively adapted for use with young children throughout the school (not just specially selected and trained conflict managers) (Fine, Lacey, Baer & Rother, 1991/1992). As well, Naomi Drew (1988) has independently developed a very similar conflict resolution or peacemaking procedure, which has resulted in a series of lessons designed for use with elementary school-age children. Although the details vary across the three programs, they all appear to involve the same basic approach to conflict resolution. As one example, Drew (1988) suggests the following six-step set of "Win/Win" guidelines for use in conflict resolution:

1. Take time to cool off, if needed. Find alternative ways to express anger.

2. Using "I messages," each person states his/her feelings and the problem as he or she sees it.

   No blaming, no name calling, no interrupting.

3. Each person states the problem as the other person sees it.

4. Each person states how he or she is responsible for the problem.

5. Brainstorm solutions together and choose a solution that satisfies both—a Win/Win solution.

6. Affirm your partner.

   Thus, there are numerous papers, curriculum guides, and procedures currently available to teachers who wish to directly train social problem-solving or conflict resolution skills in their students. Again, the interested educator is referred to the resource guide at the end of the chapter for information regarding these materials.

   In closing this section, it is important to acknowledge that the training of social skills in children is a gradual process, one that requires a considerable investment of time and energy. However, the benefits of such efforts appear to far outweigh the costs. Not only does such training promote the social development of one's current students, but may ultimately contribute to the development of a more socially effective and peaceful generation of individuals. At the same time, it is also important to recognize that the direct training of social skills in students will not solve all of the social problems that face the elementary school child, and different approaches may be needed for different kinds of social problems. For example, although training in social problem-solving and conflict resolution strategies may provide a child with effective tools for handling many interpersonal conflicts, they may not be effective in certain types of social situations, such as those encountered when a victim meets a bully. Moreover, *while* children are developing these social problem-solving skills, it may be necessary for teachers and other school personnel to develop procedures to minimize bully-victim problems in the school. To this end, the interested reader is referred to a recent book by Dan Olweus (1993), *Bullying at School: What we know and what we can do,* which details specific steps that teachers and schools can take to effectively reduce bully-victim problems in the schools.

▨ Summary and Conclusion

In this chapter, we have reviewed several dimensions of social development in elementary school-age children and delineated a series of classroom practices designed to foster social development and acceptance among classmates. From our review, several underlying themes emerge. First, schools have *implicitly* been given the obligation of promoting social development and acceptance among children. Rather than let children develop as they may, we believe that today's educators should make *explicit* attempts to develop children both socially *and* academically.

Second, interventions and general classroom practices that increase students' sense of belonging in the classroom must take into account the developmental characteristics and capabilities of the children involved. Only after teachers can fully appreciate their students' current level of functioning can they design and implement activities that encourage students along a developmental path toward higher levels of functioning.

Third, creating a positive moral atmosphere in the classroom is a first step to encouraging student development and acceptance. In order to accomplish this goal, teachers and students must become partners in creating an educational environment conducive to learning.

Fourth, teachers can also facilitate social development by providing direct training in particular social skills. In the present chapter, we highlight one area of social skills training that has received considerable attention in recent literature—the development of social problem-solving or conflict resolution skills. Given the increasing and varied number of materials and activities developed within this area in recent years, teachers interested in pursuing such training in their classrooms can benefit from many years of research and experience.

The goal of this chapter was to provide both prospective and current teachers in inclusive classrooms with background information and strategies for fostering social development and acceptance in elementary classrooms. The findings from several of the studies reviewed, as well as the descriptions of classroom practices, will hopefully help practitioners who are interested in creating classrooms that explicitly promote social development and acceptance. Careful scrutiny of the strategies and practices outlined will enable present and prospective teachers to develop and implement interventions into their everyday classroom practices.

SUGGESTED RESOURCES

GENERAL SOURCE BOOKS FOR PROMOTING SOCIAL DEVELOPMENT

AWARE: Activities for Social Development
Phyllis Elardo and Mark Cooper (1977)
Reading, MA: Addison-Wesley Publishing Co.
Project AWARE was developed at the Kramer School in Little Rock, Arkansas and field-tested from 1973 to 1977. From this effort, Elardo and Cooper have developed a teachers' handbook of practical suggestions for facilitating social development in the elementary classroom. The emphasis of the program is on the development of empathy and perspective-taking ability through regular classroom group discussions led by the teacher. The handbook provides a description of 72 different discussion activities that together address four major goals of the program: 1) increasing children's ability to understand thoughts and feelings in self and others, 2) increasing children's ability to understand and accept individual differences, 3) improving interpersonal problem-solving abilities, and 4) increasing children's respect and concern for others.

Promoting the Social Development of Young Children: Strategies and Activities
Charles A. Smith (1982) Palo Alto, CA: Mayfield Publishing Co.
In this book, Dr. Smith of Kansas State University has attempted to address two basic questions for early childhood education: "What kinds of skills do we want to nurture in children and how do we proceed to accomplish these objectives?" He has taken the rather vague goals of "improving self-concept" and "promoting social relationships" and provided specific objectives and suggestions for activities that can be used in the classroom setting to achieve these goals in children from three to eight years of age.

PREPARE
Contact: Steve Barrs, Values Education Consultant
Board of Education for the City of Hamilton
P.O. Box 556, 100 Main St. West, Hamilton, ON, L8N 3L1
(416) 521-5092
A Canadian, curriculum-based citizenship program for use with children in grades 4 to 6. The goals of the program include: "to strengthen self-esteem in the face of peer pressure"; "to deal with conflict in a positive, nonviolent manner"; "to develop an understanding of prejudice"; "to take responsibility for one's decisions." The program consists of seven curriculum units, each including a student activity guide and a teacher's guide focused on a particular theme.

MORAL DEVELOPMENT

OUR BOOK OF BIG IDEAS
Available from: The Master Teacher
Leadership Lane, P.O. Box 1207
Manhattan, KS, 66502.
Phone: 1-800-669-9633; FAX: 1-800-669-1132.
Complete Program: $39.95 (U.S.).
An Early Childhood Program designed to provide structure, content, and a record of what happens during a year of classroom community meetings. It provides a framework through which a democratic classroom can be created. The program supports the development of healthy self-esteem by fostering the capacity to recognize and solve problems, and encouraging the capacity to have friends, make friends, and be a friend.

Educating for Character: How Our Schools Can Teach Respect and Responsibility
New York: Bantam Books.
After 20 years of research and consultation in schools across the United States and Canada, Dr. Lickona offers practical guidelines and suggestions for promoting moral development in students. Topics include teaching respect and responsibility, creating a democratic classroom environment, teaching children to resolve conflicts, and cooperative learning.

Moral Reasoning: A Teaching Handbook for Adapting Kohlberg to the Classroom
R.E. Galbraith & T.M. Jones (1976)
St. Paul, MN: Greenhaven Press.
This book includes a number of lesson plans for moral dilemma discussions in both the elementary and secondary classroom based on literature.

SOCIAL PROBLEM SOLVING

The Rochester Social Problem Solving (SPS) Program
Developed by Roger P. Weissberg, Ellis L. Gesten, Nancy L. Liebenstein, Kathleen Doherty Schmid, & Heidi Hutton
Primary Mental Health Project Center for Community Study
575 Mt. Hope Avenue, Rochester, New York, 14620.
Available from:
Dr. Roger Weissberg
Psychology Department (M/C 285)
University of Illinois at Chicago, Box 4348,
Chicago, IL, 60680, USA

Specific Program References

Weissberg, R.P., Gesten, E.L, Liebenstein, N.L., Schmid, K.D., & Hutton, H. (1980). *The Rochester Social Problem Solving (SPS) Program: A Training Manual for Teachers of 2nd-4th Grade Children* (Available from Dr. Weissberg, cost: $25 (US)).

Weissberg, R.P., Caplan, M, Bennetto, L., & Jackson, A.S. (1990). *The New Haven Social Development Program: Sixth-Grade Social Problem Solving Module* (1990–91). (Available from Dr. Weissberg, cost: $40 (US)).

PATHS (Promoting Alternative Thinking Strategies)
Developed by Mark T. Greenberg and Carol Kusche
Department of Psychology
University of Washington
Seattle, WA, 98195, USA

Program References

Promoting Social and Emotional Development in Deaf Children: The PATHS Project. M.T. Greenberg and C.A. Kusche (1983) Seattle, WA; University of Washington Press (P.O. Box 50096, Seattle, WA, 98145-5096). Cost: $50.00 (U.S.), ISBN: 0-295-97227-0. Also available through Developmental Research and Programs, 130 Nickerson St., Seattle, WA, 98109, 1-800-736-2630

Rutgers Social Problem Solving Program
Developed by Maurice J. Elias & J.F. Clabby
Psychology Department
Rutgers University

Program References

Elias, M.J., & Clabby, J.F. (1992). *Building social problem solving skills: Guidelines from a school-based program.* San Francisco: Jossey-Bass.

Elias, M.J., & Clabby, J.F. (1989). *Social decision-making skills: A curriculum guide for the elementary grades.* Rockville, MD: Aspen.

Conflict Resolution Resources for Schools and Youth
The Community Board Program
1540 Market Street, Suite 490
San Francisco, CA, 94102, USA
(415) 552-1250

Program References

Sadalla, G., Holmberg, M. & Halligan, J. Conflict Resolution: An Elementary School Curriculum. (337 page text available for $42 (US) plus shipping and applicable taxes).

Conflict Resolution: An Secondary School Curriculum. (300 page text available for $42 (US) plus shipping and applicable taxes).

Children as Peacemakers
The Downtown Alternative School in Toronto
20 Brant Street, Toronto, ON, M5V 2M1
(416) 393-1882

Learning the Skills of Peacemaking:
An Activity Guide for Elementary-Age Children on Communicating, Cooperating and Resolving Conflict
by Naomi Drew (1988)
Rolling Hills Estates, CA: Jalmar Press.

General References on Social Development in Children

Daniels, A.J. (1990). Social skills training for primary age children. *Educational Psychology in Practice, 6,* 159–62. A school psychologist describes a social skills program for children experiencing peer relationship difficulties. Children involved in the program were given opportunities to work cooperatively on tasks.

Eisenberg, N. (1992). *The caring child.* Cambridge, MA: Harvard University Press. Dr. Nancy Eisenberg, a prominent researcher in the area of empathy and prosocial development, reviews research and theory on prosocial development in children in a book that is easily accessible to parents and teachers. Some topics covered include: Characteristics of Prosocial Children, Socialization in the Home, and Socialization Outside the Home: School, Peers, and the Media.

Vaughn, S. (1987). TLC-Teaching, learning, and caring: Teaching interpersonal problem-solving skills to behaviourally disordered adolescents. *The Pointer,* 31, 25–30. The author of this article describes a program designed by herself, in cooperation with three teachers and two counsellors, to improve social competence in adolescents with behavioural problems. Sample lessons are included in the description of the program that focus on the development of empathy interpersonal understanding.

REFERENCES

Aboud, F. (1988). *Children and prejudice.* Cambridge, MA: Basil Blackwell Inc.

Andersson, B.E. (February 1994). *School as a setting for development—A Swedish example.* Paper presented at the Biennial meeting of the Society for Research on Adolescence, San Diego, CA.

Arbuthnot, J., & Gordon, D.A. (1986). Behavioral and cognitive effects of a moral reasoning development intervention for high-risk behavior disordered adolescents. *Journal of Consulting and Clinical Psychology, 85,* 1275–1301.

Arbuthnot, J.B., & Faust, D. (1981). *Teaching moral reasoning: Theory and practice.* San Francisco: Harper & Row.

Armstrong, R.W., Rosenbaum, P.L., & King, S. (1992). Self-perceived social function among disabled children in regular classrooms. *Developmental and Behavioral Pediatrics, 13,* 11–16.

Aronfreed, J. (1976). Moral development from the standpoint of general psychological theory. In T. Lickona (Ed.), *Moral Development and Behavior.* New York: Holt Rinehart & Winston.

Asher, S.R., & Coie, J.D. (1990). *Peer rejection in childhood.* New York: Cambridge University Press.

Asher, S.R., & Hymel, S. (1986). Helping children who lack friends in school. *Social Work in Education,* 8, 205–18.

Asher, S.R., & Taylor, A.R. (1981). Social outcomes of mainstreaming: Sociometric assessment and beyond. *Exceptional Education Quarterly, 1,* 13–30.

Bandura, A. (1977). *Social learning theory.* Englewood Cliffs, NJ: Prentice Hall.

Barenboim, C. (1981). The development of person perception in childhood and adolescence: From behavioral comparisons to psychological constructs to psychological comparisons. *Child Development, 52,* 129–44.

Bear, G., & Richards, H.C. (1982). Moral reasoning and conduct problems in the classroom. *Journal of Educational Psychology, 73,* 644–70.

Bender, W.N., & Smith, J.K. (1990). Classroom behavior of children and adolescents with learning disabilities: A meta-analysis. *Journal of Learning Disabilities, 23,* 298–305.

Berkowitz, M.W., & Gibbs, J.C. (1983). Measuring the developmental features of moral discussion. *Merrill-Palmer Quarterly, 29,* 399–410.

Berndt, T.J. (1986). Children's comments about their friendships. In M. Perlmutter (Ed.), *Cognitive perspectives on children's social and behavioral development. The Minnesota Symposia on Child Psychology, Vol. 18* (pp. 189–218). Hillsdale, NJ: Lawrence Erlbaum.

Bigelow, B., (1977). Children's friendships expectations: A cognitive-developmental study. *Child Development, 48,* 246–53.

Bigelow, B., & LaGaipa, J. (1975). Children's written descriptions of friendship: A multidimensional analysis. *Developmental Psychology, 11,* 857–58.

Bigelow, B. & LaGaipa, J. (1980). The development of friendship values and choice. In H. Foot, A. Chapman, & J. Smith (Eds.), *Friendships and social relations in children.* New York: John Wiley & Sons.

Black, F.W. (1974). Self-concept as related to achievement and age in learning disabled children. *Child Development, 45,* 1137–40.

Blatt, M., & Kohlberg, L. (1975). The effects of classroom discussion upon children's level of moral judgment. *Journal of Moral Education, 4,* 129–61.

Brookover, W., Beady, C., Flood, P., Schweitzer, J., & Wisenbaker, J. (1979). *School social systems and student achievement: Schools can make a difference.* New York: Praeger.

Bryan, T. (1991). Social problems and learning disabilities. In B.Y.L. Wong (Ed.), *Learning about learning disabilities* (pp. 195–229). New York: Academic Press.

Bryant, B.K. (1987). Mental health, temperament, family, and friends: Perspectives on children's empathy and social perspective-taking. In N. Eisenberg & J. Strayer (Eds.), *Empathy and its development* (pp. 245–70). New York: Cambridge University Press.

Cadman, D., Boyle, M., Szatmari, P., et al. (1987). Chronic illness, disability and mental and social well-being: Findings of the Ontario Child Health Study. *Pediatrics, 79,* 805-13.

Cartledge, G., Frew, T., & Zaharias, J. (1985). Social skill needs of mainstreamed students: Peer and teacher perceptions. *Learning Disability Quarterly, 8,* 132–40.

Center, D.B., & Wascom, A.M. (1987). Teacher perceptions of social behavior in behaviorally disordered and socially normal children and youth. *Behavioral Disorders, 12,* 200–06.

Certo, N., Haring, N., & York, R. (Eds.). (1983). *Public school integration of severely handicapped students: Rational issues and progressive alternatives.* Baltimore: Paul H. Brooks.

Chandler, M.J. (1973). Egocentric and antisocial behavior: Assessment and training of social perspective-taking skills. *Developmental Psychology, 9,* 326-32.

Chandler, M.J., Greenspan, S., & Barenboim, C. (1974). Assessment and training of role-taking skills in institutionalized emotionally disturbed children. *Developmental Psychology, 10,* 546–53.

Clark, M.L., & Bittle, M.L. (1992). Friendship expectations and evaluation of present friendships in middle childhood and early adolescence. *Child Study Journal, 22,* 115–35.

Cobb, J.A. (1972). Relationship of discrete classroom behaviors to fourth-grade academic achievement. *Journal of Educational Psychology, 63,* 74–80.

Coie, J.D., & Krehbiel, G. (1984). Effects of academic tutoring on the social status of low-achieving, socially rejected children. *Child Development, 55,* 1465–78.

Colby, A., & Kohlberg, L. (1987). *The measurement of moral judgment: Theoretical foundations and research validation, Vols. 1 & 2.* Cambridge: Cambridge University Press.

Damon, W. (1977). *The social world of the child.* San Francisco: Jossey-Bass.

Damon, W. (1983). The nature of social-cognitive change in the developing child. In W.F. Overton (Ed.), *The relationships between social and cognitive development* (pp. 103–42). Hillsdale, NJ: Lawrence Erlbaum.

Dewey, J. (1933). *How we think: A restatement of the relation of reflective thinking to the educative process.* Lexington, MA: D.C. Heath.

Dewey, J. (1964). What psychology can do for the teacher. In R. Archambault (Ed.), *John Dewey on education: Selected writings* (pp. 1–15). New York: Random House.

Dickstein, E.B., & Warren, D.R. (1980). Role-taking deficits in learning disabled children. *Journal of Learning Disabilities, 13*, 33–37.

Donaldson, J., & Martinson, M.C. (1977). Modifying attitudes toward physically disabled persons. *Exceptional Children, 43*, 337–41.

Drabman, R.S., & Patterson, J.N. (1981). Disruptive behavior and the social standing of exceptional children. *Exceptional Education Quarterly, 1*, 45–56.

Drew, N. (1988). *Learning the skills of peacemaking: An activity guide for elementary-age children on communicating, cooperating and resolving conflict.* Rolling Hills Estates, CA: Jalmar Press.

Durlak, J.A., & Jason, L.A. (1984). Preventive programs for school-aged children and adolescents. In M.C. Roberts & L. Petersen (Eds.), *Prevention of problems in childhood: Psychological research and applications* (pp. 103–32). New York: John Wiley & Sons.

Edwards, C.P. (1980). The comparative study of the development of moral judgement and moral reasoning. In R.L. Munroe, R. Munroe, & B.B. Whiting (Eds.), *Handbook of cross-cultural human development.* New York: Garland.

Eisenberg, N. (1986). *Altruistic emotion, cognition and behavior.* Hillsdale, NJ: Lawrence Erlbaum.

Eisenberg, N., & Miller, P.A. (1987). The relation of empathy to prosocial and related behaviors. *Psychological Bulletin, 101*, 100–31.

Eisenberg, N. & Mussen, P.H. (1989). *The roots of prosocial behavior in children.* New York: Cambridge University Press.

Eisenberg, N., Fabes, R.A., Schaller, M., Carlo, G., & Miller, P.A. (1991). The relations of parental characteristics and practices to children's vicarious emotional responding. *Child Development, 62*, 1393–1408.

Elias, M.J., & Clabby, J.F. (1988). Teaching social decision making. *Educational Leadership, 45*, 52–55.

Elias, M.J., & Clabby, J.F. (1989). *Social decision-making skills: A curriculum guide for the elementary grades.* Rockville, MD: Aspen.

Elias, M.J., & Clabby, J.F. (1992). *Building social problem solving skills: Guidelines from a school-based program.* San Francisco, Jossey-Bass.

Festinger, L., Schacter, S., & Black, K. (1950). *Social pressures in informal groups.* New York: Harper.

Fiedler, C.R., & Simpson, R.L. (1987). Modifying the attitudes of nonhandicapped high school students toward handicapped peers. *Exceptional Children, 53*, 342–45.

Fine, E., Lacey, A., Baer, J., & Rother, B. (Dec. 1991/Jan. 1992). Children as peace-makers. *Federation of Women Teachers' Association of Ontario (FWTAO) Newsletter.* Vol. 10, No. 3, 2–10.

Freud, S. (1933). *New introductory lectures on psychoanalysis.* New York: Norton.

Galbraith, R.E., & Jones, T.M. (1976). *Moral reasoning: A teaching handbook for adapting Kohlberg to the classroom.* St. Paul, MN: Greenhaven Press.

Gans, K.D. (1985). Regular and special educators: Handicap integration attitudes and implications for consultants. *Teacher Education and Special Education, 8,* 188–97.

Garrett, M.D., & Crump, W.D. (1980). Peer acceptance, teacher preference, and self-appraisal of social status of learning disabled students. *Learning Disability Quarterly, 3,* 42–48.

Gartner, A., & Lipsky, D.K. (1987). Beyond special education: Toward a quality system for all students. *Harvard Educational Review, 57,* 367–95.

Greenberg, M.T., & Kusche, C.A. (1993). *Promoting social and emotional development in deaf children: The PATHS Project.* Seattle, WA: University of Washington Press.

Greenberg, M.T., Kusche, C.A., Cook, E.T., & Quamma, J.P. (in press). Promoting emotional competence in school-aged children: The effects of the PATHS curriculum. *Development and Psychopathology.*

Gresham, F.M. (1982). Misguided mainstreaming: The case for social skills training with handicapped children. *Exceptional Children, 48,* 422–33.

Heron, T.E., & Harris, K.C. (1987). *The educational consultant* (2nd edition). Austin, TX: PRO-ED.

Higgins, A., Power, C., & Kohlberg, L. (1984). The relationship of moral atmosphere to judgments of responsibility. In W.M. Kurtines & J.L. Gewirtz (Eds.), *Morality, moral behavior, and moral development* (pp. 74–106). New York: John Wiley & Sons.

Higgins, E.T., & Parsons, J.E. (1983). Social cognition and the social life of the child: Stages as subcultures. In E.T. Higgins, D.N. Ruble, & W.W. Hartup (Eds.), *Social cognition and social development* (pp. 15–62). New York: Cambridge University Press.

Hoffman, M.L. (1982). Development of prosocial motivation: Empathy and guilt. In N. Eisenberg (Ed.), *The development of prosocial behavior* (pp. 281–314). New York: Academic Press.

Hoffman, M.L. (1984). Empathy, its limitations, and its role in a comprehensive moral theory. In W.M. Kurtines and J.L. Gewirtz (Eds.), *Morality, moral behavior and moral development.* New York: John Wiley & Sons.

Hoffman, M.L. (1988). Moral development. In M.H. Bornstein and M.E. Lamb (Eds.), *Developmental psychology: An advanced textbook* (2nd edition, pp. 497–548). Hillsdale, NJ: Lawrence Erlbaum.

Hollinger, J.D. (1987). Social skills for behaviorally disordered children as preparation for mainstreaming: Theory, practice, and new directions. *Remedial and Special Education, 8,* 17–27.

Hops, H., & Cobb, J.A. (1974). Initial investigations into academic survival-skill training, direct instruction, and first-grade achievement. *Journal of Educational Psychology, 66,* 261–65.

Hymel, S. (1986). Interpretations of peer behavior: Affective bias in childhood and adolescence. *Child Development, 57,* 431–45.

Hymel, S., Wagner, E. & Butler, L. (1990). Reputational bias: View from the peer group. In S.R. Asher and J.D. Coie (Eds.), *Peer rejection in childhood* (pp. 156–88). New York: Cambridge University Press.

Hymel, S., Zinck, B., & Ditner, E. (1993). Cooperation versus competition in the classroom. *Exceptionality Education Canada, 3,* 103–28

Jackson, P.W. (1968). *Life in classrooms.* New York: Holt, Rinehart & Winston.

Johnson, D.W., Johnson, R.T., & Holubec, E.J. (1986). *Circles of learning: Cooperation in the classroom* (Revised). Edina, MN: Interaction Book Co.

Johnson, D.W., Johnson, R.T., & Maruyama, G. (1983). Interdependence and interpersonal attraction among heterogeneous and homogeneous individuals: A theoretical formulation and a meta-analysis of the research. *Review of Educational Research, 53,* 5–54.

Johnson, J.H., Jason, L.A., & Betts, D.M. (1990). Promoting social competencies through educational efforts. In T.P. Gulotta, G. Adams, & R. Montemayor (Eds.), *Developing social competency in adolescence* (pp. 139–68). Newbury Park, NJ: Sage.

Kaplan, P.J., & Arbuthnot, J. (1985). Affective empathy and cognitive role-taking in delinquent and non-delinquent youth. *Adolescence, 20,* 323–33.

Kasen, S., Johnson, J., & Cohen, P. (1990). The impact of school emotional climate on student psychopathology. *Journal of Abnormal Child Psychology, 18,* 165–77.

Kohlberg, L. (1958). *The development of modes of moral thinking and choice in the years 10 to 16.* Unpublished doctoral dissertation, University of Chicago.

Kohlberg, L. (1969). Stage and sequence: The cognitive-developmental approach to socialization. In D.A. Goslin (Ed.), *Handbook of socialization theory and research* (pp. 347–80). Chicago: Rand McNally.

Kohlberg, L. (1976). Moral stages and moralization: The cognitive-developmental approach. In T. Lickona (Ed.), *Moral development and behavior: Theory, research, and social issues* (pp. 31–53). New York: Holt, Rinehart & Winston.

Kohlberg, L., LaCrosse, J., & Ricks, D. (1972). The predictability of adult mental health from childhood behavior. In B.B. Wolman (Ed.), *Handbook of socialization theory and research* (pp. 1217–84). New York: McGraw-Hill.

Kruger, A.C. (1992). The effect of peer and adult-child transactive discussions on moral reasoning. *Merrill-Palmer Quarterly, 38,* 191–211.

Lewin, K., & Lippit, R. (1938). An experimental approach to the study of autocracy and democracy: A preliminary note. *Sociometry, 1,* 292–300.

Lewin, K., Lippitt, R., & White, R. (1939). Patterns of aggressive behavior in experimentally-created social climates. *Journal of Social Psychology, 10,* 271–99.

Lickona, T. (1991). Educating for character: How our schools can teach respect and responsibility. New York: Bantam Books.

Livesley, W.J., & Bromley, D.B. (1973). *Person perception in childhood and adolescence.* London: John Wiley & Sons.

Lloyd, A., C. Repp, & N.N. Singh (Eds.). (1991). *The regular education initiative: alternative perspectives on concepts, issues, and models.* Sycamore, IL: Sycamore.

Maag, J.W. (1989). Moral discussion group interventions: Promising technique or wishful thinking? *Behavioral Disorders, 14,* 99–106.

Minuchin, P., Biber, B., Shapiro, E., & Zimiles, H. (1969). *The psychological impact of school experience.* New York: Basic Books.

Moos, R.H. (1979). *Evaluating educational environments.* San Francisco: Jossey-Bass.

Nelson, C.M. (1988). Social skill training for handicapped students. *Teaching Exceptional Children, 20,* 19–23.

Olweus, D. (1993). *Bullying at school: What we know and what we can do.* Oxford, UK: Blackwell.

Parke, R.D. (1977). Punishment in children: Effects, side effects and alternative strategies. In H. Horn & P. Robinson (Eds.), *Psychological processes in early education* (pp. 71–97). New York: Academic Press.

Parker, J.G., & Asher, S.R. (1987). Peer relations and late personal adjustment: Are low-accepted children at risk? *Psychological Bulletin, 102,* 357–89.

Parten, M. (1932). Social participation among preschool children. *Journal of Abnormal and Social Psychology, 27,* 243–69.

Pearl, R. (1985). Children's understanding of others' need for help: Effects of problem explicitness and type. *Child Development, 56,* 735–45.

Pearl, R.A., & Bryan, J.H. (1979). Self-concepts and locus of control of learning disabled children. *Journal of Clinical Child Psychology, 8,* 223–26.

Peevers, B.H., & Secord, P.F. (1973). Developmental changes in attribution of descriptive concepts to persons. *Journal of Personality and Social Psychology, 27,* 120–28.

Piaget, J. (1932/1965). *The moral judgment of the child.* New York: Free Press.

Plumb, I.J., & Brown, D.C. (1990). SPAN: Special peer action network. *Teaching Exceptional Children, 22,* 22–24.

Power, F.C., Higgins, A., & Kohlberg, L. (1989). *Lawrence Kohlberg's approach to moral education.* New York: Columbia University Press.

Radke-Yarrow, M., & Zahn-Waxler, C. (1984). Roots, motives, and patterns in children's prosocial behavior. In J. Reykowski, J., Karylowski, D. Bar-Tel, & E. Staub (Eds.), *The development and maintenance of prosocial behaviors: International perspectives on positive mortality* (pp. 81–99). New York: Plenum.

Radke-Yarrow, M., Zahn-Waxler, C. & Chapman, M. (1983). Children's prosocial dispositions and behavior. In E.M. Hetherington (Ed.), *Handbook of child psychology: Socialization, personality and social development, Vol. 4.* New York: John Wiley & Sons.

Ray, B.M. (1985). Measuring the social position of the mainstreamed handicapped child. *Exceptional Children, 52,* 57–62.

Reimer, J., Paolitto, D.P., & Hersh, R.H. (1983). *Promoting moral growth: From Piaget to Kohlberg.* New York: Longman.

Rest, J. (1983). Morality. In J.H. Flavell & E.M. Markman (Eds.), *Handbook of child psychology: Vol. 3. Cognitive development* (4th edition, pp. 556–629). New York: John Wiley & Sons.

Rest, J. (1986). *Moral development: Advances in theory and research.* New York: Praeger.

Reynolds, D., Jones, D., St. Leger, S., & Murgatroyd, S. (1980). School factors and truancy. In L. Hersov & I. Berg (Eds.), *Out of school: Modern perspectives in truancy and school refusal* (pp. 85–110). New York: John Wiley & Sons.

Rholes, W.S., & Ruble, D.D. (1984). Children's understanding of dispositional characteristics of others. *Child Development, 55,* 550–60.

Richards, H.C., Bear, G.G., Stewart, A.L., & Norman, A.D. (1992). Moral reasoning and classroom conduct: Evidence of a curvilinear relationship. *Merrill-Palmer Quarterly, 38,* 176–90.

Rizzo, T.A. (1989). *Friendship development among children in school.* Norwood, NJ: Ablex.

Rubin, K.H., Fein, G.C., & Vandenberg, B. (1983). Play. In P.H. Mussen (Series Ed.), and E.M. Hetherington (Ed.), *Handbook of child psychology: Socialization, personality and social development, Vol. 4* (pp. 693–774). New York: John Wiley & Sons.

Rubin, Z. (1980). *Children's friendships.* Cambridge, MA: Harvard University Press.

Rutter, M., Maughan, B., Mortimore, P., Ouston, J., & Smith, A. (1979). *Fifteen thousand hours: Secondary schools and their effects on children.* Cambridge, MA: Harvard University Press.

Sabornie, E.J., & Kaufmann, J.M. (1985). Regular classroom sociometric status of behaviorally disordered adolescents. *Behavioral Disorders, 10,* 268–74.

Sasso, G.M., Simpson, R.L., & Novak, C.G. (1985). Procedures for facilitating integration of autistic children in public school settings. *Analysis and Intervention in Developmental Disabilities, 5,* 233–46.

Schonert, K.A., & Cantor, G.N. (1991). Moral reasoning in behaviorally disordered adolescents from alternative and traditional high schools. *Behavioral Disorders, 17,* 23–35.

Schonert-Reichl, K.A. (1993). Empathy and social relationships in adolescents with behavioral disorders. *Behavioral Disorders, 18,* 189–204.

Schonert-Reichl, K.A. (1994). Peer relationships, social behavior, and the development of moral reasoning during pre-and early adolescence. *Moral Education Forum, 19,* 21–32.

Schulman, M., & Mekler, E. (1985). *Bringing up a moral child.* Reading, MA: Addison-Wesley.

Schumaker, J.B., & Hazel, J.S. (1984). Social skills assessment and training for the learning disabled: Who's on first and what's on second? Part I. *Journal of Learning Disabilities, 17,* 422–31.

Selman, R.L. (1976). Social-cognitive understanding: A guide to educational and clinical practice. In T. Lickona (Ed.), *Moral development and behavior: Theory, research and social issues.* New York: Holt, Rinehart & Winston.

Selman, R.L. (1980). *The growth of interpersonal understanding: Developmental and clinical analyses.* New York Academic Press.

Selman, R.L., & Demorest, A. (1984). Observing troubled children's interpersonal negotiation strategies: Implications of and for a developmental model. *Child Development, 55,* 288–304.

Shantz, C. (1987). Conflicts between children. *Child Development, 58,* 283–305.

Simpson, R. (1980). Modifying the attitudes of regular class students toward the handicapped. *Focus on Exceptional Children, 13,* 1–11.

Smollar-Volpe, J., & Youniss, J. (1982). Social development through friendship. In K.H. Rubin & H. Ross (Eds.), *Peer relationships and social skills in childhood* (pp. 279–98). New York: Springer-Verlag.

Snell, M.E. (1991). Schools are for all kids: The importance of integration for students with severe disabilities and their peers. In J.W. Loyd, A.C. Repp, & N.N. Singh (Eds.), *The Regular Education Initiative: Alternative perspectives on concepts, issues, and models* (pp. 133–48). Sycamore, IL: Sycamore.

Stainback, S., & Stainback, W. (1985). *Integration of students with severe handicaps into regular schools.* Reston, VA: The Council for Exceptional Children. (ERIC Document Reproduction Service No. ED 255 009).

Stainback, W., Stainback, S., & Wilkinson, A. (1992). Encouraging peer supports and friendships. *Teaching Exceptional Children, 24,* 6–11.

Staub, E. (1988). The evolution of caring and nonaggressive persons and societies. *Journal of Social Issues, 44,* 81–100.

Strain, P.S. (1981). Peer-mediated treatment of exceptional children's social withdrawal. *Exceptional Education Quarterly, 1,* 93–105.

Stone, W.L., & LaGreca, A.M. (1990). The social status of children with learning disabilities: A reexamination. *Journal of Learning Disabilities, 23,* 32–37.

Swarthout, D. (1988). Enhancing the moral development of behaviorally/emotionally handicapped students. *Behavioral Disorders, 14,* 57–68.

Tajfel, H. (1978). Interindividual behavior and intergroup behavior. In H. Tajfel (Ed.), *European Monographs in Social Psychology: Vol. 14, Differentiation between social groups* (pp. 27–60). London: Academic Press.

Tajfel, H. (1982). Social psychology of intergroup relations. *Annual Review of Psychology, 33,* 1–39.

Turiel, E. (1974). Conflict and transition in adolescent moral development. *Child Development, 45,* 14–29.

Vaughn, S., Hogan, A., Kouzekanani, & Shapiro, S. (1990). Peer acceptance, self-perceptions, and social skills of learning disabled students prior to identification. *Journal of Educational Psychology, 82,* 101–06.

Walker, L.J. (1983). Sources of cognitive conflict for stage transition in moral development. *Developmental Psychology, 19,* 103–110.

Walker, L.J., & Taylor, J.H. (1991). Family interactions and the development of moral reasoning. *Child Development, 62,* 264–83.

Weissberg, R.P. (1985). Designing effective social problem-solving programs for the classroom. In B.H. Schneider, K.H. Rubin, & J.E. Ledingham (Eds.), *Peer relationships and social skills in childhood: Issues in assessment and intervention.* New York: Springer-Verlag.

Weissberg, R.P., & Gesten, E.L. (1982). Considerations for developing effective school-based social problem solving training programs. *School Psychology Review. 11,* 56–63.

Wentzel, K.R. (1993). Does being good make the grade? Social behavior and academic competence in middle school. *Journal of Educational Psychology, 85,* 357–64.

Westervelt, V.D., & McKinney, J.D. (1980). Effects of a film on handicapped children's attitudes toward handicapped children. *Exceptional Children, 46,* 294–96.

White, K.J., & Kistner, J. (1992). The influence of teacher feedback on young children's peer preference and perceptions. *Developmental Psychology, 28,* 933–40.

Whiting, B., & Whiting, J.W.M. (1975). *Children of six cultures.* Cambridge, MA: Harvard University Press.

Who says students don't have critiques of their school experiences? (Summer 1993). *Counseling and Human Development Newsletter, 12*(2), 10.

Yeates, K.O., & Selman, R.L. (1989). Social competence in schools: Toward an integrative developmental model for intervention. *Developmental Review, 9,* 64–100.

Yarrow, M.R., & Campbell, J.D. (1963). Person perception in children. *Merrill-Palmer Quarterly, 9,* 57–72.

Youniss, J. (1980). *Parents and peers in social development: A Piagetian-Sullivan perspective.* Chicago, IL: University of Chicago Press.

A Sociocultural Perspective on Inclusive Elementary Education: Teaching and Learning in the Zone of Proximal Development

Jacquelyn Baker-Sennett and Gina Harrison

University of British Columbia

Introduction

Each year pre-service teachers in Canada return from their teaching practicum eager to share impressions from their classroom experiences. The diversity of these experiences never ceases to amaze us. This year two pre-service teachers, Carl and Denise, taught in grade 3/4-classrooms at the same school. Denise paints a picture of her practicum classroom as creative, collaborative, and noisy. Throughout most of each day children scatter around the classroom working at learning centres or communal tables on a variety of different projects. The classroom teacher, a parent volunteer, and Denise typically spend a good part of each day circulating among the groups, observing and providing assistance.

Carl reports a very different experience. He describes his classroom as organized, efficient, and interesting. In this grade 3/4-classroom students are attentive and polite. On most days students can be found sitting at desks that are lined up in rows, paying close attention to their teacher's description of a particular historical event, or watching carefully as their teacher or a fellow student works through a math problem on the blackboard. As Denise, Carl, and the other pre-service teachers are about to embark on their careers, they are left with the question of how best to structure their own future classrooms. What is the most effective way to organize children's educational experiences?

As teachers, our classroom practices are guided by our underlying assumptions regarding how children learn. Early in our careers we grapple with the philosophical issues that will later influence teaching decisions. Are children passive recipients or active creators of their own knowledge? Do children learn better through direct instruction or through hands-on explorations? Is learning best achieved through individual or social endeavour? Our answers to these questions have important implications for everyday classroom interactions.

The purpose of this chapter is to present one of the prevailing views of educational practice. First, we will outline the basic tenets of a sociocultural perspective on inclusive education. Next, we will provide specific examples of how a sociocultural perspective can be applied to the practice of teaching, learning, and assessment in inclusive elementary educational settings. Finally, we will describe ways of creating inclusive classroom communities from a sociocultural point of view.

▣ A Sociocultural Framework for Educational Practice

A sociocultural approach to education begins with the idea that effective teaching involves understanding how educational practice is situated in social, cultural, historical, and institutional contexts. This perspective has its roots in the writings of the Soviet academic Lev Vygotsky (1896–1934). Although his career as a psychologist and educator lasted only 10 years, Vygotsky's ideas have continued to shape educational philosophy and practice throughout this century (Kozulin, 1990; Van der Veer & Valsiner, 1991). Vygotsky's contributions to psychology are based on three main premises: a) mental functioning can be understood by following its developmental origins and transitions, b) mental functioning is mediated by psychological and physical tools, and c) individual cognitive functioning originates in social activity. At first, these three premises may sound quite theoretical and far removed from educational practice, but in reality, Vygotsky's ideas serve as the building blocks for many successful teachers' classroom practice. In the following pages, we will describe Vygotsky's three premises and illustrate how they are useful teaching and learning tools in Canadian elementary school settings.

A Focus on Development

Vygotsky's first premise is that children's mental functioning can be understood by examining its developmental origins and transitions. From an educational perspective this suggests that skilled teaching involves understanding the *processes* of learning. Our goals in teaching often focus on the final product (i.e., an IQ score, what a child knows at the end of the school year, how many items he or she answered correctly on an arithmetic test). In contrast, sociocultural approaches to education emphasize the evolution of children's thinking as they work on a variety of school and everyday activities. This approach extends to a consideration of social, cultural, and historical practices. Not only is it important for teachers to be aware of their students' educational histories, but they must also have an understanding of school, district, and provincial histories and practices because all of these factors shape individual children's learning experiences.

Mediated Learning

Vygotsky's second premise is that mental functioning is mediated by psychological tools (such as language) and physical tools (including technical tools such as textbooks, computers, etc.). According to Vygotsky, mediational means do not simply make existing skills and processes more or less efficient—mediational means to structure and shape human thinking and action (Vygotsky, 1978, 1993). To provide one example of how physical tools can be understood from a sociocultural perspective, let us consider the case of a child who has been classified as learning disabled. In contemporary Canadian culture, to be classified as learning disabled, a child must meet a number of culturally predetermined requirements that involve the use of mediational means. One of the tools used to classify a student as learning disabled is the intelligence test. Another mediational mean involves funding from the government that provides resources to support special services for a percentage of the student body (McDermott, 1993; Wertsch, 1991). These mediational means are products of social, cultural, and historical forces that shape individual functioning and often go unquestioned by educational practitioners.

The above example is only one of many ways of looking at the role of mediational means in special education. Vygotsky (1993) also argued that mediational means play an integral role in the learning of special-needs children. For example, Braille, finger spelling, lip-reading, and signing are all mediational means that allow visually and hearing-impaired students to engage in compensatory modes of communication. In recent years the development of new technologies such as voice-activated computers for students with physical challenges and communication boards and specially designed typewriters for students diagnosed with autism have provided opportunities for special needs students to communicate at a level of sophistication never before thought possible (Biklen, 1993).

In addition to stressing the importance of physical tools, Vygotsky also emphasized the role of language as a mediator of children's cognitive functioning. By using language we establish ways of questioning, expressing, and thinking. Language allows us to communicate with others and with ourselves, and it is through language that we create knowledge. You may have noticed that young children spend a good deal of time talking to themselves. This activity is also known as **private speech**. Vygotsky argued that private speech is essential for cognitive development because it allows young children to guide their behaviours. Preschool classrooms are filled with the sounds of busy children engaged in self-communicating, questioning, and planning. Between the ages of about four and nine years, private speech usually evolves from talk, to whispers, to lip movements, to silent thought (Berk, 1985; Bivens & Berk, 1990).

A sociocultural perspective on teaching and learning would argue that students should be encouraged to use private speech to work through problems. In particular, children with attention deficits have a special need for learning environments that allow spontaneous private speech (Berk & Potts, 1991). Private speech serves as an important mediator of children's thinking and can provide clues to teachers as children progress on educational tasks. For example, when private speech becomes louder or more frequent than usual, it may be a signal that a student needs additional assistance. In many classrooms teachers train students to engage in effective private speech by modelling such self-talk strategies as verbalizing errors and corrections, working carefully, and providing self-praise and positive feedback. (For a critical discussion of this topic see Cole & Kazdin, 1980; Diaz, Neal & Amaya-Williams, 1990; Meichenbaum & Goodman, 1971, 1979).

Learning as a Social Activity

Vygotsky's third premise, also known as the general genetic law of cultural development, assumes that most individual mental functioning has its origins in social relationships (Vygotsky, 1978, 1981; Wertsch, 1991; Wertsch and Kanner, 1992). Vygotsky argued that:

> Any function in the child's cultural development appears twice, or on two planes. First it appears on the social plane, and then on the psychological

plane. First it appears between people as an interpsychological category, and then within the child as an intrapsychological category (Vygotsky, 1981, p. 163).

According to Vygotsky the social world is the starting point for later individual development. Thus, individual reasoning, thinking, and problem solving has its roots in social relations.

Even though Vygotsky emphasized the transition from social to individual accomplishments, in many instances problem solving remains a social endeavour. We recently spent time in one inclusive elementary classroom where groups of children worked on the cooperative planning and production of plays (Baker-Sennett, Matusov & Rogoff, 1992). At the outset, the teacher provided each group with a piece of paper that outlined issues that students need to consider when planning a play (i.e., theme, plot, characters, costumes). The children used their teacher's planning page to structure the order of their play-planning decisions. In this situation it is not easy to separate out who did the planning—teacher or students. Rather, together the teacher and students engaged in the joint activity of planning a play.

The idea that learning is a social activity maintains its importance when we consider children with special educational needs. During the playcrafting sessions we were a bit surprised to find that one student with special needs, Thom, was playing the lead role of Dracula in his group's play. A decade ago, Thom would have qualified for enrolment in a self-contained classroom and likely been labelled as moderately learning disabled. Today, we find that Thom is a fully functioning member of an inclusive classroom. When Thom told his classmates that he would like to play Dracula, one group member replied, "How can Thom play Dracula? He can't read the script." Another member responded, "Well, we can make a big Dracula cape and Ben (a strong reader) can hide under the cape. He can read the script to Thom and then Thom can say the part." Everyone took to this idea. Group members dyed a large sheet black and used it as a cape for Thom and as a hiding place for Ben. In the end, Thom practised his part and successfully memorized most of his lines. During the performance, the plan went off without a hitch, with Ben feeding Thom a few of the lines that were forgotten. Needless to say, the play was a great success and an important learning experience for all of the group members!

Taken together, Vygotsky's three basic premises have implications for educational practice and for the integration of all children into the regular classroom. As we will see in the next section, Vygotsky's developmental views regarding the role of mediation and his perspective on the relationship between social relationships and individual cognitive processes have important consequences for classroom instruction and assessment practices.

⊠ Teaching and Learning in the Zone of Proximal Development

Many developmental theorists and educators hold the view that instruction should wait until children are cognitively mature and developmentally ready to handle particular topics and concepts. Over the years, educators have created a number of assessment devices designed to measure developmental readiness for schooling, reading instruction, and other educational experiences. Based on students' performance on these tests, instruction is either provided or withheld until children are developmentally "ready." The argument behind this practice is that if children are instructed before they are ready to learn, the result will be incompetence, frustration, and possible school failure. Vygotsky took a different perspective on the relationship between development and instruction. He argued that "instruction is only good when it proceeds ahead of development" (Vygotsky, 1987, p. 212).

According to Vygotsky the most effective instruction results when teachers work within students' **zone of proximal development**, which he defined as "the distance between the actual developmental level as determined by independent problem solving and the level of potential development as determined through problem solving under adult guidance or in collaboration with more capable peers" (Vygotsky, 1978, p. 86). When children are placed in learning situations that are slightly beyond their individual levels of competence, learning can occur with the assistance of adults or more skilled children (Rogoff, 1990; Wertsch, 1979). By interacting with others in the zone of proximal development, children are able to participate in cultural activities that would be impossible for them to engage in alone. Vygotsky argued by assessing and teaching students in the zone of proximal development we are focusing on the processes by which children move from their current state of knowing to a future state, and we are assisting cognitive and social functions that are in the process of maturing as opposed to those functions that have already matured.

Scaffolded Instruction

Encouraging students to become more competent and skilled within their Zone of Proximal Development (ZPD) is a critical objective of **scaffolded instruction**. Introduced by Wood, Bruner, and Ross (1976), the metaphor of the "scaffold" refers to the process by which an adult or more capable peer assists a child in carrying out a task beyond his or her ability. Within the learning context, the teacher selectively interacts with students in the form of guided instruction (Palincsar, 1986; Rogoff & Gardner, 1984; Rosenshine & Meister, 1992). This interaction is selective because the teacher continually monitors the learning process by assessing what students can accomplish both by themselves and with assistance. Given this continual monitoring of students' potential for learning within the ZPD, the teacher provides or withdraws tutorial support based on students' task accomplishments. Thus, learning is a process of collaboration where the teacher and learner both contribute to the goal of the learner's individual accomplishments. The learner's progressive mastery of a task is dependent on selective interventions by the teacher, interventions that are carefully constructed and determined by students' needs for external assistance and their current level of task mastery (Clay & Cazdan, 1990).

This model of teaching and learning departs from the traditional view of teachers as "knowers" and students as passive recipients of instruction. Instead, student and teacher share responsibility for learning. The instructional focus for many traditional perspectives on teaching and learning involves breaking an academic or cognitive task into component parts (i.e., sequentially, temporally, or according to difficulty). In contrast, a sociocultural perspective involves the social distribution of a particular task. The task is segmented through the joint negotiation of the distribution of labour between teacher and student (Newman, Griffin & Cole, 1989).

One might expect that guided assistance occurs naturally in classroom contexts, and in some instances it does. Beed, Hawkins & Roller (1991) have identified two forms of scaffolding employed by teachers: **incidental scaffolding** and **strategic scaffolding**. Incidental scaffolding refers to the support and guidance that occurs naturally in many learning contexts, while strategic scaffolding refers to the deliberate strategies employed by the teacher to facilitate learning in the ZPD. Teachers can support learning activities that facilitate incidental scaffolding. Class discussions, show-and-tell, and field trips allow for impromptu opportunities where teachers can provide and withdraw support as students progress through learning tasks. Similarly, there are several techniques and tools teachers may employ to strategically scaffold student learning. Some useful techniques include **Teacher Modelling** (Rosenshine & Meister, 1992), **Thinking Aloud**, and **Reciprocal Teaching** (Palincsar, 1986). The following methods are only a few of the many approaches that can be adopted for scaffolded instruction, and by no means are these three methods mutually exclusive.

Teacher Modelling

Teacher Modelling emphasizes the teacher's active role as a model for the ways in which students may eventually succeed on a particular task by themselves:

1. The teacher models a task one or two times for the students. The teacher works slowly and methodically through the activity from start to finish.

2. The teacher begins the task again, modelling the steps, but this time invites student participation at any step during the process.

3. The teacher begins modelling the task then invites students to participate in working through the stages to task completion.

4. The teacher invites students to both start and complete the task independently.

Although the teacher begins the modelling process, the students themselves become models for their own task success and the success of their peers, epitomizing the transfer of responsibility and support from the teacher to the learner. Although the benefits of modelling have been investigated for decades (Bandura, 1977), it is argued that modelling is rarely practised in school settings (Tharp & Gallimore, 1988).

Thinking Aloud

Thinking Aloud is another general scaffolding technique that refers to the teacher's verbalization of his or her thought processes while working through a learning task. Through the verbalization of thoughts as the teacher works through a task, students are provided with an insight into the learning processes required for task accomplishment. Thinking Aloud may involve a series of instructional techniques that may include the following distribution of support:

1. The teacher writes a problem on the board (i.e., an addition problem).

2. The teacher proceeds by verbalizing each of the steps he or she is taking to solve the problem.

3. The teacher records the results of each of the steps on the board, continually verbalizing how he or she is thinking about the problem or task.

The Thinking Aloud technique is particularly valuable for tasks that a large number of students in the class find confusing. It is useful to hear teachers share their experiences with the learning material, and to observe how they talk themselves through difficult aspects of the problem.

Reciprocal Teaching

The scaffolding technique of Reciprocal Teaching (Palincsar, 1986) was initially devised to increase reading comprehension, however, the technique is a valuable method of providing guided assistance and support across content areas. The main objective of Reciprocal Teaching is to progressively increase students' comprehension by transferring the responsibility for the instructional process from the teacher to a student leader (Palincsar, Brown & Campione, 1993). The following steps incorporate Reciprocal Teaching:

1. The teacher begins by modelling how to generate questions, summaries, and predictions of future events. For example, the teacher may instruct the students on how to generate questions and may provide the students with a list of the key questions "who? what? when? where? why? and how?" on the blackboard.

2. The teacher asks questions about the content of a text the class has read.

3. The group discusses these questions, raises additional questions, summarizes, and clears up disagreements or misunderstandings of the text.

4. The teacher encourages students to explore increasingly complex patterns within the text once they have shown a mastery of the easier patterns.

5. A group leader is selected and given the responsibility of asking questions of the class and responding to questions created by other students.

6. The group leader provides an opportunity for the group to summarize and clarify the text passage and predict the next passage in the text.

Throughout the entire process, the teacher may assist the group leader by verbally modelling his or her own problem-solving thought processes or by prompting or reminding the leader of particular parts of the text relevant to the group leader's summary and prediction. As the group progresses, the teacher's intervention is required less frequently and intensively.

Scaffolding is intended to be a temporary support until the student has mastered a particular strategy. The pattern of withdrawal is largely dependent on the degree of mastery and fluency with which the child displays independent task accomplishments. A typical pattern of presentation and withdrawal of support has been suggested by Rosenshine and Meister (1992) and is presented in Table 9.1. This sequencing is not static, but rather it is up to the teacher to continually monitor the progression of student mastery and provide or withdraw scaffolds for learning based on students' task competency.

Scaffolded Instruction in Multicultural Educational Settings

Scaffolded instruction is possible when working with individuals, small groups, and the entire class. The techniques outlined in this section can be adapted to any number of interactions. In fact, group size can be used as its own scaffolding procedure. For example, groups of five or six students may work together on a particular task. As students become skilled, the teacher can divide the group up again into pairs. When the pairs become competent, individuals work on the task by themselves.

TABLE 9.1
General Scaffolding Technique

1. **Present the new cognitive strategies**
   a. Introduce the concrete prompt
   b. Model the skill
   c. Think aloud as choices are made

2. **Regulate difficulty during guided practice**
   a. Start with simplified material and gradually increase the complexity of the task
   b. Complete part of the task for the student
   c. Provide cue cards
   d. Present the material in small steps
   e. Anticipate student errors and difficult areas

3. **Provide varying contexts for student practice**
   a. Provide teacher-led practice
   b. Engage in reciprocal teaching
   c. Have students work in small groups

4. **Provide feedback**
   a. Offer teacher-led feedback
   b. Provide checklists
   c. Provide models of expert work

5. **Increase student responsibility**
   a. Diminish prompts and models
   b. Gradually increase complexity and difficulty of material
   c. Diminish student support
   d. Check for student mastery

6. **Provide independent practice**
   a. Provide extensive practice
   b. Facilitate application to new examples

Source: Adapted from Rosenshine & Meister (1992), The use of scaffolds for teaching higher-level cognitive strategies. *Educational Leadership 49, 26–33.*

In addition to the three techniques mentioned above, there are numerous tools that teachers may creatively use in scaffolded instruction to facilitate the teaching/learning process. A partial list of instructional tools is contained in Table 9.2.

TABLE 9.2
Examples of Instructional Tools Useful in Scaffolded Instruction

Advance organizers (i.e., handouts, overheads)

Audiotapes of text

Calculator

Captioned films

Checklist of steps

Completed samples

Computer activities

Contracts

Games for practise

Highlighted text

Interactive videodisk

Manipulatives

Mnemonics (memory aids)

Organization charts

Paraphrasing

Partial outlines

Peer notetaker

Question guides

Simplified directions

Strategy posters

Structured notes

Study guides

Summaries

Tape recorder

Volunteer tutor

Note: For additional ideas see J. Choate (1993), Successful mainstreaming. Proven ways to detect and correct special needs (Boston: Allyn & Bacon).

As illustrated in Table 9.2, verbal cues, prompts, reminders, mnemonics, and hints can be incorporated into scaffolded instruction. Records may be displayed around the classroom on cards, in students' workbooks, or in a display at a Learning Centre in the class. Since the withdrawal of the scaffold is inevitable, teachers need to gauge the appropriate time for providing and withdrawing of scaffolded assistance. As students become more apt to use these strategies spontaneously, without the use of written records, these tools may be gradually removed or made less obvious. For example, students often have difficulty remembering that the letter "i" almost always precedes the letter "e" except when the letter "c" precedes both letters. The rhyme "'i' before 'e' except after 'c'" helps us all to remember this rule. For new spellers, teachers may write this rhyme on a strip of paper and tape it to students' desks. As students make fewer mistakes with words requiring "ie" and "cei" the teacher may replace the first strip with "'i' before 'e' except after '_____,'" and then withdraw this prompt all together from those students' desks who have mastered this spelling skill.

Scaffolded Instruction in Multicultural Educational Settings

Scaffolded instruction captures the essence of learning within the zone of proximal development. Through systematic and selective support, the teacher guides learners through the stages required to complete a task and monitors the progression of their success. An important element for guiding learners' efforts successfully is the shared understanding or **intersubjectivity** of the learning experience (Rogoff, 1990). That is, for scaffolding to be effective, teachers and learners must share a common purpose and they must be aware that they do so. In essence, both teacher and learner must be aware of what the other is trying to accomplish (Dyson, 1990). One of the criticisms of contemporary educational practice is that teachers and students fail to share intersubjectivity because of a general unawareness of each other's social and cultural backgrounds. Unfortunately, in many multicultural classrooms it is common for students to experience a cultural distance between themselves and their teacher as well as between their home and school lives.

Sociocultural perspectives on educational practice provide some suggestions on how to create educational experiences that promote shared understanding in multicultural educational settings. **Culturally sensitive scaffolding** involves the use of students' prior cultural knowledge and interests as a support for school learning (Lee, 1991, 1992; Moll & Greenberg, 1990; Tharp & Gallimore, 1988; Wells, 1986). One method of culturally sensitive scaffolding involves establishing links between home, school, and community by incorporating practical community knowledge into the formal educational curriculum (Moll & Greenberg, 1990). Using this method, community members serve as sources of information for classroom curriculum, and they assist students in completing classroom projects.

Teachers working successfully with Native American students, Hawaiian students, and with ESL students throughout North America have created teaching models that build a bridge between ways of talking and thinking at home and school (Au, 1980; Tharp & Gallimore, 1988). When classroom discussions and activities are compatible with community practices, research has found that students increase participation in instructional discourse (Lee, 1992). This increased participation is associated with successful school achievement throughout the elementary and secondary school years (Lee, 1991; Tharp & Gallimore, 1988). Clearly, culturally sensitive scaffolding can serve as an important instructional tool in multicultural educational communities. The challenge for teachers involves identifying compatible and incompatible features between the elementary curriculum and home/community practices.

Toronto educators Orzechowska and Smieja (1994) argue that classroom experiences that validate children's first language abilities allow ESL children to participate fully in English language classrooms. They report that it is typical to observe

ESL students at home—reasoning, arguing, and articulating with friends and family in their first language. However, when these same children are observed at school these cognitive abilities disappear. Orzechowska, Smieja, and others argue that ESL children are silenced because they are unable to participate in English language activities. Currently, there are a number of successful educational programs designed to maximize learning in both first and second languages. As one example, Luis Moll (in press) observed the teaching strategies of a number of expert ESL teachers. He found that these teachers' classroom practices were quite compatible with a sociocultural perspective. Each of the observed teachers in Moll's study set up classroom environments that maximized development in both first- and second- language activities. For example, in one classroom a teacher routinely grouped two fluent bilingual English-Spanish speaking students with a limited English speaker. Together the group worked on assignments, wrote stories, and read books in both English and Spanish. It was the teacher's expectation that this grouping during cooperative activities would provide an English language zone of proximal development for the ESL student in addition to encouraging the student to continue to progress intellectually in Spanish at her own rate.

Dynamic Assessment

Assessing student progress is a challenge for all teachers and is a key feature of sociocultural practice. As teachers, how do we know if and when a child has mastered a particular learning task? Research has shown that those children who need the most assistance are often the same children for whom we have the most difficulty assessing. While high-achieving students may not be able to supply a correct answer when working with a teacher on a classroom problem, they are usually able to interact with the teacher in solving the problem. This is in contrast with low-achieving students who typically remain silent when unable to supply the teacher with a correct response (Newman, Griffin & Cole, 1989).

Measuring students' potential for learning within their ZPD is the goal of dynamic assessment. Rather than attaining a static measure of what students currently "know" or do not know, dynamic assessment evaluates the processes involved in student learning and the potential students demonstrate for further learning. In general, dynamic assessment attempts to accomplish three central objectives (Lunt, 1993):

1. Provides a measure of students' potential for learning and development.

2. Provides information on the processes that lead to students' success or failure at academic and cognitive tasks.

3. Provides information on ways to modify instruction and facilitate students' education and development.

Dynamic assessment has been offered as an important alternative to traditional standardized assessment methods because it allows teaching, learning, and assessment practices to occur together (Lidz, 1987, 1991). During dynamic assessment, teachers give children a task to complete and then observe the amount and type of assistance that is necessary for successful completion. In the simplest scenario students are evaluated for their mastery of a task. They are provided feedback and scaffolded support for the task, and then are evaluated again for task mastery. Thus, a measure is attained of level of performance across the processes of skill mastery, both before and after support is received.

We have already discussed the instructional relevance of the zone of proximal development. In addition to the ZPD's role in instruction, Vygotsky developed this construct as an alternative to the uses of standardized measures of cognitive performance such as the IQ test. Vygotsky provides the example of two boys, both of whom are 10 years old chronologically and eight years old in terms of mental development. He argues that both boys are mentally the same age because during assessment it is revealed that they can independently deal with tasks up to the level of an average eight-year-old. Most traditional educational perspectives would hypothesize that because their level of intellectual functioning is assessed to be the same, the course of mental development and school learning will be similar. However, according to Vygotsky, the two boys' mental development may actually follow very different developmental courses. Vygotsky goes on to suppose that the boys' teacher structures (i.e., scaffolds) learning tasks by providing opportunities for them to solve the problem with the teacher's assistance. Scaffolded assistance might involve demonstrating the entire task and then asking the boys to repeat it or offering clues or leading questions. According to Vygotsky (1978, p. 86):

> Under these circumstances it turns out that the first child can deal with problems up to a twelve-year-old's level, the second up to a nine-year-old's. Now are these children mentally the same? When it was first shown that the capabilities of children with equal levels of mental development to learn under a teacher's guidance varied to a high degree, it became apparent that those children were not mentally the same age and that the subsequent course of their learning would obviously be different.

The ZPD is a way of building diversity into assessment practices. According to Moll (in press, p. 3) "it (the ZPD) functions as a safeguard against underestimation of students' intellectual capabilities when assessed through standard, static measures or when observed in highly constrained instructional environments." Unlike many traditional assessment tools, the ZPD allows educators to assess both the individual child and the educational environment. It provides teachers with a positive view of children's potential for instruction and of their strengths displayed in joint activity, as opposed to the weaknesses that are assumed by traditional methods of assessment (Diaz, Moll & Mehan, 1986).

In North America the practice of dynamic assessment gained momentum when researcher, Ann Brown, and her colleagues challenged the rationale for using the IQ test as a measure of cognitive ability (Brown & Ferrara, 1985; Brown & French, 1979; Campione, Brown, Ferrara & Bryant, 1984). Brown and colleagues conducted a series of research studies designed to examine how children use adult prompts in testing situations and found that dynamic assessments (unlike traditional measures of IQ) were able to predict both learning speed and the ability to transfer skills across tasks and content areas. She concluded that these dynamic assessments revealed a great deal about students' cognitive abilities and processes that could not be revealed on standardized tests of intelligence.

The term "dynamic assessment" includes a range of qualitative and quantitative practices that differ according to the nature of the relationship between the child and the tester, the different ways in which potential for change is evaluated, and the types of skills that are assessed (Campione, 1989; Feurstein, 1979; Minick, 1987). Despite these variations, all dynamic assessment practices share an emphasis on assessing learning *processes* and the potential for change.

Dynamic assessment can be put to good use in situations where students appear bored, disinterested, or unmotivated to learn. When students are uninterested, it is often the case that the material is either too easy or difficult. Instruction is not effective when it falls outside a student's zone of proximal development. If after successive hints and prompts a student is unable to provide correct responses, the task may need to be simplified. Table 9.3 provides two examples of ways that dynamic assessment can be put into practice in a classroom setting.

In addition to the use of formal methods of dynamic assessment, informal classroom conferences also provide important opportunities to dynamically assess students' levels of understanding and intentions about their classroom work. Student responses during informal discussions about their work provide teachers with information about current levels of understanding, as well as a starting point for instruction in the zone of proximal development. Informal assessments do not always need to be conducted by the classroom teacher. Classmates are capable of providing both formal and informal feedback during school activities (Gianotti, 1994; Moscoe, 1994).

Clearly, dynamic assessment is not just a science but an art that successful teachers incorporate into their daily educational practices. An important assessment tool for teacher and scholar Vivian Paley is a tape recorder she sets up at activity centres and play areas throughout her classroom (Paley, 1986). At the end of the day she listens to recordings of her students as they are engaged in cooperative activities. For Paley, these tapes provide valuable information that allows her to make informal assessments about student learning and her own teaching. These

TABLE 9.3
Examples of Dynamic Assessment Techniques Useful for Classroom Purposes

PURPOSE	METHOD
Assessing the impact of teacher/peer intervention	1. Teacher records observations regarding degree of scaffolded assistance while interacting with a student or group of students.
	2. A score of 1 may represent total assistance needed to accomplish a task. A score of 5 may represent the absence of assistance for task accomplishment.
	3. The ongoing record of "assistance scores" represents a record of student progress from guided assistance to task mastery.
Assessing learning process through error detection	1. Teacher interviews students to explore learning strategies, follow error patterns, and detect strengths and weaknesses.
	2. Teacher models correct strategies or provides clues or prompts.
	3. Teacher reassesses strengths and weaknesses.
	4. Teacher can assign a dynamic score before and after mediated assistance.

recordings provide a window into children's thinking and reasoning and a blueprint for her own curriculum development.

Dynamic assessment is a very useful alternative to many of the static methods of testing students widely used in today's classrooms. Dynamic assessment focuses on students' potential and emphasizes the evaluation of learning as it develops within the zone of proximal development. Dynamic assessment alleviates the anxieties that students often feel in testing situations, because assessment is ongoing and part of the teaching and learning process.

◈ Creating Inclusive Classroom Communities

Some of the most discouraging moments in teaching occur when students are bored and uninterested. Most of us have experienced the emotional sting after being told by a student, "Why should I learn this? What difference will knowing this make for the rest of my life?" The purpose of sociocultural practice is to make learning meaningful by establishing links between informal and formal learning experiences, by emphasizing the social and cultural importance of learning, and by providing learners with the opportunities and means to eventually take charge of their own learning.

Sociocultural perspectives on education have important implications for how we create learning environments in Canada. One of the aims of a sociocultural approach to education is to create classrooms where teachers and all students view themselves as members of a learning community and where collaboration occurs in the creation and sharing of knowledge. This community approach is quite different from most traditional perspectives on learning that emphasize the direct transmission of knowledge from expert (teacher) to novice (learner) through lectures, memorization, and standardized tests.

One way that teachers can create and maintain inclusive classroom communities is by valuing the contributions of all learners. Vygotsky spent a good deal of his career dedicated to the understanding and education of individuals with special needs. In his writings Vygotsky argued for the notion that development is *qualitatively* similar for all children, thus, education is most effective when children with special needs are integrated into the mainstream classroom culture. Vygotsky felt that if children with special needs were labelled and then educated separately from their peers, development would be impeded, "Once branded a fool or handicapped, the child is placed in completely new social circumstances and his/her entire development proceeds in a completely new direction" (Vygotsky, 1993, p. 3).

Special-needs children, according to Vygotsky, will not acquire cognitive skills if they do not receive educational instruction. As one example, many educational perspectives maintain that children with moderate learning disabilities are not capable of abstract reasoning. Vygotsky argued, however, that when special-needs children are not exposed to abstract thought the result will be a "suppressing of the rudiments of any abstract thought that such children still have" (Vygotsky, 1978).

Another way that teachers can create sociocultural classroom communities is by remaining sensitive to the language environment fostered by both students and teachers. In many traditional classrooms there is one voice of authority that is continually heard—the voice of the teacher (O'Loughlin, 1992; Wertsch, 1991). When children are not allowed to question this authority they are given the message that they lack power to shape their thinking. Along these same lines, teachers need to be aware of the types of discourse that they promote (Bakhtin, 1981, 1986). In any classroom, only a few students have access to the same sophisticated language skills that teachers have acquired. Research has found that the few students who possess these specialized and often highly technological vocabularies are routinely validated, while the rest of the students are left feeling mystified, powerless, and removed from the learning process (Wertsch, 1991). The inclusive classroom teacher validates each child's personal ways of knowing and talking by recognizing that thinking is shaped by a range of sociocultural experiences and practices. Teachers can come to understand and validate students' ways of knowing by visiting the homes and neighbourhoods of at-risk and special-needs students, by observing during play and recess time, and by encouraging students and parents to share information about activities that occur outside of school. All of this information can provide useful clues about how classroom instructional activities may be designed and adapted to encourage inclusion.

Summary and Conclusion

It is an error to see only illness in abnormality. In an abnormal child, we perceive only the defect, and therefore, our teachings about these children and our approaches to them are limited to ascertaining the percentages of their blindness, deafness or distortion of taste. We dwell on the "nuggets" of illness and not on the "mountains" of health. We notice only defects that are miniscule in comparison with the colossal areas of wealth that handicapped children possess (Vygotsky, 1993, p. 68).

In this chapter we have presented an introduction to the ideas of Lev Vygotsky and his followers that form the foundation for a sociocultural perspective on inclusive education. We have emphasized three major premises of Vygotsky's writings: mental functioning can be understood from a developmental perspective, children's cognitive development is mediated by cultural tools, and individual cognitive functioning originates in social activity. We have also discussed the practice of teaching within the zone of proximal development, and we have provided examples of ways that teachers can facilitate student learning in the ZPD through such practices as scaffolded instruction and dynamic assessment. Finally, we have stressed the importance of creating inclusive classroom communities of learners, and have provided some suggestions for fostering these communities from a sociocultural point of view.

Although the ideas presented in this chapter have focused on our role as teachers, they apply equally well to our role as learners. We can learn tremendous amounts from one another, and in many school districts throughout Canada individuals involved in mentor and apprenticeship programs, parent-teacher organizations, and action-research groups are taking a sociocultural approach to reform educational practice. Vygotsky's lesson was that what we cannot do alone, we can often accomplish with the assistance of others. This is an important lesson as we continue to develop as teachers and learners in the zone of proximal development.

SUGGESTED RESOURCES

A sociocultural perspective provides important research evidence and rationale for inclusive education. However, this movement is still in its infancy, and to date few educational materials have been developed from this point of view. Educators interested in exploring the ideas presented in this chapter in further detail may consider the following materials.

Writings on Special Education by Vygotsky

Vygotsky, L. (1993). *The collected works of L.S. Vygotsky: Volume 2, The fundamentals of defectology.* New York: Plenum Press. This volume contains Vygotsky's major writings, speeches, reports, and comments on the topics of abnormal psychology, learning disabilities, and special education. Although written near the beginning of this century, it is surprising how contemporary Vygotsky's ideas are with respect to inclusive education.

Classroom Examples of Sociocultural Practice

1. John-Steiner, V., Panofsky, C., & Smith, L. (1994). *Sociocultural approaches to language and literacy.* Cambridge: Cambridge University Press. This edited volume provides readers with both theoretical and practical information on ways of understanding language and literacy development from a sociocultural perspective. The volume provides particularly useful information on deaf education, private speech, and parent-child reading practices.

2. Newman, D., Griffin, P., & Cole, M. (1989). *The construction zone: Working for cognitive change in school.* Cambridge: Cambridge University Press. This book provides transcribed dialogue and analysis of classroom lessons in arithmetic, social studies, and science. Classroom and after-school programs were all developed from a sociocultural perspective. The authors are involved with the Laboratory of Comparative Human Cognition at the University of California at San Diego, where author, Michael Cole, hosts an active internet (E-mail) users group for researchers and educators interested in sociocultural approaches to education.

3. Tharp, R., & Gallimore, R. (1993). *Rousing minds to life: Teaching, learning, and schooling in social context.* Cambridge: Cambridge University Press. Tharp and Gallimore draw on Vygotsky's ideas to present classroom examples of successful teaching and learning programs that have been implemented over the past two decades. The book provides extensive information on the Kamehameha Elementary Education Program (KEEP), a Hawaiian educational program designed for at-risk ethnic minority children.

Dynamic Assessment

1. Lidz, C. (1991). *Practitioner's guide to dynamic assessment.* New York: Guilford Press. This book contains information on classroom dynamic assessment practices. An appendix includes contact numbers and addresses for individuals who are involved in implementing dynamic assessments in Canadian classrooms.
2. For information on workshops based on Reuven Feurstein's methods of dynamic assessment (Learning Potential Assessment Device), contact the following address: Hadassah-WIZO-Canada Research Institute, 6 Karmon Street, P.O. Box 3160, Beit Hakerem Jerusalem 96308 Israel.

Journals/Newsletters

Three journals have recently been established for the purpose of communicating information related to sociocultural issues. Subscription information is contained below.

1. Journal: *Mind, Culture, and Activity: An International Journal.*
   Editors: Michael Cole, Yrjo Engestrom, Olga Vasquez
   Subscription: Laboratory of Comparative Human Cognition, 0092
                  University of California at San Diego, La Jolla, CA
                  92093 USA
2. Journal: *Culture and Psychology*
   Editor: Jaan Valsiner
   Subscription: SAGE Publications, 6 Bonhill Street, London EC2A 4PU, UK
3. Newsletter: *Socio-Cultural Research News*
   Editors: Pilar LaCasa and Jacquelyn Baker-Sennett
   Subscription: Fundacion Infancia y Aprendizaje. Carretera de Canillas,
                  138, 28043 Madrid Tf. 759 68 92 (FAX: 300 35 27)

REFERENCES

Au, K. (1980). Participation structures in a reading lesson with Hawaiian children: Analysis of a culturally appropriate instructional event. *Anthropology and Education Quarterly, 11,* 91–115.

Baker-Sennett, J., Matusov, E., & Rogoff, B. (1992). Social processes of creativity and planning: Illustrated by children's playcrafting. In P. Light & G. Butterworth (Eds.), *Context and cognition: Ways of learning and knowing.* (pp. 93–113). Hertfordshire: Harvester-Wheatsheaf.

Baker-Sennett, J., Matusov, E., and Rogoff, B. (1993). Planning as Developmental Process. *Advances in Child Development and Behavior.* In H. Reese (Ed.), Advances in child development and behavior (Vol. 23, pp. 253–81). San Diego: Academic Press.

Bakhtin, M.M. (1981). In M. Holquist (Ed.), C. Emerson & M. Holquist (Trans.), *The dialogic imagination: Four essays by M.M. Bakhtin.* Austin: University of Texas Press.

Bakhtin, M.M. (1986). In C. Emerson & M. Holquist (Eds.), V.W. McGee (Trans.), *Speech genres and other late esays*. Austin: University of Texas Press.

Bandura, A. (1977). *Principles of behavior modification*. New York: Holt, Rinehart & Winston.

Beed, P., Hawkins, E., & Roller, C. (1991). Moving learners toward independence: The power of scaffolded instruction. *The Reading Teacher*, 648–55.

Berk, L. (1985). Why children talk to themselves. *Young Children, 40*, 46–52.

Berk, L., & Potts, M. (1991). Development and functional significance of private speech among attention-deficit hyperactivity disordered and normal boys. *Journal of Abnormal Child Psychology, 19*, 357–77.

Biklen, D. (1993). *Communication unbound: How facilitated communication is challenging traditional views of autism and ability/disability*. New York: Teachers College Press.

Bivens, J., & Berk, L. (1990). A longitudinal study of the development of elementary school children's private speech. *Merrill-Palmer Quarterly, 36*, 443–63.

Brown, A., & Ferrara, R. (1985). Diagnosing zones of proximal development. In J.V. Wertsch (Ed.), *Culture, communication and cognition: Vygotskian perspectives* (pp. 273–305). Cambridge: Cambridge University Press.

Brown, A., & French, L. (1979). The zone of potential development; implications for intelligence testing in the Year 2000. *Intelligence, 3*, 255–77.

Campione, J. (1989). Assisted assessment: a taxonomy of approaches and an outline of strengths and weaknesses. *Journal of Learning Disabilities, 22*, 151–65.

Campione, J., Brown, A., Ferrara, R., & Bryant, B. (1984). The zone of proximal development: implications for individual differences and learning. In B. Rogoff and J.V. Wertsch (Eds.), Children's learning in the "zone of proximal development." *New directions for child development, 23*. San Francisco: Jossey-Bass.

Choate, J. (1993). *Successful mainstreaming: Proven ways to detect and correct special needs*. Boston: Allyn and Bacon.

Cole, M.P., & Kazdin, A.E. (1980). Critical issues in self-instruction training with children. *Journal of Child Behavior Therapy, 2*, 1–23.

Diaz, S., Moll, L.C., & Mehan, H. (1986). Sociocultural resources in instruction: A context specific approach. (In California State Department of Education, Evaluation, Dissemination), *Beyond language: Social and cultural factors in schooling language minority children*. (pp. 187–230). L.A.: Assessment Center, California State University.

Diaz, R.M., Neal, C.J., & Amaya-Williams, M. (1990). Social origins of self-regulation. In L. Moll (Ed.), *Vygotsky and education: Instructional implications and applications of socio-historical psychology*. (pp. 127–54). Cambridge: Cambridge University Press.

Dyson , A. (1990). Weaving possibilities: Rethinking metaphors for early literacy development. *The Reading Teacher, 44*, 202–13.

Feurstein, R.A. (1979). *The Dynamic Assessment of Retarded Performers: The Learning Potential Assessment Device, Theory, Instruments and Techniques*. Baltimore, MD: University Park Press.

Gianotti, M. (1994). Moving Between Worlds: Talk During Writing Workshop. In G. Wells (Ed.), *Changing schools from within: Creating communities of inquiry.* (pp. 37–60). Toronto: OISE Press.

Kozulin, A. (1990). *Vygotsky's Psychology: A biography of ideas.* Cambridge, MA: Harvard University Press.

Lee, C. (1992). Literacy, cultural diversity, and instruction. *Education and Urban Society, 24,* 279–91.

Lee, C.D. (1991). *Signifying as a scaffold to literary interpretation: The pedagogical implications of a genre of African-American discourse.* Unpublished doctoral dissertation, University of Chicago.

Lidz, C. (1991). *Practitioner's guide to dynamic assessment.* New York: Guilford Press.

Lidz, C.S. (1987). *Dynamic assessment: An interactional approach to evaluating learning potential.* New York: Guilford Press.

Lunt, I. (1993). The practice of assessment. In H. Daniels (Ed.), *Charting the agenda: Educational activity after Vygotsky* (pp. 45–70). London: Routledge.

McDermott, R.P. (1993). The acquisition of a child by a learning disability. In S. Chaiklin & J. Lave (Eds.), *Understanding practice: Perspectives on activity and context.* Cambridge: Cambridge University Press.

Meichenbaum, D.H., & Goodman, J. (1971). Training impulsive children to talk to themselves: A means of developing self-control. *Journal of Abnormal Psychology, 2,* 115–26.

Meichenbaum, D.H., & Goodman, J. (1979). Clinical use of private speech and critical questions about its study in natural settings. In G. Zivin (Ed.), *The development of self-regulation through private speech.* New York: John Wiley & Sons.

Mehan, H. (1993). The construction of an LD student: A case study in the politics of representation. In J. Lave and S. Chaiklin (Eds.), *Understanding practice: Perspectives on activity and context.* Cambridge: Cambridge University Press.

Minick, N. (1987). Implications of Vygotsky's theories for dynamic assessment. In C.S. Lidz (Ed.), *Dynamic assessment: An interactional approach to evaluating learning potential* (pp. 16–40). New York: Guilford Press.

Moll, L. (in press). Teaching second-language students: A Vygotskian perspective. In D. Johnson & D. Roen (Eds.), *Richness in writing: Empowering ESL students.* New York: Longman.

Moll, L., & Greenberg, J. (1990). Creating zones of possibilities: Combining social contexts for instruction. In L.C. Moll (Ed.), *Vygotsky and education* (pp. 319–48). New York: Cambridge University Press.

Moscoe, T. (1994). Conferences: Planned Transactions. In G. Wells (Ed.), *Changing schools from within: Creating communities of inquiry.* (pp. 61–80) Toronto: OISE Press.

Newman, D., Griffin, P., & Cole, M. (1989). *The construction zone: Working for cognitive change in school.* Cambridge: Cambridge University Press.

O'Loughlin, M. (1992). Rethinking science education: Beyond Piagetian constructivism toward a sociocultural model of teaching and learning. *Journal of Research in Science Teaching, 29,* 791–820.

Orzechowska, E., & Smieja, A. (1994). ESL learners talking and thinking in their first language: Primary ESL students sharing picture books with a bilingual assistant. In G. Wells (Ed.), *Changing schools from within: Creating communities of inquiry* (pp. 129–50). Toronto: OISE Press.

Newman, F., & Holzman, L. (1993). *Lev Vygotsky: Revolutionary scientist.* London: Routledge.

Paley, V. (1986). On listening to what the children say. *Harvard Educational Review, 36,* 122–31.

Palincsar, A.M. (1986). The role of dialogue in providing scaffolded instruction. *Educational Psychologist, 21,* 73–98.

Palincsar, A.M., Brown, A.L., Campione, J. (1993). First-grade dialogues for knowledge acquisition and use. In E. Forman, N. Minick, & A. Stone (Eds.), *Contexts for learning: Sociocultural dynamics in children's development* (pp. 43–57). Oxford: Oxford University Press.

Rogoff, B. (1990). *Apprenticeship in thinking: Cognitive development in social context.* New York: Oxford University Press.

Rogoff, B., & Gardner, W. (1984). Guidance in cognitive development: An examination of mother-child instruction. In B. Rogoff and J. Lave (Eds.), *Everyday cognition: Its development in social context* (pp. 95–116). Cambridge: Harvard University Press.

Rosenshine, B., & Meister, C. (1992). The use of scaffolds for teaching higher-level cognitive strategies. *Educational Leadership, 49,* 26–33.

Rueda, R. (1990). Assisted performance in writing instruction with learning disabled students. In L. Moll (Ed.), *Vygotsky and education: Instructional implications and application of sociohistorical psychology.* (pp. 403–26). Cambridge: Cambridge University Press.

Tharp, R.G., & Gallimore, R. (1988). *Rousing minds to life: Teaching, learning, and schooling in social context.* Cambridge: Cambridge University Press.

Van der Veer, R., & Valsiner, J. (1991). *Understanding Vygotsky: A quest for synthesis.* Cambridge: Basil Blackwell.

Vygotsky, L. (1978). *Mind in society.* Cambridge: Harvard University Press.

Vygotsky, L. (1981). The genesis of higher mental functions. In J.V. Wertsch (Ed.), *The concept of activity in Soviet psychology.* Armonk, NY: M.E. Sharpe.

Vygotsky, L. (1987). *The collected works of L.S. Vygotsky. Vol. 1.* New York: Plenum.

Vygotsky, L. (1993). In R. Rieber & A. Carton (Eds.), *The collected works of L.S. Vygotsky: Vol. 2, The fundamentals of defectology.* New York: Plenum.

Wells, G. (1986). *The meaning makers: Children learning language and using language to learn.* Portsmouth, NH: Heinemann Educational Books.

Wertsch, J. (1979). From social interaction to higher psychological process: A clarification and application of Vygotsky's theory. *Human Development, 22,* 1–22.

Wertsch, J. (1991). *Voices of the mind: A sociocultural approach to mediated action.* Cambridge, MA: Harvard University Press.

Wertsch, J., & Kanner, B. (1992). A sociocultural approach to intellectual development. In R. Sternberg & C. Berg (Eds.), *Intellectual development.* Cambridge: Cambridge University Press.

Wood, D.J., Bruner, J.S., & Ross, G. (1976). The role of tutoring in problem solving. *Journal of Child Psychology & Psychiatry, 17,* 89–100.

Parents and Teachers as Partners: Family Functioning and Teacher/ Parent Collaboration

G.M. Kysela

L. McDonald

S. Brenton-Haden

J. Alexander

University of Alberta

J. Cunningham

Edmonton Separate School Board

Introduction

Until recently, researchers and practitioners working with children exhibiting characteristics described as learning difficulties (disabilities), developmental delays (or disabilities), and behavioural disorders have focused on the child as having the "disability" or "handicapping" conditions. This **disability model**, based on psychological and biological theories of human pathology, yielded practices and tools designed to diagnose and remediate the "disabilities" within the child in the context of our educational systems and schools.

The emergence of two innovative theoretical views, namely **ecological theory** (Bronfenbrenner, 1979) and the **transactional theory of development** (Sameroff & Fiese, 1990), made researchers and practitioners reconsider the utility of the concepts of learning disability, developmental disabilities, and behaviour disorders. These two theoretical views shift the focus for developmental and learning difficulties from the child to an ecological emphasis. The emphasis is on the *transaction* between children and significant other people and environments, as the sources of developmental variance, and hence, the learning difficulties or disabilities and behavioural disorders children appear to exhibit.

Until the emergence of these recent theories, the construct of learning disability, for example, was seen as a hypothetical process variable (English & English, 1958), a hypothetical construct that was presumed to exist but was not observable. The process within the student is thought to have specific properties (e.g., information-processing difficulties) and effects (e.g., difficulties in child learning) quite independent of those conditions that led to its initial inference. In our opinion, however, there is reason to question the existence of such a specific process within the child. The research reviewed in this chapter leads to the proposition that the learning difficulties a child exhibits in school are largely, if not completely, a product of the child's unique characteristics, in terms of information processing and retrieval, *and* family and educational environmental experiences, that have had an ongoing influence upon the child's learning and development. Thus, working together with parents and students becomes an essential condition of teaching children with special needs in typical classrooms within our elementary schools.

In this chapter, we first present two case studies that exemplify typical problems children and families encounter. Then our Family Adaptation Model of family functioning is described, which provides a structure for understanding family issues in these case studies and synthesizes current research and practices with families of children exhibiting learning and developmental difficulties. Next, current research with families of children exhibiting learning difficulties, developmental disorders, and behaviour problems is structured within the dimensions of this model. Finally, future directions for collaborations with and support to families and children with learning and development problems are suggested within the context of the Family Adaptation Model.

CASE STUDIES

Robert

Robert was a difficult baby from the day he was born. He wiggled, squirmed, and screamed his way through his first year of life. Robert eventually moved beyond the colicky, infant stage and settled into his role as a rambunctious, often oppositional child who got into everything both at home and in the neighbourhood. During Robert's preschool years, his parents were often in conflict over child-rearing. His mother felt that Robert's father often gave in to Robert's unreasonable demands in order to avoid conflicts. Robert's father, on the other hand, felt that his wife was an inflexible worrier. This resulted in the mother feeling abandoned and on her own to raise this difficult child. A further feeling of isolation developed when the father's family supported him in his belief that Robert was just an active boy whose mischievious behaviours weren't overly serious. The family discord between the parents' approaches to child rearing led to an inconsistency in dealing with Robert's behaviour.

When Robert was three years of age, a third child was born. This child had Down's Syndrome and was very sickly. This additional responsibility increased the mother's stress. She was now even more isolated from the community as neighbours began to refuse to visit with her or have her and her children in their homes because of Robert's undisciplined behaviour.

During this time, unable to draw upon the support of friends and relatives in the community, the mother's only source of support came from literature on coping with hyperactive children and a friendship with a psychologist.

When Robert entered kindergarten, the mother visited with his new teacher to establish a working relationship that would benefit Robert, the teacher, and the family. Continued communication was helpful in dealing with Robert's impulsive and inappropriate behaviour and his seeming inability to be reasoned with.

The school district's psychologist completed an assessment on Robert, diagnosing Attention Deficit Disorder and recommending a trial program of drug intervention using Ritalin. Both parents were upset at the diagnosis and recommendation for drug intervention before trying other less aggressive treatment possibilities, and rejected this proposed intervention.

When Robert was in grade 1, the child with Down's Syndrome died after a lingering illness.

Throughout Robert's first four years of school, the mother met regularly with teachers in order to plan consistent approaches to managing Robert's behavioural difficulties. None of his teachers ever made her feel responsible when his behaviour was unacceptable. The mother felt that although Robert was not an easy child to work with, he and she have always been treated with dignity and respect by caring teachers.

Robert is now in a regular grade-4 class in which a significant number of students have varying special needs. Grade four is considered a milestone in the school system, as behavioural and academic expectations are considerably higher. Additionally, students generally have a variety of teachers for different subjects, each of whom may have different expectations, teaching styles, and routines. These changes have been difficult for Robert to handle. Fortunately, Robert is an intelligent child who has maintained math and reading scores appropriate to his age and grade in school in spite of his poor work habits.

His four teachers, usually operating independently of one another, attempted to implement various management strategies with little success. No collaborative planning was carried out until a number of conflicts had occurred. Although his parents had requested continuous communication, they were not contacted until November of grade 4. A collaborative team was established and included the school counsellor, Robert's teachers, and his parents. The teachers spoke of the difficulties they had been encountering and it was concluded that more frequent exchanges were necessary. A subsequent meeting with a developmental pediatrician was also held, the result being that for the first time both parents realized the severity of the social difficulties their son was encountering on a daily basis, and acknowledged the position expressed by the pediatrician that medical intervention was necessary

before the situation further worsened. A further result of this meeting was the realization by both parents of the need for consistent child-rearing strategies. Robert's parents and his teachers would need to support one another for this to be achieved.

Robert has responded very well to medication. Life for this boy and his teachers has improved significantly. The mother, however, still feels the need for more support than she is currently receiving, in the form of ongoing communication rather than waiting until conflicts occur.

Since the school has adopted a policy of inclusion with the philosophy that the focus of schools should be on parents as intervention agents, it is essential that parents receive the help, support, and skills they need to manage demands both at home and in the community. These needs are best met through working within the collaborative framework.

Kim

Kim's birth was a difficult one, involving a brief period of oxygen deprivation. In spite of this, his development appeared normal and he reached all developmental milestones age-appropriately with fluent speech by 2 1/2 years.

When he was three years old, he fell, striking his head. He became very ill and had numerous grand-mal seizures. He lost the ability to speak and his sense of balance was affected. Once a medication was found to control the severity of the seizures, only mild ones occured. Kim is now nine years old and these mild seizures are still almost continuous. His speech is severely delayed, and he uses one or two words to express whole thoughts. He drools, walks with a shuffling, lurching gait, and often falls out of his chair while sitting. He is a big boy who can be oppositional and difficult to manage when frustrated or angry.

Before entry into the school system, the family worked hard to help Kim relearn the skills lost. They are very patient and full of hope, yet they are operating without the usual support network of extended family and close friends, or parent support groups such as the Epilepsy Society, as they are new Canadians with limited ability to speak or understand English.

When Kim entered school, his parents could see that his teacher had inadequate support to deal with his learning difficulties. Classes were too large and there were other children with special needs as well. Results of an assessment requested by the school resulted in Kim's placement in an opportunity room during the mornings and a regular grade-1 classroom in the afternoons. His grade-2 assignment was full-time placement in an opportunity classroom with an enrolment of 10 children with learning difficulties. In this setting, Kim's behaviour became so difficult to manage that school personnel had his special needs reclassified in order that he qualify for a more segregated setting.

The parents were asked to place Kim in a special education classroom with five other children, all classified as moderately mentally handicapped. Kim's parents' request to visit the classroom was denied but they were shown pictures of the class. The children's mentally handicapping conditions were evident in the pictures and Kim's parents decided this was not what they wanted for their child.

Kim's parents' goal for their child was meaningful integration into a school community. If this was to happen, they felt he needed normal children as role models from whom he could learn social and academic skills. The family had been teaching Kim at home and he could now read at a mid-grade-1 level and perform math operations at the grade-2 level. They wanted Kim to continue to learn and to improve his communication skills, outcomes that were unlikely if he was placed with children whose abilities were lower than his own. The parents rejected the placement recommendation, removed Kim from the school district, and enrolled him in a regular grade-3 classroom in a school that espouses the philosophy of inclusion.

In the new school, the staff examined Kim's file forwarded by the previous school district. Information contained in the file forewarned them of Kim's frequent violent outbursts, leading to a consultation with Kim's parents, the school counsellor, and a district psychologist. They discussed ways of dealing with the disruptive behaviour should it occur, and shared information regarding the nature of Kim's epileptic condition. Kim's mother was also consulted regarding the creation of Kim's individual program plan.

Each time Kim's parents were invited to meet with staff at the new school, they were nervous both because of communication difficulties as new Canadians and because they were expecting to be told their son could not remain in a regular school. The staff was sensitive to this fear and did their utmost to reassure the parents that this school and this classroom was the very best place for Kim—that Kim belonged and was a valued member of the school community.

Early in the year, the school received funding for a half-time teaching assistant to support Kim's teacher in the inclusive process, as he learns to use inclusive teaching strategies such as partial participation, multilevel instruction, cooperative learning groups, and circles of friends.

The Family Adaptation Model

In looking at Robert and Kim's case studies, it is easy to identify certain family issues. The parents had concerns about the adequacy of their own parenting skills; difficult behaviours creating friction within the family unit; feelings of isolation from the community, friends, and family; difficulties in managing and organizing team meetings; and educational planning. These issues pose questions as to the functioning of the family and how well the family has adapted to the parenting challenges posed by a child with learning difficulties. If family adaptation is considered to be an important factor affecting child development, then we must review the literature to try and identify an appropriate and practical model of family adaptation for use with families that include a child with serious learning difficulties.

A number of family intervention studies (Achenbach, Phares, Howell, Rauh & Nurcombe, 1990; Barrera, Rosenbaum & Cunningham, 1986; Belsky, 1985; Davis & Rushton, 1991; Seitz, Rosenbaum & Apfel, 1985) suggest that the family-focused approach has beneficial, immediate effects for teachers, students, and their families. An examination of the intervention procedures used in many of these studies demonstrates the effects of interventions that target family stress management, parent-child interactions, coping and problem solving, resources and supports, and family perspectives. What remains unclear, however, is exactly what aspects of these interventions are effective and under what circumstances. Few studies have isolated the components in such a way that their individual and combined influences on family functioning and child learning processes can be examined systematically. What is needed is a multidimensional framework to assess the needs of children and their families along several of these dimensions simultaneously.

When considering family functioning from the view of family systems theory, this perspective includes the family's relationship to other social structures, for example, social services or educational institutions. In addition, the family is seen as being interactive in nature, with each member affecting the beliefs and actions of other members. Thus, a change in the family system, such as the birth of a child, will lead to changes throughout the system (Bailey & Simeonsson, 1988; Olson & Kwiatkowski, 1992). Few studies have tried to isolate individual components of early intervention programs in order to examine individual and combined influences on family functioning. An exception is in the study of the effects of social support on family stress. Crnic, Greenberg, Ragozinn, Robinson, and Basham (1983) provided an overview of studies in this area. They reported that parental social supports have both direct and indirect positive effects on child development, family stress, and adaptation.

In successful family functioning, families are felt to regard challenges and hardships as a natural part of family life over the life cycle. Families deal with these challenges by utilizing their unique repertoire of strengths and capabilities that enable them to adapt. Furthermore, families will utilize the resources of their social network and the community to enable them to cope with daily stresses and strains (Dunst, 1993). These fundamental assumptions about family functioning underlie the Family Adaptation Model presented in this chapter.

The Double **ABCX Model** has served as the basis for our model and was developed by McCubbin and Patterson (1981) as an extension of Hill's classic family stress theory and ABCX family crisis model. In this model, the letters ABCX represent the stressor event (A), the family's crisis-meeting resources (B), the family's definition or interpretation of the crisis event (C), and the family crisis itself (X). McCubbin and Patterson (1981) extended Hill's model to address the issue that no event occurs in isolation and introduced the concept of "pile-up" stressors. Thus, the ABCX model allows the teacher to consider both the presence and impact of these variables on family functioning. More recently, McCubbin and McCubbin (1991) proposed the **Resiliency Model of Family Stress, Adjustment and Adaptation**. They directed our attention towards critical elements of family functioning during illness or stressful times. The McCubbin model has attempted to examine the relationship between family functioning variables over time. Previous studies with families of children with special needs or disabilities that made use of this model include Bristol (1987); Gallagher and Bristol (1989); Lavee, McCubbin, and Olson (1987); Reddon, McDonald, and Kysela (1992); and Redington (1992). In each of these studies, the dimensions of the model were found to be helpful in explaining some of the ways in which families coped with stressors and demands. They each reported mediating effects of family supports and parental appraisals when considering the effects of demands and stressors on family adaptation. Huang (1991) also recommended that further studies using the T-Double ABCX Model should consider the relationship between stressors, resources, perceptions, and adaptation measures among other populations.

McCubbin and McCubbin (1991) have suggested that pile-up of demands and the family's capability to meet those demands are dynamic and interactional dimensions. We have developed the Family Adaptation Model, a derivative of models such as T-Double ABCX, in order to characterize the ways families meet the demands placed upon them. The models, shown in Figures 10.1 and 10.2, identify family appraisals, personal and social supports, and family coping strategies as mediating dimensions between demands/stressors and family adaptation. It is the effects of these mediating variables that are addressed in this chapter.

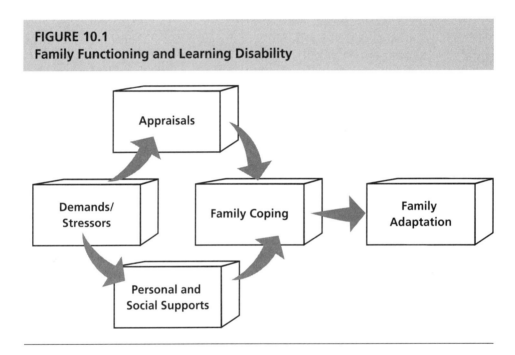

FIGURE 10.1
Family Functioning and Learning Disability

The Family Adaptation Model characterizes how demands/stressors affect family adaptation through family coping processes; these processes involve parental use of personal and social supports and are directed by global and specific appraisals of their situation. Family coping is seen as the process of using these supports and appraisals to reduce the effects of demands and stressors on family functioning and subsequent adaptation. One assumption of this model is that this is an ongoing process of family adaptation in response to demands and stressors of varying magnitude and intensity. Unlike the T-Double ABCX Model, there is only

FIGURE 10.2
Family Profile Diagram

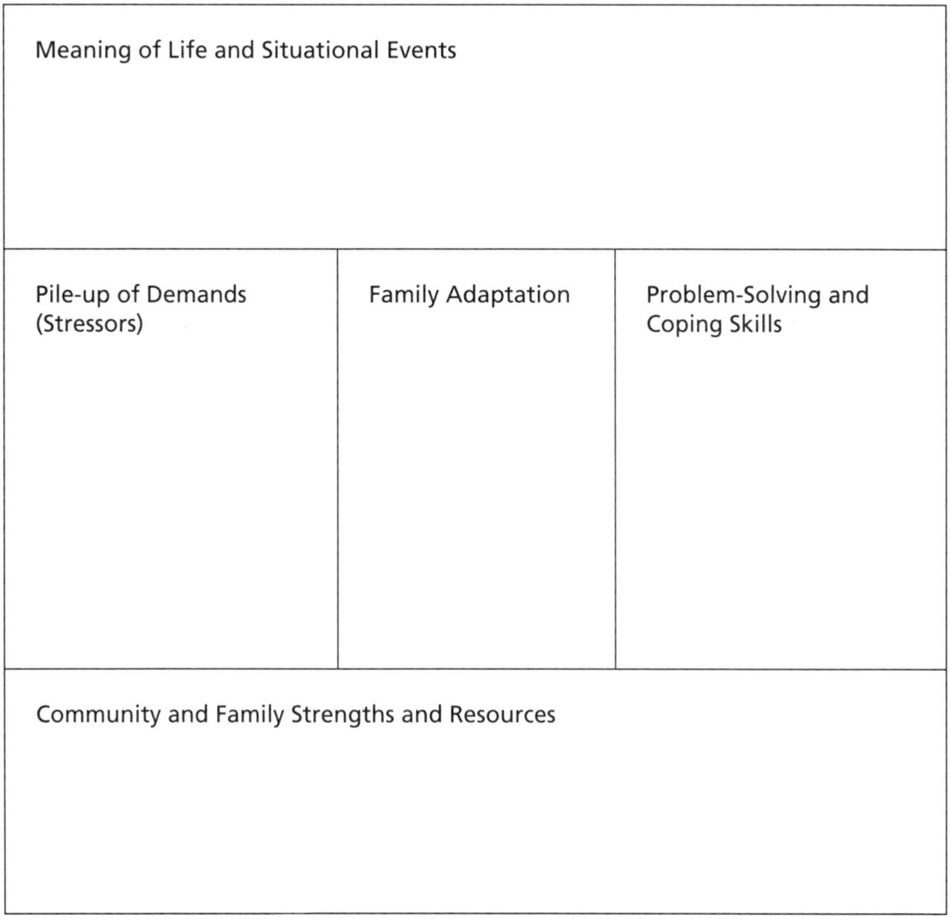

Meaning of Life and Situational Events		
Pile-up of Demands (Stressors)	Family Adaptation	Problem-Solving and Coping Skills
Community and Family Strengths and Resources		

one proposed process of family adaptation rather than an adjustment and adaptation phase. Measures of these five dimensions developed by other family researchers are utilized to assess parental perceptions of each dimension. Another assumption of the model is that the process moves from left to right and when satisfactory adaptation is attained, the cycle reiterates back to the beginning involving a consideration of new demands or stressors on family capabilities.

⊞ Synthesis of Family Systems Research Using the Family Adaptation Model

The purpose of this section of the chapter is to organize existing literature pertaining to families of children with learning and development problems within the Family Adaptation Model. The dimensions of the model are most critical to the understanding of families who experience pile-ups of demands or stress because of their attempts to deal with their child's special needs. The stressors affecting families, family's strengths, capabilities, and resources available to them, appraisals and perspectives influencing their judgments, and coping patterns assisting adaptation are discussed.

Demands/Stressors

Families of children identified with learning and developmental difficulties may be faced with numerous challenges and demands. Their children must deal with difficulties in academic learning. In addition, they may experience problems with family and peer relationships. Parents, especially those with children with severe learning difficulties, often report a sense of powerlessness and lack of support with the problems they face (Tausig, 1985).

Bronfenbrenner (1979) stressed the importance of examining the bidirectional influences of individuals on each other, the settings, and setting characteristics when examining learning problems encountered by a child in the school system. He pointed out that children are affected by, and affect, significant adults in their lives, and therefore it is critical that behaviour in the home, as well as at school, be examined. In this area, then, teachers and parents may want to discuss demands that the family views as stressing their capacity to function in the accomplishment of day-to-day goals and tasks.

The occurrence of stress within families having a child with special needs has been found to be much higher than for families without a child having a special need. Predictors of stress included the mother's perceived spousal support and perceived control. A high level of both spousal support and perceived control were found to be positively correlated to lower levels of stress reported by mothers of children with disabilities (McKinney & Peterson, 1987). In terms of parental outcomes with the stress of parenting a child with special needs, the research indicates the presence of stress to be two to three times more prevalent in mothers of children with disabilities than in mothers of children without disabilities (Anstey & Spence, 1986; Singer & Irwin, 1990). In responding to this stress, parents, in particular mothers, may experience a decline in psychological well being. Emotional adjustment has been found to be negatively affected by the demands placed on the parents by the child's special needs (Byrne & Cunningham, 1985).

Personal and Social Supports

Fathers of children with special needs, in particular, are not very different from most ordinary fathers in the extent of their contribution to child care, but the difficulties faced by mothers are often increased. It has been suggested that feelings of inadequacy in the father may result in additional problems for the mother if she has to cope with the needs of the child as well as those of family and husband (McConkey, 1985; Russell, 1986).

Dyson (1989) points out that not only parents are affected by the presence of child in the family with special needs. Siblings are also affected in terms of self-concept, behaviour problems, and social competence. In measuring adjustment in these areas, brothers and sisters of children with special needs were found to be similar to siblings of nonhandicapped children in terms of psychological adjustment. However, behaviourally, siblings of children with difficulties were found to be less active in extracurricular activities. Brothers of children with special needs were found to be less aggressive, less active, and tended to have fewer externalizing behaviour problems than brothers of nonhandicapped children. Furthermore, in a comparison of siblings of children with mental disabilities to those of children with physical or sensory disabilities, the first group showed better behaviour adjustment, higher self-concept, and more social competence.

The age of the child with special needs was also found to be a determining factor in sibling adjustment. More behaviour problems were reported in siblings as the age of the child with special needs increased. However, this finding was also mediated by the age gap between the sibling and the child with special needs; the larger the age gap, the better the siblings' behaviour adjustment. Additionally, mother's education and a larger family size were positively correlated with sibling adjustment (Dyson, 1989).

The contribution of family environment to perceived stress and demands has been studied by a few investigators using the **Moos Family Climate Model** (Family Environment Scale; Moos & Moos, 1976, 1983). This model has been used to examine the family environment in terms of three major domains of family functioning. The Relationship domain addresses support among family members, commitment to family environment, and family cohesion. The Personal Growth domain is concerned with family and child developmental directions and personal goals. The third dimension, System Maintenance, examines the degree of structure, clarity, and openness to change. More specifically, this dimension assesses the extent of possible change in the family, the existence of control and order, and evaluation of the personal cost involved in a family's efforts at change.

Using this model with families having a child described as learning disabled, Margalit and Almougy (1991) noted trends in family climate, which included decreased personal growth, and consequently less familial satisfaction and poorer family interrelations. These families' functioning problems included limited emotional expression, decreased opportunities for conflict resolution, and less cohesion and support.

Margalit and Heiman (1986) used a questionnaire and interview format to compare families of children with and without learning disabilities. They found, in families in which there was a child diagnosed as having a learning disability, a greater emphasis on organization and control and less encouragement of free emotional expression or personal independence. Parents reported fewer opportunities for intellectual activities, and also exhibited greater need for family members to reach personal achievements. Margalit and Almougy (1991) hypothesized that students diagnosed as having learning disabilities would be rated by parents as less competent in areas related to academic functioning, and that in families where there is a child diagnosed as having a learning disability, there would be more emphasis on achievement and fewer opportunities for leisure activities. These authors found that mothers of children in which a child was diagnosed as having a learning disability viewed their families as demonstrating more conflict, placing more emphasis on achievement and religion, and providing fewer opportunities for intellectual and recreational activities.

Ziegler and Holden (1988, p. 99) concluded, based on work performed by professionals in a clinical setting with families in which there was a child diagnosed as having a learning disability, that it is necessary to understand both the child's learning profiles and the nature of the family strengths and resources. They concluded that family functioning is a powerful mediator in child outcomes. Children and adolescents diagnosed as having learning or attention problems seem to do best in families whose lives reflect several related traits: "the child is expected to function with normal children; concerted efforts at compensation in both learning and self-control are reinforced; aspects of the child's difficulty are accepted as neither fully under the child's nor the family's control; the parents maintain their commitment and concern for the child at the same time as a certain detachment from the problem, so that none of the family members is overwhelmed by frustration."

In collaborating with parents, teachers may wish formally to take into account the personal and social supports available to families to assist them in meeting the pile-ups being experienced. In our research with families of young children with special needs (Reddon et al., 1992), we found that these social and particularly intrafamily supports were very powerful moderators of stressors.

Appraisals

Several family resources were identified by Wallander, Varni, Babani, and Banis (1989), and Hauser-Cram and Krauss (1991) as appraisal factors that mediate the pile-up of stressors in the family with an identified child with special needs. These family appraisals were categorized as either psychological resources or utilitarian resources. Psychological resources such as a high degree of family cohesion, independence, achievement, activity, and organization within the family were found to mediate stress levels within the family. Lower family conflict was also found to predict greater self-esteem for both the child with the special need, parents, and siblings. In general, there is a positive relationship between child adjustment and family psychological resources and appraisals. Utilitarian or practical resources found to strengthen the coping ability of families were financial stability and education levels of parents. It was suggested that the "education level of parents may contribute to cognitive ability related to appropriate parenting of the special needs child" (Wallander et al., 1989, p. 160).

Stoll Switzer (1990) concluded that it is essential to examine family factors associated with academic progress for children diagnosed as exhibiting learning disabilities. Families were identified through clinical investigation, including full psychoeducational evaluation of the child, information from professionals working with the child, informal and formal meetings with family members, formal treatment of parents, and research interviews. She identified two family appraisal factors that help children reach their potential. The first family factor involved acceptance of the learning problem. Parents who displayed a persistence in investigating early signs and symptoms of a learning disorder and sought assistance in early identification and placement were more likely to have a child who was achieving at a higher level than those parents who did not pursue these early indications of a learning problem. We would argue that the higher levels of achievement were perhaps due to the early intervention in addition to the positive effects of family adaptation.

The second factor proposed by Stoll Switzer as an important component for success was role delineation for the child by parents. The way the family perceived their child determined the role of the child. As the family was assisted to view their child as capable, the child's role shifted from one of diminished maturity and achievement expectations to a role that accommodated changes and an increase in achievement demands. The child subsequently seemed to be more able to learn from school instruction.

Based on these findings, Stoll Switzer (1990) observed the importance of assisting families in early identification and placement of the child having a learning problem in school, followed by the establishment of a cooperative working relationship between home and school. Suggestions included parental participation in support workshops to help parents understand the learning problems their child might be experiencing, as well as the importance of the two factors mentioned above. Stoll Switzer suggested a close link between the two factors, acceptance of the learning problem and role delineation, and school success for the child with a learning problem. In addition to this acceptance and role delineation process within the family, there is also the need for a process to make teachers more aware of family factors associated with academic achievement. Sensitive, open, and honest communication within the family and between the family and school staff was seen by Stoll Switzer to foster optimal child and family development. In support of this, Faerstein (1986) found that when parents were given an honest appraisal of their child's problems, mothers, in particular, exhibited coping mechanisms that enabled them to function effectively, regardless of their emotional response to the diagnosis. Therefore, the collaborative development, between parents and teachers, of an Individual Educational Plan (IEP) may be an opportune time to identify family appraisals and supports and assist parents in the two processes mentioned by Stoll Switzer.

Ziegler and Holden (1988) made use of parental prompting to aid the process of grieving in families of children diagnosed as exhibiting learning disabilities. These authors felt that parents must be helped to use their understanding to aid their child in the management of the frustrations experienced in learning. In this approach, an established foundation for family involvement is maintained through monthly contact and periodic short-term contracts to help the child and family overcome problems encountered at each developmental stage. Follow-up ensures the update of educational plans and continued advocacy for the child (for example, at the beginning of each new school year). A focus for this approach remains the family's understanding of their child's learning problems in order that parents may be able to differentiate between the potential effects of the learning problem their child exhibits and the needs and style unique to the family.

Ziegler and Holden (1988) proposed several advantages to their approach. In each session with the family, something "new" is offered, since visits are spread out over time. It is easier to maintain realistic optimism through monthly sessions than is the case in weekly sessions. Ziegler and Holden also proposed that a long-term view of on-going contact is more easily maintained.

Family Coping

Orlando and Bartel (1989) cautioned against the use of a pathology model when examining family coping patterns with a child diagnosed as exhibiting a learning disorder. A coping or transactional perspective is preferred as it permits greater focus on how families cope successfully with their child's needs and also allows an examination of strengths as well as weaknesses within the family and child. These researchers concluded that a critical element to the success of coping behaviour in families is the level of skill demonstrated by parents in assisting their child. Teachers working collaboratively with parents can provide information on assisting in children's learning, thus facilitating a parental sense of efficacy in this area.

Several family characteristics emerged in studies of families in which a child has been identified as having a special need or handicapping condition, such as higher levels of depression and lower degrees of perceived maternal competence. These parents were also more likely to engage in avoidance or wishful thinking coping strategies (Breslau & Davis, 1986; Goldberg et al., 1986; Frey, Greenberg & Fewell, 1989). These emotion-focused coping strategies were related to higher levels of distress as compared to a problem-focused (information-seeking) approach, which appears to reduce the distress to a significant degree. Mothers involved in emotion-focused strategies tended to remain involved in a cycle of self-blame, withdrawal, and internalizing feelings of frustration.

Stoll Switzer (1990) identified family engagement with achievement behaviour as a distinguishing factor associated with child progress. Several activities by parents seemed related to their children's progress. Parents who helped their child develop work habits and positive attitudes about school were often engaged with their child in school-like tasks, were able to work daily on appropriate rewards and incentives, and used techniques like modelling and prompting. These interventions may lead children to approach academic difficulties more positively.

A second factor identified by Stoll Switzer (1990) was the method of parental discipline. A firm rational manner of support and encouragement with verbal give-and-take helped the child develop an internal locus of control, which was associated with greater success in school. In other words, an authoritative rather than authoritarian method of discipline seemed to contribute to academic success. Again, these activities and orientation can be facilitated by teachers through their collaborative efforts with families.

Orlando and Bartel (1989) suggested that a family's adjustment to a child with special needs has several characteristics. These characteristics were identified as assistance with material resources, opportunity for emotional expression (provided through support groups), definition and understanding of the supposed disorder or handicapping condition (including implications for schooling and careers), and strategies for helping parents assist the child. They also identified the need to define alternative interventions that could be practised within the family. Orlando and Bartel (1989) outlined three major types of family involvement in intervention. Enhancing family involvement in intervention can lead to increased feelings of parental efficacy, greater repertoire and depth of parenting skills, which results in better coping skills.

The first intervention identified by Orlando and Bartel (1989) addressed the nature of the intervention. They proposed a preventive, developmental approach for parents and teachers that includes teaching by example, provision of approval for appropriate behaviour, specific rule teaching, and setting of expectations and limits.

The second type of intervention involved the parents as intervention agents. There is the expectation that children can learn to be the agent of their own learning, as a full participant in the learning and development process. Siblings are also viewed as effective supports for their family members, acting as models of appropriate behaviour and providing encouragement and reinforcement to the child identified as having a learning difficulty.

The third type of intervention concerns the learning environment. Orlando and Bartel (1989, p. 335) concluded that "for most children the desired learning environment is the home." Support for these conclusions is presented in the research of Sah and Borland (1989) in their work with families of children described as gifted-learning disabled. These children were identified on the basis of teacher nomination using behavioural checklists, and a detailed plan was developed to schedule and structure the child's activities in the home. Parents were taught techniques to facilitate the child's adherence to the schedule. These authors found that structuring home activities with the active participation of the family resulted in a decrease in organizational problems. As well, attempts to develop more effective parental discipline skills led to a decrease in problem behaviours and improvement in achievement at school. These results suggest a causal link between home organization and academic behaviour/achievement and provide an excellent example of family/school partnerships.

The common theme to be found in each of the approaches presented is the concern with, and emphasis given to, the importance of interventions that address the family members as a whole. Ziegler and Holden (1988) acknowledged the critical role played by parents in helping their child with special needs. Orlando and Bartel (1989) recognized the parent as central to all intervention attempts.

Ziegler and Holden (1988) recognized three key aspects of children's development that are affected by the supposed presence of a problem. These aspects of development include self-esteem, the ability to manage frustration, and a sense of self-control. Maintenance of children's sense of self-esteem requires that children, parents, and teachers make changes in their expectations. For children to maintain a feeling of confidence in their ability to control behaviour, their sense of self-control must be actively reinforced by both parents and teachers.

For children to be supported in their development in these three areas, interventions should address both the child and the family to maximize healthy development. Ziegler and Holden (1988) continued by suggesting there is a recurrence of these three aspects, self-esteem, self-control, and frustration/tolerance, during each developmental stage. To address this recurrence, they suggested a family therapy model for intervention that includes these three major goals. To aid the child with self-control skills, parents could learn behavioural skills that provide structure for the child in terms of behavioural goals. Parents and children would be assisted to identify strengths and weaknesses the child may have, and parents made aware of the child's perception of parental pride and support.

Consideration of all the information on the dimensions identified in the preceding pages gives a fairly accurate picture of family adaptation. The development of a model of family adaptation is an important step in understanding the strengths, needs, and concerns of families with children with special needs. In its initial stages, the Family Adaptation Model was developed with parents of preschool children with special needs. However, the model has great potential for teachers and other professionals working with families with older children.

Implications for Collaborative Involvement Strategies

The Family Adaptation Model identified five dimensions of family adaptation that provided starting points for the analysis of collaborative involvement between parents and teachers. These dimensions included Demands/Stressors, Personal and Social Supports, Appraisals, Family Coping, and Family Adaptation. The first four dimensions will be reviewed in order to discuss the types of collaborative involvement that might be developed with families, which will have a positive impact on the fifth dimension—Family Adaptation.

Demands/Stressors

It appears that families of children with learning and developmental disabilities experience higher levels of stress than other families. The two main themes discussed within this dimension included the reciprocal nature of the interaction between parent and child and family stress management. Given the reciprocal nature of parent-child interactions, teachers may assist parents by helping them identify successful strategies for interaction with their child in order to have a positive impact on the development of skills and competencies. Parents may feel less stressed if they can see that their efforts have resulted in positive gains for their child. For example, in Kim's case study, Kim's parents were very interested in helping him learn new social and academic skills so that he could attend an inclusive education program. In spite of Kim's gains, the school district decided to place him in a segregated classroom. The school staff could probably have reduced the stress on the parents by working with them to identify skills they could work on at home that would help ensure that Kim would do well in an inclusive classroom. Instead, the family worked in isolation and finally located an inclusive education placement on their own.

Teachers can also help families cope with stress by identifying specific coping strategies for solving stressful situations. It is not being suggested that teachers try to "counsel" families, but that they help parents identify successful coping strategies and unsuccessful coping strategies. For example, in Robert's case study, in grade 4 Robert was involved with *four* different teachers with *four* different sets of expectations. The parents felt that the teachers were not acting in a coordinated fashion and were not communicating with them as promised. It would have been very helpful if Robert's grade-3 teacher could have prepared the family for transition to grade 4. A planning meeting with the parents and the four teachers could have been arranged while Robert was in grade 3 or at the beginning of grade 4. Family stress could have been avoided or lessened if the transition had been more carefully planned. Other useful stress management approaches include systematic relaxation, self-control, and exercise habits. Teachers and counsellors could assist families to develop these competencies and use them with their children at home and in the community. Probably one of the most empowering strategies a teacher can use is to help parents identify stress management strategies that have been successful for them in the past.

Personal and Social Supports

The nurturance of couples' support for each other and extended family support is essential to enhance family adaptation to the difficulties encountered in dealing with a child's learning problems. Teachers may help contextualize the child's difficulties within the framework of family, school, community, and the changing demands placed upon their child in these different environments. The family members may then be able to identify the supports that are currently available and the additional supports that are needed. As well, from this analysis, it will be clearer that the child with a learning problem has capabilities in a variety of areas. Robert's mother could have benefited from the support of husband, friends, and relatives after the birth of her child with Down's Syndrome. Teachers or counsellors may have helped the mother discuss her support needs with her husband, or identify someone within her family or circle of friends who could have provided some support. Instead, the mother had to rely on literature and a professional for necessary support at a very difficult time in her life. It is very likely that Robert's father could have also benefited from a discussion of supports that were available to him.

Single-parent families will be most vulnerable in terms of support and may find membership in a support group or groups to be especially valuable, particularly with other single-parent family members. It is clear that interactions aimed at helping families identify support needs and accessing necessary supports will have a positive impact on healthy family adaptation. This, in turn, will enhance the learning environment of the child with challenges.

Appraisals

Positive appraisals such as learning to accept the learning problem and viewing a child as capable of growth are important steps toward positive family adaptation. Teachers may help parents develop and maintain positive appraisals by helping them focus on their child's strengths in addition to their child's needs. Parents involved in our research have expressed frustration with teachers and school personnel who only talk to the parents when problems develop. These parents also indicated that IEPs sometimes focus on all of the things the child is presently unable to do, instead of presenting a more balanced picture of strengths and needs. For example, discussions between Robert's parents and the kindergarten teacher and school staff most often focused on Robert's impulsive and inappropriate behaviour. They failed to point out that Robert had two close friends and loved to participate in outside games. Perhaps the family would have been more willing to accept the diagnosis of Attention Deficit Disorder and try the trial program of drug intervention if they felt that school staff had Robert's best interests in mind.

Teachers can also suggest strategies to help parents maintain healthy perspectives and attitudes. For example, **reframing** is a technique in which parents are encouraged to think about a situation that is viewed as negative by one or both parents in a more positive light. When parents having problems with negative appraisals develop more positive attitudes about the capabilities and unique characteristics of their children, they may value their child more extensively as an equal family member.

Family Coping

A variety of coping and problem-solving strategies have been employed by families resulting in positive adaptation to their child's special needs. Some of these strategies include family decision-making approaches, family esteem and confidence, seeking out additional information regarding their child's needs, and obtaining support from family, friends, and professionals. As well, healthy families maintain levels of organization and flexibility that support the adaptation process. Teachers can be particularly helpful if they help parents to identify those effective coping strategies currently in use (such as those mentioned above), as well as those strategies that are not helpful. For example, Kim's family went through a stressful time when they felt compelled to move their child from one school district to another. They were able to get through this particularly stressful time by relying on the support of family and close friends. This was a coping strategy that had been helpful to both parents in the past. Additional research on effective coping strategies would be beneficial to identify effective coping skills for clinical use.

It is clear that teachers and parents must work together within a parent-school collaborative partnership. Parent involvement in the educational process is a complex issue. For example, Dissent (1985) suggested that often intervention techniques mentioned by well-meaning educators are too complex or burdensome for the average family. The parents may feel a loss of control because the intervention is primarily under the control of the professional. The parents' feelings of failure are heightened if the child does not reach targets set or if parental expectations are unrealistically high (Lorenz, 1986). Lorenz continued by noting that parents are dependent on rare meetings with professionals, resulting in the perception that although the parent role as teacher in the home is a primary one, their involvement is perceived by professionals as secondary. Green (1985) also identified the fact that the specificity of skills tends to exclude fathers and/or working parents. Little was said here as well about the needs of single-parent families. Teachers are encouraged to work collaboratively with families and encourage parents to participate in their child's development. They are also cautioned to make sure that parents are encouraged to be involved to the degree to which the parents feel comfortable.

Calliste (1993) pointed to a degree of confusion between the terms involvement, collaboration, participation, and partnership and suggested that while parents may be involved, it may not be in the form of true partnership. This perception is suggested to be due, perhaps, to a lack of clarity about parents' role as compared to a focus on professionals and their role.

The area of collaboration between home and school in children's learning and behaviour and emotional difficulties is problematic. School professionals need to include awareness and assessment of the needs of parents including parental attitudes and value systems, attitudes toward education, and parental willingness and/ or ability to be involved in the child's education for whatever reason (economic, organizational, emotional). Calliste (1993) stressed the need to understand the reluctance, for whatever reason, for some parents to become the teacher rather than the parent.

School professionals must strive to overcome the feelings of isolation often expressed by parents by providing support and advice to facilitate links with community and support groups, and working toward breaking down the barriers between schools and community. As well, the aim must be to actively involve parents in every stage of service provision (Halliwell & Williams, 1991). "If partnership is to be realized, parents must be able to evaluate each stage of the collaboration" (Calliste, p. 79).

As well, from the school's perspective, positive attitudes are needed by the whole school with direct support to classroom teachers and classmates. School professionals, to be maximally effective, must be positive in contacts with parents, aim to work flexibly with parents at home, and transfer family coping and adaptation skills to these parents. All of this is only possible through close collaboration with all persons involved with the special-needs child.

▣ Conclusion

Directions are presented in this paper with regard to intervention implications. It is essential to maintain a family-focused approach to collaboration that involves the family as a whole in terms of interactions among family members, coping resources, problem-solving capabilities, and stress and crisis management.

Intervention should strive to promote an emphasis on both organization and personal independence within the family. Basic to this is an understanding of the nature of the family's style of functioning and the child's learning profiles. The several dimensions of the Family Adaptation Model address these concerns from the perspectives of family involvement and collaboration with families in which there is a child with special needs.

The focus should be on supporting parents' preferences for coping and problem-solving approaches as well as respecting their appraisals of the situations. Where necessary, teachers and parents may collaborate in developing parental skills to enhance family flexibility and training to manage demands. Parents can develop a perception of their child as an academically competent person, capable of becoming an active participant in learning and development. Thus, the goal becomes collaborating with parents to maintain their child's sense of self-esteem, self-control for learning, as well as management of the child's frustrations encountered in learning. Families should be encouraged to support their child in a systematic way. Parents must also receive support to feel confident in their role as advocates for their child within the school system. The development of a cooperative working relationship between the home and school, in an environment of open, honest communication, should be encouraged. This collaborative process will ultimately benefit the child, the family, and the educators.

SUGGESTED RESOURCES

If we wish to be effective in assessing and assisting parents of children with learning difficulties, we must provide a variety of tools that will fit the various styles, strengths and preferences of the families we serve. Some of these tools involve using formal assessment measures, a structured family interview and graphs, pictures, charts and other written materials that will help family members identify the strengths and capabilities that will help them meet the needs of their child (and their entire family system if they wish).

Formal Assessments

These include the Life Orientation Test (LOT), Family Crisis Oriented Personal Evaluation Scales (F-COPES) or the Family Inventory of Resources for Management (FIRM). They should only be used if parents wish to receive in-depth information in these areas. As soon as possible after the checklists have been completed, parents should receive feedback about their scores on the assessments. These family assessment measures can be found in McCubbin and Thompson (1991).

Checklists

Checklists usually give teachers information about family members' interests and needs. They do not necessarily help family members identify strengths. They can be helpful if teachers address the concerns raised on the checklists. Review the checklists with family members before giving them out to parents. Highlight (or delete) any statements that may lead parents to believe that they can receive help that you are not willing or able to provide. Emphasize that you may not be able to provide all the support they request on the checklist. Be clear about your responsibilities and limits.

Family Profile—Fill in the Blanks (See Figure 10.2, p. 233).

This profile process allows parents to write down their own strengths, stressors, resources, and perceptions in a way that parallels the model mentioned earlier in this paper. It could also be used by teachers to organize the information received from formal assessments.

Genograms, Ecograms, Circle of Friends Pictures

These forms offer family members an opportunity to identify all of the people with whom they have contact, and then assess their level of satisfaction with the support they receive. The teacher can present the family members with a variety of charts and ask family members with which ones they would be most comfortable.

Pictorial Analogies such as Teeter-Totter

These models offer another way for parents to document the various aspects of family functioning such as stressors, perceptions, strengths, and resources. Again, the interventionist should ask the family to complete the form that they would find most helpful.

Structured Interview

A structured interview can contain a variety of open-ended questions based on a specific topic. The listening and interpersonal communication skills of the teacher are very important when conducting structured interviews. The teacher must be prepared for a wide variety of responses and be appreciative of the information given by the parents. Many parents find the structured interview to be a helpful, nonintrusive way of gathering family information.

To Summarize, Helpful Assessment Tools Include:

- Formal assessments
- Checklists
- Family profile—Fill in the blanks
- Genograms, ecograms, circle of friends pictures, MAPS
- Pictorial analogies such as: Teeter-totter, weight lifter, and weights
- Structured interview
- Combination of any of the above

Alternatively or perhaps in addition teachers and parents could work together on a strategic approach to problem solving such as the "WE CAN" approach of Shank and Turnbull (1994). This model was developed for teachers to use for structuring lessons for their students to work together and attain common goals (Johnson, Johnson, Holubec & Roy, 1984). It is reasoned that because "positive interdependence exists among students' goal attainments, students seek outcomes that are beneficial to all individuals with whom they are linked cooperatively" (Shank, 1991, p. 43).

REFERENCES

Achenbach, T.M., Phares, V., Howell, C.T., Rauh, V.A., & Nurcombe, B. (1990). Seven-year outcome of the Vermont Intervention Program for low-birthweight infants. *Child Development, 61,* 1672–81.

Anstey, T.J., & Spence, N. (1986). Factors associated with stress in mothers of intellectually disabled children. *Australia and New Zealand Journal of Developmental Disabilities, 12,* 249–55.

Bailey, D.B., & Simeonsson, R.J. (1988). Assessing needs of families with handicapped infants. *The Journal of Special Education, 22,* 117–27.

Barrera, M.E., Rosenbaum, P.L., & Cunningham, C.E. (1986). Early intervention with low-birth-weight infants and their parents. *Child Development, 57,* 20–33.

Belsky, J. (1985). Experimenting with the family in the newborn period. *Child Development, 56,* 407–14.

Breslau, N., & Davis, G. (1986). Chronic stress and major depression. *Archives of general psychiatry, 43,* 309–14.

Bristol, M.M. (1987). Mothers of children with autism or communication disorders: Successful adaptation and the T-Double ABCX Model. *Journal of Autism and Developmental Disorders, 17,* 469–86.

Bronfenbrenner, U. (1979). *The ecology of human development: Experiments by nature and design.* Cambridge: Harvard University Press.

Byrne, E.A., & Cunningham, C.C. (1985). The effects of mentally handicapped children on families: A conceptual review. *Journal of Child Psychology and Psychiatry, 26*, 847–64.

Calliste, J. (1993). Partnership with parents: A model for practice. *Educational Psychology in Practice, 9*, 73–81.

Crnic, K.A., Greenberg, M.T., Ragozinn, A., Robinson, A.B., & Basham, N. (1983). Effects of stress and social support on mothers of preterm and full term infants. *Child Development. 54*, 209–17.

Dangel, R., & Polster, R. (Eds.). (1984). *Parent-training: Foundations of research and practice.* New York: Guilford Press.

Davis, H., & Rushton, R. (1991). Counselling and supporting parents of children with developmental delay: A research evaluation. *Journal of Mental Deficiency Research, 35*, 89–112.

Dissent, T. (1985). Parentology: A critique. *Educational and Child Psychology, 2.*

Dunst, C.J. (1993). Implications of risk and opportunity factors for assessment and intervention practices. *Topics in early childhood special education, 13*(2), 143–53.

Dyson, L. (1989). Adjustment of siblings of handicapped children: A comparison. *Journal of Pediatric Psychology, 14*, 215–29.

English, H.B., & English, A.C. (1958). *A comprehensive dictionary of psychological and psychoanalytical terms.* New York: David McKay Co.

Faerstein, L.M. (1986). Coping and defense mechanisms of mothers of learning disabled. *Journal of Learning Disabilities, 10*, 592–95.

Frey, K.S., Greenberg, M.T., & Fewell, R.R. (1989). Stress and coping among parents of handicapped children: A multidimensional approach. *American Journal on Mental Retardation, 94*, 240–49.

Gallagher, J.J., & Bristol, M. (1989). Families of young handicapped children. In M.C. Wang, M.C. Reynolds, & H.J. Walberg (Eds.), *Handbook of special education: Research and Practice. Vol. 3. Low incidence conditions* (pp. 295–317). New York: Pergamon.

Goldberg, S., Marcovitch, S., MacGregor, D., & Lojkasek, M. (1986). Family responses to delayed preschoolers: Etiology and father's role. *American Journal of Mental Deficiency, 90*(6), 610–17.

Green, H. (1985). Parents and professionals as partners: Some problems and perspectives. *Educational and Child Psychology, 2.*

Halliwell, M., & Williams, T. (1991). *Pathway: Making decisions about the education of pupils giving concern.* Windsor: NFER-Nelson.

Hammill, D.D. (1990). On defining learning disabilities: An emerging consensus. *Journal of Learning Disabilities, 23*, 74–84.

Hauser-Cram, P., & Krauss, M.W. (1991). Measuring change in children and families. *Journal of Early Intervention 15*, 288–97.

Hill, R. (1958). Generic features of families under stress. *Social Casework, 39*, 150.

Huang, I.C. (1991). Family stress and coping. In S.J. Bahr (Ed.), *Family research: A sixty year review, 1930-1990, Vol. 1.* New York: Lexington Books/MacMillan Inc.

Johnson, R.T., Johnson, D.W., Holubec, E.J., & Roy, P. (1984). *Circles of learning: Cooperation in the classroom.* Alenadrai, Va: ASCD.

Lavee, Y., McCubbin, H.I., & Olson, D.H. (1987). Life events and transitions on family functioning and well-being. *Journal of Marriage and the Family, 49,* 867–73.

Lorenz, S. (1986). Managing director or plumber's mate: Parent-centred approaches to intervention. *Educational and Child Psychology, 3.*

Margalit, M., & Almougy, K. (1991). Classroom behavior and family climate in students with learning disabilities and hyperactive behavior. *Journal of Learning Disabilities, 24,* 406–12.

Margalit, M., & Heiman, T. (1986). Family climate and anxiety in families with learning disabled boys. *Journal of the American Academy of Child Psychiatry, 25,* 841–46.

McClellan, A. (1990). *Patterns of stress and supports in families with handicapped children: Assessment and intervention.* Unpublished master's thesis. The University of Alberta, Edmonton, Alberta.

McConkey, R. (1985). Working with parents: A practical guide for teachers and therapists. London: Crown Helm: Bookline.

McCubbin, H.I., & McCubbin, M.A. (1991). Family stress theory and assessment: The T-Double ABCX Model of family adjustment and adaptation. In H.I. McCubbin & A.I. Thompson (Eds.), *Family assessment inventories for research and practice* (pp. 3–32). Madison WI: University of Wisconsin-Madison.

McCubbin, H.I., & Patterson, J.M. (1981). *Systematic assessment of family stress, resources and coping: Tools for research, education and clinical intervention.* St. Paul, MN: Department of Family Social Science.

McCubbin, H.I., & Thompson, A.I. (1991). *Family assessment inventories for research and practice.* Madison WI: University of Wisconsin-Madison.

McKinney, B., & Peterson, R. (1987). Predictors of stress in parents of developmentally disabled children. *Journal of Pediatric Psychology, 12,* 133–50.

Minuchin, S. (1974). *Families and family therapy.* Cambridge: Harvard University Press.

Moos, R.H., & Moos, B.S. (1976). A typology of family social environments. *Family Process, 15,* 357–71.

Moos, R.H., & Moos, B.S. (1983). Adaptation and the quality of life in work and family settings. *Journal of Community Psychology, 11,* 158–70.

Olson, J., & Kwiatkowski, K. (1992). *Planning family goals: A systems approach to the IFSP.* Tucson, AZ: Communication Skill Builders.

Orlando, J.E., & Bartel, N. (1989). Cognitive strategy training: An intervention model for parents of children with learning disabilities. *Reading, Writing, and Learning Disabilities, 5,* 327–44.

Perosa, L., Hansen, J., & Perosa, S. (1981). Development of the structural family interaction scale. *Family Therapy, 8,* 77–90.

Perosa, L., & Perosa, S. (1982). Structural interaction patterns in families with a learning disabled child. *Family Therapy, 9,* 175–87.

Reddon, J., McDonald, L., & Kysela, G. (1992). Parental coping and family stress I: Resources for and functioning of families with a preschool child having a developmental disability. *Early Child Development and Care, 83,* 1–26.

Redington, C.J. (1992). *Adaptation and functioning in families: A rural perspective.* Unpublished master's thesis, The University of Alberta, Edmonton, Alberta.

Russell, P. (1986). Working with parents: A framework for collaboration and partnership. *Educational and Child Psychology, 3.*

Sah, A., & Borland, J.H. (1989). The effects of a structured home plan on the home and school behaviors of gifted learning-disabled students with deficits in organizational skills. *Roeper Review, 12,* 54–57.

Sameroff, A.J., & Fiese, B. (1990). Transactional regulations and early intervention. In S. J. Meisels & J.P. Shonkoff (Eds.), *Handbook of Early Childhood Intervention* (pp. 119–49). Cambridge: Cambridge University Press.

Seitz, V., Rosenbaum, L.K., & Apfel., N.H. (1985). Effects of family support intervention: A ten-year follow-up. *Child Development, 56,* 376–91.

Shank, M.S. (1991). Cooperative family problem solving: An intervention for single parent families with a child who has a disability. Ann Arbor, MI: UMI Dissertation Publications.

Shank, M.S. & Turnbull, A.P. (1994). Cooperative family problem solving: An intervention for single-parent families of children with disabilities. In G.H.S. Singer & L.E. Powers (Eds.), *Families, Disability and Empowerment: Active coping skills and strategies for family interventions* (pp. 231–54) Baltimore: Paul H. Brookes.

Silver, L.B. (1989). Psychological and family problems associated with learning disabilities: Assessment and intervention. *Journal of the American Academy of Child and Adolescent Psychiatry, 28,* 319–25.

Sines, J.O. (1987). Influence of the home and family environment on childhood dysfunction. In B. Lahey & A. Kazdin (Eds.), *Advances in clinical child psychology, Vol. 10* (pp. 1–54). New York: Plenum Press.

Singer, G.H., & Irwin, L.K. (1990).Family support: Emerging practices, issues and questions. In L.H. Meyer, C.A. Peck, & L. Brown (Eds.), *Critical issues in the lives of people with disabilities* (pp. 271–312). Baltimore: Paul H. Brookes.

Stoll Switzer, L. (1990). Family factors associated with academic progress for children with learning disabilities. *Elementary School Guidance & Counselling, 24,* 200–06.

Tausig, M. (1985). Factors in family decision-making about placement for developmentally delayed individuals. *American Journal of Mental Deficiency, 89,* 352–61.

Wallander, J.L., Varni, J.W., Babani, L., & Banis, H.T. (1989). Family resources as resistance factors for psychological maladjustment in chronically ill and handicapped children. *Journal of Pediatric Psychology, 14,* 157–73.

Ziegler, R., & Holden, L. (1988). Family therapy for learning disabled and attention-deficit disordered children. *American Journal of Orthypsychiatry, 58,* 196–210.

Using Computers to Support Teamwork in Inclusive Elementary Classrooms

Leonard P. Haines
Gladene Robertson

University of Saskatchewan

Introduction

A central premise of this chapter is that the use of technology plays a vital role in supporting special-needs learners within the classroom. An equally important premise is that collaborative interactions between teams of parents and professionals, for the purpose of design and delivery of individualized instructional programs for students, lie at the heart of successful inclusionary classrooms. The content of the chapter will illustrate how technological supports for both students and teachers, combined with the needed network of human resources, are powerful factors in the creation of effective inclusive classrooms.

The Inclusive Classroom Context

The movement toward increasingly inclusive education for children with special needs has emerged along with other significant, and often related, changes within present-day classrooms. For the most part, these changes are more than superficial trends or fads. In most cases, they represent deep-level changes and fundamental restructurings of philosophies and practice. For example, the traditional teacher-directed classroom, which stressed decontextualized basic skills lessons and independent student exercises, is giving way to classrooms in which teachers emphasize integrated curricula, thinking skills and strategies, cooperative group learning, resource-based learning, and self-directed projects (Gardner, 1993; Nolan & Francis, 1992; Perkins, 1991). In addition, curricula have become more holistic, engaging students in tasks that combine listening, speaking, reading, and writing in meaningful problem-solving contexts (Drake, 1993). Authentic process evaluations and assessment often incorporating portfolio or project formats have been encouraged (Farr & Tone, 1994; Herman, Aschbacher & Winters, 1992; Kemp, 1993).

As restructuring movements appeal for integrated and individualized educational practices, there has been a simultaneous, yet philosophically divergent, call for uniformity of curricula and conformity of evaluation procedures. An example of the latter is an active movement toward accountability and monitoring of standards through the use of province-wide and nation-wide tests.

Both the student-centred and standard-focused philosophies of education have passionate proponents and both co-exist within a climate of financial restraint and diminishing resources for schools. To establish credibility, those who support the restructuring and inclusionary movements have an obligation to demonstrate the validity and effectiveness of the practices they espouse. Any such demonstration must clearly delineate the realities associated with the proposed changes.

First, consider the challenges. Some students may require extra time and assistance to master the skills and strategies that their classmates acquire more readily. Other students may need ongoing adaptation of teaching materials and methods in order to progress successfully. Still others may exhibit behaviours that impede their own and other students' progress in the classroom. Given the present-day realities of large class enrolments combined with limited personnel and material resources, teachers are facing major challenges to provide needed support to individual students.

Next, consider the opportunities. In the new classroom context, educators view self-directed learning, interaction, collaboration, and higher-order thinking skills as essential to learning (Redding, 1991). Accordingly, students who once might have been excluded from attending classrooms with their peers will have the opportunity to participate in and benefit from instruction that emphasizes interesting and meaningful content with a problem-solving focus. However, still to be answered are questions regarding the practices that will minimize obstacles and optimize students' successful participation in this inclusive classroom context.

The Technological Context

During the 1980s and 1990s there have been dramatic innovations in computers and related technology. New generations of hardware routinely incorporate major advances in speed, storage capacity, innovations, and price-performance ratio. Software developers have taken advantage of hardware advances to create more powerful, flexible, and innovative applications.

Two major developments of the mid-1990s have been in the areas of multi-media and networking. Multimedia involves the integration of video, audio, and text from multiple sources, all controlled by the computer (Schwier & Misan-chuck, 1993). Advances in this area, particularly in computer speech recognition and speech output, have the potential to provide special-needs learners, their parents, and teachers with the support needed for successful inclusive classrooms. Computer networks, both locally and widely distributed, have revolutionized the way people work and communicate (Sproull & Kiesler, 1991). The world-wide Internet has given rise to virtual communities of users organized around common interests and goals. Computer networks have also arrived in the classroom, creating "virtual schools" that extend the parameters of classroom walls around the world (Noden & Moss, 1993).

Despite the potential of hardware and software advancement to enhance and even transform instruction, the effective use of technology in the classroom is often a slow process marked by various obstacles. Hasselbring (1991) has pointed out that the presence of computers and related technology has expanded greatly in the schools in recent years. However, there is still an insufficient number for them to be used effectively within the curriculum. At the same time, rapid innovation in both hardware and software has resulted in widespread obsolescence in the technology used in schools. As well, educational software has characteristically been of low quality, untested for effectiveness, and often used inappropriately. Pre-service and in-service programs have been inadequate for preparing teachers to use computers effectively (Norvak & Berger, 1991). There is a pressing need to close the gap between the state of the art in computer technology and the effective use of this technology to assist students within inclusive classrooms.

The Special Education Context

The ways in which services are provided to students with special needs have changed dramatically in recent years. The effectiveness of the traditional special education practice of providing services for students in settings outside the classroom has long been questioned for students with mild exceptionalities (Dunn, 1968). However, the inclusive education movement (Stainback & Stainback, 1990) and the closely related Regular Education Initiative (REI) (Will, 1986) have extended the principle of classroom placement to all students. There has been a progressive trend toward educating students with special needs in regular classrooms rather than labelling and segregating them from their peers (Sanche & Dahl, 1991). However, simply placing all students in classrooms will not ensure quality educational experiences. It is important to seek out and use the most effective practices to ensure that they receive quality education in inclusive settings.

While the individualization of instruction for each learner has been identified as a desirable and effective instructional practice in general (Bloom, 1976), this approach has been seen as the instructional cornerstone for learners who have special educational needs (Bloom, 1984; Wang & Birch, 1984). The segregated individual tutorial and small-group instructional models of the past made it possible for special educators to tune instruction to the skill levels and learning characteristics of the student. However, the REI and its central themes **delabelling** and **inclusion** (Gartner & Lipsky, 1987) have changed the context in which individualization takes place. The emerging challenge is to accomplish individualized instruction within classrooms containing 20 or more students with diverse characteristics and needs.

For special education resource teachers, these changes in how individualization is viewed and practised have accelerated the trend toward providing support service for students with special needs in the regular classroom and decreased the focus on "pull-out" settings and programs. This change of instructional setting has resulted in an evolution of roles that has precipitated a search for effective models of practice to guide the resource teacher in providing appropriate support to students in the classroom (Slavin, Karweit & Madden, 1989). Emerging techniques include adaptive instruction (Salend, 1994), cooperative learning (Slavin et al., 1989), peer-mediated interventions (Stone & Campbell, 1991), and use of technology (Male, 1994). The service-delivery model best suited to delivering this range of techniques, **collaborative consultation** (Idol, Paolucci-Whitcomb & Nevin, 1986), means that resource teachers and other professionals now provide services that range from indirect (e.g., offering materials and information) through to direct (e.g., co-teaching, in-class tutorials), all within the regular classroom. The key factor in the collaborative approach is the willingness and ability of the resource teacher, classroom teacher, parents, and others involved in the student's education to plan and work effectively together (Friend & Cook, 1992). The collaborative model places an increased emphasis on communication skills, joint planning and decision making, and shared responsibility. There is a pressing need to develop new tools and techniques to support and facilitate the process of collaboration itself.

Integrating Contexts: The Vision

Technology can be used as much more than a vehicle for supporting and delivering traditional schooling. In considering this issue, Collins (1991) has pointed out that even if technology is initially used in schools to reinforce traditional practices, it will exert a transforming effect upon the teaching-learning environment. Dwyer, Ringstaff, and Sandholtz (1991) have described teachers' responses to the introduction of technology into their classrooms as progressing through a series of phases: entry, adoption, adaptation, appropriation, and invention. They observed a parallel evolution of these teachers' instructional practices toward use of more team teaching, interdisciplinary project-based instruction, collaborative tasks, and individually paced instruction. A vision that combines inclusive education, special education support, and technology will need to take into consideration the transformational effect of these factors working in concert in the classroom.

Inclusive classrooms are emerging as child-centred, collaborative, and active/interactive (Collins, 1991; Dwyer, 1994; Dwyer et al., 1991). Student groupings are carefully designed to accomplish specific goals, and are best described as flexible, temporary, and heterogeneous. Special education services are delivered as inconspicuously as possible through collaborative planning, in-class assessment techniques, and small-group instruction. Computers and related technology are used both directly and indirectly to support students: directly, by assisting as needed with mobility, communication, and instruction; and indirectly, by serving as tools for collaborating teams consisting of parents, classroom teachers, special educators, related professionals, and students. Computers may also be used in new ways to guide and support the ongoing collaborative planning and decision making that is central to the operation of the team and vital to the successful individualization of instruction for students in the inclusive classroom (Haines, Sanche & Robertson, 1993).

▣ Technology and Instruction

Technology in Special Education: Overview

The use of technology has a long history in the education of special-needs students, particularly for persons with sensory or mobility impairments. For persons with visual impairment, technologies such as the Optacon (a device that translates print to a tactual form) and the Kurzweil Personal Reader (a machine that converts print to synthetic speech) have been an integral part of enhancing their independence and enriching their lives. It is important to note, however, that the newer, more advanced technology is not inherently more useful than earlier, simpler devices. The white cane, for example, might still be the best mobility tool in many specific situations. The same may be said of other technologies. The key to successful application of new technology to assist students in inclusive classrooms is the careful, appropriate fitting of the technology to the specified needs of the individual and the unique requirements of the setting.

It is beyond the scope of this chapter to describe the full range of special education technology. Lewis (1993) and Male (1994) have provided valuable, in-depth treatments. Lewis's volume emphasizes detailed descriptions of hardware, software, and their uses. Male places emphasis upon computer software and its integration into the classroom as tools for both students and teacher. The authors of this chapter have emphasized the use of the computer as a tool to *direct* and *facilitate* the activities of a collaborative team working to support students in inclusive classrooms. It is important to ensure that students are provided with the best possible combination of assistive technology for augmentative communication, mobility, assistive listening, low vision, and environmental control (Lewis, 1993). Beginning with the assumption that assistive technology is in place, professional educators may move on to examine how computers can be used to support teaching and learning.

Computer Support for Teaching and Learning

Even a cursory review of the growing literature on computer utilization shows that the computer is being used mainly for **computer-assisted instruction** (CAI) rather than as a tool for **computer-managed instruction** (CMI). In contrast to CAI, in which the computer is used as a medium for instruction, CMI uses the information handling power of the computer to support instructional delivery by the teacher. The distinction here is between the use of the computer to provide instruction directly to the student (CAI) and the use of the computer as a tool supporting the work of the teacher (CMI).

In a review of CAI and CMI, Lillie, Hannum, and Stuck (1989) noted a disproportionate amount of research literature devoted to CAI. They found that emphasis disconcerting since they considered the potential benefits of computer use for CMI to be much greater. Some years earlier, Baker (1978) argued that CMI might have greater potential for positive impact on the schools than almost any other means of computer use. Support for this position can be found in a study by Kulik, Bangert, and Williams (1983). After completing a meta-analysis of 45 studies of CAI and CMI, they concluded that the use of CMI contributed as much or more as the CAI programs to student achievement gains in schools. A major practical limitation in the use of computers for CAI appears to be the amount of instructional time currently available for individual students. Woodward and Gersten (1992) reported a ratio of 1 computer per 30 students and an average of only

15 minutes of CAI time per student per day. In contrast, a teacher using CMI to assist with the decision-making and management aspects of individualizing instruction could influence the achievement of many students, whether additional hardware was available or not.

Lillie et al. (1989) reviewed the main systems of CMI currently in use in North America. They classified CMI software into three categories: **integrated learning systems**, **subject-specific instructional management systems**, and **generic instructional management systems** (p. 55). Descriptions of the first two categories indicate that both are relatively closed systems in which instruction is limited to a single subject or curriculum, to administratively relevant information, and to the computer system over the teacher's professional expertise. Generic instructional management systems, on the other hand, place greater emphasis on the teacher being in charge of teaching the subject and curriculum. Further, the systems can be customized to fit the local school's curriculum and unique instructional objectives. Perhaps the greatest potential contribution generic CMI systems can make to instruction is to assist teachers in identifying and addressing students' individual needs. However, even these generic CMI systems place more emphasis on record keeping and reporting on instruction than supporting the teacher in ongoing planning and teaching. What seems very clear is that CMI has a great deal more potential to support the work of teachers than has been realized thus far.

In seeking out and using the most effective practices to ensure quality education for all students in inclusive classrooms, collaborative planning and instructional delivery emerges as an approach with great potential. It is in this collaborative context that the authors envision a new emphasis for CMI. There is considerable promise in the use of the computer to support collaborative teamwork through communication, instructional planning, teaching, record keeping, and reporting.

◈ Computers and Collaboration

In this section a connection is made between two powerful concepts—computer support and collaborative instructional delivery. Computers are tools that can systematize and expedite repetitive tasks. They can organize, store, retrieve, manipulate, and display information rapidly. They also have the capability to facilitate communication. Collaboration reflects a movement toward teacher empowerment through active and interactive involvement in shared planning and decision making. Efficient and effective communication is essential to collaborative interactions. Computers can facilitate collaborative teamwork by providing support for joint planning, communication, reporting, and any other activities in which the team routinely engages.

Collaboration and Teamwork

Friend and Cook have defined collaboration as: "… a style for direct interaction between at least two co-equal parties voluntarily engaged in shared decision making as they work toward a common goal" (1992, p. 5). As a style of interaction, collaboration involves knowing a repertoire of social, communication, and problem-solving skills, and using them effectively during professional interactions. Certain fundamental assumptions can be identified. Collaboration is voluntary, requires parity amongst participants, is based on mutual goals, depends on shared responsibility for participation and decision making, and involves shared resources and accountability. The collaborative style of interacting can be used in a variety of teamwork situations, such as consultation, assessment, teaching, and problem solving.

The concept of teamwork has gained wide acceptance, and has even been mandated in some special education laws. There are many different kinds of teams to fulfil different functions, from Teacher Assistance Teams (Chalfant, Pysh & Moultrie, 1979) to teaching teams (Bauwens, Hourcade, & Friend, 1989). Abelson and Woodman (1983) have reported several reasons why the use of teams can improve decision making. In comparison with decision making by individuals, team decision-making sessions are preferable because:

- Greater knowledge and experience are available

- More approaches to solving a problem are available

- Greater communication and understanding of the decisions occurs

- Participation in decision making increases acceptance of the decision

Despite these potential benefits, Kaiser & Woodman (1985) found that the effectiveness of team functioning is adversely affected by a number of factors:

- Lack of experience and training at working together

- Territoriality and lack of trust

- Unclear roles and accountability

- Limited parental involvement

- Unsystematic assessment procedures

- Loosely organized decision-making and planning procedures

The way around these barriers appears to lie in improving communication skills and collaborative values of team members, and in systematizing the decision-making procedures used by the team.

An examination of current models of collaborative instructional planning (e.g., Friend & Cook, 1992; Dettmer, Thurston & Dyck, 1993) reveals some shared steps in the delivery process underlying the individualization of instruction. When teams work collaboratively, they routinely and repeatedly engage in the following activities as they plan and deliver instruction to students:

- Identification: definition of the problem, anticipate desired outcomes, and consider related information

- Information Gathering: assessment of the learner and setting

- Reflection: consideration of information to generate an instructional plan

- Teaching: implementation of the instructional plan

- Monitoring: evaluation of the student's response to the instructional plan

- Reporting: communication of information about the instructional delivery

Within this model, the Reflection, Teaching, and Monitoring stages are repeatedly worked through as necessary, thereby allowing the team to continuously adjust instruction based on the student's progress.

There are many more dimensions to collaboration than the instructional delivery model above (Friend & Cook, 1992). However, this model provides an organizational framework that could focus and systematize the work of collaborative teams, thereby addressing some of the main factors that reduce the effectiveness of team functioning.

Using the Computer to Support Teamwork

The potential to influence student performance by using CMI to support the work of the teacher has been established. Given the importance of teamwork to inclusive education, CMI could be extended to use of the computer to support collaborative team interactions. In particular, it is important to provide support for the instructional delivery process and to reduce those factors that limit team effectiveness. These goals motivated the design and development of computer software called Instruction CoPlanner (Haines, et al., 1993; Robertson, Haines, Biffart, & Sanche, in press).

Instruction CoPlanner: Design and Operation

The Instruction CoPlanner software consists of several elements, all designed to facilitate and support collaborative teamwork. The central element of the program is a **CoPlanner Worksheet**, which supports the cooperative work of a team planning for students in inclusive settings. The team usually consists of at least the classroom and resource teachers, and may include an educational psychologist, social worker, educational consultant, the parent, and the student for whom the plan is being developed. Teams begin by initiating a "project" for or with the student. Group members then participate individually or together in the project by contributing information from their perspectives and areas of expertise, to the project worksheet for the student. The worksheet displays a question-driven, five-stage model of collaborative instructional delivery. Those five stages are Information Gathering, Reflection, Teaching, Monitoring, and Reporting. The work of the team is captured in detail by CoPlanner while an ongoing **Project Summary** is routinely developed in the process. All products of the joint work of the team can be stored on computer, edited, and printed.

A second feature of Instruction CoPlanner that supports collaborative teamwork is the on-line **Communication** system. A personal notepad allows each user to store thoughts privately, and later call them up to assist with decision making. Using the electronic mail and conferencing systems, members of the team can keep each other informed by posting messages or reports to any or all team members in the collaborating network. This system facilitates ongoing interaction between meetings or when face-to-face meetings are not possible. An educational psychologist, for example, may observe the student at a time when other members of the team are teaching. The psychologist can leave an interim report on CoPlanner, or send one electronically, for any or all of the team to read when each logs on and uses the software.

A **Tools** database is a fourth element supporting collaboration. Tools are methods and forms for use in assessment and instruction. The database can be searched by name, tool properties, or curriculum areas. New assessment or teaching tools can be readily added to CoPlanner, and tool reports and actual tools can be printed for immediate use by any member of the team.

The final major element of Instruction CoPlanner is a **Reporting** system for planning and preparing progress reports for a student with special needs. A series of guiding questions helps the collaborating team to consider the content and delivery plan for a report. The most current version of the Project Summary can be imported, and edited into a printable report. This feature saves time for those responsible for reporting the student's educational progress.

Instruction CoPlanner has two other features to support users: a password **Security** system and on-line **User Help.** The security system restricts access to the software and student files through the use of passwords while the Help system consists of context-specific **Balloon Helps** and a complete on-line **Manual**. Taken together, these elements of CoPlanner are intended to support collaborative teams of educators as they design and deliver programs of instruction to students in inclusive classrooms. Consistent with the concept of computer-supported instruction, the software serves as an instructional support system for collaborative planning rather than a medium for student instruction.

◈ CoPlanning for Martin

Meet Martin Clark—blue eyes, red hair, freckles, and nine years old. Although he has always lived close to Attwood Elementary School, he attended the neighbourhood school with his friends for only half of his kindergarten year, then not again until this year. Due to his aggressive and disruptive behaviour in kindergarten, he was removed and placed in a Social Learning Classroom in a school across the city. Last year the school district adopted an inclusionary policy, which meant that all students in segregated special education programs would be moved back into their local schools. To assist in implementing an inclusionary policy, the school district provided their teachers, administrators, and special education and other support staff with in-service preparation on collaboration and the use of Instruction CoPlanner.

Martin began this year in the third grade with the support of a collaborating team consisting of Donna (the classroom teacher), Cindy (the teacher associate), Don (the principal), Wanda (the resource teacher), Derek (the psychologist). Marie (his teacher from the Social Learning Classroom), and Martin's parents. He is now near the end of his first year at his home school. In the following case study, we trace Martin's progress and the work of the team through their use of Instruction CoPlanner.

Beginning Martin's Project

The team met for the first time the week before the school year started so they could begin co-planning for Martin. At this meeting they spent time getting to know one another and working through their beliefs and goals about Martin's classroom program. The team worked together to create a feeling of belonging for the parents, as well as to help them understand the co-planning process and their role in it. Work began on Martin's project with the team creating a new Instruction CoPlanner file for Martin. The team agreed that their first priority was to assist Martin in acquiring classroom behaviours necessary for success. Wanda began a CoPlanner file for Martin, and the team arrived at consensus decisions about the reasons for beginning the project. The outcomes they would like to see as the year progressed were also mutually defined (see Figure 11.1). Marie provided information on Martin's program and progress in the Social Learning Classroom. They agreed to meet two weeks later, after school was in progress, to begin the next steps in the project.

FIGURE 11.1
Beginning an Instruction CoPlanner Project for Martin

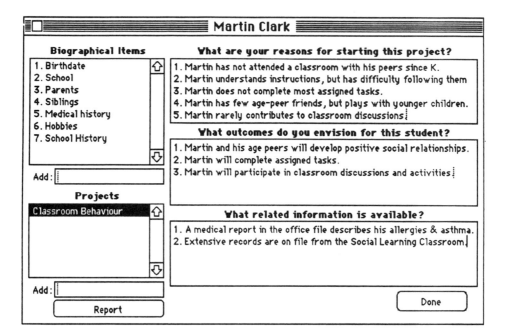

Information Gathering

During the second week of school, the team met again to begin their plan to study Martin's classroom behaviour. Donna reported that Martin was fitting into class routines fairly well, but that the concerns outlined at the first meeting remained valid. Wanda began the CoPlanner session by opening Martin's file, and the team selected the target areas of Personal/Social Values and Skills, and Independent Learning for the project. Within the CoPlanner worksheet, the following questions guided their joint planning:

- What additional information is needed and where can it be found?
- When can the needed information best be obtained?
- How can the needed information be obtained?
- Who can best collect this information?

The team used the CoPlanner Tools database to search for, list, and describe the assessment tools related to Martin's need areas. The assessment plan they decided upon included a parental interview and review of past records to be completed by Wanda. Derek was to carry out classroom observations on two occasions. Donna volunteered to conduct an interview with Martin, complete a rating scale with his parents, and carry out direct observation during class activities. The worksheet displaying their plan is shown in Figure 11.2.

FIGURE 11.2
Instruction CoPlanner Information-Gathering Worksheet

Worksheet:Classroom Behavior				
Project: Oct. 08, 1994	Information Gathering Plan			
	What additional information is needed, and where can it be found?	When can the needed information best be obtained?	How can the needed information be obtained?	Who can best collect this information?
Independent Learning	1. Developmental background and educational history from: a) parents b) Student File. 2. Time-on-task data.	1a) Interview on Wednesday, 13 Oct.,3:30, Donna's room. b) during week of Oct. 11 2. During journal writing: Monday, Oct.11 & Wed. Oct. 13; 9:15 to 9:45	1a) Parent semistructured interview b) Review cumulative folder. 2. Classroom on-task observations using the Restricted Academic	1. Resource Teacher (Wanda) 2. Psychologist (Derek)
Personal and Social Values & Skills	1. Self-awareness; from Martin 2. Behavioral information; from teacher & parents 3. Behaviours during group activities.	1. After cooperative learning group in social studies, Thurs, Oct. 14. 2. Forms to be returned by 22 Oct. 3. During cooperative learning groups in social studies, week of 11 Oct.	1. Student interview using Cooperative Learning Self-evaluation form. 2. Behaviour Rating Scale; parents and Martin 3. Discussion tool.	1. Classroom teacher (Donna) 2. Donna and parents 3. Donna while observing groups.

The team agreed to meet two weeks later to review the information they had gathered and continue planning together. In the meantime, Wanda continued her ongoing co-teaching times in Donna's classroom and gathered observational information on Martin and several other students needing instructional support. She recorded her observations as CoPlanner notes (see Figure 11.3).

Prior to the team meeting to consider the new assessment results, Wanda sent a summary of her classroom observations to each of the team members for consideration (Figure 11.4).

FIGURE 11.3
Wanda's Observational Notes on Martin's Classroom Behaviours

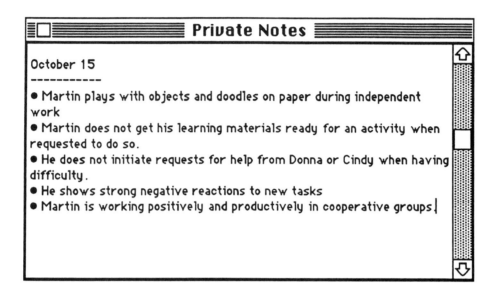

Private Notes

October 15

• Martin plays with objects and doodles on paper during independent work
• Martin does not get his learning materials ready for an activity when requested to do so.
• He does not initiate requests for help from Donna or Cindy when having difficulty.
• He shows strong negative reactions to new tasks
• Martin is working positively and productively in cooperative groups.

Reflection

Donna began the subsequent meeting by opening Instruction CoPlanner to the Reflection section of the worksheet and led the team through sharing and discussion of the information they had collected. The information and decisions resulting from consideration of the guiding questions in the worksheet are presented below:

"What is the learner able to do?"

• Martin's on-task behaviour is 10 to 20% during writing tasks.

• He responds positively to small-group instruction and discussion.

• He enjoys hands-on projects.

• Disturbance of other students is not a concern.

• Martin interacts positively with peers in small group discussions.

"What related behaviours does the learner show?"

• Martin plays with objects and doodles during independent work.

• He does not have learning materials ready for activities.

FIGURE 11.4
Mail Message to Team Members

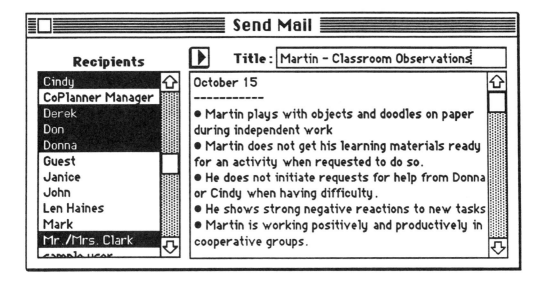

• Martin does not ask for assistance when experiencing difficulty.

• He hides, loses, or destroys his written work.

• Martin does not interact with peers during unstructured times.

"What strategies and skills need strengthening?"

• Martin needs to start, sustain engagement, and complete tasks.

• He needs to make successful transitions between activities.

• Martin needs to initiate interactions with peers.

• He needs to request assistance during tasks when needed.

"What approaches, techniques, and materials are most effective?"

• Charts of completed work have motivated him.

• Small, cooperative learning groups have been effective.

• Extra time for completion of projects has been beneficial.

• Personal choice of his project topic has sustained his attention.

"What new approaches, techniques, materials should be introduced?

• A contract system for task selection and completion, with rewards.

- Self-monitoring charts: task preparation and work completion.
- Cognitive coaching: modelling, role playing, feedback on social skills.
- Teach cooperative group process roles (recorder, encourager, facilitator).

Teaching

At the same meeting, the team completed the Teaching section of the Instruction CoPlanner worksheet. This involved developing their instructional decisions into an action teaching plan:

"Where can this learner's instructional needs best be met?"

- Martin will remain in Donna's classroom for all instruction.

"When will the needed instruction be provided?"

- Contacts and charts: begin next Monday, 12:45.
- Cognitive coaching: begin Tuesday morning, 10:30.
- Cooperative Learning Skills: begin Thursday, 9:45.

"How can the needed instruction best be delivered?"

- Contracts and charts: provide an orientation session and follow-up.
- Cognitive instruction: whole-class instruction, small group follow-up.
- Cooperative Learning: whole-class model, small group follow-up.

"Who will deliver the needed instruction?"

- Donna will initiate contracts and charts; Cindy and parents follow-up.
- Wanda, Donna, and Cindy will jointly deliver cognitive coaching.
- Donna and Wanda will co-teach Cooperative Learning Skills.

The team left the meeting enthused about the plan, their contributions to it, and their joint roles in implementing the teaching Martin would require. They agreed to a brief meeting the following week to prepare a plan to keep track of Martin's responses to the instruction they had decided upon.

Monitoring

Don began the next meeting by starting CoPlanner and opening Martin's Monitoring worksheet. This last phase of their instructional planning was guided by a series of monitoring questions and resulted in the following decisions:

"What learning outcomes will be monitored?"

- Starting, sustaining engagement, and completing tasks.
- Making successful transitions between activities.
- Initiating positive interactions with peers.
- Requesting assistance during tasks when needed.

"When will the learning outcomes be monitored?"

- During independent writing assignments.
- During peer partner learning and unstructured times.
- During cooperative learning activities.

"How will the learning outcomes be monitored?"

- Classroom observation: anecdotal records, frequency counts.
- Self-evaluations completed by Martin.
- Examination of completed work samples.

"Who will monitor the learning outcomes?"

- Wanda will do formal observations (anecdotal comments/counts).
- Donna will administer and collect self-evaluations.
- Cindy and Donna will collect and analyze work samples.

"Where will the learning outcomes be monitored?"

- In Donna's classroom.

With an instructional plan in place to suit Martin's needs, and a plan to keep track of his progress, the team had completed the crucial first steps in implementing an effective educational program. Over the following weeks they met at regular intervals to discuss progress and adjust the program as required to ensure Martin's ongoing success. Between meetings, they exchanged information using the CoPlanner mail system to maintain continuous communication.

Reporting

Although Martin's parents had been members of the planning team from the outset, they were not as fully aware of day-to-day and overall progress as were the teachers delivering the instruction. The team decided that it would be helpful to prepare and deliver progress reports to the Clarks on a regular basis. The goal was to provide a descriptive profile over time of Martin as a learner. This profile would provide the parents and others who might become involved in his education with detailed summaries of Martin's academic and social growth. The CoPlanner reporting system helped them with this task. Wanda and Donna together kept Martin's CoPlanner Project Summary up to date as the work of the team progressed, so written reports could be readily prepared. The team completed a Report Planning worksheet to guide the process. Wanda, Donna, Cindy, and Don met with the Clarks, including Martin, once a month to report his progress, both orally and in writing.

Reflections on CoPlanning

Martin experienced a successful return to his neighbourhood school. His success was due largely to the ways in which his parents, teachers, and support staff worked together to plan and implement an educational program designed specifically for Martin's capabilities and needs as a learner. In particular, Martin's team shared the decision making and subsequent delivery of instruction, and they stayed in close communication as Martin progressed. Instruction CoPlanner played a significant role in their success by focusing and systematizing their decision making and by supporting ongoing communication, sharing of information, and reporting.

Conclusion

The key to effective inclusionary practice lies in establishing support networks based on shared collaborative skills and values. These networks or teams often generate more, and potentially better, solutions when solving problems, and they exert more power in making decisions than do individuals who are working in isolation. In part, this effectiveness is because of the team's combined experience and knowledge but, as well, their successes are based on the ongoing respect and support they offer to one another. When they work together as collaborative teams, educational professionals, paraprofessionals, parents, and students are in close, regular communication. Since decision making is shared, there is increased acceptance of decisions and a resultant joint optimism about the programs they have planned.

Teachers can use technology for many purposes and in many ways in the inclusive classroom. Computers can contribute meaningfully to instruction by serving as tools and tutors for teaching and learning. We can expect the presence of computers to exert transformational effects upon the nature of the teaching and learning that takes place in these classrooms. Nevertheless, instructional planning and delivery must remain a fundamentally human process.

SUGGESTED RESOURCES

Books

Lewis, R.B. (1993). *Special education technology: Classroom applications.* Pacific Grove: Brooks/Cole. This book focuses on methods for the practical integration of technology to enhance effective instruction. It describes a range of technological supports for teaching and accessibility. Augmentative communication devices, mobility aids, environmental control devices, assistive listening devices, low-vision aids, and devices that translate from one medium to another are described. Lewis also includes appendices of resources available to teachers.

Male, M. (1994). *Technology for inclusion: Meeting the special needs of all students.* Boston: Allyn and Bacon. This book has the goal of providing content to help readers reflect on the questions that they would like answered as they pursue how computers may be used by their special-needs students. The author also reviews a variety of applications of computer technology that will empower students and enhance classroom instruction. It utilizes both case studies and scenarios as part of the content presentation.

Journals/Magazines/Published Proceedings

Closing the Gap, P.O. Box 68, Henderson, MN, USA 56044. This monthly newsletter that contains software and hardware reviews and articles covering a range of applications is published by a professional organization of the same name. Once a year it publishes a comprehensive resource directory that is a comprehensive guide to the selection of microcomputer technology for special education and rehabilitation. It also hosts a major international conference on special education technology.

Educational Leadership, 1994, 51(7). Special Issue: "Realizing the promise of technology."

Exceptional Children, 1994, 61(2). Special Issue: "Technology-based assessment within special education."

Journal of Special Education Technology. This journal is published by the Technology and Media Division of the Council for Exceptional Children. The purpose of the journal is to provide readers with information regarding research and practice in the application of educational technology toward the development and education of exceptional children. Peabody College, Box 328, Vanderbilt University, Nashville, TN 37203.

Technology and Teacher Education Annual

This annual is a compilation of the papers published for the Society for Technology and Teacher Education by the Association for the Advancement of Computing in Education and represents a good cross section of topics intended primarily for the teacher educator. For example, the 1993 Annual includes papers in the areas of Inservice and Graduate Education, Integrating Technology into Methods Classes Instructional Technology,

Multimedia, Concepts and Procedures, Technology Diffusion, Pre-service Teacher Education, Instruction Design, Research, Mathematics and Science, Telecommunications, and Simulations. The address of the Association for the Advancement of Computing in Education is P.O. Box 2966, Charlottesville, VA 22902 USA. (Telephone: 1-804-973-3987 or FAX 1-804-978-7449 or E-mail: AACE@VIRGINIA.EDU).

Software/Hardware Publishers

EDMARK: P.O. Box 3218, Redmond, WA 98073–3218. (Telephone: 1-800-362-2890)

MECC: Software Plus. #1 - 12760 Bathgate Way, Richmond, BC V6V 1Z4. (Telephone 1-800-663-7731)

Sunburst: 920 Mercer Street, Windsor, ON N9A 7C2 . (Telephone: 1-800-321-7511 or FAX: 914 - 947 - 4109)

The Learning Company: 6493 Kaiser Drive, Fremont, CA 94555. (Telephone: 1-800-852-2255)

Tom Snyder Productions: 90 Sherman Street, Cambridge, MA 02140. (Telephone: 1-800-342-0236)

REFERENCES

Abelson, M., & Woodman, R. (1983). Review of research on team effectiveness: Implications for teams in schools. *School Psychology Review, 12*, 125–36.

Baker, F.B. (1978). *Computer managed instruction: Theory and practice.* Englewood Cliffs, NJ: Educational Technology.

Bloom, B. (1984). The 2 sigma problem: The search for methods of group instruction as effective as one-to-one tutoring. *Educational Researcher, 13*, 4–16.

Bloom, B.S. (1976). *Human characteristics and school learning.* New York: McGraw-Hill.

Bauwens, J., Hourcade, J.J., & Friend, M. (1989). Cooperative teaching: A model for general and special education placement. *Remedial and Special Education, 10*, 17–22.

Chalfant, J., Pysh, M., & Moultrie, R. (1979). Teacher assistance teams: A model for within building problem solving. *Learning Disability Quarterly, 2*, 85–96.

Collins, A. (1991). The role of computer technology in restructuring schools. *Phi Delta Kappan, 73*, 28–36.

Dettmer, P., Thurston, L.P., & Dyck, N. (1993). *Consultation, collaboration, and teamwork for students with special needs.* Boston: Allyn and Bacon.

Drake, S.M. (1993). *Planning integrated curriculum.* Alexandria, VA: ASCD.

Dunn, L. (1968). Special education for the mildly retarded: Is much of it justifiable? *Exceptional Children, 35*, 5–22.

Dwyer, D. (1994). Apple Classrooms of Tomorrow: What we've learned. *Educational Leadership, 51*, 4–10.

Dwyer, D.C., Ringstaff, C., & Sandholtz, J.H. (1991). Changes in teachers' beliefs and practices in technology-rich classrooms. *Educational Leadership, 48,* 45–52.

Farr, R., & Tone, B. (1994). Portfolio and performance assessment: *Helping students evaluate their progress as readers and writers.* Fort Worth: Harcourt Brace.

Friend, M., & Cook, L. (1992). *Interactions: Collaboration skills for school professionals.* New York: Longman.

Gardner, H. (1993). *Multiple intelligences: The theory in practice.* New York: Basic Books.

Gartner, A., & Lipsky, D.K. (1987). Beyond special education: Toward a quality system for all students. *Harvard Educational Review, 57,* 367–95.

Haines, L., Sanche, R., & Robertson, G. (1993). Instruction CoPlanner: A software tool to facilitate collaborative resource teaching. *Canadian Journal of Educational Communications, 22,* 177–87.

Hasselbring, T.S. (1991). Improving education through technology: Barriers and recommendations. *Preventing School Failure, 35,* 33–37.

Herman, J.L., Aschbacher, P.R., & Winters, L. (1992). *A practical guide to alternative assessment.* Alexandria: Association for Supervision and Curriculum Development.

Idol, L., Paolucci-Whitcomb, P., & Nevin, A. (1986). *Collaborative consultation.* Austin, TX: Pro-Ed.

Kaiser, S.M., & Woodman, R.W. (1985). Multidisciplinary teams and group decision-making techniques: Possible solutions to decision-making problems. *School Psychology Review, 14,* 457–70.

Kemp, M. (1993). *Watching children read and write: Observational records for children with special needs.* Melbourne: Nelson.

Kulick, J.A., Bangert, R.L., & Williams, G.W. (1983). Effects of computer-based teaching on secondary school students. *Journal of Educational Psychology, 75,* 19–26.

Lewis, R.B. (1993). *Special education technology: Classroom applications.* Pacific Grove, CA: Brooks/Cole.

Lillie, D.L., Hannum, W.H., & Stuck, G.B. (1989). *Computers and effective instruction.* White Plains, N.Y.: Longman.

Male, M. (1994). *Technology for inclusion: Meeting the special needs of all students.* Boston: Allyn and Bacon.

Noden, H., & Moss, B. (1993). Virtual schools: Reading and writing. *The Reading Teacher, 47,* 166–68.

Nolan, J., & Francis, P. (1992). Changing perspectives in curriculum and instruction. In C.D. Glickman (Ed.), *Supervision in transition: 1992 Yearbook of the Association for Supervision and Curriculum Development.* Alexandria, VA: ASCD.

Norvak, D.I., & Berger, C.F. (1991). Integrating technology into preservice education: Michigan's response. *Computers in the Schools, 8,* 89–101.

Perkins, D.N. (1991). Educating for insight. *Educational Leadership, 49,* 4–8.

Redding, N. (1991). Assessing the big outcomes. *Educational Leadership, 49,* 49–53.

Robertson, G., Haines, L., Biffart, W., & Sanche, R. (article in press). Using the computer to support collaborative instructional planning. *Teaching Exceptional Children.*

Salend, S.J. (1994). *Effective mainstreaming: Creating inclusive classrooms.* New York: Macmillan.

Sanche, R., & Dahl, H. (1991). Progress in Saskatchewan toward integration of students with disabilities. *Canadian Journal of Special Education, 7,* 16–31.

Sanche, R., Haines, L., & Robertson, G. (1994). Instruction CoPlanner: Computer technology supporting collaborative decision-making across the curriculum. *Journal of Technology and Teacher Education. 2,* 155–66.

Schwier, R., & Misanchuk, E. (1993). *Interactive multimedia instruction.* Englewood Cliffs, NJ: Educational Technology Publications.

Slavin, R., Karweit, N., & Madden, N. (1989). *Effective programs for students at risk.* Boston: Allyn and Bacon.

Sproull, L., & Kiesler, S. (1991). *Connections: New ways of working in the networked organization.* Cambridge, MA: MIT Press.

Stainback, W., & Stainback, S. (Eds.). (1990). *Support networks for inclusive schooling: Interdependent integrated education.* Baltimore: Paul H. Brookes.

Stone, J., & Campbell, C. (1991). Student to student: Curriculum and the development of peer relationships. In G. Porter & D. Richler (Eds.), *Changing Canadian schools: Perspectives on disability and inclusion* (pp. 239–56). North York, ON: The Roeher Institute.

Wang, M.C., & Birch, J.W. (1984). Effective special education in regular classes. *Exceptional Children, 50,* 391–99.

Will, M.C. (1986). Educating children with learning problems: A shared responsibility. *Exceptional Children, 52,* 411–15.

Woodward, J., & Gersten, R. (1992). Innovative technology for secondary students with learning disabilities. *Exceptional Children, 58,* 407–21.

A Thematic Review and Some Further Considerations

Jac J. W. Andrews

University of Calgary

Introduction

The authors in this book have presented their views regarding the best ways to accommodate student diversity in today's schools. As one reviews the authors' practical suggestions, common themes emerge. First, many of the authors indicate that *group effort* is often more beneficial than individual effort in the teaching and learning transaction. Second, many of the authors suggest that teachers need to be *proactive and adaptive* in addressing the unique learning needs of their students. Third, many of the authors appear to advocate for an *educational climate* that maximizes student opportunity and potential, and develops acceptance and appreciation of individual differences.

This chapter has two parts. In the first part, major themes from the text are presented and expanded. The second part of the chapter provides an overview of three conditions that can enable teachers to better accommodate student diversity in their classrooms. These very important conditions are administrative leadership and support, professional training and development, and educational research.

◈ Themes

Group Effort

One of the major underlying themes in this book is that people should work together. Many of the authors have recommended that teachers collaborate with one another, form partnerships with other professionals and parents, and promote cooperative learning experiences among their students. As noted by Costa (1991, p. 12) "together, individuals surface ideas, then bounce and batter them about, thereby eliciting thinking that surpasses individual effort. As individuals engage in problem solving, conversation, and consensus seeking, multiple perspectives are expressed, dissonance created and reduced, discrepancies perceived and resolved, and alternatives weighed."

Teachers Working Together

Teaming approaches provide an opportunity for teachers to collaborate with their colleagues in order to address the complexities of student management and instruction. Concomitantly, teachers, administrators, and specialists within the school need to learn to collaborate with parents and professionals outside the school to take advantage of the available resources from the community that can be used to better meet the needs of students.

For many people, it is not easy to work with others. Some people feel uneasy because they lack experience working in groups and some people are generally uncomfortable in sharing their ideas with others. Hence, team members might need to learn how to interact and problem-solve with others within a group. As noted in this book, important skills to master include ways to deal with one's own feelings, how to be supportive of others, handle resistance, resolve conflict, set goals, and listen to others. These collaborative skills can lead to effective decision making and empower teachers and other group members to take responsibility for student outcomes and make significant educational changes.

Successful development, implementation, and maintenance of collaborative and cooperative groups requires a collaborative work ethic and environment within the school. According to Phillips and Mccullough (1990), when a collaborative work ethic is assimilated throughout the entire school, it empowers teachers to support each other and help one another solve problems. In working towards a collaborative work environment, teachers should have opportunities to meet with one another to discuss the problems they are facing, and pool their expertise and resource materials (Idol & West, 1991).

Collaborative efforts must be highly regarded and promoted by school administration. Principals can facilitate collaboration among teachers by encouraging them to collectively find ways for dealing with student diversity, providing time for them to interact with one another during the school day, and reinforcing their collaborative efforts (Johnson, Pugach & Devlin, 1990). Principals can provide leadership in the process of collaboration by showing commitment to ongoing professional development opportunities that can better prepare teachers with the essential skills for collaboration and by modelling collaboration with teachers and others in appropriate situations (Idol & West, 1991).

Teachers Working with Parents

Currently, there is a greater emphasis on the role of parents in educational problem solving and decision making. As noted in this book, teachers are becoming increasingly aware of the importance of knowing more about their students' families for addressing their needs and for working in partnership with parents.

Both teachers and parents can benefit from school-home partnerships. Teachers can find out from parents more information about how students approach their learning and gain assistance with respect to program planning and instruction. Parents can find out more about their child's strengths and weaknesses and get help from teachers in enhancing their child's functioning at home and in school. However, in order for parent-teacher partnerships to be successful, schools must provide a school climate that is perceived by parents as open, friendly, and helpful. Moreover, schools must promote a philosophy of partnership and make sure that parents are treated the same ways as teachers during collaborative activities (Henderson, Marburger & Ooms, 1986).

School-home partnerships can also be aided when teachers are cognizant of the diversity of families. Families differ in terms of employment, cultural background, values and beliefs, parenting skills, challenges and hardships, attitudes towards education, and family functioning and subsequent adaptation. When teachers know more about family attitudes and feelings regarding education and the school environment, they can form more mutually beneficial relationships with parents.

Students Working Together

Many authors in this book have pointed out that students' academic and social development can be enhanced when they are given opportunities to successfully interact with their peers in a variety of cooperative and collaborative activities. However, it is important to note that just like teachers, many students will not find it easy to work with their peers. They will also need to learn how to collaborate with one another in order for them to realize the mutually beneficial consequences of group effort.

To develop and sustain successful group activities, students need to be given sufficient opportunities to work with others in the classroom and be supported by their teacher for their collaborative efforts. However, collaborative and cooperative methods have to be carefully planned and appropriately orchestrated.

Teaching approaches that promote student collaboration can also develop important social skills. Many students have social interaction problems and experience interpersonal difficulties. Collaborative learning methods can be used as a way to provide continuity between the teaching of academic and social skills.

Proactive and Adaptive Teaching

Another underlying theme throughout this book is that teaching students with diverse needs in regular classrooms requires teachers to be instructionally proactive and adaptive. However, remember that adaptive instruction "is **not** isolated individualized instruction (a child sitting along completing a worksheet); it may involve ordinary or even greater amounts of direct group instruction [highlight added]" (Reynolds & Birch, 1988, p. 72). According to Wang (1993), teachers who take a proactive and adaptive approach to teaching: 1) identify and monitor students' learning characteristics, 2) prepare educational plans based on students' abilities, needs, and interests, 3) modify school environments to correspond to student differences, and 4) use direct and indirect interventions in a variety of settings and grouping arrangements to build students' basic skills and develop their higher-order thinking skills so that they can be adaptive to changes in their environment.

Identifying and Monitoring Students' Learning Characteristics

In the past, assessment practices were used most often to make predictions about students' learning and to place students in programs according to their ability levels and the expectations that teachers had about their potential for success (Reynolds & Birch, 1988). Currently, assessment practices are considered to be a much more integral part of instruction.

Informal assessment practices are becoming increasingly relied upon as a primary source of information for teachers. Although teachers use test data routinely to make educational decisions about their students, testing is only part of the process that enables teachers to gain more insight about their students and design and deliver appropriate instruction.

When teachers are identifying their students' learning characteristics, they should consider the following principles of assessment. First, tests typically estimate students' performance from isolated samples of behaviour at one point in time. To better appreciate a student's functioning in a particular area, it might be better to use a multiple assessment approach (e.g., the combined use of observation techniques, work sample analysis, and checklists) that can be used under different circumstances and at different times and offer a more robust indication of students' performance in a particular subject area. Second, teachers should know the purpose of their assessment. Is the information obtained from the assessment going to be used to develop an intervention program, evaluate students' progress, compare students' performance with their peers, or be used to assist students in their understanding of their own functioning? Third, as noted in this book's chapter on assessment, teachers should consider the extent to which the assessment technique measures what it is supposed to measure, and the degree to which the information gained from the assessment technique is accurate and reliable.

As assessment practices have become more concurrent with instruction, teachers have become more interested in how students' learning can be better addressed. The aim has become to observe students' performance with respect to a variety of tasks and conditions, and determine the type and degree of instructional procedures necessary to successfully develop students' learning and better their ability to deal with the task demands.

Preparing Educational Plans

Results from assessment practices form the basis of educational plans for students. Flexible planning is required for accommodating student diversity. Moreover, the focus of the plans should be more on the learner than on the curriculum. Hence, along with covering important content it is also important that students learn how to better direct their own learning, work cooperatively with others, and become independent decision makers and problem solvers.

According to Clark and Peterson (1986, p. 267), "teacher planning does influence opportunity to learn, content coverage, grouping for instruction, and the general focus of classroom processes." Some factors that influence planning include teacher-related factors (e.g., teachers' knowledge, skills, competence, and motivation to plan), environment-related factors (e.g., demands for content coverage and accountability), and student-related factors such as interest in subject matter, background knowledge, and use of learning strategies (Schumm, Vaughn, Haager, McDowell, Rothlein & Saumell, 1995).

Modifying School Environments to Correspond to Student Differences

Increasing diversity within classrooms demands teachers to be more responsive to the individual needs of students. However, teachers do not need to construct lesson plans for each student. Rather, teachers can develop lesson plans for the entire class that incorporate individualized learning objectives.

Students benefit from teachers who provide structure and clarity in their lessons and who facilitate student thinking, problem solving and decision making. Students also benefit from teachers who summarize and reinforce the content of lessons when necessary, pace their lessons appropriately, and maximize student engagement.

According to Rosenshine and Stevens (1986), teachers should review the previous day's work, present new content and skills, provide opportunity for student practice of skills, check for student understanding, and reteach concepts if necessary.

Using Direct and Indirect Interventions

According to Meyen (1990); Vergason and Anderegg (1991), and Bos and Vaughn, (1991), direct instruction, learning strategies instruction, and guided instruction (sometimes referred to as mediated or scaffolded instruction) have stood the test of time, research, and application as effective practices for students with diverse needs.

Direct instruction is an adaptive group-based approach to teaching that focuses on the development of students' basic skills. The critical instructional features of direct instruction include an explicit step-by-step teaching strategy, student mastery for each step, fast pacing, error-free learning, teacher-directed activities towards independent work, use of adequate, systematic practices with a range of examples, and cumulative review (see Gersten & Carnine, 1986; Gersten, Woodward & Darch, 1986). Students involved in direct instruction have demonstrated substantial gains in achievement (Becker & Carnine, 1981; Bourbeau, 1984; Darch, Carnine & Gersten 1984; Doyle, 1983).

Strategy-based instruction is premised on the view that learning is an active and constructive process (Shuell, 1986; Wittrock, 1986) involving the learner's control and regulation of cognitive processes used to acquire, store, retrieve, and apply knowledge. Teaching students to assume control over the learning process by showing them and having them practise learning strategies has been shown to have value for all students.

Among the better known strategy programs are The Learning Strategies Curriculum (Deshler, Warner, Schumaker & Alley, 1983) for learning disabled adolescents, Informed Strategies for Learning (Paris, Cross & Lipson, 1984), which focuses on reading comprehension; and The Strategies Program for Effective Learning and Thinking (SPELT) (Mulcahy, Marfo, Peat & Andrews, 1986), which is an inclusive learning and thinking curriculum that can be implemented across all subject areas from the elementary to high school curriculum.

Guided instruction is a way that teachers can help their students bridge the gap between their present capabilities and learning goals. In guided instruction, teachers work with students on academic tasks that are too difficult for the student to accomplish independently but can be carried out successfully through the teacher's guidance, modelling, and demonstration. Gradually, there is a shift from teacher-regulated activity to student-regulated learning and an increased willingness to participate in the learning process (Brown & Ferrara, 1985).

Guided instruction is sometimes referred to as scaffolded instruction (Tharp and Gallimore, 1988) or mediated instruction (Haywood, 1987), and comes from the sociocultural theory of learning where the teacher focuses on the process of learning and encourages the student by providing support as he or she develops new knowledge and skills. Gradually, teacher support is reduced and the responsibility for learning is placed in the hands of the students.

The most important underlying factor in successfully teaching and managing students with diverse needs is the establishment and maintenance of classroom climate. Teachers need to develop positive personal relations with their students in order to engage them in collaborative and cooperative learning activities.

Classroom Climate

Classroom environments need to be safe and secure places for the students where they can feel comfortable expressing their views and where diversity is clearly accepted. Environments should be conducive to peer interaction and be perceived as positive and accommodating.

Presenting a Positive Attitude

Attitudes are learned and influenced by the degree of knowledge and amount of experience an individual has with particular people and situations (Smith, Price & Marsh, 1986).

Some school activities that reflect a positive attitude towards teaching students with diverse needs include: 1) experienced teachers mentoring new teachers; 2) parents working as volunteers within the classrooms; 3) teachers being honoured for their collaborative efforts and instructional innovations; 4) teachers making adaptations and modifications in their teaching; 5) teachers using programs and activities that match students' abilities and interests; and 6) teachers using peer teaching or tutoring approaches in their classrooms.

Showing Acceptance and Appreciation

The importance of valuing diversity is recognized by Barth (1990) who says "I would prefer my children to be in a school in which differences are looked for, attended to, celebrated as good news, as opportunities for learning ... What is important about people—and about schools—is what is different, not what is the same" (p. 514–15).

It would be very difficult for successful teaching and learning to take place in the absence of strong and respectful teacher-student relationships. Teachers can build bonds with students and between students by creating a classroom community that recognizes the importance of interpersonal relationships and that reinforces the idea of sharing and working together.

Promoting Self-Identity

Schools should be a place where individuality is valued and validated. As pointed out by Branthwaite (1985), a person's self-confidence and feelings of self-worth influence the way he or she interacts with others. Students must be able to view themselves positively in order to have satisfactory interpersonal relationships. Moreover, a positive self-concept is the foundation for developing acceptance and respect for others who are different from ourselves.

Teachers can promote students' positive self-perceptions by providing opportunities for students to experience harmonious and beneficial social interactions. Additionally, teachers can be good listeners, respect the views of their students, and communicate their belief in them as competent learners.

Conveying a Sense of Belonging

Students need to feel safe and secure, experience a sense of belonging and affection (Maslow, 1968), and believe that they are legitimate members of the classroom. Teachers should strive to create classroom communities where students' needs and interests are accommodated and their contributions are valued. For students to feel they belong in the classroom, they need to be able to fully participate in the general routines and rituals of the classroom. In some cases, students will need supports to be part of the rituals of the classroom.

Maintaining High Expectations

Teachers should have high expectations for all their students. Students need teachers who can inspire them, build their confidence, and challenge them to reach their potential. Students should be praised for their efforts towards meeting learning expectations and for the successful steps made in meeting performance standards (Scruggs & Mastropieri, 1992).

Showing Sensitivity and Empathy

For teachers to be sensitive and empathic towards their students, they need to be able to view the world from their students' perspective. When students feel that their teachers respect them and understand their thoughts and feelings, they are much more likely to relate positively with their teacher and feel comfortable within the classroom. As noted by David Aspy and Flora Roebuck, "students learn more and behave better when they receive high levels of understanding, caring and genuineness, than when they are given low levels of them" (cited in Rogers, 1983, p. 199).

It is becoming increasingly necessary for teachers to be aware of the different cultural and ethnic backgrounds of their students and be sensitive and empathic to their diverse social experiences. Teachers can show their sensitivity and empathy by 1) giving students a chance to share some of their cultural experiences with one another, 2) encouraging students to discuss their feelings regarding their immigration to Canada, 3) structuring student groups in ways that allow everyone in the class to learn about each others' differences, 4) creating learning centres that highlight cultural diversity, 5) reminding students of multicultural events in the community, and 6) taking students on field trips that expose students to various forms of diversity.

Enhancing Motivation

Students' interest in learning can be enhanced by showing them ways to be successful in their learning. Successful learners are not passive recipients of information. Rather, they set goals for themselves, implement strategies to achieve their goals, monitor their work, and evaluate their efforts. Many ineffective learners are not motivated to learn because they lack the ability to reflect upon and regulate their learning.

Some students attribute their successes to luck rather than to their own efforts and attribute their failures to factors beyond their control. Students who attribute success and failure to factors beyond their control are very often less willing to engage in academic tasks compared to those students who attribute their performance to controllable factors such as effort (Weiner, 1984). Teachers can help their students make more appropriate attributions by training students to relate their failures to insufficient effort and their successes to perseverance and appropriate strategy use. Effort feedback related to successful achievement enhances students' motivation and skills (Schunk, 1982), and improves their sense of control (Fulk & Mastropieri, 1990).

Scruggs and Mastropieri (1992) point out that some students have poor motivation because they view school as an endless series of assignments. They suggest that teachers can improve their students' attitudes toward school work by helping them set goals and monitor their progress toward meeting those goals. Moreover, they can increase students' effort by rewarding their quick and efficient task completions with either "free time" or some desired activity.

Modelling

Modelling is the acquisition of behaviours as the result of observing other people (Bowd, McDougall & Yewchuk, 1994). An effective model is someone who clearly demonstrates a skill or process that informs the learner about what she or he needs to do to achieve the desired goal (Wood, 1993).

As noted throughout this book, an important goal for students is to learn how to cooperate and collaborate with others. Teachers can promote student cooperation and collaboration by encouraging student discussion and interaction, and structuring learning experiences that allow students to build positive and beneficial relationships with one another.

◈ Enabling Conditions

Administrative Leadership and Support

Teachers need support from their principals to deal with the problems and issues related to teaching students with diverse needs in the classroom. Supportive leadership from school district superintendents and school principals can positively impact program development and teachers' instructional efforts with respect to student diversity (Good & Brophy, 1989; Reynolds, Martin-Reynolds & Mark, 1982; Thousand & Villa, 1991).

In a study conducted by Miles and Simpson (1989), teachers reported that they were willing to teach students with diverse needs in their regular classrooms on the condition that they be part of the planning process and provided that certain modifications recommended by them were adopted (e.g., reduced class size, provision of support services, and paraprofessional assistance in the classroom). One implication from this study is that if school administration helps teachers help themselves deal with student diversity, then programs and practices might be strengthened.

When teachers believe that their principals have a positive attitude with respect to student diversity, they have more confidence that they will get more administrative support relative to the initiation, development, and implementation of innovative approaches for teaching students with diverse needs. According to Wood (1993) principals should assist them by:

- Arranging for in-service training activities for teachers and participating in these activities

- Consulting with other principals and administrators who have successfully implemented programmes for meeting the diverse needs of students

- Supporting within school teaming approaches for instructional planning and classroom teaching

- Developing a collaborative network with administrators and teachers from other schools, and with parents and professionals in the community

- Designing procedures to evaluate school-based programs

Professional Training and Development

Many teachers believe that they are underprepared to teach students with diverse needs (Post & Roy, 1985). Moreover, teacher federations acknowledge that teachers are not provided with sufficient professional training and development (Csapo, 1981). According to a survey of provincial Deputy Ministers of Education in Canada, regular classroom teachers across Canada are not being adequately prepared to teach students with diverse needs in regular classrooms (Hill, 1988).

Pre-Service Training

Present and future teacher education programs will need to place more emphasis on training teachers to effectively educate students with diverse needs in regular education classrooms (Brophy & Good, 1986; Simpson, Whelan & Zabel, 1993). However, beyond enhancing future general educators with diversity-related teaching skills, teacher preparation programs should provide courses and experiences that reflect an overall vision that pervades the entire curriculum (Galuzzo & Pankratz, 1990). Teachers are facing the enormous challenge of educating an increasing population of students with diverse needs while being in the midst of extensive educational reform (Gable, McLaughlin, Sindelar & Kilgore, 1993). Therefore, they need to have the knowledge base and skill competencies that will help them assume new roles and responsibilities and address the increasing diversity in their classrooms.

It seems clear that university faculties of education and public schools should develop a partnership and jointly prepare teachers to renew schools and educate a broad range of students who have different backgrounds and abilities. Teachers in training should share a common core of professional content and experience and understand the mission and circumstances of schools (Goodlad & Field, 1993) that will allow them to successfully apply programs and approaches to reach the desired educational goals.

Based on the directions recommended by the authors of this book, students in faculties of education should be provided with educational experiences that develop their competencies in areas such as 1) collaboration and consultation skills that will help them work with others to solve problems and design programs related to teaching heterogeneous groups of students, 2) teaching methods that will enable them to provide adaptive instruction to students with diverse needs, 3) assessment techniques that allow them to better understand the developmental potential of their students and inform them of ways to better accommodate their learning and behavioural capabilities, 4) management techniques for dealing with students who have behavioural difficulties, 5) multicultural activities that help students appreciate diversity, and 6) microcomputer applications that can assist teachers with some of their responsibilities and prepare students for a world that will involve higher technologies.

In line with the above suggestions, Lovitt (1993); Pugach (1992); Simpson, Whelan, & Zabel (1993); and Gable et. al. (1993) offer the following recommendations for pre-service teacher training:

- Prospective teachers should have field experiences with excellent teachers in a variety of locations and across different levels of schooling.

- Prospective teachers should have opportunities to work in schools that have a wide range of ethnic diversity in order to learn about other cultures.

- Prospective teachers should have the chance to work collaboratively with specialists.

- Prospective teachers should be given a number of experiences with parents to learn how to interact with parents and become aware of the roles they can play in students' education.

- Prospective teachers need to be taught various ways to instruct, manage, and assess students in classrooms and be given opportunities to practise these procedures.

- Prospective teachers should be given opportunities for reflection to clarify what they have learned from practise and consider how their teaching affects each student.

- Prospective teachers should be given opportunities to learn to balance group needs with those of individuals, to accommodate social differences, and to facilitate self-esteem among students who are neglected or rejected by their peers.

- Prospective teachers should be extensively trained in current technological advances in education.

- Prospective teachers should have training that emphasizes both the attitudes and skills required for successful collaboration.

- Prospective teachers should become knowledgeable about the services that can be provided by nonschool systems such as medicine, mental health, welfare, corrections, and day-care, and learn how to access and coordinate these services to best serve their students.

In-service Training

In-service training programs can help teachers who are working in schools acquire the knowledge and skills that can address their identified needs. In-service training programs provide schools with a mechanism for ongoing staff development. Staff development efforts provide opportunities for all of the teachers in the school to renew their commitment to teaching, set educational goals, design instructional strategies, and practise learned skills in their classrooms. According to Murray (1993) effective staff development programs require:

- An educational climate that supports collegiality and collaboration and encourages experimentation and risk taking

- The use of research paradigms, effective teaching models, and principles of adult learning and change

- The participation and leadership of teachers and administrators who share responsibility for decision making

- Resources and sufficient time to have comprehensive staff development and appropriate incentives and rewards for the participants

- The congruence of visions for change with goals, processes, and support structures

Educational Research

One of the most effective ways of improving the education of students in Canada is through research studies involving Canadian teachers and students. Researching what works within educational contexts is a time-consuming and often prosaic task that "requires dogged pursuit of reliable answers to research questions and protracted public scrutiny of one's data and their interpretation" (Kauffman, 1993). Nevertheless, within the last couple of decades, school-based research has contributed to more effective practice in classrooms (e.g., Becker & Gersten, 1982; Brophy, 1983; Deshler, Schumaker, Alley, Warner & Clark, 1982; Emmer, Everston & Anderson, 1980; Greenwood, Carta & Hall, 1988; Wong, 1986) and, therefore, has proven to be a worthwhile endeavour.

Advances in educational knowledge and practice through applied research programs require substantial funding. Unfortunately, funding for educational studies in Canada is very limited. While acknowledging the reality of limited resources throughout Canada to carry out research and development, it is important to strengthen the empirical base of education and ensure that accountable strategies and approaches are being used.

According to a variety of educational researchers (Fuchs & Fuchs, 1990; Hollowood, Salisbury, Rainforth & Palombaro, 1995; Lovitt, 1993; Scruggs & Mastropieri, 1994) some future directions in research might include:

- To investigate more effective instructional procedures to promote knowledge that transfers across situations

- To investigate better routines for teachers that can reduce their paperwork and stress

- To investigate how intensive the instructional context needs to be to create effective and efficient learning in integrated and inclusive settings

- To investigate the relationship among curriculum methods, instructional methods, and learner outcomes in inclusive educational settings

- To investigate alternative assessment approaches that can better inform teachers about what to do with their students and how much improvement their students are making on the skills and behaviours that are being taught to them

- To investigate collaborations among parents and teachers with respect to such things as the types of information that should be shared, the frequency that information should be shared, and the formats that can be used to share information

- To investigate the nature of collaborations among and between school personnel and outside professionals regarding student diversity

- To investigate the validity and degree to which peer collaborations, effective teaching skills, positive classroom atmosphere, administrative support, and professional development can be implemented in schools that are less successful in accommodating learner diversity

▣ Conclusion

This chapter has brought together the major themes in this book for teaching students with diverse needs and has presented some salient enabling conditions for ensuring quality education for all students. The challenge that resides within us is to prepare ourselves with the knowledge and skills that can help us deal with the multifaceted and complex nature of today's classrooms. Change efforts are pivotal to the future success of all schools facing increasing student diversity. With this point in mind, I end this book by paraphrasing Skrtic (1991):

Change efforts are successful in schools if people
want change and if people act to change.

SUGGESTED RESOURCES

Buzzell, J.B., & Piazza, R. (1994). *Case studies for teaching special needs and at-risk students.* Albany, New York: Delmar Publishers Inc.

Morsink, C.V., Thomas, C.C., & Correa, V.I. (1991). *Interactive teaming: Consultation and collaboration in special programs.* New York: Merrill.

Porter, G.L., & Richter, D. (Eds.). (1991). *Changing Canadian schools: Perspectives on disability and inclusion.* North York, ON: The Roeher Institute.

Samuels, M., Burrows, I., Scholten, T., & Theunissen, D. (1992). *Asking the right questions: Assessment and programme planning for adults with learning difficulties.* The Learning Centre, Calgary, Alberta.

Villa, R.A., Thousand, J.S., Stainback, W., & Stainback, S. (Eds.). (1992). *Restructuring for caring and effective education: An administrative guide to creating heterogeneous schools.* Baltimore, MD: Paul H. Brookes.

Wang, M.C. (1992). *Adaptive education strategies: Building on diversity.* Baltimore, MD: Paul H. Brookes.

REFERENCES

Alberta Education (1992). *Integrated services review.* Yellowhead school division, No. 12, Edmonton, AB: Alberta Education.

Barth, R. (1990). A personal vision of a good school. *Phi Delta Kappan, 71,* 512–71.

Becker, W., & Carnine, D. (1981). Direct instruction: A behaviour therapy model for comprehensive educational intervention with the disadvantaged. In J. Bijou & R. Ruiz (Eds.), *Behaviour modification.* Hillsdale, NJ: Lawrence Erlbaum.

Becker, W.C., & Gersten, R. (1982). A follow-up of Follow Through: The later effects of the direct instruction model on children in fifth and sixth grades. *American Educational Research Journal, 19,* 75–92.

Bos, C.S., & Vaughn, S. (1991). *Strategies for teaching students with learning and behavioural problems* (2nd edition). Toronto: Allyn and Bacon.

Bourbeau, P. (1984). *An experimental analysis of the generalization of teaching skills from the classroom to trained and untrained bank settings in the community.* Unpublished doctoral dissertation. University of Oregon, Eugene.

Bowd, A., McDougall, D., & Yewchuk, D. (1994). *Educational psychology for Canadian teachers.* Toronto: Harcourt, Brace & Co.

Branthwaite, A. (1985). The development of social identity and self-concept. In A. Branthwaite & D. Rogers (Eds.), *Children growing up* (pp. 34–42). Philadelphia: Open University Press.

Brophy, J.E. (1983). Classroom organization and management. *The Elementary School Journal, 83*(4), 265–86.

Brophy, J., & Good, T. (1986). Teacher behaviour and student achievement. In M.C. Wittrock (Ed.), *Handbook of research on teaching* (3rd edition, pp. 328–75). New York: Macmillan.

Brown, A., & Ferarra, R. (1985). Diagnosing zones of proximal development. In J.V. Wertsch (Ed.), *Culture, communication, and cognition* (pp. 273–305). Cambridge: Cambridge University Press.

Centre, Y., Ward, J., Parmenter, T., & Nash, R. (1985). Principals' attitudes toward the integration of disabled children into regular schools. *The Exceptional Child, 32*, 149–61.

Chomicki, S., & Kysela, G. (1993). Teacher attitudes towards mainstreaming: What do they think and what do they need? A literature review. *Exceptionality Education Canada, 3*(4), 61–79.

Clark, C.M., & Peterson, P.L. (1986). Teachers' thought processes. In M. Wittrock (Ed.), *Handbook of research on teaching* (255–96). New York: Macmillan.

Correa, V.I. (1990). Advocacy for teachers. *Teaching Exceptional Children* (Winter), 7–9.

Costa, A.L. (1991). The school as a home for the mind: A climate for thinking. In. R. Mulcahy, R. Short, & J. Andrews (Eds.), *Enhancing learning and thinking* (11–20). New York: Praeger.

Csapo, M. (1981). Teachers' federations in the mainstream. *B.C. Journal of Special Education, 5*(3), 197–218.

Darch, C., Carnine, D., & Gersten, R. (1984). Explicit instruction in mathematical problem solving. *Journal of Educational Research, 4*, 155–65.

Deshler, D.D., & Schumaker, J.B., (1984). An instructional model for teaching students how to learn. In J.L. Graden, J.E. Zins, & M.J. Curtis (Eds.), *Alternative educational delivery systems: Enhancing instructional options for all students* (pp. 391–411). Washington, DC: NASSP.

Deshler, D.D., Schumaker, J.B., Alley, G.R., Warner, M.M., & Clark, F.L. (1982). Learning disabilities in adolescent and young adult populations. Research implications. *Focus on Exceptional Children, 15*, 1–12.

Deshler, D.D., Warner, M.M., Schumaker, J.B., & Alley, G.R. (1983). Learning strategies intervention model: Key components and current status. In J. McKinney & L. Feagans (Eds.), *Current topics in learning disabilities, Vol.1.* Norwood, NJ: Ablex.

Doyle, W. (1983). Academic work. *Review of Educational Research, 53*(2), 159–99.

Eisner, E.W. (1991). What really counts in schools. *Educational Leadership, 48*, 10–17.

Emmer, E.T., Evertson, C.M., & Anderson, L.M. (1980). Effective classroom management at the beginning of the school year. *The Elementary School Journal, 80*(5), 219–31.

Fuchs, D., & Fuchs, L.S. (1990). Making educational research more important. *Exceptional Children, 57*(2), 102–07.

Fulk, B., & Mastropieri, M.A. (1990). Training positive attitudes: "I tried hard and did well." *Intervention in School and Clinic, 26*, 79–83.

Gable, R.A., McLaughlin, V.R., Sindelar, P., Kilgore, K. (1993). Unifying general and special education teacher preparation: Some cautions along the road to educational reform. *Preventing School Failure, 37*(2), 5–10.

Galuzo, G.R., & Pankratz, R.S. (1990). Five attributes of a teacher education program knowledge base. *Journal of Teacher Education, 41*, 7–14.

Gersten, R., & Carnine, D. (1986). Direct instruction in reading comprehension. *Educational Leadership, 43*(7), 70–78.

Gersten, R., Woodward, J., & Darch, C. (1986). Direct instruction: A research based approach to curriculum design and teaching. *Exceptional Children, 53*, 17–31.

Good, T.L., & Brophy, J.E., (1989). School effects. In M.C. Wittrock (Ed.), *Handbook of research in teaching* (pp. 570–602). American Educational Research Association.

Goodlad, J.I. (1990). *Teachers for our nation's schools.* San Francisco: Jossey-Bass.

Goodlad, J.I., & Field, S. (1993). Teachers for renewing schools. In J.I. Goodlad & T.C. Lovitt (Eds.), *Integrating general and special education* (pp. 229–52). Toronto: Maxwell Macmillan Canada.

Greenwood, C.R., Carta, J.J., & Hall, V.R., (1988). The use of peer tutoring strategies in classroom management and educational instruction. *School Psychology Review, 17*, 258–75.

Haywood, H.C. (1987). A mediational teaching style. *The Thinking Teacher, 4*(1), 1–6.

Henderson, A.T., Marburger, C.L., & Ooms, T. (1986). *Beyond the bake sale: An educator's guide to working with parents.* Washington DC: National Committee for Citizens in Education.

Hill, J.L. (1988). Integration in Canada: Implications for the certification of regular education teachers (RETS). *Canadian Journal of Special Education, 4*(2), 123–31.

Hollowood, T.M., Salisbury, C.L., Rainforth, B., & Palombaro, M.M. (1995). Use of instructional time in classrooms serving students with and without severe disabilities. *Exceptional Children, 61*(3), 242–53.

Idol, L., & West, J.F. (1991). Educational collaboration: A catalyst for effective schooling. *Intervention in School and Clinic, 27*(2), 70–78.

Johnson, L.J., Pugach, M.C., & Devlin, S. (1990). Professional collaboration. *Teaching Exceptional Children* (Winter), 9–11.

Kauffman, J.M. (1993). How we might achieve the radical reform of special education. *Exceptional Children, 60*(1), 6–16.

Lovitt, T.C. (1993). Retrospect and Prospect. In J.L. Goodlad and T.C. Lovitt (Eds.), *Integrating general and special education* (pp. 253–74). Toronto: Maxwell Macmillan Canada.

Mallory, B.L., & New, R.S. (1994). Social constructivist theory and principles of inclusion: Challenges for early childhood special education. *The Journal of Special Education, 28*(3), 322–37.

Maslow, A. (1968). *Toward a psychology of being.* New York: D. Van Nostrand.

Meyen, E. (1990). Quality instruction for students with disabilities. *Teaching Exceptional Children, 22*(2), 12–13.

Miles, B.S., & Simpson, R.L. (1989). Regular educators' modification preferences for mainstreaming mildly handicapped children. *The Journal of Special Education, 22*(4), 479–91.

Mulcahy, R.F., Marfo, K., Peat, D., & Andrews, J. (1986). *A strategies program for effective learning and thinking (SPELT): Teachers' Manual.* Edmonton: Cognitive Education Project, University of Alberta.

Murray, L.B. (1993). Putting it all together at the school level: A principal's perspective. In J.L. Goodlad and T.C. Lovitt (Eds.), *Integrating general and special education.* Toronto: Maxwell Macmillan Canada.

Odell, S.J. (1989). Developing support programs for beginning teachers. In Assisting the beginning teacher (pp. 19–38). Reston: VA: Association of Teacher Educators.

Paris, S.G., Cross, D.R., & Lipson, M.Y. (1984). Informed strategies for learning: A program to improve children's reading awareness and comprehension. *Journal of Educational Psychology, 76,* 1239–52.

Paris, S.G., & Oka, E.R. (1986). Self-regulated learning among exceptional children. *Exceptional Children, 53*(2), 103–08.

———. (1986). Children's reading strategies, metacognition, and motivation. *Developmental Review, 6,* 25–56.

Phillips, V., & Mccullough, L. (1990). Consultation-based programming: Instituting the collaborative ethic in schools. *Exceptional Children, 56*(4), 291–304.

Post, L., & Roy, W. (1985). Mainstreaming in secondary schools: How successful are plans to implement the concept? *NASSP Bulletin, 69,* 71–179.

Pugach, M.C. (1992). Unifying the preservice preparation of teachers. In W. Stainback and S. Stainback (Eds.), *Controversial issues confronting special education: Divergent perspectives* (pp. 255–69). Toronto: Allyn and Bacon.

Reynolds, B.J., Martin-Reynolds, J., & Mark, F. (1982). Elementary teachers' attitudes towards mainstreaming educable mentally retarded students. *Education and Training of the Mentally Retarded, 17,* 171–76.

Reynolds, M.C., & Birch, J.W. (1988). *Adaptive mainstreaming: A primer for teachers and principals* (3rd edition). New York: Longman.

Rogers, C. (1983). *Freedom to learn for the 80's.* Columbus, OH: Bell and Howell.

Rosenshine, B., & Stevens, R. (1986). Teaching functions. In M.C. Wittrock (Ed.), *Handbook of research on teaching* (3rd edition, pp. 376–91). New York: Macmillan.

Schumaker, J.B., & Sheldon, J. (1985). *Learning strategies curriculum: The sentence writing strategy.* Lawrence, KS: University of Kansas.

Schumm, J.S., Vaughn, S., Haager, D., McDowell, J., Rothlein, L., & Saumell, L. (1995). General education teacher planning: What can students with learning disabilities expect? *Exceptional Children, 61*(4), 335–52.

Schunk, D.H. (1982). Effects of effort attributional feedback in children's perceived self-efficacy and achievement. *Journal of Educational Psychology, 7,* 548–56.

Scruggs, T.E., & Mastropieri, M.A. (1992). Effective mainstreaming strategies for mildly handicapped students. *The Elementary School Journal, 92*(3), 389–409.

Skrtic, T.M. (1991). The special education paradox: Equity as the way to excellence. *Harvard Educational Review, 61*(2), 148–206.

———. (1991). *Behind special education: A critical analysis of professional culture and school organization.* Denver: Love Publishing Co.

———. (1994). Successful mainstreaming in elementary science classes: A qualitative study of three reputational cases. *American Educational Research Journal, 31*(4), 785–811.

Shuell, T.J. (1986). Cognitive conceptions of learning. *Review of Educational Research, 56,* 411–36.

Simpson, R.I., Whelan, R.J., & Zabel, R.H. (1993). Special education personnel preparation in the 21st century: Issues and strategies. *Remedial and Special Education, 14*(2), 7–22.

Slavin, R.E., Madden, N.A., & Leavey, M. (1984). Effects of team assisted individuation on the mathematics achievement of academically handicapped and nonhandicapped students. *Journal of Educational Psychology, 76,* 814–19.

Smith, T.E.C., Price, B.J., & Marsh, G.E. (1986). Mildly handicapped children and adults. St. Paul, MN: West Publishing.

Stainback, W., & Stainback, S. (1989). Common concerns regarding merger. In S. Stainback, W. Stainback, & M. Forest (Eds.), *Educating all students in the mainstream of regular education* (pp. 255–74). Baltimore, MD: Paul H. Brookes.

Swicegood, P., & Parsons, J. (1989). Better questions and answers equal success. *Teaching Exceptional Children, 21,* 4–8.

Tharp, R.G., & Gallimore, R. (1988). *Rousing minds to life: Teaching, learning and schooling in social context.* New York: Cambridge University Press.

Thousand, J.S., & Villa, R.A. (1991). A futuristic view of the REI: A response to Jenkins, Pious, & Jewell. *Exceptional Children, 57,* 556–62.

Veenman, S. (1984). Perceived problems of beginning teachers. *Review of Educational Research, 54,* 143–78.

Vergason, G.A., & Anderegg, M.L. (1991). Beyond the regular education initiative and the resource room controversy. *Focus on Exceptional Children, 23*(7), 1–7.

Wang, M.C. (1993). The theory and practice of adaptive education. In M. Wang (Ed.), *Adaptive education strategies: Building on diversity* (pp. 1–37). Paul H. Brookes.

Weiner, B. (1984). Principles for a theory of student motivation and their application within an attributional framework. In R. Ames & C. Ames (Eds.), *Research on motivation in education: Student motivation* (Vol. 1, pp. 15–38). New York: Academic Press.

Wittrock, M.C. (1986). Students' thought processes. In M.C. Wittrock (Ed.), *Handbook of research on teaching*. New York: Macmillan.

Wong, B.Y.L. (1986). A cognitive approach to teaching. *Exceptional Children, 53*(2), 169–73.

Wood, J.W. (1993). Mainstreaming: A practical approach for teachers (2nd edition). Toronto: Maxwell Macmillan Canada.

To the owner of this book

We hope that you have enjoyed *Teaching Students with Diverse Needs: Elementary Classrooms,* first edition, and we would like to know as much about your experiences with this text as you would care to offer. Only through your comments and those of others can we learn how to make this a better text for future readers.

School _____ Your instructor's name _____

Course _____ Was the text required? _____ Recommended? _____

1. What did you like the most about *Teaching Students with Diverse Needs: Elementary Classrooms?*

   _____

   _____

   _____

2. How useful was this text for your course?

   _____

   _____

   _____

3. Do you have any recommendations for ways to improve the next edition of this text?

   _____

   _____

   _____

4. In the space below or in a separate letter, please write any other comments you have about the book. (For example, please feel free to comment on reading level, writing style, terminology, design features, and learning aids.)

   _____

   _____

   _____

   _____

Optional

Your name _____ Date _____

May Nelson Canada quote you, either in promotion for *Teaching Students with Diverse Needs: Elementary Classrooms* or in future publishing ventures?

Yes _____ No _____

- - - - - - - - - - - - - - - FOLD HERE - - - - - - - - - - - - - - -

Nelson

TAPE SHUT

MAIL ➤ POSTE

Canada Post Corporation / Société canadienne des postes

Postage paid
if mailed in Canada

Port payé
si posté au Canada

Business Reply

Réponse d'affaires

`0107077099`   **01**

TAPE SHUT

0107077099-M1K5G4-BR01

Nelson Canada
College Editorial Department
1120 Birchmount Rd.
Scarborough, ON M1K 9Z9

PLEASE TAPE SHUT. DO NOT STAPLE.